THE
SUPERLAWYERS

THE
SUPER-
LAWYERS

The Small and Powerful World
of the Great Washington Law Firms

by Joseph C. Goulden

Weybright and Talley
New York

LIBRARY OF CONGRESS CATALOG CARD NUMBER: 72-75461

MANUFACTURED IN THE UNITED STATES OF AMERICA

For George
and Phyllis
and Dick
and Judy,
some friends who got us by.

For Bob Sobel,
with the best
wishes + warm
regards. /
Joseph C Goulden
May 1972

Contents

Prologue

I wrote Clark Clifford so that the letter would arrive by Friday, asking for an interview at his convenience the following week. "My goal is an objective study of lawyers who practice before the Federal government," I wrote, "—who and how, and what they contribute to the process." I acknowledged an awareness of the bar canons on publicity and client-lawyer confidentiality, and quoted a remark Charles Horsky, another Washington Lawyer, once made to the effect that writing (and talking) about a law practice requires walking a path "between the Scylla of tedious platitude and the Charybdis of professional inhibitions." It was a carefully written letter, one designed to get me through the doors of Washington's major law firms.

Late the following Thursday afternoon, when I had already scrubbed Clifford as an interviewee for that week, and had begun thinking of another approach, the phone rang.

The voice of instant warmth—resonant, with a halting deliberativeness that gave you time to digest what was said, but not enough to interrupt; a voice calculated to inform and to make you listen; a sort of early-day Everett McKinley Dirksen; the voice I used to hear in White House briefing rooms as a journalist late in the Johnson Administration, and at occasional Pentagon press conferences, and before Senate committees. "This is Clark Clifford," the voice said. It continued. What a wonderful idea for a book, and I'm glad someone is doing it, and I'm certainly looking forward to reading it when it is published. And you certainly show an understanding of the problems a lawyer faces when he talks for publication. Now, you want to come in this week, but I'm afraid this week is about over, isn't it, and I have to go down to Texas tomorrow for the dedication of President Johnson's library. Now if it isn't *absolutely* essential that you see me this week, I wonder if I could ask you to put off our interview until very early next week? Would I be troubling you too much to ask you to drop around late on Monday afternoon, say five o'clock or so? I can give you more time then, because it's late in the day, and we won't be interrupted.

We made the appointment, and exchanged a few pleasantries about Johnsonian barbecues and journalism, and rang off. And an hour or so later the realization swept over me, and I stopped whatever I was doing and thought about it. Hot damn, this is *how* Clark Clifford does it. Not for him the efficient secretary intermediary—Mr. Clifford is busy this week, he could see you next week, now when shall we work you in?—no, a few caresses of my ego, a veritable apology that a former President wanted the same hours as did I, and *could* I wait a day or so? And a hint that he was setting aside some very special time for me—

God, I thought, I am doing Clark Clifford a favor by interviewing him.

I told this to another writer a few days later. "Jesus," he said, "Clifford sure conned you."
"No, I don't think so," I replied.

Because he deals with Presidents, Cabinet members, and obscure government clerks with equal finesse, Clark Clifford is at the very pinnacle of the very specialized professon which is the subject of this book: The Washington Lawyer. I define the Washington Lawyer as an attorney who practices before the Federal government in the nation's capital. Clark Clifford is not a typical Washington Lawyer. For one thing, no such creature exists, as we shall discover in considerable detail. Second, he is so much better at what he does, and makes so much more money at it, than most (if not all) other Washington Lawyers that he is in a category to himself. Clifford accomplishes things in Washington about which other attorneys dare only dream. At some time in the future Clifford might be emulated, even surpassed; he need not fear duplication. And, finally, the mystique exemplified by Clark Clifford is both blessing and curse for attorneys who practice in the same town with him.

The curse is the notion that Washington Lawyers are in fact influence-peddlers, attorneys who rely upon know-who rather than know-how; men who use friendships within the government, or bribery or other corruption, to accomplish extralegal ends for clients. The backslap, not the brief, is assumed to be their tool. To much of the nation the words "Washington Lawyer" mean the gurgle of good whiskey, and two-inch steaks in the rear of a dimly lit restaurant, and even a frisky feminine laugh. The high proportion of former government officials among Washington Lawyers, and their continuing close friendships at the agencies where they once worked, are accepted as further evidence of "insider's influence." The formula is simplistic: Clark Clifford is friendly with the President, and the President controls the government. Ergo, what Clifford wants, Clifford gets, with a single phone call. Such is the myth.

The blessing is that the public image of the Washington Lawyer, unfounded though it might be, brings them clients who would otherwise make do with their hometown lawyers, or a letter to a Congressman. Having a Washington Lawyer is a modern status symbol for the corporate executive. And necessary, in many instances, to be sure. But the corporate executive all too often *thinks* he is receiving special services—after all, his house counsel doesn't socialize with the Commissioner of Internal Revenue—and he *pays* accordingly. Which is to say, dearly.

"Out there in the country, out there past Pittsburgh and before the Coast, out there where the Federal government is still viewed as a strange creature confined behind a high wall, they think of Washington Lawyers as some sort of . . . well, some kind of Himalayan guides. We are creations of a mythology, and captives of a mythology—and also benefactors of a mythology. If someone wants to make you into a legend (or your profession into a legend), why fight it? The pay's good." This from a partner in Arnold and Porter, a firm which has been a power in Washington (and hence the nation) for a quarter of a century.

"All I do, really, is practice law. It's nothing different from what my Yale classmates do in New York or Boston or Philadelphia or Chicago. I research and write briefs, and argue my cases, and try to keep my clients happy, and I cut the grass every second Saturday morning. I'm not a superlawyer, I'm not a man who backslaps John Mitchell or George Romney—hell, the most influential man I've met this year was an Assistant Secretary of Transportation who goes to our church. Sure, we talk. We talk about the weather, and the merits of station wagons. Big stuff." This from a specialist in transportation law, a man who was involved in two landmark rail merger cases, but who is completely unknown outside the tight circle of fellow practitioners in the field.

"In 1962 I was on a first-name basis with everyone in Jack Kennedy's Cabinet. On January 21, 1969 [the day after Richard Nixon's inaugural] the only Cabinet officer I knew was [Secretary of State] Bill Rogers, and him through legal connections. The only other one I've met since is Hodgson, the Secretary of Labor, but him only once, at a social function." This from Charles Horsky, a partner in prestigious Covington and Burling, Washington's largest (and best, by most measures) law firm, a man who was a White House adviser under Presidents Kennedy and Johnson.

The Washington Lawyer is an important figure in contemporary America because he is often the interface that holds together the economic partnership of business and government. In the decades following the New Deal, at a pace that sharply accelerated during the 1960s, some Washington Lawyers directed a counter-revolution unique in world economic history. Their mission was not to destroy the New Deal, and its successor reform acts, but to conquer them, and to leave their structures intact so they could be transformed into instruments for the amassing of monopolistic corporate power. Attorney General John Mitchell, whose credentials as a capitalist are beyond reproach, said in a 1969 speech, "In 1948, the nation's two hundred largest industrial corporations controlled forty-eight percent of the manufacturing assets. Today, these firms control fifty-eight percent, while the top five hundred firms control seventy-five percent of these assets. The danger that this super-concentration poses to our economic, political, and social structure cannot be overestimated." A benevolent government has made possible this concentration: one with the trappings but not the reality of regulation, one which stifles competition in the name of an "orderly" market.

Lee Loevinger, formerly a member of the Federal Communications Commission, now an attorney in Washington, once opined, "The most pervasive social institution of the modern age, the most characteristic social problem of the exponential growth of recent years, is bureaucracy. It is like a passionless mob, which can capture and conquer man *unless he is wise enough to subdue it and shape it to his own purposes.*"* The Washington Lawyer is the man American business depends upon to "subdue . . . and shape" the Federal government.

The Washington Lawyer in recent decades has stepped beyond the attorney's traditional role as legal representative. The Washington Lawyer accepts government as an existential fact and tries to direct what it does to the benefit of his corporate clients. The Washington Lawyer affects public policy when it is being shaped in the Congress and the regulatory agencies and in the executive departments, either as a proponent of original ideas or in reaction to those from elsewhere. He is a markedly more sophisticated man than knee-jerk conservatives of the 1930s, for he recognizes the government as a source of subsidies, as a partner in legalized price fixing, as a deterrent to competition. The lawyer's historic role was that of advising clients how to *comply* with the law. The Washington Lawyer's present role is that of advising clients how to *make* laws, and to make the most of them.

Here we must draw a distinction between the Washington *L*awyer and the Washington *l*awyer. The District of Columbia Bar Association estimates that there are 15,000 licensed lawyers in the Washington metropolitan area—7,000 in private practice, 8,000 with the government, in attorney positions. Ray-

---

* Emphasis added throughout, unless otherwise noted.

mond Garrety, the association's executive director, stresses that these figures are largely guesswork, and for several reasons. Until April 1, 1972, attorneys practicing in Washington courts were not required to join a bar association. Effective that date, the D.C. Court of Appeals required attorneys to join a lawyers' association as a condition of practicing law. The ruling, however, did not apply to attorneys who practice exclusively before Federal regulatory agencies or act as lobbyists for trade and industry associations. The D.C. bar group itself has 5,200 members. The Federal Bar Association has 4,300 members; however, many of these persons live elsewhere in the United States, and the FBA does not break down its membership by locations. And as Garrety notes, many of the "Washington" lawyers actually conduct strictly local practices in suburban Maryland and Virginia. So, too, for many of the lawyers working in Washington—men who write wills and defend criminal cases and handle real estate and other non-Federal commercial transactions, leading the same professional lives as attorneys in Boston or Denver or Kansas City. There are also the non-practicing attorneys who deal with the Federal government as lobbyists or trade association officials, five hundred to six hundred of them, by Garrety's informed estimate. Finally, the government contains "lawyers" at all levels who do not practice law, ranging downward from Richard Nixon through Foreign Service officers holding non-legal assignments in the State Department and FBI agents.

"How many 'Washington Lawyers' are there by your definition?" Garrety asked me. "Make up your own number—it's as good as anyone else's."

To further confuse our statistics, not all Washington Lawyers are based in Washington. Each morning's airline shuttle flights from New York are laden with lawyers from the factory-firms of Wall Street en route to business at the Securities and Exchange Commission, the Justice Department's antitrust division, the

Federal Trade Commission, and elsewhere. The larger New York law firms—Cravath, Swaine and Moore; Paul, Weiss, Rifkind, Wharton and Garrison, to name two of a dozen—maintain Washington offices, partly for logistical and administrative convenience; but as one prominent Wall Street name told me, "You can't practice securities law from your desk in New York. You must get down to Washington at least once a week and give the SEC a pat on the ass. I'll go see a Commissioner even when I don't have anything specific to talk about. Hell, you can't let them forget who you are, because the time may come when you want to get a message across in a hurry. And I'm not talking about 'fixing' any proceedings, either, so don't you get any wrong ideas. But there are times in a securities practice when you want to get something through the Commission in a hurry, and, my boy, that's when you'd better have close acquaintances. And I don't mean any GS-13 staff attorney, either; I mean a *mover*." This man lives in New Jersey; if you threw a rock from his office window you would hit the New York Stock Exchange; his "knowledge" of Washington is what he sees on a cab ride from National Airport to the SEC Building and back again to the Jockey Club or the Sans Souci ("the only places in town fit to eat"). Why, then, does he consider himself a "Washington" Lawyer? "Because I make my money there, that's why. I've got young fellows to do the daily running; I sit up here and hustle the clients."

The statistical vagaries and qualifications notwithstanding, Washington is a heavily lawyered city. Washington has slightly less than one-half of one percent of the United States population, and almost five percent of the lawyers. And law is truly a growth industry, both for firms and for individual practitioners. "A frontier town for lawyers," says Lloyd Cutler of Wilmer, Cutler, and Pickering. When Earl W. Kintner left the chairmanship of the Federal Trade Commission in 1961 he deliberately sought out a small office, and found one in Berg, Fox, and Arent. "There were nine people here in 1961. I brought over two more from the FTC. Now we are up to eighty-five, which makes us second largest in the city." At its present rate of growth, Arent, Fox, Kintner, Plotkin and Kahn could well be over the one-hundred mark by the time this book reaches print. Covington and Burling, the city's largest firm, grew from eighty-five lawyers in 1960 to the present one hundred thirty. Arnold and Porter went from thirty-five to seventy; Wilmer, Cutler and Pickering from ten to fifty-six; Hogan and Hartson, from thirty-seven to seventy-six. (Because of the latter firm's strong local orientation, however, purists wouldn't include it under our definition.) The number of lawyers is up twenty-five percent in the past decade, and no one expects a reversal of the trend.

"If we didn't accept a single new client, and just held on to what we have now," a Covington and Burling partner told me, "we'd continue to grow. Every time the Federal government sneezes, you can hear the coins rattle in our cash register."

Another lawyer, in a smaller firm: "Ecology and the pollution laws are going to mean as much law business for Washington as did the creation of the Securities and Exchange Commission. Another thing: you now have the public-interest lawyers, the Naders. They are already making us corporate types work a hell of a lot harder in the agencies. I spent more than seventy-five hours answering one public-interest petition at the FCC, questions that wouldn't have been raised three years ago. Multiply that by what's happening all over town, and you begin to get the idea."

Seventy hours of legal service, at this lawyer's hourly fee of $60, amounts to a $4,200 fee. Hence the corporate lawyers have a truly ambivalent attitude about the Nader-bar: They are angered that the public-interest lawyers are chipping away at their comfortable control of the regulatory agencies, yet corporate lawyers share an instinct common to most of us—the love of making money. And they are being paid handsomely to contest the challenges the Naders pose to the corporate state.

Because Washington Lawyers are so diverse, generalizations are dangerous. Yet here are some of the things I have concluded after studying them, which will be discussed in the following pages:

■ ■   Isolated misuse of influence is easy to find, yet any Washington Lawyer who bases his practice upon "connections" is foolhardy. As former White House adviser Daniel P. Moynihan has noted, "a miracle of American national government" is the "almost complete absence of monetary corruption at all levels of government, and especially at the top." Not nearly as much of what happens in Washington is reported as the press likes to think, but every bureaucrat lives with the awesome knowledge that any under-the-table deal he makes possibly could be spread over the front pages of *The Washington Post*. A lawyer who relies upon a political friendship to force a lower-level bureaucrat to make a questionable decision risks being hit by the ultimate weapon of the Civil Service: the leaked memo. Administrations change. And when they do, the search begins for scandal. Further, as one attorney told me, "Sure, I made friends with all the Democrats I could when I first started practicing here in 1962, and I'm identified with the Republican Party. But I can't risk my entire professional life on the outcome of a national election—hell, if I wanted to do that, I'd be a politician, not a lawyer." Which is *not* to suggest that Washington Law is devoid of politics. One of the more charming success stories of the Nixon Administration has been the newly expanded Washington office of the Wall Street law firm of Mudge,

Rose, Guthrie and Alexander. Before 1969 the firm included two other names—those of President Nixon and his Attorney General, John Mitchell. The Phoenix firm of Mitchell's Deputy Attorney General, Richard Kleindienst, suddenly decided it needed an office in Washington when the Republicans came to power. Myer Feldman, longtime aide to John F. Kennedy, both in the Senate and in the White House, joined a three-lawyer firm in 1965; it is now past twenty, and Mike Feldman is a rich man. Or the relatively obscure new firm of Reeves and Harrison, which according to its listing in *Martindale and Hubbell*, the legal directory, specializes in "general, administrative and international practice." Marion Edwyn Harrison, a founding partner, features in his biography in the directory the fact that he was co-chairman of the Nixon-Agnew campaign in Virginia in 1968. Another member, Patrick J. Hillings, records that he was a Republican Congressman from California from 1951 to 1959, and a special assistant to John Mitchell in the 1968 campaign. Another member, as of January 1971, is Murray M. Chotiner, who has worked for Nixon, on and off, since 1946, last as a White House counsel. Another member, Robert Sagle, is secretary of the J. Edgar Hoover Foundation, which he runs from the office. The firm was formed in early 1969.

■ ■ The Washington Lawyers' longtime dominant influence on the regulatory agencies results from a combination of factors, of which influence is but one of many. The corporate lawyers have more resources—money, experience, and manpower—than do government lawyers. "Put my name on this, and I'll kill you, but litigating against a government lawyer is a piece of cake," says one attorney. "I don't care what the government puts out about 'higher-caliber-of-lawyers' and that bull. On a man-to-man basis, the private bar kicks the crap out of them." High turnover is another factor; it is not uncommon for eight to twelve government lawyers to share responsibility for an FTC case as it goes through the agency and the courts. The private bar is omnipresent. The private bar stacks the industry advisory committees that shape agency policy. The private bar dominates the bar association committees that recommend new legislation. Some members of the private bar recruit venal Congressmen to perform bloody hatchet work on recalcitrants. A prime example: in 1959 a skittish Federal Power Commission chairman *volunteered* to a Congressional subcommittee the fact that Washington Lawyer Tommy Corcoran had arranged private meetings with FPC members just before a decision was reached in a crucial pipeline case. The subcommittee subsequently clubbed not Corcoran, but the very Commissioners who complained of the *ex parte* contacts. (See chapter 4: "Tommy the Cork Corcoran: The Lawyer as Acrobat.")

A good deal of the Washington Lawyer's clout is by virtue of delegated power. "When I used to look across my desk and see Lloyd Cutler, I didn't think of him as an attorney, but as an emissary of General Motors," says a former Senate committee staffer. "You know that he's speaking for $40 billion, and that's a lot of voice, regardless of the identity of the man doing the talking." Another Congressional veteran: "It's silly for a home-state client to hire a lawyer when he wants to get a message to us. Hell, my boss isn't dumb enough to ignore a constituent, or to give him any special treatment just because he's hired a guy with a wave in his hair and a hundred-dollar briefcase. But businessmen seldom realize they can speak for themselves."

America's governmental system is so constituted that some Washington Lawyers constantly violate the public interest, without violating public statutes. These lawyers pervert the Federal government for the financial benefit of private corporate clients. Through legalistic maneuvering, they helped their clients keep on the marketplace a host of consumer products—ranging from pharmaceuticals to pesticides and automobiles—which are gravely dangerous to the American citizen. Through what is euphemistically called "effective representation," some of them wheedle billions of dollars of tax breaks and public subsidies from a pliant Congress and Federal bureaucracy." When criticized for emasculating laws designed to protect the public, they lapse into well-rehearsed speeches about "everyone has a right to a lawyer, whether he's a corporation or an indigent criminal defendant." Agreed. But some Washington Lawyers frequently go beyond the advocate's role in representing industries and become an extension of management. An example: Covington and Burling is among the more self-consciously dignified firms in town, one prideful of its sweet scent of probity. And two of its senior partners—H. Thomas Austern and Stanley Temko—are the legal technicians who have helped manufacturers keep on the market a vast variety of pharmaceuticals and foodstuffs for years after the Food and Drug Administration challenged their value. (See chapter 1, "Covington and Burling: The Pinnacle of Power.") There are dropouts. Robert Wald, formerly Washington Lawyer for the Lorillard cigarette interests, quit in 1971 because of personal misgivings about the industry he represented. Wald told *The Wall Street Journal*'s Jonathan Kwitny: "I haven't the slightest doubt that cigarets cause lung cancer. I had to come home every night and face my kids saying, 'Daddy, why do you work for a cigaret company?' "

The Washington Lawyer is a smart man who works long hours and earns good money for doing so. In six successive interviews I asked lawyers their "normal" working hours. The responses ranged from ten to fourteen hours; three worked at least one day of the weekend; all took a briefcase home at night. Five of these men were seniors in major firms, the sixth only four years out of the government. Each of the first five, surprisingly, considered their present schedule "light." Ernest Jennes, one of the top men at Covington and Burling, said he frequently "worked around the clock" when he was younger and litigated cases in court. Said another, "It's all very glamorous, being on a committee that gets you to the White House when you submit the final report—you listen to a speech by the President, and your name is in the paper the next morning, in paragraph seventeen, and you get a couple of handshakes that week at the Federal City Club. What doesn't show is that at seven o'clock the morning of the big day, you were at your desk with a cardboard cup of White Tower coffee and an uneatable sticky roll, rewriting a brief some young associate had produced, in the hopes you could put it in final form before you went to the White House at noon." About one-third of Arnold and Porter's lawyers are out of town at any given time, meeting with clients or trying cases. The firm keeps three dozen New York–Washington airline shuttle tickets on hand, already filled in, so brisk is travel there. (The firm also maintains an East Side apartment for partners caught in New York overnight; it is occupied, most days.)

But the money. Ah, the money. Of the fifty-five partners in Covington and Burling, almost half are in the six-figure bracket, by reliable inside estimate, with the top handful near or above $200,000. A trifle more for partners at Arnold and Porter. A pittance less at Wilmer, Cutler, and Pickering. Legend credits the redoubtable Clifford with earning $1 million on a single case, $25,000 for less than a week's work on another. (See chapter 2, "Superclark: Mr. President, I Think You Should . . .") Income is something a man discusses only with the tax collector and (sometimes) his wife. But there are guidelines: The Washington Lawyer works 1,200 to 1,400 hours a year* that are "billable" to specific clients. The straight-billing rate ranges from $35 per hour for a very junior associate in a large firm to $250 for the name members of the name firms. Retainers from corporate clients—money that isn't always reflected in the per-hour billings—adds a substantial amount to income. The fresh-from-the-campus salary for newly hired associates at a firm of the caliber of Arnold and Porter is now $17,500. A man who "makes partner" in seven years can expect an annual income of $60,000 up.

According to a Census Bureau survey, District of Columbia law firms had an average income of $102,096 in 1967, compared with a national average of $4,724. "Law firm," however,

---

* Or more. Covington and Burling, through formal memo in the 1960s, told partners and associates it expected them to "bill" a minimum of thirty-five hours per week, which comes to 1,660 hours for a forty-eight-week year.

included single practitioners as well as partnerships, so the study's sole value is to offer verification of what everyone suspected: Washington Lawyers earn more than those elsewhere (with the exception of New York lawyers).

The following pages introduce some of the more interesting and important Washington Lawyers and their firms—what they've done, what they (and others) think of themselves, how they go about their business, what impact they've had upon our national life, the challenge they face from the newly powerful public-interest bar. This is not intended as a roster of the Washington legal profession. There are enough lawyers in Washington to fill sixteen yellow pages of the phone book. Washington Law is highly specialized, and highly fragmented, and I was highly subjective in choosing what and whom to write about; if a phase of it bored me, I avoided it. Hence you won't find a word in these pages about such things as tariff and patent law, even though several hundred Washington Lawyers work in these fields, profitably and presumably happily. Similarly, after some preliminary research I backed away from Hogan and Hartson, one of Washington's older and larger firms because (a) of its local orientation, and (b) what "national" characteristics it has are duplicated, more or less, at Covington and Burling. Rich and powerful as it is, Hogan and Hartson for the moment is not nearly as important in Washington Law as such individuals as John Banzhaf, the young George Washington Law School professor who is busily training brigades of legal guerrillas for raids on the Federal bureaucracy, and William Dobrivir, the drop-out Covington and Burling lawyer who has, among other things, stripped the Reservist general's stars off the shoulders of Senators Barry Goldwater and Strom Thurmond. Such men as Banzhaf and Dobrivir have the potential to tilt the balance of power in Washington Law, provided the movement launched by Ralph Nader can become a permanent, ongoing force without succumbing to leaden institutionalization.

Bar association canons being what they are, attorneys in Washington and elsewhere well may shudder at a book highlighting individual practitioners. As a journalist (and a citizen) I find it somewhat foolish that an entire profession would declare itself off limits to outside, objective scrutiny. The Washington Lawyer is a public figure; collectively, he is a public institution, veritably an estate of government. And any institution which accepts the responsibility of wielding immense power also accepts the responsibility of critical outside examination. The core of this book is material gleaned from interviews with more than seventy Washington Lawyers and more governmental officials than I care to count. More detailed source information can be found in the Bibliography.

Covington and Burling:
The Pinnacle of Power

To reach the inner sanctum of Covington and Burling, Washington's premiere law firm, one rides the elevator to the seventh floor of the eight-story office building at 888 16th Street Northwest, across Lafayette Park from the White House, and steps into the subdued ambience of old and dignified money. The living room is that of a very, very tasteful home, its furnishings so congruous with the light-hued wood paneling that, think as you may the next day, not a single individual piece comes to memory. A constant—and most silent—flow of lawyers (all wearing coats and ties and *white* shirts) and secretaries over the carpeted floor, figures whose silence detaches them one from the other, heads bobbing politely in the general direction of the receptionist, lips rippling into what *could* be a smile. Dignity. Covington and Burling people, be they lawyer or functionary, do not banter. They hold their file folders snugly under their arms, and they do not swing their briefcases as they walk to the elevator, and (Blackstone forbid!) the secretaries do not chew gum or carry lighted cigarettes or come to work bra-less. Not a glance at The Visitor, for when someone enters Covington and Burling, regardless of his business, he is entitled to privacy, and thus one must ignore even the existential fact that The Visitor is sitting in open view on the sofa. Walk on, silently and briskly, and close the door behind you.

Enter John Sapienza stage right, down the dim circling stairway from the eighth floor. Not a big man, but husky of frame, with a Bahamas-quality tan in mid-spring; face round and heavy-bottomed, remindful of Jose Ferrer, or even Anthony Quinn. John Sapienza is one of the better tax lawyers in the country, and he would rather be doing something else this afternoon. A journalist—well, after all, Covington and Burling neither wants nor needs publicity. "We have always prided ourselves on keeping well in the background," Sapienza remarks. But as chairman of the Covington and Burling management committee he is willing to listen to questions about the firm, if not answer them.

Up the stairway to a smaller but no less luxurious reception area, past an incredibly beautiful brunette receptionist (this one smiles) and into Sapienza's corner office. An ambivalent panorama. To the right rear of Sapienza's desk, visible through the full-wall windows that face visitors' chairs, is the White House, framed by the verdant green of Lafayette Park. To the left, across 16th Street, the headquarters building of the AFL-CIO. George Meany's office is also on the eighth-floor corner; the curtains and offset windows are such that you can't see

Meany's cigar smoke, but peer carefully and there is the United States flag behind his desk. ("I never knew that," a partner was to exclaim later, when I casually mentioned who occupied the office. His eyes flickered toward Meany's window for the rest of our interview.)

We talk about what Sapienza and another partner, Ernest Jennes, call "the box we're in." Covington and Burling takes most seriously the canons on publicity and client confidentiality, they tell me. Yes, it does. Not like *some* firms whose partners were quoted extensively in a *Fortune* Magazine article on lawyers. Covington and Burling isn't criticizing the talkative barristers, mind you, for to do so runs afoul of yet another canon, and backbiting isn't Covington and Burling's style. It is simply stating its own standards, and if others do not meet them, well . . .

And Ralph Nader. This Man Nader, engaged in a Nader's Raiders study of the firm. This Man Nader wanted to interview every partner and every associate in the firm, and on the record. This Man Nader wanted access to Covington and Burling's office files. This Man Nader wanted to move researchers into the firm—physically—for whatever time was required for his study. This Man Nader . . .

Sapienza is too controlled a man to shudder, but even saying the name is distasteful to him. "I don't know why," he said, "we receive so much attention. After all, we're only a bunch of lawyers trying to conduct a practice."

Which does not exactly do justice to the truth. Covington and Burling is not just another law office. It is, in fact, Washington's oldest, largest, and probably best national law firm. At one time or another, it has performed legal services for most blue-chip corporations in America. Unlike many firms, Covington and Burling doesn't list representative clients in *Martindale and Hub-*

bell, the quasi-official legal directory. But, estimates one partner, "We've done things for, I'd say, twenty percent of the companies on *Fortune*'s list of the five hundred top corporations." GM, AT&T, du Pont, CBS, American Airlines—you get the idea. Because of the diversity of talent afforded by its sheer size, Covington and Burling is perhaps the only law firm in Washington that can assign a specialist to handle any problem a client has before the Federal government, from defending a criminal antitrust case to obtaining an arms export license or convincing the Food and Drug Administration of the safety of a patent medicine or fancy new combination drug. Covington and Burling lawyers possess that special confidence that comes from expertise and power, and think in commensurately grand terms.

John G. Laylin, a senior partner who specializes in international work, matter-of-factly illustrated this point to me one morning during a casual conversation. First, Laylin showed me a glass bowl, half filled with rocks the size of golf balls and covered with water. "This is something I'm spending half my time on right now," Laylin said. "These nodules are rich in cobalt, nickel, and copper. A client of mine found them in fifteen thousand feet of water, in the middle of the ocean. Now, the law on mining of deep-sea resources is very vague. These nodules are found in high concentration in a certain area; in other areas, nearby, they are nonexistent. My client has spent millions of dollars locating them."

Laylin handed me a photograph album with pictures of the nodules littering the ocean floor, taken with deep-sea exploration equipment. "What we want is exclusivity," he said, "the right to stake a claim to what we have found, and to extract the minerals. Why, the way the law stands now, the Russians could park right alongside us, and start pulling them up, too." So Laylin was spending many hours weekly on a treaty establishing an international body to regulate exploration of sea-bed resources seaward of the two-hundred-meter line. The United States government submitted a draft treaty—lawyer Laylin's handiwork, basically—to a United Nations committee in August 1970. On another front, as chairman of a special American Bar Association subcommittee, Laylin is mobilizing bar support of the treaty; the morning we spoke he interrupted our conversation three times in scheduling a meeting with out-of-town lawyers on the committee.

But obtaining an international treaty is a staggeringly complex task. Drafts must be circulated and debated and rewritten; even if the United Nations accepts the final version, member nations still must ratify it. In the meantime, all those nodules remain on the ocean floor, and Laylin's client (whom he would not identify) is restless. What, then, is an interim solution?

For a law firm powerful enough to cajole the United States government into drafting an international treaty, requesting legislation from Congress is a routine exercise, even if a time-consuming one. Under a bill drafted by Laylin in 1971, any person subject to United States jurisdiction would be required to obtain a Federal license before doing any undersea mining work. Reciprocal protection would be given other nations passing similar legislation.* In other words, no claim-jumping. "No state can by itself establish a rule or principle of international law," Laylin wrote in a draft paper on sea-bed law, "but any state can sow seeds which can grow into a 'general practice accepted as law.' "

And this is what Laylin is doing—on behalf of a fee-paying Covington and Burling client, but in an undertaking bearing the imprimatur of both the United States government (which is to say, all of us) and the American Bar Association. Such is the stuff of big-time Washington Law.

---

* Laylin's bill was still before Congress in October 1971 with favorable prospects for passage.

To paraphrase Dorothy Parker's classic line about Hemingway, influence is the use of power with grace. Covington and Burling does not overpower the Federal government, nor does it shove it around. The graceful technique is to smother, to overwhelm, and always with good-natured tolerance of the bureaucrats. Although it is the foremost law office in a political town, Covington and Burling is not a blatantly political firm; one partner, John Douglas, son of former Senator Paul Douglas, managed to run a key committee for Senator George McGovern's Presidential campaign without once getting his name into the papers. Nor is Covington and Burling a firm laden with charismatic, business-drawing names. Of its one hundred nineteen lawyers, only two were prominent outside (a) Washington and (b) the legal profession. One was former Secretary of State Dean Acheson, so near retirement from the early 1960s through his death on October 12, 1971, that some younger men in the firm avow they *never* saw him. The other is John Lord O'Brian, longtime guru of Establishment foreign policy, now in his nineties; his name continues on the firm's letterhead, but he no longer practices. "We just don't seem to go into the things that attract wide public attention," a partner told me somewhat primly. "Of course, we don't need that kind of 'advertising.' "

Covington and Burling's clout rests on factors far more substantial than politics and personality. Quality work explains much of the firm's success—but not all of it, for lawyers there are quick to point out there are men of equal or greater legal skills in offices elsewhere in the city. More important, perhaps, is longevity—the ongoing practice over the decades that transforms a law firm into an institution. The founders of Covington and Burling set out to create a firm that would service the nation's corporations in the nation's capital at a time of increasing Federal strength. They succeeded.

The firm's name partners, Edward P. Burling and Judge J. Harry Covington, were men of totally disparate personality. The austere, taciturn Burling was a man out of an old *Saturday Evening Post* success story. He grew up in rural Eldora, Iowa, where he worked in a grocery store at age eleven, and went on to Grinnell College and Harvard Law School. Partner and friend Acheson wrote in his memoirs that Burling's exposure to "the life of the intellect" at Harvard "fatally weakened his natural drive toward the acquisition of power." After graduation Burling returned to the Midwest to practice in Chicago for almost a quarter of a century.

Covington spent his early years as a Congressman from the Eastern Shore of Maryland, an easygoing area whose life-style is that of the Old South. A Wilsonian Democrat, Covington swung the Maryland delegation away from Champ Clark at the 1912 Democratic convention, and President Wilson thereafter relied upon him as a close adviser in the House. One key assignment, culminating in success in 1914, was managing the bill creating the Federal Trade Commission. One of the FTC act's authors, George Rublee, had met Burling at Harvard Law, and practiced briefly with him in Chicago before starting his own corporate office in New York. During the First World War, Covington resigned from Congress to accept an appointment by Wilson as Chief Justice of the District of Columbia Supreme Court.

Rublee, meanwhile, went to work with the Allied Maritime Transport Council, which pooled and allocated Allied shipping tonnage for world use. He persuaded his old law partner, Burling, to come to Washington as general counsel for the United States Shipping Board, and one of the first persons he introduced him to was Judge Covington.

After two years on the bench, the gregarious Covington tired of the secluded life of a judge. Burling found Washington life exciting and had no particular desire to return to Chicago. So on January 1, 1919, the two men formed Covington and Burling.

The firm was known variously as Covington, Burling and Rublee; Covington, Burling, Rublee, Acheson and Shorb; and Covington, Burling, Rublee, O'Brian and Shorb, in succeeding decades. But after Acheson left the firm in the 1940s to rejoin the State Department, it reverted to the original title, and a decision was made not to add the name of each new partner. A fortunate choice, now that the firm is up to fifty-five partners. In verbal shorthand, Washington Lawyers refer to the firm as "Covington" or "C&B."

Let us pause a moment for historical perspective, for "The Washington Lawyer" did not exist in 1919. Whatever Federal practice the city had in those days had grown in response to isolated and highly specialized situations. Right after the Civil War, when the industrial revolution began to boom across America, patent attorneys dominated "Washington Law." (Of the four firms listed in the 1880 edition of *Martindale and Hubbell*, the legal directory, two listed their specialties as patent law.) Next came the public land lawyers, who practiced before the General Land Office; then specialists in wheedling pensions for widows and orphans of Civil War veterans. In a historical sketch of Washington attorneys published in 1952, Covington and Burling partner Charles Horsky noted a distinct change around 1915, when firms began advertising an expertise in practice before the Interstate Commerce Commission and advising on the Food and Drug Act. The story survives (perhaps it is apocryphal) of the lawyer who refused to leave the War Department for a high position in the Bureau of Internal Revenue because he was confident the wartime income tax was a temporary expedient which would be repealed when peace came.

Howard Westwood, another Covington and Burling partner

with a keen appreciation of history (his office walls are covered with Civil War scenes), states that the early regulatory agencies did not generate much business for local lawyers. "Most of the ICC work, for instance, was done by lawyers in Chicago, the major railroad headquarters. The FTC wasn't very active. There always have been what we called 'Indian lawyers,' mostly in claims court. But that was about it." Horsky describes circa-1919 Washington as "a country law town, where an attorney started to work at ten and broke at two for the day, with maybe a lunch in between. Everyone knew everyone else, and the Federal practice wasn't that big or important, except for people who did the routine administrative work in the agencies.

"Now, Mr. Burling was different. He had worked like a bastard in Chicago, trying to eke out a living, not knowing anybody when he came to town, having to build a practice from the ground up. You don't shake off that sort of background; if you work hard as a young lawyer, you'll continue."

Despite his many years in Washington, Judge Covington also lacked the commercial connections essential to a successful local practice. What, then, do two lawyers in their mid-fifties do in launching a Washington law office?

Practice *national* law. Covington and Burling, according to Westwood, "saw the need for representation before the Federal government. Judge Covington had been in Congress in the New Freedom Days of President Wilson; he had a feeling for the direction the Federal government was taking. I suspect, in a vague way, he figured the impact of the Federal government on businessmen around the country was bound to increase—and the concerns of businessmen along with it. When a man is concerned, he wants a lawyer, and these two partners wanted to be that lawyer."

The two partners were uniquely complementary. According to Acheson, Covington was a "great talker . . . an encyclopedia of American politics, of Maryland history, a rare raconteur, an authority on 18th- and early 19th-century furniture, aquatints, and prints, a gourmet of talent, a great bird shot, and the best-natured man one could wish to know." (To summarize: the sort of man to attract big-business clients.) After joining the firm in the 1930s, Charles Horsky frequently rode the Pennsylvania Railroad's Congressional train to New York with Judge Covington. "The train would leave Union Station at four-thirty in the afternoon, and on any given chair car Judge Covington would know at least six people. It was a true education to walk through the train with him. The same thing coming back—constant handshaking." Knowing government bureau chiefs, and judges, and members of regulatory agencies, is one level of advantage; more important for the firm, however, was Covington's friendship with the ruling elders of the du Pont family of Delaware. ("A train can't go through Wilmington without at least one du Pont getting aboard," says Horsky, "and the Judge always knew him.") Because of this relationship, Covington and Burling early became Washington counsel for the vast du Pont enterprises, and through du Pont, for General Motors Corporation, then a subsidiary.

Judge Covington produced the clients; Ed Burling produced the legal work. "You know," Horsky said, "you asked why we got where we did. One thing that can't be understated is this. Mr. Burling was one hell of a good lawyer. There was something else, too. If he had to hire assistants, as he eventually did, he wanted good ones—not the friend of a friend, or someone's son who needed a job, or some old worn-out government lawyer who wanted a place to rest. Mr. Burling was also extraordinarily lucky: very early along [1921], he hired Dean Acheson, who had the charisma to attract clients also, and who could handle himself in a courtroom; and he hired Paul Shorb. Mr. Burling told Shorb he wanted someone to become a specialist in tax law, because taxes were going to be a big field. Well, Shorb became Washington's first real tax attorney, and the best, too."

When Acheson joined Covington and Burling in 1921, the firm had six lawyers—"happily overworked, chronically disorganized, and pleasantly prosperous." One business mainstay in those years was a multitude of claims, both by and against the United States. Some of the shipping claims came to the firm because of Burling's stint on the War Shipping Board; others, apparently, because George Rublee became a favored tennis partner of the King of Sweden while on a prolonged social tour of Europe before the war. When Sweden needed an American lawyer to seek compensation for vessels commandeered by the Allies, she turned to Rublee's firm. Acheson was hired specifically to press a $16-million claim on behalf of Norway. This taste of international experience started Acheson on a somewhat circuitous route to the position of Secretary of State.

"The firm grew enough in the twenties on its tax practice that by the time of the New Deal, it had attracted a cadre of topnotch guys," Horsky states. "Burling wanted the best, and he was willing to pay for it. He had the ability to sense who was good—he did all the interviewing himself—and not to be impressed by grades alone. So in the early 1930s, when the corporations began worrying about 'Washington,' and thinking about hiring a law firm here, Covington and Burling had fifteen or twenty good lawyers. When the 1933–35 boom came, this cadre immediately wanted help, so there was a tremendous increase in size right away.

"In a way, this relates right to our present problem of trying to stay at a controllable size. There is always a tendency to take on more work than you can do, then hire people to do it. But growth is natural, and the way it comes about makes it hard to control.

"You are a lawyer, and you want someone to help you with a case. You hope to get a very good person—otherwise, why bother with hiring him? You rely upon this man, and give him more and more responsibility. In three to five years, he is in a lead position, and *he* needs someone to help him. It's silly for an experienced attorney to spend his time running down citations in the library. So he hires an assistant, and the cycle continues."

As a corporate law firm, Covington and Burling soon became the legal spearhead of big business's attempt to blunt the revolutionary thrust of the New Deal. As old-time Wilsonian Democrats, theoretically partners Covington and Burling could have been expected to tolerate—even applaud—what was happening. But the pragmatic Covington knew enough about politicians (even those in the White House) to suspect that any "political philosophy" contained a good deal of sham, and as an Eastern Shoreman he was intrinsically conservative on the powers of government. "Judge Covington was outraged by a good deal of what the New Deal set out to do, and he was certainly no friend of the New Dealers," Horsky recollects. But Covington, who didn't take his industrialist clients nearly as seriously as they might have believed, couldn't bring himself to rage against Roosevelt. "Hell," he would tell the du Ponts, "*every* government is going to tax you." Burling was also pragmatic. "I disagreed with the New Deal strongly," he told a *Washington Post* reporter in a ninetieth birthday interview in 1960, six years before his death. "But it was a great benefit to lawyers because so many businessmen all over the country began squealing about what was happening to them and had to hire lawyers. And when you ask me about bureaucracy, I say, 'Oh, I'm for it. How would I eat otherwise?' "

Which is not to suggest that Covington and Burling simply yielded the field to the New Deal, and obediently accepted its economic reforms. H. Thomas Austern, one of the very early partners, quickly became the country's expert on the National Recovery Administration, and he drafted numerous Blue Eagle industry codes. (Just as quickly, unfortunately, his specialty evaporated. "When the Supreme Court declared NRA unconstitutional in the sick chicken case," Horsky says, "half of what poor Tommy knew became irrelevant.")

Covington and Burling was just as obliging when a client chose to fight the New Deal. Rural electrification, for example. The Public Works Administration had a program to bring electrical power to the backwoods of America, to the farmhouses and isolated hamlets long ignored by the monopoly utilities. A utility holding company—based in New York, but with subsidiary operating companies strewn across the continent, the consumers far removed from the owners—hired Covington and Burling to scuttle the program. Edward Burling went into Federal court in Oklahoma and obtained an injunction halting a PWA project which conceivably could have cost the holding company a handful of customers. Acheson chuckled in his memoirs that the injunction stopped Secretary of the Interior Harold L. Ickes "in his tracks" because other lawyers followed Burling's example and obtained more than forty injunctions in parallel cases around the country. To Burling's credit, he did warn the holding company it faced almost certain defeat when the case was decided, and that it should take advantage of the time provided by the litigation to regroup. "If the time were used to extend electric lines to rural areas and send rates down," Acheson wrote, "the cooperatives would find getting started much tougher than if the companies held an umbrella over rates." But the company wouldn't follow Burling's advice, and eventually retained a harder-nosed New York law firm to handle the case. It lost, just as Burling had predicted.

Burling's thinking in the PWA case reflects a philosophical changeabout in the law firm during the mid-1930s about what advice should be given clients about relations with the Federal government. Burling's decision, in essence, was that Federal power would not be diminished. The 1936 election results demonstrated (to him, at least) that the vast majority of the American people supported the basic thrust of the New Deal. Burling was a pragmatic man, and also a shrewd lawyer. By his analysis, industry deserved a quid pro quo from the government. In return for submission to regulation, industry should be given protection from "harmful competition." Burling knew his corporate clients well enough to realize the phoniness of their plaints that they be permitted to operate "competitively, in a free enterprise system." Never in its history has American business sought any such thing. From the earliest stirrings of the industrial revolution, the American businessman has fought savagely to establish monopoly control—in oil, in railroads, in sugar, in farm produce, in capital. Because of the counsel of such men as Burling, industry realized by 1936 that the buccaneer days of capitalism were over, that the public would not tolerate a return to an economic system in which the businessman was sovereign. How, then, could business subtly seize control of the reform movement and turn a historic trend to its own advantage?

What follows is basic to an understanding of what the Washington Lawyer is all about, and why America, during the past three decades, has been transformed into a corporate state, one in which the overlap of government and industry is nigh total, and which is neither socialism nor capitalism. It is a case study of an entire industry which willingly submitted itself to governmental control, and of the economic benefits it has been able to reap over the past thirty-five years because of a regulated monopoly. And the prime mover in the episode is the law firm of Covington and Burling.

The United States domestic airline industry was conceived in the early 1930s in a freewheeling competitive situation. Subsidies for air-mail contracts enabled a handful of lines to establish national trunk lines within a few years. Government regulation was minimal: a subsidized line had to meet token safety standards, and the Post Office Department doled out mail contracts through competitive bids. But no restrictions whatsoever were placed upon the freedom of unsubsidized carriers to fly over any route or into any territory. Further, entering the airline business required nominal capital investment: The airways were free, and navigational and other operational facilities were maintained or subsidized by the government. A fledgling airline did not have to buy right-of-way, lay rails, pave highways, or tunnel through mountains; any citizen with an airplane could enter business. As passenger traffic volume increased during the decade, competition—chiefly from the wildcat independent lines—resulted in substantial reductions of passenger and air express rates.

Faced with the awesome reality of free enterprise, the trunk airlines began looking for protection. First, they formed the Air Transport Association, to provide the industry with "the coordinating and stimulating force of a central pool of experience, ideas and strength." The ATA has said of itself that "the general policies which motivate its activities express the desire of its membership for joint action and a united front."

The ATA president, Colonel Edgar S. Gorrell, had an uncle who was an officer of the National Canners Association, which had been one of Covington and Burling's first clients, chiefly in pure food cases. Gorrell asked for a recommendation of a good Washington law firm, and the uncle sent him to H. Thomas Austern, who handled the canners' problems. "The airline industry was about to repeat every error of the land-grant railroads," Austern told me. "They came here with a three-bit problem—mail contracts—that was symptomatic of a lack of forward thinking." Too busy to handle the case, Austern turned the airline companies over to Howard Westwood. "I studied the situation and quickly decided that one of the things Gorrell needed was the kind of legislation that the motor carriers and railroads had, regulating rates and routes and entry into the business and the like," Westwood says.

During a complicated three-year Congressional fight, Westwood and the ATA pushed a bill which in effect transformed American commercial aviation into a closed market. The bill forbade anyone to engage in air transportation without first proving to the satisfaction of a newly created Civil Aeronautics Board that the applicant was "fit, willing and able" to perform the proposed service, and that the service was required in the "public convenience and necessity." Scheduled carriers already operating were not required to make similar proof, and the act directed the CAB to issue them operating certificates—so-called "grandfather certificates." The eighteen scheduled lines receiving the grandfather certificates constituted the ATA membership. They are also the major carriers that constitute the core of the modern airline industry.

This bill, which the Administration supported, ostensibly was written by the Interstate Commerce Commission, which had had four decades of experience in regulating rail and truck traffic. Such was not the case. As the Celler subcommittee developed in 1956 hearings, it was written during January and February 1937 in meetings in rooms 212 and 214 of the Carlton Hotel in Washington. Attending were ICC officials, Gorrell of the ATA, lawyers from United, Trans World, American and Chicago and Southern airlines, and Howard Westwood, the latter as attorney for the ATA. The senior ICC official present explained that the private site was necessary because "we were doing this work overtime—nights and Sundays—and the offices of the Commission were closed, and the guards would not let people come in who were not employees of the Commission."

Although the Post Office and Commerce departments were directly concerned with the bill because of their involvements in commercial aviation, they were neither informed of nor invited to the secret Carlton Hotel tête-à-têtes. The resulting bill went directly to Congress with Administration backing, with nothing said of its composition by a Covington and Burling lawyer.

A careful reading of Gorrell's Congressional testimony on behalf of the CAB act makes clear the ATA's desire for immunity from competition. "Today," he told one committee, "a person without any appreciable finances, if he desires to take the chance, can start a line as a common carrier." A statement of the American capitalist dream? No, a plea on behalf of closing the market.

As Gorrell put it, "Now, not many people are willing to go into the business today and put their money into it, thereby making an investment, unless there is some proper protection against fly-by-night companies whereby some irresponsible companies cannot come along with a lot of secondhand planes and cut prices right out from under legitimate operators. A system that permits such an operation permits no protection for an orderly growth of the business between the points to be served."

Fly-by-night companies. Secondhand planes. Pejorative words —and ones peculiarly applicable to the origins of ATA member companies themselves. A National Airlines president once boasted his line "started out in 1934 with two Ryan four-passenger single-engine planes, not much larger than Lindbergh's *Spirit of St. Louis*." When Pan American made its first flight, a winter service in Alaska, President Juan Trippe says, "the passenger was glad to use it even though he had to ride with a cold nose in a single-engine open-cockpit job." A businessmen's belief in free enterprise and competition is in inverse proportion to the amount of the market he controls.

Persons within the Roosevelt Administration warned of the

economic consequences of the aviation plan lawyer Westwood
wrote for the ATA. Postmaster General James A. Farley noted
that the government had spent "hundreds of millions of dollars
in the building of airports, installation of beacon lights, etc., and
direct subsidies paid to the contractors. Now that the financial
position of these lines is being constantly improved, it would
appear wise to go very slow in granting them perpetual contracts with exclusive franchises . . ." The Post Office Department
solicitor, Karl A. Crowley, said, "This bill provides a perfect
plan for creating monopoly of air transport in this country."
And the Commerce Department warned that the bill "would
produce an undue advantage to the three or four powerful airlines which are already well entrenched and a detriment to the
weaker ones." Despite these protests, the CAB act passed, a feat
for which Howard Westwood receives modest credit in bio-
graphic notes when he writes articles for bar journals.

The ATA achieved its desired monopoly. The trunk airlines
operating under the old "grandfather certificates" handle ninety-
plus percent of airline passenger traffic, and use the CAB to
limit severely the entry of competitors. As former CAB chairman Ross Rizley once complained, the effect of the grandfather
clause "is to give advantage to the large carriers since they are
far better able to support the costs of a drawn-out, complicated
proceeding. Legal fees and payment to high-priced economists
mount very rapidly." (For more on the tribulations small companies face at the CAB, see chapter 5, "Ruling the Regulators:
Just Who's Doing What to Whom?")

For decades thereafter Covington and Burling lawyers helped
the established airlines defend their position in CAB hearings.
One partner who joined the firm in the late 1950s told me he
was immediately assigned to work on aviation cases under
Westwood's direction. "This was a very busy time at the CAB,"
the attorney said. "The CAB was holding major inquiries into

the airline fare structure, operations of non-scheduled airlines, freight operations, and route designations. During one period C&B handled four separate matters, each of which required some seventy days of formal hearings." Covington and Burling's client was American Airlines, which paid seven-figure legal fees for the representation.

As a general practice, only three Covington and Burling lawyers signed briefs filed with the CAB. Why? "That's right," the lawyer replied, "but that doesn't begin to reveal the number of persons who might have been involved. Count the library work, and the people who do economic research, and you could have six or eight people contributing to a single pleading. Of course, you *could* list them all. But that's not so good taste, and it could work against you. Why flaunt it?"

Because it specializes in corporate representation before the Federal government, Covington and Burling will not accept just any client who walks in the door or is referred to the firm by an out-of-town lawyer. The firm will not soil its hands with a divorce proceeding, even for a corporate president it has represented in administrative matters for years. "When this sort of thing arises," one partner told me, "we discreetly refer the client to a list of three firms in Washington that have expertise in domestic relations. We just don't want to get involved in this sort of case." Nor will the firm accept run-of-the-mill criminal cases, other than what its lawyers are assigned through the District of Columbia court's plan for indigent defendants. In successive interviews three senior partners told me they had *never* represented a criminal defendant, despite careers at the bar totaling three-quarters of a century. "If I was appointed to defend someone today," one of these men said, "I'd have to scout around the office for one of our recent graduates who had taken a criminal procedure course and was up on the latest law. You

know, I'm not even sure I could locate the criminal courts here
in the District."

One Covington and Burling partner said the firm avoids criminal work for two reasons. The firm's built-in expenses are such
that few criminal defendants can afford the per-hour fee of $50
upwards. Second, "it's just outside our field. We are administrative lawyers, and our entire operation is geared that way. Criminal work is an entirely different procedural field, and we don't
think we can spend the time on it to develop the expertise you
need." Conversely, when a corporate client faces criminal action, Covington and Burling is capable of conducting a first-rate
defense, replete with bargaining with prosecutors and trading
off one defendant against another to lessen the damage. Covington and Burling's operating rule is the same in both criminal
and civil proceedings: the firm represents the client and is
bound to protect his interests. If a "public policy" issue is involved, presumably someone else will be present to protect the
general public. Witness the price-fixing cases involving manufacturers of electrical equipment—a white-collar scandal with
implications far beyond the routine criminal case.

When the case began to unfold before Federal grand juries in
1959, General Electric retained Covington and Burling to conduct an internal investigation to determine the culpability of
individual executives. For weeks partner Gerhard Gesell (now a
U.S. District Court judge in Washington) took sworn statements from GE officials, trying to determine just how strong
a case the government could develop from GE documents and
witnesses and what defense the company should offer. (To avoid
a conflict of interest, Covington and Burling did not defend
individual employees who were indicted, since what was good for
them was not necessarily good for the company, and vice versa.)
Gesell soon concluded that the Justice Department had GE in
an inextricable bind, and that the company should make the

best deal possible. He recommended that GE plead guilty to the corporate criminal indictments, the fines for which would be relatively minimal. At the same time, however, Gesell demanded some munificent swap-offs from the prosecution.

Based upon what happened, Gesell's strategy was as follows: He needed something in the official record absolving GE directors and top management of any responsibility for the price-fixing. By restricting blame to lower-echelon officials, GE hoped to lessen treble antitrust damages which GE customers were certain to seek in civil suits. And, second, he would stipulate just enough evidence to enable the court to accept a guilty plea —but not any material really useful to plaintiffs in the forth-coming civil suits.

The Justice Department accepted the arrangement, agreeing to nol. pros. the case against Arthur F. Vinson, a divisional vice president and the ranking indicted officer, and to put into the court record some carefully worded language about who knew what concerning the criminal conspiracy. Assistant Attorney General Charles Whittinghill told the court that the government "could not properly argue to a jury that there is no reasonable doubt" as to Vinson's complicity. Then Whittinghill and Gesell went into an agreed-upon script, one written to plead GE guilty with as little pain as possible, either to its image or to its pocket-book.

"Before pleading in this case," Gesell said, "inasmuch as this is the only one of the cases involving General Electric where there have been any allegations concerning the company's board of directors, I would like to ask the government if they have a statement they wish to make with respect to that before I plead. I understand they do."

Gesell "understood" correctly, for in fact he had already read Whittinghill's statement. "In response to the request of General Electric," the prosecutor said, "the government makes this statement: The government has not charged and does not claim that any member of 'the General Electric board of directors, including Mr. Ralph J. Cordiner and Mr. Robert Paxton [board chairman and president, respectively] had knowledge of the conspiracies pleaded to in the indictments, nor does the government claim that any of these men personally authorized or ordered commission of any of the acts charged in any of the indictments."

The script completed, Gesell said, "Your honor, with that statement, General Electric pleads guilty in this case."

In a letter to stockholders after the court proceeding, GE claimed it pleaded guilty and *nolo contendere* to the various criminal indictments "only when it appeared that the company would be held legally responsible for what had been done by a few officers and employees, *in spite of the innocence of the directors and top management*." Under close examination, however, Whittinghill's statement does not go quite so far as to say affirmatively that Cordiner and Paxton were innocent, only that the government "did not charge or claim" they were guilty. The line is thin but real.

The trial court out of the way, Gesell next moved to keep grand jury records away from city and state governments which had been bilked of millions of dollars by the corporate price-fixers. The victimized governments—and a few private customers—pleaded they could not possibly amass the same evidence, showing the extent of their losses, were they denied access to the government's case—details which were compiled, after all, at the taxpayers' expense. Gesell had kept GE officials off the public witness stand, however, and he did not intend to let the consumers win a backdoor victory. Regardless of the public-policy issues, he maintained, the testimony should not be released. U.S. District Judge J. Cullen Ganey agreed, over Justice Department opposition. Noting the plight of the swindled governments, he nonetheless ruled that "such considerations do not outweigh the policy of secrecy."

All in all, an exemplary legal performance, and Gesell received laudatory pats on the back from his colleagues at Covington and Burling, and some kind words from GE Chairman Cordiner. Then, unexpectedly, a rear-guard action by Senator Estes Kefauver, and a further challenge to Gesell's legal ingenuity.

Kefauver said the guilt pleas without trial, and the grand jury secrecy, "meant that the American people would have no access to the details of the conspiracies." Kefauver moved for hearings by the Senate subcommittee on antitrust and monopoly, which he chaired. And Gesell moved to stop him, working through the complaisant Senator Roman Hruska (R., Neb.), a subcommittee member. At a closed meeting of the subcommittee Hruska argued vigorously against pursuing the cases any further, saying Congress should not put itself into the position of gathering evidence for use by a plaintiff in a private suit. Were the companies required to testify publicly, Hruska maintained, they almost certainly would damage their defenses in subsequent civil trials. On and on Hruska rambled, with a legal erudition his colleagues had never before detected. Surely someone had coached this cornpatch solon. And, sure enough, someone had: After repeated Hruska references to a "legal memorandum," one of Kefauver's staff people peeked over the Senator's shoulders and saw a document prepared by Gerhard A. Gesell of Covington and Burling. Kefauver told Hruska, in effect, If you are going to act as an attorney for GE, I'll even things out, and act as attorney for the citizens they cheated. Hruska fumed, but couldn't stop public hearings. Nor could Kefauver stop Hruska from asking batting-practice questions—big, soft and slow—to serve up to GE Chairman Ralph J. Cordiner. "Hruska was not officially recognized as counsel of record for Cordiner," colum-

nist George Dixon wrote the next day, "but the Nebraska law-
maker acted as if he were a combination mouthpiece and press
agent for the harried magnate." Dixon continued:

> The Republican Mr. Hruska pretended to be throwing
> searching questions at the high-voltage tycoon, but be-
> came so blatant as defender and apologist that even Cor-
> diner began to look a bit embarrassed. I hadn't heard such
> vicious cross-examination since a department store Santa
> Claus asked me if it wasn't true that I loved my mommy
> and poppy and that I was the dearest, sweetest and best
> little boy in the whole, wide world . . .
>
> Chairman Kefauver had difficulty in holding onto his
> judicial mien when the GOP solon asked the witness if he
> didn't think it would be terrible to tighten the antitrust laws.
> This ripped through Cordiner's defenses so brutally he
> broke down and agreed the present laws were "amply
> severe."

One morning in 1947 the Iranian Ambassador to the United
States telephoned John G. Laylin, a senior partner at Covington
and Burling, and asked him to come to the embassy immediately. The matter was urgent, the Ambassador said, and he
would be appreciative if Laylin would hurry. The firm had done
no work for Iran previously; curious about the summons, Laylin
dropped whatever work he was doing and caught a cab.

"When I got there and sat down, the Ambassador asked what
I liked to drink," Laylin recollects. "I told him that I was a
Scotch man, but that I normally didn't drink anything that
early. After all, it was only ten in the morning.

"The Ambassador smiled. 'Mr. Laylin,' he said, 'after what I
am going to tell you, I think you are going to need a drink. I
have just been authorized to hire you to get the Russians out of
my country.'

" 'Mr. Ambassador,' I said, 'I think I would like to have a Scotch.' "

And thus began a period of cold-war diplomacy which veritably made Covington and Burling an arm of the United States Department of State, orchestrating activities of friendly allied governments so they did not conflict with Washington's foreign policy goals.

Covington and Burling's international practice is unique in several respects. As do a score of other New York and Washington firms, it advises foreign governments and companies in routine commercial matters. But unlike the others, it is also a prime mover in shaping foreign policy—both of the United States and of its client governments. And in numerous instances the goals of its clients and Washington overlap.

In the case of Iran, Laylin says, "the Russians had overstayed their welcome" after the Second World War ended, and both the Iranians and Washington wanted them out. A formal treaty obligated the Soviets to withdraw by March 2, 1946, but they stalled, pressing for Iranian recognition of a pro-Soviet autonomous regime created in Azerbaijan, and for a joint Soviet-Iranian company to exploit oil resources in the north of the country. Because of a strong pro-Soviet element in its parliament, the Iranian government did not have complete freedom of action, and Ambassador Hussein Ala maneuvered to persuade the United States to take the matter to the Security Council on its own initiative. Secretary of State James Byrnes was sympathetic, but replied Iran would be better received if it acted on its own. The visit to Laylin followed.

Laylin helped the Ambassador draft Iran's case for presentation to the United Nations Security Council; after some months of haggling, the Soviets appeared to have won their two points and withdrew the troops. Whereupon the Iranian parliament repudiated the oil consortium agreement and sent troops into Azerbaijan to reestablish authority in the breakaway region.

Summarizing his efforts, Laylin says, "This was the only time in the postwar period the Soviets were bargained out of anything."

Dean Acheson had left Covington and Burling in 1941 to reenter government; from August 1945 to June 1947, when the firm was rebuilding its international practice, he served as Under Secretary of State, the department's number-two position. Laylin, however, insists that Acheson "had absolutely nothing to do" with Covington and Burling representing Iran and Greece, two nations with whose affairs Acheson dealt intimately in his official capacity. "The Iran case came about this way," he said. "Immediately after the war I handled a routine case for Saudi Arabia. An Arabist in the State Department apparently was impressed. Anyway, shortly thereafter, when Iran asked this man to recommend a United States lawyer for the Soviet problem, he listed three firms—Covington and Burling was among them—and told what I had done for Saudi Arabia. That's why the [Iranian] Ambassador called me in. Right after we won the Iranian case in the United Nations, the Greek Ambassador said to me, 'Congratulations! You ran the Russians out of Iran. Now you are going to run them out of Greece.' "

The Greek case, considerably more complicated, involved much closer liaison with former partner Acheson, and it is also a nigh-classic case of the overlaps between government and the quasi-public world of the Washington Lawyer. Greece was near collapse in the winter of 1946–47 because of guerrilla activity, economic turmoil and inept government; Acheson writes in his memoirs that the situation there "deteriorated rapidly during January and February 1947" and that by late February "all signs pointed to an impending move by the Communists to take over the country."

On February 18, 1947, Covington and Burling formally consummated its agreement with the Greek government. P. Economou-Gouras, chargé d'affaires of the Greek embassy in

Washington, spelled out the terms in a letter to Laylin and John Lord O'Brian, another senior partner in the international field:

> You are to act as our sole legal advisers in the United States on all matters brought by Greece to the attention of the Security Council of the United Nations and on all questions involved in the application of Greece for loans from the Export-Import Bank, and from the International Bank for Reconstruction and Development [the World Bank].
>
> It is understood that you are not to be asked to undertake any work that may conflict in any way with the foreign policy of your government, and that you may reserve the right to withdraw at any time as our advisers if in your opinion any proposed course of conduct will conflict with the policy of your government.
>
> You have stated it will not be satisfactory to answer isolated questions but that within the scope of your work you must be kept fully informed and consulted on all developments. The embassy and our country will, of course, be free to follow your advice or not as we think best promotes the interests of Greece, but we fully understand and will respect your desire to withdraw as counsel in the event that your advice is not followed on any matter of importance.

Economou-Gouras agreed to pay Covington and Burling "in accordance with your customary scale of charges on a time basis," and enclosed a $5,000 retainer. But the amount actually received by Covington and Burling for the case indicates Greece was not a normal commercial client. The fees for three years totaled only $52,263, a pittance for the amount of work done by the firm. The Iranians paid less than $50,000. Laylin, however, denies Covington and Burling got into the case on behalf of the State Department or any other Federal agency.

Three days later, on February 21, Secretary of State George C. Marshall directed Dean Acheson "to prepare the necessary steps for sending economic and military aid" to Greece; shortly thereafter, economically strapped Britain formally announced her intention to cease aid to Greece and Turkey within six weeks, and the chain of events which led to establishment of the Marshall Plan was under way. Financially, Covington and Burling worked with State Department officials to lobby $400 million in economic and military aid through Congress, paying particular attention to Republican Senator Arthur Vandenberg. Diplomatically, Laylin and O'Brian wrote speeches for the Greeks to present both in the Security Council and in the General Assembly. The issue there was support of guerrillas in Greece by Yugoslavia, Albania, and Bulgaria. "I never spoke for Greece in the debates, but I sat in the audience or right behind their delegates, and I offered my thoughts," Laylin says. "It was ninety-nine percent legal work." A Soviet veto killed a U.S. resolution in the Security Council asking for cessation of external aid to the guerrillas, but with Laylin's guidance Greece managed to push the same document through the General Assembly.

According to the record of UN debates, the U.S. and Greek positions were indistinguishable during the entire episode. Yet Laylin attempts to draw a clear distinction between *representing* a foreign government—"which we never do"—and *advising* a foreign government. "I would not go to the State Department and say I am speaking for the government of Greece," Laylin says. "I say I am advising the Greeks, and that the Prime Minister, or Foreign Minister, has asked me to say 'this is the position of Greece.'" When working for a foreign client, Laylin says, "I make clear that I am an American, and I am not going to do anything against the high policy of my government; if it ever gets to that point, I'll withdraw. But that does not mean I am reluctant about telling people in the State Department that something I am advocating is a good thing for my client *and* the United States, too."

The distinction carries with it an independence that Laylin says he would not have if he acted as the agent of a foreign client. "If a lawyer is acting as the representative of a foreign government, and instructions come from the home office—the foreign ministry, or the chief executive officer—he has to follow them. This holds also for the Ambassador. But I can come back to them and say, 'I don't think this is so good, and I don't think you should do it.'

"Let me give you an example, concerning a country I'll have to leave nameless. The country was the beneficiary of a considerable amount of United States financial aid. It fell down in a deal involving a shipment of grain and was sued for certain demurrage charges for the shipping, something relatively simple relating to slowness in paperwork. The case was pretty clear-cut against the country. The foreign ministry wanted to plead sovereign immunity and get out of the suit. It was silly. At most, the country would save $300,000 or so. But in doing so it would jeopardize literally tens of millions of dollars of future aid, because the United States government would be most upset.

"The Ambassador did not have guts enough to tell the foreign minister he was doing a stupid thing. We can speak candidly, for the worst thing they can do, if the foreign minister is offended, is to fire us. We are not dependent upon any one client—but the Ambassador is." The country followed Laylin's advice and paid the claim.

Laylin and other firm partners frequently—but non-specifically—speak of Dean Acheson's "attractiveness" in obtaining new clients. Acheson rejoined the firm on January 21, 1953, the day after leaving the office of Secretary of State. He registered as an agent of a foreign government in only one instance: in

August 1959, to aid the Venezuelan government in its success-
ful attempt to extradite the ousted dictator Marcos Perez Jime-
nez for trial for fiscal corruption. But as a private citizen,
Acheson spoke with the authority of a former Secretary of State
on issues involving foreign governments which Covington and
Burling has represented. He argued to the House Foreign Affairs
Committee in 1970 against commercial strictures against South
Africa, and he had friendly words for the junta government of
Greece. And Acheson also did favors for Presidents, the public awareness of which is not harmful to a Washington Lawyer.
President Kennedy used Acheson to pass word to the West
German government he wanted a different German Ambassador in Washington, and the sooner the better, and to help
through the NATO crisis precipitated by Charles de Gaulle's
withdrawal of France. President Johnson first utilized Acheson
as an adviser on civil rights matters, and found him a faithful
follower of his Vietnam policy. And President Nixon brought
Acheson out of retirement in 1971 to help beat down an attempt by Senator Mike Mansfield to cut U.S. troop commit-
ments to NATO.

Laylin is the Covington and Burling partner responsible for
training new associates who intend to work in the international
field. He looks for men with a background parallel to his own:
an emphasis on political science, history, and government in
undergraduate school, then a heavy load of international law
courses. After his own graduation from Harvard Law, in 1928,
Laylin interviewed at Sullivan and Cromwell, the big New York
law firm. This was the era when one could make a serious case
for the position that Sullivan and Cromwell outranked the State
Department in the conduct of United States foreign policy. Both
John Foster and Allen Dulles came through the firm, and Laylin says John Foster Dulles "arranged for an appointment for
me to work with Dwight Morrow, who was then our Ambassa-

dor in Mexico City. I learned much there about how business is done with foreign nations. It was invaluable." (Covington and Burling, which avoids hiring lawyers from the government, makes an exception in the international field: it actively scouts the Foreign Service for bright people.) After two years with Morrow, Laylin returned to Sullivan and Cromwell; although he yearned for an international practice, some homework was in order. "Talk all you want to about being an 'international lawyer,' " Laylin says, "first you've got to learn to be a good lawyer. I handled all sorts of small cases; the principles are pretty much the same—how to develop a factual situation; what is important to your case; where to draw the issue; how to argue it."

Laylin's early cases at Sullivan and Cromwell involved foreign nations that were going off the gold standard, and how the change in monetary standards could be reconciled with obligations to foreign bondholders. Lawyers who understand the intricacies of gold trade are very rare; hence a special assignment early in the New Deal. When President Roosevelt decided to take the United States off the gold standard, Sullivan and Cromwell loaned Laylin to the Administration as an adviser. Working with Dean Acheson, then the acting Secretary of the Treasury, Laylin in time wrote the specific language that abrogated the gold standard. His assignment ended, Laylin prepared to return to New York, but Acheson persuaded him to come to Covington and Burling as a partner.

Row upon row of leather-bound volumes of court pleadings and briefs in Laylin's office display the diversity of his foreign practice the past 35 years.* A border dispute between Iran and Iraq. Another between Pakistan and Afghanistan. Claims for

* So, too, does the list of foreign decorations which Laylin has acquired over the years: Commander, Order of the Lion, Finland; Commander, Order of Dannebrog, Denmark; Sitara-I-Pakistan; and Comendador of Order of San Carlos, Colombia.

compensation for U.S. owners of sugar mills confiscated by the Castro government in Cuba. "In one case before the Foreign Claims Settlement Commission," Laylin says, "we received an award for $110 million." A deep sigh. "Only there was no money to collect." An attempt to obtain compensation for the Cerro Corporation, a U.S. copper company nationalized by the Allende government of Chile. A more or less continuous case involving Colombia's payments (or lack thereof) on bonds sold in foreign markets. A seventeen-year court fight on behalf of Denmark to force the United States to pay compensation for forty vessels requisitioned in 1941. ("The Danish owners were promised treatment equal to that of U.S. companies; when time came to settle, lawyers down at the Maritime Commission wanted to take off fifty percent. We worked seventeen years, but we got the equal treatment.")

But Covington and Burling's longest-time client has been Pakistan, for which it has served as permanent solicitor around the world. "We have advised them from the beginning, when they first came into existence in 1947." The first case involved a dispute with India over water rights in the Indus River basin. Laylin prepared a World Court brief, but India refused to accept the court's jurisdiction. And what followed is why Laylin thinks international law is a fascinating way to make a living. "In international law," he told me, "you about have to create your own forum. If you have a really hot dispute, they certainly are not going to arbitrate." So Laylin began searching for someone to whom he could argue Pakistan's cause. He learned that India had asked the World Bank for financing of a dam on its side of the Indus—one which would enable it to halt the flow of water to Pakistan. "I persuaded the World Bank and its directors to adopt a policy under which they would not lend money for structures on international rivers before the parties had agreed on an equitable distribution of water," Laylin said. India protested the regulation, for she knew exactly why it was being proposed, and by what lawyer. But India also needed the dam, so she agreed to negotiate a settlement of the Indus issue with Pakistan. To tighten the lid on his victory, Laylin also succeeded in persuading the International Law Commission, a UN group, to pass a declaration on the rights of riparian states to waters from international rivers.

Laylin worked fourteen years on the Indus River case, and very profitably. Pakistan paid legal fees ranging as high as $125,-000 per year during the period, according to foreign agent registration statements filed by Covington and Burling with the Justice Department. Also remunerative is a commercial and political intelligence operation Covington and Burling runs for the Hong Kong General Chamber of Commerce. The firm periodically reports on "proposed legislation introduced in Congress and on matters raised with the Tariff Commission and with other agencies concerning imports in which the members of the Chamber and/or Federation [of Industries] may be interested." In 1968 alone Covington and Burling received $33,450 for its reports on tariff matters. But foreign representations carry with them the potential for nickel-and-dime cases a firm as august as Covington and Burling would normally shun—for instance, a lease dispute between Guinea and the New York World Fair Corporation, and a row between client Canada and Ghana over who was responsible for repairs to a nine-inch-tall brick fence and retaining wall separating their respective embassies.

And there is also the danger of political embarrassment, both external and internal.

In 1970 five young associate members of the firm became disturbed over Covington and Burling's work on behalf of South African Airways, which is government-owned. Because of South Africa's apartheid policies, the airline would not accept black passengers on flights from New York. When the airline faced loss of its landing rights at Kennedy International Airport in New York, Covington and Burling defended it, first before the New York State Commission on Human Rights, then in United States District Court. The representation disgusted the group of associates.

"How could we in good conscience work for an airline that discriminated against American citizens?" one of these lawyers asked me several months after leaving Covington. "There are certain fundamental principles to which this nation is committed, morally and legally, and here we were, trying to uphold an abominable violation of them." The group took its protest to the firm's management committee and argued that Covington and Burling should drop the case. "It was all very friendly, all very polite, but the management committee wouldn't budge."

This incident, and others, convinced the young lawyer he wasn't "partner material," and he left the firm several months later. He notes, however, that the internal dispute did not adversely affect the group of protestants. "As a matter of fact," he said later, "one of them was made partner in 1971, so I suppose things worked out okay." Covington and Burling also won the airline case.

Laylin bridled—politely, I admit, but I know a bridle when I see one—when I asked him about the South African case. "Hell," he snapped, "I'm a lawyer, not a reformer. *We* are lawyers. We act as counsel. We are not presumptuous enough to pass judgment on the form of government of a client which happens to be a foreign nation, no more than we would ask a domestic client whether he is a Democrat or a Republican."

In the airline case, according to Laylin's version, South Africa "got a little choosy about who it would issue visas, as is its right. *All* airlines require visas before you can fly overseas, and the policies are set by the government. So why single out South African Airways?"

Well, I asked Laylin, isn't the visa requirement aimed at blacks, as alleged by the firm's dissident associates? And does Covington and Burling feel comfortable helping a foreign government enforce a racist policy?

Yes, Laylin conceded, the policy is directed against blacks. "Blacks *and* agitators. South Africa doesn't want them; it decided as a matter of national policy to keep them out. But that isn't our business. I don't give a second thought to the matter."

Actually, Laylin continued, Covington and Burling once had an even more intense internal dispute over representation of a nation at the other end of the political spectrum. "We were attorneys for Poland before it went Communist. On that occasion, we resigned at the insistence of one or two partners—not including Mr. Acheson, I might add. I was dead against resigning. We were helping them to prepare paperwork for an Export-Import Bank loan for construction of coal cars that would service all of Europe. The coal was badly needed, for this was the period of great economic stress, the years right after the war. The State Department was most upset at our decision, for Americans in Poland were having trouble obtaining counsel. I argued, but I lost, and we had to drop Poland."

Laylin was silent a minute. "You know," he finally continued, "some of these younger people don't seem to understand the proper role of a lawyer. We're not here to save the world, or to force our own ideas on someone else, but to represent clients."

For its size, Covington and Burling is markedly unorganized. "This isn't really a law firm," Charles Horsky told me. "Actually, it's a conglomeration of fifty law practices." For managerial efficiency, some large firms are split into departments —for litigation, for corporate work, for taxes, for various regulatory matters. A concomitant of such a tightly structured organization is close supervision, which lawyers, as professional

men, tend to find galling. At the other extreme are firms decen-
tralized to the point where there is no continuity of experience,
with lawyers taking in turn, almost in roster fashion, whatever
case comes into the office. Covington and Burling attempts to
walk a middle ground between departments and the free-float-
ing system. Most of the senior men are better in one particular
phase of law than others, but they are not necessarily bound to
practice before the SEC, the Internal Revenue Service, or the
ICC.

A partner who desired anonymity gave me an illustration to
show how the Covington and Burling system works:

"I became an expert in communications law—or so they say
—because in the 1940s one of our clients wanted to buy a
television station, and I had dealt with him on other matters. I
studied, and I learned how to handle proceedings at the FCC.
And I suppose I spend more time on communications matters
than anything else.

"But if the Echo Broadcasting Company—to make up the
name of a client—has a tax problem, I'll carry it as far as I can,
then consult with someone in the office who is a tax expert. If
Echo intends to file a registration statement with the SEC so it
can sell stock to the public, an SEC specialist would draft the
papers, but I'll go over them carefully to ensure that all the
representations are accurate, and that they do not unwittingly
violate any of the myriad FCC rules and regulations.

"In other words, there are very few of us who do only one
thing. You might think that a lawyer's experience would be
more varied in a small firm. That is not true. Let's be realistic.
In an office of nine men, how many people can you have learning tax law? Or SEC law? Or doing litigation?"

A five-member management committee does whatever routine decision-making is required to keep the firm going. "Every
partner in the firm has equal voice in the way our affairs are

conducted," a member of the committee told me. "There are some firms around the country—I can think of one in Cleveland, and in Dallas and on the Coast, and right here in Washington, for that matter—that are dictatorial, with one man in complete control. Not every lawyer likes to be involved in the routine of administering an office—they'd rather practice law." A lawyer who is a partner is tantamount to being director of a corporation; the management committee is comparable to a corporate executive committee. Theoretically, a thirty-five-year-old freshly elected partner had equal stature with the venerable Dean Acheson, who worked with the firm, on and off, for half a century. In practicality, however, the process isn't quite one-man-one-vote. "I would hope," said a partner, "that at fifty years of age, I would be more persuasive than a younger man. If not, I'm not much of a lawyer."

New clients go through a screening committee, which detects possible conflicts of interest. But the court of first resort is the partner who has initial contact with the prospective client. If for some reason he doesn't like the case, he is entitled to reject it without further referral to the screening committee. Seldom is a rejected client passed on to the committee. "We have that much individuality—and business," says a partner.

Finding new bodies to feed into this ever-expanding legal machine keeps a senior partner occupied for most of the spring. Unlike most Washington law firms, Covington and Burling seldom hires directly from the government. Of the fifty-five partners in the firm as of mid-June 1971, twenty-nine were Harvard Law graduates. (The next greatest representation is Yale, nine graduates; no other law school supplied as many as five partners.) Eleven had clerked for U.S. Supreme Court Justices. "The top law grads and the clerks," one partner said. "That's where they come from. We don't find any need to hire from government to get experience, because we have a wide range of experience right in the firm. What would we do with a former chairman of the FTC? Hell, show me anybody in Washington who knows more about the FTC than Tommy Austern and I'll give you the keys to the office. Or the CAB. Remember, Howard Westwood *created* the CAB." Covington and Burling does not frown at nepotism, however. Edward Burling, Jr., and J. Harry Covington, Jr., are among the current partners. William P. Bundy, Acheson's son-in-law, worked with the firm for three years before joining the government in 1951, first with the CIA, then with the Defense and State departments.

But Covington and Burling does recognize the value of government service, so much so, in fact, that it has a more or less permanent slot reserved for its lawyers, and a very important one. The Solicitor General's office is tantamount to attorney for the Federal government. So far as Washington Lawyers are concerned, its most important function is deciding which Federal cases are to be appealed to higher courts. If the Food and Drug Administration loses a proceeding at the trial court level, for example, FDA attorneys must convince the Solicitor General the case should be pursued further. There are twelve lawyers in the office, and for the past two decades one has always come from Covington and Burling—generally for a two-year term, with a partnership when he returns to private practice. To the Washington legal fraternity the slot is known as "The Covington and Burling Seat." But a partner insisted to me that if a lawyer enters government service, he must sever all connections with Covington and Burling, and he is not guaranteed a job if he resigns. "We might say, 'We hope you come back,' but nothing firmer than that," the partner said. No less an authority than Dean Acheson candidly stated the value of high-level government service. When he returned to Covington and Burling after six months as Under Secretary of the Treasury in 1933, "considerations of law, propriety and good taste ruled out departmental practice. This left—in Washington—practice before the courts and administrative tribunals, where one's conduct was a matter of public record . . . My short venture from private practice into government service did not hurt; on the contrary, it improved my practice. I had become known . . . throughout the business community as a 'sound' man." Conversely, after his term as Secretary of State from 1949 to 1953, Acheson says he was "controversial," and not nearly so valuable a drawing card. Corporate clients conceivably could have been concerned about candidate Richard Nixon's sneering references to "Dean Acheson's College of Cowardly Communist Containment."

New lawyers are permitted to ask for work in a particular field—but don't necessarily get it. A partner who is active in recruiting says he tells graduating seniors, "We'll give you varied enough experience so that you'll have a background in almost anything a lawyer can do in Washington. But rotate from field to field too much, and you'll become a dilettante." One disgruntled former associate who resigned after two years asserted, "You'll hear anything at the interview. You might be promised international work, but if they happen to need an FTC flunky the week you come in, that's it, baby, and don't come crying to the headhunter who hired you." The firm elders can't seem to understand why twenty-four-year-old graduates aren't content to plunge headfirst into the esoterica of maritime or patent law. One partner supposedly coordinates assignments of associates; however, there is much tugging and pulling among partners who need help, and a new lawyer might find himself splitting his time between three or four overseers. A man can say no to an assignment once. The second time, he is getting onto dangerous ground. "If a man goes into three or four areas without being happy, you begin to ask whether it's him or you who is wrong, and this is when you might advise him he might want to do something else."

A new associate can also expect a grinding schedule; night and weekend work is the norm, and there are whispered stories of the senior partners who delight in assigning a complicated brief at five o'clock on Friday afternoon, with a Monday morning deadline. Testing, you understand—a man must prove his *commitment* to the firm, and his ability to churn out top-quality work under pressure, without fretting about what the wife and kids are doing this evening. For partners, the rule is unwritten and thus all the more binding: you are not required to work any specific number of hours, only to "carry your share of the load." Hence Covington and Burling is as bustling at midday Saturday as are other firms at midday Tuesday; fewer secretaries, of course, for they must be paid overtime, and partners wear sports clothes, but the legal factory grinds on.

But Covington has advantages which some lawyers don't appreciate until they are outside the firm. Logistical support. Stenographic pools that work evening shifts, producing crisp electric-type copies of briefs and pleadings. Messengers who get your papers across town on time. The largest private law library anywhere. "One advantage I have in practicing at the NLRB [National Labor Relations Board]," Charles Horsky told me, "is that we have a better file of NLRB cases than the NLRB does. Hell, they borrow stuff from us." A complete legislative history of every major act passed since 1919—Congressional committee hearings, floor debates, indexes of court decisions. Nine full-time librarians, a bindery, a microfilm room, enclosed cubicles so that lawyers can research in privacy and silence, a sun-filled reading room with upholstered chairs. "A lot of money goes in here," partner H. Thomas Austern told me after a tour, "but it's worth it."

Covington and Burling decides within five to seven years after a man graduates from law school whether he is to be promoted to partner. "If you take a man in, it pretty well means you expect to practice law with him the rest of your life," a senior man said. "It's hard to tell him you've changed your mind when he is already a partner." The selection process is ritualized. One Monday afternoon in mid-June of each year the firm's partners gather in what Charles Horsky calls "Jack Valenti's theater downstairs"—the screening room of the Motion Picture Association of America on the ground floor of the building (Covington and Burling does not possess a conference room large enough to seat all its partners). One partner says, "There's seldom much debate. The management committee has recommendations, and most of us have a good idea of who is good." Three to five new partners are selected annually, and after each vote someone phones upstairs and invites the man to "come down for a moment." The ceremony is fixed: he is told the partners present have voted to offer him a partnership, and is asked, "Will you accept?" Horsky says, "Somehow he always says yes." Applause and handshakes, and circulation of an announcement memo through the office the same afternoon.

Election to partnership carries with it the probability that the lawyer will be a moderately wealthy man within his lifetime. As of June 1971 Covington and Burling had 5,226 "shares" outstanding. The distribution is a discreetly held secret, and three partners told me no hard formula existed on how the shares are divided. The amorphous guidelines relate to (a) how much money a lawyer brought into the firm via fees; (b) how much future income his clients represent; (c) how much he earned in previous years; and (d) the size of his family, and other personal obligations. The number of shares has steadily increased, for Covington and Burling gives a man a "raise" by increasing the number allocated to him, not by cutting someone else's quota. The allocations are recommended by the management committee, and are approved by a partnership vote. One veteran partner remembers only one argument over allocations—

from a senior man who did not think he was entitled to the number of shares voted him, and tried to decline an increase. (He did not win.) But this veteran does add, "One reason we've had no disputes, I suppose, is that the amount of money to be divided is continually growing."

Not all men who come to Covington and Burling are willing to do what is necessary to be invited to "Jack Valenti's theater downstairs" to accept a partnership. A young lawyer who was most unhappy when he resigned from Covington and Burling, after a year's work there, bit into his veal cutlet in a small Italian restaurant north of K Street and chewed reflectively a minute before giving me an opinion of his old firm. "Covington and Burling is the top law firm in the country in terms of legal expertise, no doubt about that," he finally said. "You pay top dollar, but you get top work.

"Why is it good? Because it has made money, lots of it, by representing the big corporations, and therefore can afford to hire the best legal minds available. It's a tradition—don't hire anyone who isn't top-notch. When you get people who know they can be very rich in a few years' time, you don't have to give even lip service to pro bono work, or the public interest. Money. If you don't want to be rich, you get out."

This young lawyer wasn't naive about Washington Law. He worked and lived in Europe before graduation, and he had spent time in Washington. He had heard all the law school sto- ries about Covington and Burling being a corporate firm; he knew what it did, and for whom. Why, then, did he go into the firm?

"Fifteen thousand dollars a year is one reason," he said. "But I had to see for myself whether it was as bad as I had heard. It was, even worse. The moral blindness. The idea that the only way to do business was to gut the regulatory agencies. The complete disdain

for any interest other than that of the corporation clients. Look at Tommy Austern. Nine years he managed to keep the Geritol case going. [See chapter 5, "Ruling the Regulators: Just Who's Doing What to Whom?"] Could anyone be proud of a stunt like that?"

Covington and Burling does not like to hear such comments from former Bright Young Men, even secondhand. "We seem to spend an inordinate amount of time during our job interviews explaining that corporations have a right to legal representation," a senior partner says. "I'm always getting questions like, 'Will I *have* to represent corporations? Or anyone else who comes along?' One year the question was, 'What, for example, would Covington and Burling do if you were asked to represent Eichmann?' " Covington and Burling now has the answers (although, for the record, no one who asked the question was hired): A young associate took a court appointment to defend a member of the American Nazi Party in a criminal action. "The lawyer was Jewish, too, and I think maybe he went out of his way to prove something to himself." Another partner quotes with distaste Robert F. Kennedy's angry private remark that Edward Bennett Williams, the noted Washington criminal attorney, should have been disbarred because he let client Jimmy Hoffa take the Fifth Amendment more than one hundred times before the Senate rackets committee. The Bill of Rights, this man says, is a very encompassing guarantee, and it protects corporations and individuals alike, and once you start waiving it for one party, you eventually waive it for all. "The public interest—what is it? Who can define it?" asks John Sapienza. He defines "public policy" as an act of Congress that has been upheld by the courts. "I don't recognize the onmipotence of a Federal official, and I have no qualms whatsoever about challenging a new law in the courts. That is part of our system."

And Sapienza went into a litany of corporate faith which I heard repeated so many times in Washington law offices that I could mouth the words along with the speakers: If the "public interest" suffers because of one-sided legal representation, the persons concerned with the "public interest" should find some lawyers of their own, either through the government or through private groups. Covington and Burling isn't obligated to pull its punches just because it is facing push-over opposition. Don't gripe at us if we win a drug case at the FDA—gripe at the FDA for not hiring better attorneys. Or at Congress for not providing enough money to hire them. Or at yourself for not being willing to pay the taxes to provide the money to hire the better attorneys. And so forth.

When public-interest law became fashionable in Washington in the late 1960s, many firms rather ostentatiously announced formal programs of free or low-fee work. (See chapter 10, "The New Washington Lawyers: Balancing the Scales.") Arnold and Porter, for instance, adopted a policy of committing ten percent of the firm's time to notable causes. Covington and Burling said nothing, but watched with a good deal of detached amusement. "We had been doing this sort of thing in our own unorganized, unstructured, unpublic way," a senior partner states, "long before it became 'the thing to do' in Washington Law." Two outsiders agree. Professor Monroe Freedman, of the George Washington University law faculty, and a keen critical observer of Washington firms, states, "C&B has long done this kind of work and shunned the credit." And the American Civil Liberties Union, which uses Covington and Burling as an informal legal labor pool, gave the firm a twenty-five-year award for meritorious service a few years back.

Covington partners stress that the firm does not demand public-interest work on a collective basis, but simply lets a new man know he can do as much or as little as he wishes, so long as he earns his keep in the office. "I'd never tell a kid what to do," states Thomas Austern. "It's not our business whether he plays a piano in a whorehouse or in a church." Some examples: Early partner George Rublee bargained desperately with Joseph Goebbels in the late 1930s to ransom Jews from Nazi Germany. His then assistant, Austern, remarks, "I couldn't even begin to tell you the number of weeks Rublee worked on this deal, because we don't count things that way." Charles Horsky, as a member of the Maryland board of education, played a quiet but dominant role in desegregation of public schools in suburban Montgomery County. The fight against the Three Sisters Bridge, which would destroy a scenic Potomac landmark. A ruling that District of Columbia courts would consider alcoholism a disease, not a crime. A $100,000, eighteen-month fight to stop the U.S. Navy from selling the offshore Puerto Rican island of Culebra. "Conscience work," says one outside critic, "giving society a few cents change from all the profits it makes." Perhaps—perhaps not. "It's a sad commentary on our society," notes public-interest lawyer Benny Kass, "but we judge a person's sincerity today by how much money he is willing to give to a cause. On that criterion, Covington and Burling is damned sincere."

Covington and Burling makes no pretense at rapport with all its clients, and their policies. "Sometimes you really have to grit your teeth," one man told me in a moment of rare candor about client-firm relations. "I see things I find personally repugnant. But I don't suppose I'd like all my clients if I practiced criminal law, or real-estate law." Sapienza insists that Covington and Burling does draw a line: "If a corporation is polluting a river, for instance, we'll advise of its rights under the law, and how to go about complying with the law. But if some corporation came in here and said outright, 'To hell with the law, we're not going to follow it, and we want you to fight the government as long as we can,' we wouldn't represent him." Sapienza and his colleagues are somewhat testy about what they feel are suggestions that they really don't give a damn what happens to the country. A broader view—that is what is needed, they say. A firm that pollutes might employ three hundred men whose families are dependent upon its staying in business; the practices probably were legal when the factory began operation; management is sincere about obeying the statutes. The lawyer's task is to find a mode of compliance that doesn't put the company out of business. And if doing so means haggling with the Federal government, and tough bargaining, so be it—that's how Covington and Burling lawyers earn their living. "You've got to remember," remarks partner Ernest Jennes, "that we are human beings and citizens as well as lawyers. Our wives and our children breathe this air, and so do we."

Each Monday noon, there is a steady stream of Covington and Burling partners out the front door of 888 16th Street NW, trim men in their forties and fifties and sixties who walk with the controlled stride of tennis players, and with that special confidence of success and comfortable living, the Ivy League come to middle age. The partners turn right past the entrance, stroll a short half-block to H Street turn right again, and a few paces farther vanish into the stiff-collared gloom of the Metropolitan Club, which is, understandably, Washington's finest. The Partners Luncheon. Social, yes, but not in a boisterous sense, for protocol is such that a partner doesn't even sip a glass of dry sherry before taking his place at the luncheon table. Cold vichyssoise and dignity, and low-murmured table talk about developments in the firm's major cases, and what the FTC will be saying in Matter A this week, and how soon the FCC will act in Matter B, and what sort of nonsense can be expected from this new Assistant Secretary of something, and how his views might affect Matter C. Lunch, then a speaker, never a campaigning politician or a Cabinet officer, but someone who might . . . well, *broaden* partners. William Lawrence, the political journalist; Senator Charles Mathias of Maryland, chairman of the Senate District Committee; a partner, David E. McGiffert, formerly Under Secretary of the Army, and an expert on military manpower. But the program is secondary: The Partners Luncheon is a chance for members of Covington and Burling to see one another in the flesh and be reassured everyone still exists.

In the Covington and Burling pecking order, the more senior partners enjoy offices on the seventh and eighth floors of 888 16th Street NW, or the coveted spacious corner offices on the floors below, with two-wall windows. My first two weeks in the firm I spent in the upper echelons of the firm, geographically and otherwise. Then one morning at 8:30 I found myself on the fifth floor for a chat with a young associate. I nodded at a pretty young secretary I met in the corridor, then stopped in my tracks. Yes, I had heard correctly. This young Covington and Burling secretary, four floors from the boss, was whistling the title song from Jesus Christ Superstar. *When I came back through the reception area an hour later, I encountered her again. "This must be a pretty interesting place to work," I remarked.*

She wrinkled her nose noncommittally. "A pretty safe place, too," she said. It was after nine o'clock now, and her whistling was done for the day.

Superclark:
Mr. President, I Think You Should...

*"Clark Clifford—the secret there is that he intimidates peo-
ple. He doesn't make statements, he pronounces judgments. It's
a lot like talking to God—or listening to God, to be more accurate. He draws himself up and he says these things, and you
have to believe him, yeah, you want to believe him, for anyone
who speaks with such authority must be right. It's not law, but
it's effective. I couldn't get away with it. Look at me [five feet
four inches, 125 pounds maximum]—do you think I could
sound Olympian?"*

—*A Washington Lawyer, talking about
the "why" of Clark Clifford.*

Lights dim, the three-way lamps at their lowest level, drawn drapes intercepting both the glare of the late afternoon spring sun and the vista of the White House. Soothing, and one's eyelids droop involuntarily, not from drowsiness, but from . . . *security.* Refuge from whatever troubles bothered you elsewhere in Washington, on the streets or in the bureaucracy. Clark McAdams Clifford. Fingers spread and interlocked into a neat little teepee at midriff level (a superiority sign, according to body-linguist Julius Fast). Feet crossed at the ankles, chair tilted to the exact angle where he can swing his feet back and forth without dragging his shoes on the floor. Hands flicking to grasp broad lapels on the suit like those men used to wear in the late 'fifties and early 'sixties or to run along the thin necktie. The desk checkerboarded with neat stacks of paper, each held down by a medallion paperweight. Walls formal, barren of the political memorabilia so common to the Washington Lawyer, even the former Deputy Assistant Secretary who inevitably manages to procure the General Services Administration stock photograph to-my-good-friend-and-colleague-in-government of whatever President happens to be in office. Clifford wants no such distractions on his premises.

Control. Never yield the initiative—but never seem to be grabbing for it, either. Clark McAdams Clifford's look says okay-first-question and I ask it, and the feet swing, and the teepeed hands slowly rise across his chest, and the eyes are with me, unblinking, and is it a smile or the permanent expression of a quizzical listener, the locked-on face that is unrevealing of emotion because it never changes? Whatever, the face grips me, and the teepeed hands open toward me, and Clifford is talking about my first question, which had something to do with his return to practice in 1969 after his year as Secretary of Defense. Certainly, that is fine to hear, and that is a very good question, and I think it shows insight. But first, would you mind if I gave you a little background on how I came to practice law in Washington? Now, not all of this will be useful to you, but you might find an item of color or two, and you go right ahead and interrupt me when you want to do so. Yes. Yes, certainly, and suddenly I am not hearing an answer to my question about 1969, but an account of Clark Clifford's first day in court in St. Louis, Missouri, in 1929, and the fact that he had evaded me by exactly forty years does not disturb me at all. I am too busy listening to the Gospel as spoken by Clark Clifford, and scribbling furiously through a legal pad, and we didn't return to 1969 for almost two hours. So what? Control.

Senator Stuart Symington, Clifford's longtime personal friend and fellow Missourian, used the same word a few days later. "Clark Clifford is the most controlled man I have ever met," Symington told me. "He can listen to facts without letting his emotions trip him up, and not be distracted by things that don't matter. He controls himself as well as a situation. Coffee bothered him, so he gave it up. The same thing with alcohol, just like that." Symington is a patrician man in his seventies, one who served as Secretary of the Air Force before coming to the Senate. He has seen—and held—Washington power for more than a quarter of a century. He paused before continuing, as if wary of overstatement, but he said it anyway: "Without question, Clark Clifford is the most powerful private citizen who has been in town since I've been here. He's a lawyer who does not have to look for business, because people come to him, not vice versa."

Superclark. Mr. Smooth. (Someone even wrote a movie with that title, based on Clifford.) A "curious hybrid of Rasputin, Perry Como, and Mr. Fix," in the unfriendly words of New Leftist David Horowitz of *Ramparts*. "The man who started stopping the Vietnam War," in the words of a former Johnson Administration official who likes Clifford. "The son of a bitch who walked out on the President," in the words of another, who doesn't. The Man with the Million-Dollar Fee (of which we shall say more later). "A publicity hound; a man who operates on reputation, not law, and who knows every shortcut in Washington," the bitter comment from a senior partner in a large firm that shuns public attention. "The tops—the guy who can solve that special problem after every other law firm in town has stumbled over their feet." This from a former Senate staff member whose boss was unfriendly with Clifford. Any list of Washington Lawyers extant—compiled either by the lawyers or by the people who watch them closely—has Clark Clifford at or near the top.

One litmus test of a Washington Lawyer's effectiveness—a quality that does not necessarily relate to his ability—is the identity of the corporations that seek out his services. Corporation executives are not universally intelligent, but you do find a concentration of pragmatism in the blue-chip suites. And here is a sampling of the corporations who thought Clark Clifford could do them good as a Washington Lawyer: Standard Oil of California. Hughes Tool. American Broadcasting. Continental Airlines. TWA. El Paso Natural Gas. The du Pont Corporation. Time, Inc. General Electric. W. R. Grace Shipping. The late, lamented Pennsylvania Railroad. FMC. Kerr-McGee Oil. Phillips Petroleum.

That is one Clifford hat. Another—if they are distinguishable —is that worn by Clark Clifford the Presidential adviser. Clifford masterminded Harry Truman's 1948 campaign, the one he wasn't supposed to win. Clifford wasn't for Jack Kennedy until after Los Angeles, but was in good grace enough thereafter to handle the Ike-JFK transition details. Clifford was one of the first men summoned to the White House by Lyndon Johnson in November of 1963, and by every insider's account except LBJ's, a suddenly dehawked Clifford was responsible for the turnaround in U.S. war policy in March 1968. As a Cabinet officer Clifford did not participate in the 1968 campaign—although his law partner, former CIA official Thomas D. Finney, helped direct Senator Eugene McCarthy's Presidential bid. And as of mid-1971 Clifford was the chief foreign policy adviser to Senator Edmund Muskie, who he early decided was the most likely prospect to win the Democratic Presidential nomination. Resiliency. But save for his ten months as Secretary of Defense, Clifford has not been on a Federal payroll since he resigned from the Truman White House staff in 1950. "Clark is a wonderful fellow," President Kennedy once said, tongue planted mischievously in cheek. "In a day when many are seeking a reward for what they contributed to the return of the Democrats to the White House, you don't hear Clark clamoring. All he asked in return was that we advertise his law firm on the backs of one-dollar bills."

Clifford is unique among Washington Lawyers because what he does is not exactly law. "Most corporations do not have a good understanding of Washington," he told me. "Their basic attitude is an antipathy to government. Fifty years ago, the corporate executive did not have to concern himself with Washington. Government had not inserted itself into the business and economic life of the country. The corporate executive could go through life without giving a damn about Washington. Especially the New York executives." But from the vantage point of the Truman White House, Clifford realized the New Deal had wrought a fundamental change in business-government relations "and that corporations needed help in finding ways to get along with government." But not as a lawyer. The routine practice, he said, "does not interest me in the least. If a company represented had a whole series of matters before the Federal Power Commission, I would have to go out and hire a specialist. When I started my practice, I wanted to be the higher-level policy adviser. They [the corporations] can get that kind of routine service anywhere.

"What a lawyer ultimately wants is to become a senior adviser and counselor. The value of his advice is not based on the hours he spends, but on his years of experience, his understanding of law and government, and clients are willing to pay a premium for that sort of representation. I have never charged by the hour. We sit down and agree on a reasonable fee." What is Clifford's definition of reasonable? Hire him and find out, one of his associates suggested. But anyone who takes the elevator to his softly lighted twelfth-floor office at 815 Connecticut Avenue NW can be reliably admonished to bring a minimum of $5,000.

There is a story, perhaps apocryphal, of the corporation general counsel in the Midwest who asked Clifford what his company should do concerning certain tax legislation. After several weeks Clifford responded, "Nothing," and enclosed a bill for $20,000. Unaccustomed to the Clifford style, the general counsel testily wrote that for $20,000 he certainly was entitled to a more complete explanation of the recommendation. He got it. "Because I said so," Clifford said in letter two, and billed the corporation for another $5,000.

But drop-in, one-time clients are rare. "The basis of our practice is a number of corporations we have on a retainer basis." The number ranges from thirty to forty; in mid-May 1971 there were thirty-four. "Some of the corporations use us sparingly, but when a problem comes up, it is important to get our view, quickly."

"The Clifford firm" formally is Clifford, Warnke, Glass, McIlwain and Finney; as of June 30, 1971, it had seven partners (including Clifford) and four associates, all living comfortably in the shadow of the name figure. According to one outsider who has close professional contacts with the firm: "It's easy not to look past Clark, and think the rest are ciphers or dodos or high-grade legal clerks. Any man in the firm could make it big under his own flag. But why worry? Money is more important in this business than publicity." And another: "There's clout in that firm that doesn't show on the surface—and by surface I mean Clark." Paul Warnke was a Covington and Burling partner from 1957 to 1966, when he went to the Pentagon, first as general counsel, then Assistant Secretary for International Security Affairs. Clifford brought him into the firm in 1969. Samuel D. McIlwain was in the Reconstruction Finance Corporation and the Justice Department under Truman, and then counsel for the Senate Finance Committee in 1957–58. Larry L. Williams was an antitrust trial lawyer for Justice from 1948 to 1965. Carson M. Glass also spent a decade at Justice. Clifford hires directly from the government. "We have to," he told me, "because we are specialists in dealing with the government."

Because of his Mr. Insider reputation, corporations quite logically expect something besides a scholarly brief when they come to Clifford. Clifford thinks it a "bromide" that Washington Lawyers are considered to be influence-peddlers (or influence-purchasers). He hears the word without a grimace, but the inner pique adds tartness to his mellow baritone. "You have a few people who go around saying who they have in their pocket, and how many Congressmen and commissions they can control. Well, I've never seen any evidence it was anything other than talk. They shouldn't do it—it hurts all of us.

"When a new company comes up to us, in the course of discussing the problem, I have a little speech I always make to them. I have made it so many times that my colleagues say they can recite it along with me. It goes something like this. Now this isn't verbatim, but it's the gist of what I say:

"There is one point I wish to make clear. This firm has no

influence of any kind in Washington. If you want to employ someone who has influence, you will have to go somewhere else. First, because I am not sure what the term 'influence' means, but that is inconsequential; second, because whatever it is, we don't have it.

"What we do have is a record of working with the various departments and agencies of government, and we have their respect and confidence, and that we consider to be a valuable asset."

So what is Clifford's magic? Control, says Stuart Symington. Command, says another friend. Clout, says a wide swath of the Washington bar.

Go back to St. Louis, Clifford said at the outset of our interview. The skills he acquired there and the training he honed in the White House with President Truman are responsible for whatever success he has enjoyed as a Washington Lawyer.

For a man of such messianic ability, say some of the more blasphemous wits around Washington, Clark Clifford's birth date was quite appropriate: Christmas Day, 1904. His father, an auditor for the Missouri Pacific Railroad, earned enough money to keep the family on the fringe of St. Louis society. His mother was a lecturer of sufficient talent to perform professionally, specializing in children's fairy tales. Her brother, Clark McAdams, was known through Missouri as the crusading liberal editior of the *St. Louis Post-Dispatch.* Clifford polished his charm as a student actor at Washington University, receiving his law degree in 1928. Clifford had brains—he finished second among 350 persons who took the Missouri bar examinations that year—and he had self-confidence. Jacob Lashley, whose law firm specialized in defending corporations in personal injury cases, lectured to one of Clifford's law classes. After he finished, Clifford politely asked if he could "sit in your office and see how it works." Clifford didn't want a salary—simply a toehold into St. Louis's leading law office. Lashley said come ahead.

"I had my heart set on being a trial lawyer," Clifford told me, "but it was a very large firm and for a while I found myself with practically nothing to do but run errands. I finally went to a judge and asked for appointments to defend indigent defendants in criminal cases. This was all right with the firm because I had so little to do; in fact, I was there at my request more than theirs. Within a few weeks I had my first case, and thereafter I kept a steady stream of clients going upriver to the state penitentiary. My first case involved a man named John Piper, who was charged with stealing an automobile. I spent three days trying his case. And oh, but did I prepare! I read the life of Clarence Darrow and other famous criminal lawyers, and I wrote out a ringer of a jury speech.

"The jury went out and came back in fifteen minutes and gave John Piper twenty years. I was crushed. I thought my career was at an end. The judge saw I was hurt, and he called me up and said he was going to appoint me to another case right away. I started to protest, because I didn't want any more, but he stopped me. 'Clark,' he said, 'it's like getting thrown from a horse, or going down in a plane. You've got to get right back up or you'll be gunshy and never do it again.' So I took another case, and wow-ee! Boy! They sent him up again!

"All this time I kept trying to forget poor John Piper. This poor fellow—he wasn't much older than I was, and there he sat, in the state penitentiary. I did my best to forget it, but each Christmas, just about the time I thought I'd forgotten about him, here would come a Christmas card from poor old John Piper in the state pen.

"I kept on trying cases, and getting licked, until my twelfth or fourteenth came along, and I got a verdict—'I sprung one,' was the expression—and man, did I feel good. It was like being thrown into the creek by your dad to learn to swim; you consume an awful lot of water, but you learn how to swim.

"An interne has to work on people to become a doctor, and he sends some to the graveyard. Well, I sent mine to the state penitentiary."

The Lashley firm, meanwhile, began trusting Clifford with small cases, and "I began trying them." Clifford makes the process sound easy. It wasn't. Stuart Symington, who became friendly with Clifford during this period in the cheerful surroundings of the St. Louis Racquet Club, says simply, "He was the best trial lawyer in St. Louis. How did I get to know him? Well, I've always been attracted to attractive people, and he was one of the best." For the next fifteen years Clifford was one of St. Louis's busiest—and most successful—trial lawyers. "In one year alone, around 1930 or 1940, I forget which, I tried just under forty cases. I would try one during the day, and prepare one at night.

"What I didn't know was that this was the greatest period of training an individual can go through. It was enormously helpful in every other endeavor in my life. Why? Well, here is what a trial lawyer does:

"First, he is confronted by a voluminous collection of facts. What he has to do is winnow through them and find out which are most salient. He must organize them so he can understand them and put them into an orderly, logical sequence. Then comes the burden of proving his case—that is, presenting the facts as articulately and persuasively as possible, in an effort to guide those who are going to make the decision. That is what you are doing, whether you are a salesman, or a corporate executive, or a Washington Lawyer.

"But very few men receive the unusual and pressure-filled course of training a trial lawyer does. Very few have to go through the onerous discipline, when you acquire these traits so deep inside you they are second nature."

When Clifford joined the White House staff, he says, "I found very early this was an enormous asset. A man with this kind of training can sit and listen to the recitation of a lot of facts as they are laid on the table, and not always in an orderly fashion. At some stage you are called upon to present an opinion, or write a memo. Now, this is a discussion and dialogue in the presence of the President.

"I began to recognize early there was a useful advantage—and I might say I made the most of it."

Clifford was past draft age when the Second World War began, and had three young daughters. (His wife, Margery Pepperell Kimball, was from a Boston family and heiress to a firearms fortune; they met on a postgraduation European tour.) When Clifford began talking about entering the Navy, Stuart Symington protested. "I told him he was crazy, that he didn't have enough money to go off to war, that he should stay home and take care of his family." Clifford grinned and enlisted, and was soon a Navy officer assigned to San Francisco, helping to break supply logjams for the Pacific fleets. His wife went home to Boston for the duration. By the spring of 1945 Clifford was a thirty-eight-year-old lieutenant commander restlessly awaiting the end of the war. Then he got a call from the White House from an old St. Louis business client, James K. Vardaman, naval aide to President Truman. "Jake wanted to go to the Potsdam Conference, and he wanted somebody to look after his White House office while he was gone. He didn't want a Regular Navy man, because he didn't think much of the Navy. So he called me in for 'temporary duty.' It was to be three weeks or so."

Clifford couldn't find enough naval work to occupy his time, so he began looking around for something to do. "Mr. Truman had held over Judge Sam Rosenman, who had been a counsel to

President Roosevelt. The Judge was grossly overworked and had no one helping him. The naval aide's office was not very important, so I began to help out Rosenman. When Truman and Vardaman returned, Rosenman said, 'Why not keep this young fellow here? He might be helpful.' Well, that started me." At the end of 1945 Truman appointed Vardaman to the Federal Reserve Board, and Clifford became the naval aide. When Rosenman resigned a few weeks later to practice law, "that left this great vacuum in the White House, and I began gradually to fill it, writing speeches and memos. On June 1, 1946, Mr. Truman talked with me and said it would be better if I left the Navy and assumed the position of White House counsel."

Power. Now Clifford was truly an insider. A man who puts words into the mouth of the President, and who spoke for him in the Federal government, and who possessed the most esteemed and coveted privilege in Washington—direct, no-knock-on-the-door access to the President of the United States. Clifford's title of counsel is not fully descriptive of his importance to the Truman Administration, for then as now he was far more than a lawyer.

As a writer, he could produce speeches peculiarly suitable for the Missouri syntax and delivery of the President. Both a political speech and a jury speech, after all, have the same purpose: to give an audience the facts you want them to hear, and to persuade them to accept them as presented.

As a pacifier of the renowned HST temper, he dissuaded the President from foolish public outbursts. During a 1946 railroad strike, Mr. Truman intended to make a shrill, polemical speech urging, "Let's give the country back to the people. Let's . . . hang a few traitors and make our country safe for democracy." Clifford was the only staff member with the guts to say, "Mr. President, this just won't do." Truman substituted a more moderate speech.

As a press adviser Clifford convinced the President that there are times when he should keep his mouth shut; if he didn't know enough about a subject to comment intelligently, he should say nothing.

As an adviser Clifford spoke for Truman in dealings with high officials within the executive branch, the Congress, even the judiciary. The injudicious exercise of delegated authority— failure to realize that your power is derived, not real—has toppled many a young White House staff member who came to confuse himself with the President. Not Clifford. Whatever personal beliefs Clifford possessed he kept tightly inside himself; he didn't try to push his own programs, but those of the President. In a sense, he created a protective facade for himself: Although he lacked the cruasading fire and ebullience of the prototypical New Dealer, he was no less the liberal, and he realized that Truman's success depended upon adherence to liberalism—not, as many big Democrats recommended in the postwar years, a swing to the middle of the road. As an apolitical figure Clifford didn't attract the fire of Congressional conservatives, neither to himself nor to the President. And a man who acts on behalf of the President can learn in a very short time the way the Federal government operates, because people answer his phone calls and his questions.

As a major-domo Clifford both worked for the President and played with the President. Early in his White House stay Mr. Truman began inviting Clifford to come along on the festive weekend poker parties aboard the Presidential yacht *Williamsburg*. The group would leave the pier at the Maine Avenue Navy Yard on Friday evening and spend that night and Saturday cruising south down the Potomac through tidewater Virginia, drinking bourbon and playing cards. The regular guest list included such men as Chief Justice Fred Vinson, Secretary of Commerce W. Averell Harriman, Senator Clinton Anderson, and Symington. To round out the party Clifford would often invite a new Senator the President liked—Lyndon Baines Johnson of Texas. (Only two things about the weekends disturbed Clifford: he didn't like to play poker, because he was no good at it, and lost money, and because of an ulcer he could not drink bourbon. So he sat and listened, and learned and remembered more than the revelers.)

And Clifford gradually took another role as well—that of political adviser. By mid-1947 the Truman Administration showed obvious signs of strain. The reconversion of the economy, the catch-up demands of unions, which had been constrained during the war, the resultant stiffening of business, labor strife, the near collapse of agriculture, public fears of expanding Soviet power—all these problems seemed to point inevitably toward a Republican victory in 1948. Clifford began talking to politicans around the country, and to labor leaders; in November 1947, a year before the election, he wrote a coldly pragmatic forty-three-page memo to Mr. Truman which could be titled "The Selling of the President 1948." "The basic premise of this memo—that the Democratic Party is an unhappy alliance of Southern conservatives, Western progressives, and big-city labor—is very trite, but it is also very true," Clifford wrote. "And it is equally true that the success or failure of the Democratic leadership can be precisely measured by its ability to lead enough members of these three misfit groups to the polls." Clifford told the President how to go after each of these groups:

▌▌ He thought it "inconceivable that any policies initiated by the Truman Administration, no matter how 'liberal,' could so alienate the South in the next year that it would revolt. As always the South can be considered safely Democratic. And in formulating national policy, it can be safely ignored."

▋▋   Court the Western states by concentrating on "reclama-
       tion, floods and agriculture."

▋▋   It was dangerous to assume that "labor has nowhere
       else to go in 1948. Labor can stay home . . . The labor
       group has always been politically inactive during pros-
       perity. When they are well fed, they are not interested.
       They will probably be well fed in 1948. Labor leaders
       should be invited to the White House to flatter them—
       but to talk on general issues. To invite advice on spe-
       cifics, and then not follow it, is to court trouble."

Clifford didn't think the third-party candidacy of former Vice
President Henry Wallace was dangerous, but nonetheless said
he should be defused; "every effort must be made now . . . to
dissuade him and to identify him and isolate him in the public
minds with the Communists."

On the President's own image, Clifford counseled simultane-
ous courting of the left-intellectuals and the prairie-Populists.
"The 'right' may have money, but the 'left' has the pen. If the
intellectual can be induced to back the President, he will do so
in the press, on the radio, and in the movies. He is the 'idea
man' for the people." Get rid of whatever residual Wall Street
image had been inherited from President Roosevelt by "easing
out" such men as Averell Harriman, James Forrestal, Robert
Lovett, and John J. McCloy—all essential in wartime, but now
overly conspicuous displays of business influence.

"The public has a tremendous interest in its Chief Executive
and is invariably hungry for news about him," Clifford wrote.
"It does not want those stereotyped gestures so done to death in
past years. No one really cares anymore about round-the-world
fliers, or the little girl with the first poppy of the Disabled Veterans, or the Eagle Scout from Idaho." Instead, Clifford said,
invite Einstein to lunch at the White House and at the next press
conference mention that they talked about peaceful uses of

atomic energy—and drop the name of an important current book he has on the nightstand. "A President who is also a candidate must resort to subterfuge," Clifford said. "He cannot sit silent; he must be in the limelight . . . He must resort to the kind of trip Roosevelt made famous in the 1940 campaign—the 'inspection tour.' No matter how much the opposition and the press pointed out the political overtones of those trips, the people paid little attention, for what they saw was the Head of State performing his duties." And Truman should make foreign policy pronouncements, not the State Department.

Truman accepted the memo as his basic campaign document, and the election went just about the way Clifford had predicted, with one exception: The Dixiecrat movement cost Truman four Southern states. But by stressing farm and reclamation matters he captured many traditionally Republican agricultural states and the whole tier of eleven Western states (excluding Oregon), where the GOP had expected to make gains. Stung by passage of the Taft-Hartley Act over Mr. Truman's veto (Clifford wrote the veto message), the American Federation of Labor for the first time organized a national political group—Labor's League for Political Education—and produced landslide margins in key Eastern states. The 1948 election was the high-water mark of Clifford's association with President Truman. Thereafter, he got what he wanted from the Truman White House. And thereafter he was a man whose counsel was actively solicited by Democratic politicians who wanted to gain or retain the Presidency.

The next year, in a sense, was anticlimactic. Clifford could look into the past and wonder, "How do you top this?" He had written the Defense Reorganization Act of 1947, which created the Department of Defense, thereby concentrating America's war-making might into a single agency. He had played a crucial role in persuading Mr. Truman to accept George Kennan's containment concept of dealing with Soviet expansion in Europe—

the cornerstone of U.S. cold-war policy. Fascinating years, yes, but they were beginning to wear on Clifford.

"I had developed a theory about government," he told me, "that after four or five years, you ought to get out. Why? Well, there are several reasons. You enter a period of diminishing returns for your effort. There is the increasing physical exhaustion. We began with a meeting with the President at eight or eight-thirty every morning, and rarely did we get away from the White House until long after dark, and you took things home. You have this . . . well, we called it, 'the daily crisis,' for one always seemed to happen. When you are young and strong you can take it, and even enjoy it, but after four or five years you are worn out physically, and I mean it.

"After years on the periphery of the policy-making area, you develop areas of resistance. You come up with an idea, and you could guarantee in advance those men in government who would take the opposite position, just because you favored something.* Clifford feuded with Dr. John R. Steelman, the White House economic adviser, over fiscal and labor policies, and with James Forrestal, the first Secretary of Defense, over U.S. policy toward Israel. And many Congressmen were revising their initial surface judgment that Clifford was a handsome, articulate, and harmless young man. The 1948 election removed much of his protective anonymity and revealed him as a true power in the crowd around President Truman. And Clifford says, "I was doing a lot of speech and memo writing, and I suppose it is a lot like newspapering and journalism: everything I wrote sounded the same."

* Clifford encountered the same problem two decades later as Secretary of Defense. He told *Armed Forces Management* in a 1968 interview, "There is a certain type of attrition which goes with this job. If the gentle Lord Himself were in charge here, after a time He would begin to find that areas of resistance had been created. This is inevitable if one is willing to take part in important policy decisions and to make the tough decisions."

Money was another factor. In 1943, when he left his St. Louis law practice to enter the Navy, Clifford earned about $30,000. Through the fall of 1949 his salary as White House counsel was $12,000; Congress then raised it to $20,000. But with three daughters approaching college age Clifford decided it was time to return to private life. Missouri Democrats wanted him to run for the United States Senate, but he turned them down: he was in debt (a St. Louis friend had loaned him almost $25,000 to supplement his White House pay); he had no taste for elective politics. So Clifford's obvious choice, and one which he says didn't take him long to make, was to return to law. But where, and how?

"Dean Acheson [then Secretary of State] counseled against starting my own law firm," Clifford says. "He told me, 'There are a number of successful firms here. There's hardly a place for a new one—go into an existing office.' " Clifford could have done so; Covington and Burling, for instance, talked to him about accepting a partnership. His old St. Louis firm offered him a position as resident partner in Washington. But Clifford decided to open his own office. "I had this visceral feeling I would never be happy unless I gave it a try . . . I looked at what I considered to be my assets: A wide range of trial experience in St. Louis which few men have. The Navy. Four or five years in the White House, the best spot there is to learn how the United States government works. Combining all these experiences, I thought it would be worthwhile to try it. It was. I was successful from the very start. From the first week on, I was busy."

Clifford and a longtime friend, Edward H. Miller, opened Clifford and Miller on February 1, 1950. "I kept the firm small, deliberately, just one partner and two younger men." (Miller died before the year ended.) "I wanted a smaller firm, one that would specialize in handling problems corporations have with the United States government. I felt there was a place for a man who had had broad practical experience in Washington, legal experience rather than political. You tick off some of the names around town. [He did, but lawyer that he is, asked me not to quote him.] They went up by the political route. I went up the legal route. I could offer something that would be important to a corporate client."

What is that "something"?

Clifford doesn't like the word influence, so let's use another: access. People in government had become accustomed to answering Clark Clifford's phone calls when they came from the White House; they answered them now from Clifford and Miller. Insight. From his St. Louis days, Clifford knew how businessmen thought; from his White House days, he knew how bureaucrats thought. Find a common ground of consensus. Let's work this thing out together. Flexibility. In 1952 Clifford worked hard to obtain legislation authorizing pipelines to increase the price of natural gas, a bill of great benefit to client Phillips Petroleum. With the help of the oil industry's great friend, Senator Robert Kerr, of Oklahoma, Clifford succeeded. Whereupon Truman vetoed the bill. Undeterred, Clifford and Kerr went to the Federal Power Commission and through eloquent persuasion managed to convince the FPC it had authority to raise prices *without* the legislation. Why no one ever noticed this authority previously is something unmentioned by history. In addition to Phillips, Clifford's first-year clients included the Pennsylvania Railroad, the Radio Corporation of America, Standard Oil of California, Howard Hughes, and newly independent Indonesia.

The gas bill veto was enough to shatter any subconscious thoughts Clifford might have entertained about building a law practice on Truman's name. So did another early case, this one on behalf of Howard Hughes's TWA. Arch-rival Pan American, seeking an increase in European routes, sought Civil Aeronautics Board approval of the purchase of American Overseas Airlines. TWA paid Clifford $50,000 to fight the transaction, and he won. Whereupon Truman intervened, as the President is authorized to do in cases involving international flights, and the CAB reversed itself. The end result was that Pan American obtained competitive routes with TWA to Paris and Rome. All TWA salvaged was new landing rights in Frankfurt and London.

From the beginning, Clifford knew his White House background made him a marked man, and that is one reason he kept his firm small. "Practicing law in Washington," he told me, "is a lot like combat, when a soldier is walking through a minefield. You have to make only one misstep and you are through. I want to know what is going on here, every day," and he leaned over and rapped the wooden window sill with his clenched knuckles for emphasis.

"I could fall on my face tomorrow. I have been in and out of government for more than twenty years, and I have been adviser to Presidents. Yet I am not conscious of any instance in which I have been charged with any impropriety. That is not an accident. First, you don't get into a position which is improper, or, second, looks like you are improper."

The knives have occasionally flashed in his direction. Hearst scandalists Jack Lait and Lee Mortimer wrote in *USA Confidential* that Clifford "charged $25,000 per consultation in the White House, where he practiced law while on the U.S. payroll." They retracted. The House Commerce Committee, during a 1950 study of Washington lawyer-lobbyist relations with the regulatory agencies, ran across Clifford's name only once during months of work. At the same time he represented Phillips Petroleum, he lunched eight or ten times a year with FPC member Frederick Stueck, an old law school friend from Washington University. But as Stueck said, Clifford "does not represent them [Phillips] in any natural-gas matter. What did we talk about? The things that people who have known each other for twenty-five years talk about. While in school we were rather close friends. We sang on the glee club together." So far as he knew, Stueck said, Clifford had represented Phillips on a tax matter ("I recall his telling me about a very large tax case involving in excess of a million dollars which he argued before the Supreme Court") and a stockholder suit. "He does not have anything to do with the natural-gas end of their business," Stueck said in 1960. The committee did not seek to question Clifford, accepting Stueck's account.

But oh the Republicans have tried to topple Superclark. In 1953, when Attorney General Herbert Brownell staffed the Justice Department with prosecutors trained under the rackets-busting Thomas E. Dewey, and the GOP still believed all its old campaign oratory about "corruption in Washington," a major drive was directed against Clifford. Clifford knows this is true, for a "friend" slipped him a memorandum from the Justice Department which said, in effect, "Let's make a real effort to see what we can find on Clark Clifford." After all, here was this former White House lawyer, a Missouri-gang crony of Jake Vardaman and Harry H. Vaughan, making scores of thousands of dollars a year as a lawyer, and only a few months after leaving the public payroll. Certainly some shenanigans *must* be involved . . . if only we can find them. "The Administration has the machinery—the investigators, the rooms full of file cabinets, the time and energy to run down everything. Well, they didn't get anything, for there was nothing to find. They worked over everyone who had been around Mr. Truman, and what did they find but some deep freezes and a tax collector? Although I must say, I'm glad I didn't have one of those deep freezes."

Time and again in discussing Clifford with other Washington Lawyers I detected resentment that he made so much money with such little apparent effort. Clifford these days never enters a pleading on behalf of a client; he is seen in Congress even less than the President (who must go once annually for the State of the Union message); there is no evidence he could even locate the FCC or the SEC without the services of a cabdriver. He stays in his office, and he has an inordinate amount of time to devote to Democratic politics, and to monitoring President Nixon's Vietnam policies, and golf (at Burning Tree, most often with Stuart Symington). Someone who performs so little visible work must have a magic button he presses once or twice a day to make the Federal government perform regulatory and tax miracles for his clients.

Perhaps so. But one of Clifford's friends suggested I read what David E. Lilienthal, chairman of the Tennessee Valley Authority, wrote about Clifford in his diary. I did. An entry for April 1951, a year after Clifford left the White House.

> Lunched with Clark Clifford. He told me the whole details of his last year, his first year of law practice after leaving the White House. It is a simply unbelievable story. He practices alone; his partner died two and a half months after they began; he hired four young lawyers; five stenographers. In this establishment—a one-man performance— he earned probably as much as any professional man in the country, amusement field included, and more than any lawyer. He said he came out even on the year, after paying off his debts . . . buying a house, outfitting a law office, etc. He is uneasy about what will happen after Truman is out, if he is; if he will keep any of his clients—which is nonsense, as he is a very able man with or without Truman.
>
> He looks like the wrath of God, ten years older than two years ago. Troubled with his stomach, his nerves, wakes up at three a.m. How can this have happened to him, who

never had any limit on how hard he could work? I told him what I had said when his wife raised the same questions with me months ago; that this was nonsense; he was selling his only asset of health and family life for too little; that he ought to cut down and give attention to capital gains possibilities. He has a sense of insecurity (financial) that is hard to fathom, considering the facts. He is a fine man, did a great job with the President, best man in the White House since I've known about things. I told him he must remember he will be expected to render public service again . . . , as Clark Clifford, not as Harry Truman's helper.

Clifford says those days are over—that his practice is organized to the point where he spends ten hours daily in the office, not sixteen. "I still keep a close watch on every case that comes into the office, and I'm advised on any major decisions," Clifford told me. "But I'm gradually cutting my percentage of the work. Every year since I left the Pentagon I've passed on more and more authority and responsibility to the other partners." Could the firm ever become "institutionalized," as is Covington and Burling? "Oh, I don't know," Clifford said. "We have some pretty good lawyers around here, I must say." Nonetheless a corporate client who seeks out Clark Clifford wants some attention from the top man—not on a daily basis, mind you, for an associate is going to do the detail work, but Clifford will speak with the client on the first visit, and he is going to keep one of his shrewd eyes on the problem as it progresses. "We keep the number of our clients at a point where I can spread out over all of them," he says. "In our particular kind of law, it's important that we be available when someone needs us. I'm here all the time—if you are a client, and want to call, nine times out of ten I am here. I take a one-week vacation every year, and tag two weekends onto it. That's all. I am here from nine in the morning until seven o'clock at night, day in and day out, with a half-hour lunch. I also get in on Saturday for a 'clean-up' day."

In his younger days Clifford dabbled in international work. He represented the late Matthew Fox, a West Coast entrepreneur, who tried to obtain commercial monopolies in the new Republic of Indonesia, and traveled frequently to Djakarta in the early 1950s. Old cases tend to generate new ones, and often in unexpected directions. At one time Matty Fox was married to Yolande Betbeze, a one-time Miss America. Miss Betbeze later became a friend of Algerian Ambassador Cherif Guellal, serving as an unofficial hostess at his embassy. Guellal resigned as Ambassador when Algeria broke diplomatic relations with the United States so he could remain in Washington as a discreet unofficial representative of his government. The political feud notwithstanding, Algeria wanted to cooperate with U.S. business. A Clifford client, El Paso Natural Gas Company, wanted access to Algeria's resources. Enter Clifford, with Miss Betbeze acting as intermediary between him and Guellal. Clifford says he spent "eight or nine days" in Algeria talking with government officials. "They are developing industry and petroleum, and felt I could be of help in advising them," he says of the matter. But rarely will Clifford leave the country, even in response to the pleas of a former Miss America. "I let one of the other partners go," he said. "I feel obligated to stay closer around the office."

"He is a man whose silken smoothness and handsome good looks are almost cloying to an Easterner of the big cities, until one observes that the smoothness stems from genuine good manners that accompany an impressively analytical mind."

—*Theodore White, in* The Making of the President 1960.

Throughout the Eisenhower years, Clifford's name was constantly linked—politically and professionally—to three United States Senators in a unique position to benefit clients of a Washington Lawyer: Lyndon B. Johnson, the Senate majority leader; Robert Kerr, whose love affair with the oil industry was one of the more stirring romances of Congressional history, approached only by his affection for the aerospace corporations; and Stuart Symington, who for two decades believed everything the generals and the military industrialists told him, and voted appropriations accordingly. That Clifford prospered under a Republican Administration is not admissible as proof that his practice is nonpolitical. A more accurate deduction is that he pursued power elsewhere in the city—in Congress, rather than in the executive branch.

People who don't like Clifford have applied what he considers to be an unwarranted cause-and-effect formula to his friendship with Symington. McDonnell Douglas Corporation, based in St. Louis, has received a rich gush of defense contracts; Symington, from St. Louis, sits on the Armed Services Committee, which votes much of this money; Clifford has done occasional legal odd jobs for McDonnell Douglas. A profitable coincidence? Clifford told me, "I've never had anything to do with procuring contracts; I don't do that sort of work."

In the late 1950s, when Johnson and Symington broke their friendship in a dispute over whether defense or space warranted more spending, Clifford made what could have been a disastrous choice. Both Johnson and Symington were maneuvering for the Democratic Presidential nomination, and Johnson has an acutely Arabist view of personal relations: "My enemy's friend is my enemy." Clifford must have gulped a few times, but he decided to stay with Symington, and Johnson put his name high on whatever he calls his list of undesirables. Clifford thought Symington was an attractive compromise candidate.

The East wouldn't take Johnson. Kennedy was too young, and Catholic besides. Adlai Stevenson—did anyone really want to retread *him* again? Hubert Humphrey, deep Southern trouble. Who else? Clifford put together an informal brain trust for Symington, and raised money for him, and wrote speeches, and told him whom to talk to, and what about, and waited for the deadlock . . . It never came, of course, and life could have become very unpleasant for Clark Clifford, for the Kennedys judged friends on the basis of where they stood *before* the Democratic national convention. But Clark Clifford, as usual, was someone different. Kennedy recognized Clifford's personal obligation to Symington. Kennedy also needed a link to the old Truman wing of the party, the Midwesterners who were hard-core Stevensonites. And Kennedy also had first-hand knowledge of Clifford's adroitness in handling delicate legal matters. When Kennedy published *Profiles in Courage* in 1957, columnist Drew Pearson claimed in a broadcast that Theodore Sorensen actually wrote the book, with the Senator taking credit. The statement was false, and Kennedy wanted Pearson to withdraw it—but not under pressure that would make a lasting enemy of the columnist. He deputized Clifford, a Pearson friend, to show him the original handwritten notes and manuscript. Most diplomatically, Clifford convinced Pearson he was wrong, and the desired retraction was published.

So, soon after the convention, feelers from the Kennedy people encountered feelers from Clifford, and by the end of the summer he was in the candidate's innermost circle, right along with Joseph Kennedy, Sorensen, Kenny O'Donnell, Lawrence O'Brien, Pierre Salinger, John Bailey, and Robert Kennedy. Again, an important decision: Kennedy obviously intended to rely upon his father and the Irish Mafia to run the campaign, and Clifford was an outsider. What, then, could he do? The most important job of all, for someone who had no intention of taking a position *in* the Kennedy Administration (assuming, as Clifford did early, that Kennedy did win) but who intended to do a great deal of business *with* the Kennedy Administration. Clifford would handle the transition from Eisenhower to Kennedy. He went to work in early fall drafting a document detailing the practical authority a new President had to make changes within the bureaucracy, and how, and spelling out a timetable for the key appointments. Before noon the day after election Clifford flew into Hyannis Port, and handed the President-elect a thick handbook containing his recommendations. And for the next two months Clifford met almost daily with Kennedy and liaison officials from the Eisenhower Administration, the man responsible for handing the reigns of government from one President to another.

The new Democratic Administration gave Clifford a chance to reenter government service, and on matters both mundane and momentous. Soon after the inauguration Mrs. Kennedy decided to renovate the White House, and hopefully to restore some class to its declining rooms. The President could remember only the public furor when Harry Truman decided to add the famed South Porch to the executive mansion. Leave things alone, he begged his wife. According to Pierre Salinger, she was "warned, begged, and practically threatened" not to undertake the restoration. She prevailed, of course, but only after the President asked Clifford to draft a charter for a Committee on the Fine Arts to provide for public scrutiny of the project. Clifford and partner Carson Glass also wrote the incorporation papers for the White House Historical Association, a nonprofit group created for the sole purpose of marketing White House guide books. The association's earnings—more than $100,000 per year —are funneled directly to the White House for the purchase of historic furnishings. Clifford has been an association director since its founding.

At another level, Kennedy appointed Clifford to the Foreign Intelligence Advisory Board, a very quiet Presidential advisory committee with watchdog powers over the Central Intelligence Agency and the foreign activities of the various military and domestic agencies (such as the FBI and the Atomic Energy Commission). And after the Bay of Pigs debacle, Kennedy detailed Clifford to find out how the government could have committed such a blunder. (Lawyer that he is, Clifford did not begin this task with the accepted preconception that the CIA was at fault; although he won't discuss Presidential assignments in this particular field, it can be reliably stated that his report faulted the Pentagon more than the CIA. One direct result was Defense Secretary Robert McNamara's decision to merge all Pentagon intelligence activities into a single Defense Intelligence Agency.)

Clifford's well-publicized rapport with Kennedy also had an immeasurable impact upon his law practice. Clifford is insistent that he has never capitalized upon friendship with Kennedy or any other President, that any client who thinks otherwise is self-illusioned. That is Clifford's story, for the record, and he has a standing challenge to anyone to produce evidence to the contrary. And finding it is difficult, for Clifford has a keen instinct for avoiding proceedings where his activities might get into the public record. A classic example was his role in saving shareholders in the vast du Pont empire uncounted millions of dollars through special tax legislation.

In 1949 the Justice Department brought an antitrust suit against ownership of General Motors stock by the Christiana Securities Corporation, the holding-company subsidiary of E. I. du Pont de Nemours. The government charged that beginning in 1915, Christiana bought GM stock in a deliberate attempt to dominate GM, and that du Pont had obtained "an illegal preference over its competition" in the sale of paint, chemicals, and other products to GM. Christiana owned some 63 million shares of the 281 million GM shares outstanding. The complex case dragged through the courts for a decade, twice going to the U.S. Supreme Court before the government won and Christiana was ordered to divest itself of all GM stock within ten years—a $3-billion dump.

Clifford was not involved in the antitrust trial, in which Covington and Burling represented du Pont. "After the suit was all over, and the decision entered, Crawford Greenewalt, the du Pont president, called one day and said he had to see me. He said the divestiture problem was extremely serious, and laid out two alternatives. One was for du Pont to distribute the GM shares to its own shareholders on a pro rata basis. But they had a ruling from Internal Revenue Service that if this was done, the distribution would be taxed as though it were ordinary income. Now this was stock acquired back in the teens and twenties, at a considerably lower price, less than $10 a share. Greenewalt said it would be 'extremely unfair' to tax this as ordinary income, and I agreed.

"The other alternative was to sell the GM shares on the open market, at six million shares a year for ten years. This is more GM stock than is traded in a normal year, and it would have had a devastating effect upon the value of the shares. When you have this annual dumping, the price wouldn't hold, because everybody would know of the overhang. This was terribly unfair both to GM and to people who already owned its stock.

"What Greenewalt wanted from me was a different approach to the problem, and we were employed to handle it. We thought it out a great deal, and reached the decision that these were peculiar circumstances that warranted special legislation. We wrote a bill providing that du Pont could distribute the stock to its shareholders, and they would pay taxes as if it was a return of capital—which it was—which meant they'd pay capital gains, not ordinary income rates." (In lay language, this means a maximum of twenty-five percent of the difference between the acquisition price and the distribution price.)

"Then we made what has been called an exceedingly erudite decision—to get Mr. Greenewalt down here to lobby his own legislation. He was here for weeks, going home on weekends. We set it up so that he personally visited every member of the Senate Finance Committee and the House Ways and Means Committee. He was here for the duration. We helped him in working up his presentation for each individual member.

"Why use him as a lobbyist rather than me? Well, two reasons. First, he had prestige in the business community. The Senators and Representatives were rather flattered to be visited by one of the top five business leaders in the country. Second, he had lived with this problem for a great number of years, and he could describe the impact of the decision upon du Pont and GM shareholders from personal knowledge."

Because he did not escort Greenewalt, Clifford was not required to (and did not) register as a lobbyist for du Pont. This task fell to John Sharon, then with the firm of Cleary, Gottlieb, Steen and Hamilton, which registered as du Pont's agent. (Sharon later joined the Clifford firm, then went with Abe Fortas when Fortas resigned from the Supreme Court in 1969.)

In the Senate Finance Committee, Senator J. Allen Frear (D., Del.) ran interference for his du Pont constituency, estimating at one hearing that the "tax penalty" resulting from the forced sale would be "close to $1 billion." Justice Department witnesses were cool toward the bill, one declaring that the possibility of such special-interest tax relief would encourage companies to seek out merger partners, knowing they were protected against loss if ordered to divest. But Greenewalt's personal courting prevailed. The bill passed by overwhelming majorities. By one Treasury computation, the bill Clifford wrote made the wealthiest du Pont family members liable for a tax of about $7.25 per share, rather than the $45 per share they would have paid had the law not been changed. But the du Ponts still weren't satisfied. By 1964 the stock had risen to near $100, and much of it remained undistributed. On their behalf Clifford argued to IRS that the tax should be based on the 1962 price, which would reap the Treasury around $465 million. What more does the government want? Clifford demanded. He noted that civil antitrust laws were not intended to be punitive. And he asked IRS to change its interpretation of the 1962 act to adjust for the increase in the GM value.

The ruling had been made by Robert Knight, the general counsel of the Treasury Department. By 1964 he was in private practice with Shearman and Sterling, a New York tax firm. Clifford called him in the summer of 1964. Knight relates, "He asked me whether the fact that his clients produced a lot of revenue was the kind of factor that would permit a reconsideration." Clifford also asked whether Knight would consider returning to Treasury temporarily to restudy the highly complex question. A few weeks later, in fact, Secretary of the Treasury C. Douglas Dillon did summon Knight back to Washington as a special consultant. He underwent a furious round of briefings by Clifford and Christiana Securities officials, and on November 20, 1964, reversed his 1962 decision and gave the du Pont people what they wanted. Saving for the du Ponts: $56 million to $100 million, according to IRS estimate.

Senator Paul Douglas (D., Ill.) angrily asked whether if GM stock had fallen in value, IRS would have changed the rules to collect more money from du Pont. He doubted it. He declared to the Senate Finance Committee: "Very frankly, it seems to me this has been a heads-I-win, tails-you-lose ruling—heads du Pont wins, tails the government loses." Senator Albert Gore (D., Tenn.) charged that the "last-minute change in a Treasury ruling [was] negotiated and issued in secrecy and contrary to a clear intent of Congress." The entire episode smacked of favoritism, Gore declaimed; "stranger yet was the fact that [Knight] first learned of his possible selection as special consultant . . . by way of a telephone call from a Washington lawyer for the du Pont interests, Mr. Clark Clifford . . ." He suggested that every government official involved "share in whatever rewards are given out for service well beyond the call of duty to the rich and privileged."

Covington and Burling, du Pont's original counsel in the case, is a tolerably competent law firm, one whose expertise is recognized as far north of Washington as Wilmington, Delaware, du Pont's headquarters. Why, then, I asked Clifford, had du Pont turned to him as special counsel?

"This was a complicated question involving not only Congress but also the Treasury and Justice Departments, as well as a specialized knowledge of government," Clifford told me. "This was not in their [Covington and Burling's] line, but in ours. That's all." In fact, he said, "Greenewalt asked around a good deal about who could handle his problem, and I understand that Covington and Burling mentioned me."

Clifford's fee, by reliable account, was a ten-year retainer, which ultimately brought his firm approximately $1 million.

Clifford did almost as well in helping General Electric clean up the mess left by its involvement in the electrical equipment price-fixing cases. GE and certain of its officers had already pleaded guilty to criminal indictments in 1961 when Clifford entered the case at the request of Charles E. Wilson, former GE board chairman called out of retirement to plan defense of hundreds of damage suits filed by bilked GE customers (chiefly governments and utilities) Wilson had known Clifford since their service together in the Truman Administration, and he got Clifford to interrupt a Florida golfing vacation to join the defense. For the next year Clifford spent one day weekly at the GE headquarters in New York, trying, in his words, "to set some kind of policy to enable us to find a way out of this serious difficulty." GE's recruitment of Clifford caused stirs in government because of his friendship with Kennedy, prompting Attorney General Robert F. Kennedy to declare at a press conference that regardless of Clifford's connections, he would be treated the same as any other lawyer.

The Federal government agreed to settle its $70 million of claims for slightly more than $7 million—thereby setting a pattern for negotiations in hundreds of other cases brought by other governments around the nation.

Clifford is also credited—or blamed—with helping GE wangle a tax ruling permitting deductions of the treble damages as an expense of doing business. A Senate subcommittee headed by Senator Philip Hart (D., Mich.) poked around this affair for several years without discovering any evidence of a Clifford involvement. The reason, Clifford states, is quite simple: "I had nothing to do with it. I got out after the treble damage cases. This was something entirely different. But because you are connected with a company in a particular case, you tend to be associated with every blasted detail."

Clifford denies ever approaching a President on behalf of any client. He does *not* deny the obvious advantages of being known as a friend and adviser of the President, but he asserts in the next breath that the relationship carries special problems. "If you are going to maintain your standing with the President *and* the bar," Clifford told me, "you can't work on a matter involving a client. Usually the sort of things you'll be called upon to do, on behalf of the White House, are so broad no individual client is involved." Several times, Clifford indicated, a President has asked him for an opinion on something that could touch his law practice. "You have a legitimate out. You explain the circumstances to him [the President]. If he goes ahead and asks your advice, you give it to him.

"Sometimes a group of companies will come to you with a position directly contrary to the policies of the Administration. We tell them, 'We are not available for that kind of job.' " This policy is not so much an unwillingness to buck the Administration as it is an acceptance of the probability that Administration policy won't change. Clifford is shrewd. He won't diminish his reputation by taking a patently hopeless case, and he won't waste whatever friendship points he has outstanding at the White House by asking for a favor he has no chance of receiving. Clifford cited an example: "Some companies from a basic industry wanted changes in tariff policies. I knew what President Kennedy felt on the question, and I happened to agree with him, too. I said we were not available and gave them a reference elsewhere. I just stay out of this sort of thing."

Clifford's severest test of Presidential versus client loyalties came during the steel price showdown in the spring of 1962. Kennedy had persuaded the United Steel Workers to forgo large wage increases in negotiations that spring to cool inflation, and he thought he had reciprocal agreement from the manufacturers not to boost prices. Within a week after the contracts were signed, Roger Blough, president of United States Steel, informed the President that his company intended to raise prices by about twelve percent.

Kennedy called Clifford to the White House and told him to go to New York immediately to meet with Blough. The exact conversation is something that Clifford won't repeat, even at this late date. But it can be summarized as follows: Clifford reminded Kennedy he represented a major steel company. That doesn't matter, the President said, this is something special; I am going to draw a line with Roger Blough. Arthur Goldberg [then

Secretary of Labor] has already rented a hotel suite. You go in there with Roger Blough and the other steel people, and you stay there until they agree to roll back their prices.

Clifford ticked off a list of the horrible things that would happen to United States Steel and the other big steel corporations. Antitrust investigations. A thorough probe of their market practices. A tax audit. "The first thing I did was remind them of Kennedy's order halting Defense Department purchases of steel from companies that had raised prices. That is an awful amount of steel. The tax thing, too. No large corporation would like a thorough tax examination. The tax people could always find something, and the expense of going through such an investigation would be tremendous."

Clifford's stature gave his warnings chilling credibility. Blough fumed and frothed and said nasty things about the White House. But when he and Clifford left the hotel suite two days later, he had agreed to roll back the steel prices.

In 1959 the Revlon Corporation, the cosmetics manufacturer, retained Washington Lawyer Max Kampelman for advice on how to handle the scandal over rigged television quiz shows. Revlon sponsored the ultra-popular "$64,000 Question," which had the highest rating of any network show during the period. When disgruntled contestants revealed that the drama was contrived hokum, Kampelman spent several intensive weeks interviewing persons connected with the program and studying documents. He concluded that President Charles Revson was clean—that the culprits were the persons who staged the show. "Revson told me how he used to watch the show and cheer and holler for whoever was about to win the $64,000 jackpot. He was telling the truth, too," Kampelman says.

Kampelman gathered several suitcases of documentary material, wrote a summation report, and took it all to the Senate committee conducting the investigation. "I gave them every-thing; I opened it up completely. When they looked at the mate-rial, they decided they had no reason to call Revson, and they told him to forget about it." Kampelman was quite happy at this point, for putting a client before an investigative committee un-necessarily is an act of foolishness akin to Russian roulette. But a public relations man argued that Revson should demand the right to testify at the televised hearings to "clear his name." Kampelman said this would be rank folly: Revson is dogmatic, speaks a highly ethnic version of English, and dresses like . . . well, he does manufacture women's cosmetics, and his sartorial taste anticipated mod fashions by more than a decade. "It couldn't help but be a disaster," Kampelman said.

Kampelman, fortunately, had a way out of the case. Since his original retainer came from the Revlon Corporation, not Revson personally, he concluded that the interests of the two parties were not strictly parallel, and that what Revson was doing was not necessarily to Revlon's advantage. Revson pleaded; now that he had agreed to enter a den of lions voluntarily, he wanted someone to come along and hold his hand. Kampelman put him in touch with Clark Clifford.

"I was in on this all the way. I took Revson to Clifford's office, and we went through the papers and laid it out, the whole back-ground. Clark couldn't have spent more than a handful of hours on the case, him and his whole firm, hell, he couldn't have, and that includes the hearings. Just as I thought, the committee clob-bered Revson. They knocked his brains out.

"Anyway, several days after the testimony, Clark called and asked what I thought he should bill Revson. I was surprised, for I thought he would have settled something like this in advance, and I didn't know what to say. Clark continued, 'I was thinking about sending him a bill for $25,000.' I whistled, because that was pretty steep, by my standards, and Clark heard me. 'When

Revson gets the bill,' he said, 'he'll cuss and call me a son of a bitch and the whole business. But he'll pay it. And next year, when he's down in Miami Beach playing gin rummy with his buddies, he'll talk about his 'friend Clark Clifford' and his 'lawyer Clark Clifford,' and how much the so-and-so charged him— and it'll be worth $25,000 to him.' He did it, too."

"One reason the President likes Clark Clifford," a White House official told me in a private conversation in early 1968, "is that Clark made it on his own in Washington. Like it or not, one measure of a man is how much money he can make. Clifford has never been dependent on Johnson. When he tells Johnson something, it's because he thinks it is sound advice, and not necessarily what Johnson wants to hear." This man spoke a few days before Clifford became Johnson's Secretary of Defense— an appointment that changed the entire course of the Administration.

Clifford and Johnson had only cursory contact after LBJ's break with Stuart Symington in the late 1950s. The split was more a mutual coolness than a feud. Johnson simply struck Clifford from the list of persons he telephoned and saw regularly, and Clifford did not volunteer his advice. But several days after President Kennedy's assassination, Johnson called Clifford and invited him over for "a little talk." Johnson asked Clifford deep questions about the White House organization under Harry Truman, and the mechanics of the Eisenhower-Kennedy transition. Publicly, Johnson was saying, "Let us continue." Privately, he was quietly planning his own government. "Clark," he finally said, "you're now my transition expert." They talked for almost five hours, and when Clifford finally walked out of the White House into the November night, the breach was healed.

Once again, power. To plan, with co-intimates James Rowe and Abe Fortas, the high strategy of the 1964 campaign. To advise, in long evening conversations, on what the President should do in the slowly expanding war in Vietnam. To counsel on high-level appointments. When Robert Kennedy resigned as Attorney General in 1964 to run for the Senate, Clifford could have had the job. He refused. He wanted his independence. And his law practice, which did not suffer from the hours Clifford spent at the White House. During a rambling conversation with reporters in 1967 Johnson remarked that "my friend Clark" earned $1.3 million the previous year.

And always control. There are parallels between the techniques used by Clifford the lawyer and Clifford the Presidential adviser. For instance, the Bobby Baker investigation produced evidence that Don B. Reynolds, a suburban Maryland insurance agent who sold the President a high-risk $100,000 life policy, had been pressured into buying advertising time on the Johnson TV station. Later, at Baker's suggestion, Reynolds gave Mr. and Mrs. Johnson a high-fidelity phonograph. Walter Jenkins, a longtime Johnson aide, allegedly did the pressuring, and Republicans on the Senate rules committee wanted to put him under oath about the transactions. Clifford defused the danger inherent in putting Jenkins before hostile questioners by getting the Democratic majority to accept his testimony in affidavit form. The Senators readily accepted Clifford's story that Jenkins was "too busy with the transition" to testify. Clifford also told Johnson to speak out on the various Reynolds charges in a situation he could control—an impromptu press conference. Johnson did so, in a rambling monologue, and the conference was at an end before anyone could pin him down with specific questions. Thereafter the subject was off-limits to the press. With Fortas, Clifford also devised a solution to Johnson's "Bobby Kennedy problem." By early summer 1964 Johnson feared Kennedy was maneuvering for the Vice Presidential nomination. He could not stand the man (in private he constantly referred to Kennedy as "that little shit") and didn't want him in his Administration. The Clifford-Fortas solution: Rule out the possibility of *any* Cabinet officer taking the nomination.

Clifford's success in handling these and other discreet Presidential missions reinforced Johnson's confidence in him. And on Vietnam, Clifford reciprocated with repeated endorsements of what Johnson was doing. As Clifford was to say later, he thought U.S. involvement in Indochina was "based upon sound and unassailable premises," and was "thoroughly consistent with our self-interest and our responsibilities." Clifford's first vivid awareness of the dangers posed by the fighting in Indochina came during a transition conference with President Eisenhower one day before President Kennedy's inauguration. General Eisenhower warned that an insurgent victory in Laos could put all of Indochina into Communist hands, and that the United States should be prepared to intervene unilaterally. Clifford accepted unquestioningly General Eisenhower's domino theory—and also what he was being told about "progress" by U.S. military and diplomatic officials. A trip to Vietnam in the fall of 1965, as chairman of the Foreign Intelligence Advisory Board, confirmed his "belief in the correctness of our policy." So, too, did a 1966 trip with Johnson to Manila for a conference with allied nations involved in the war. Clifford felt "we were on the right road and that our military progress was bringing us closer to the resolution of the conflict." Within the councils of the Administration Clifford was a superhawk, arguing against bombing pauses on the grounds that Hanoi would interpret them as signs of weakness, and telling Johnson not to negotiate until he reached a position of strength.

Stuart Symington, whose own disillusionment with Vietnam began in mid-1966, found he could no longer talk about the war with his old friend "because he was so for it."

And then, in the fall of 1967, the first seeds of doubt. Johnson sent Clifford and General Maxwell Taylor to persuade Asian and Pacific allies to commit more troops to the war. Their pleas "fell on deaf ears" in country after country; not a single ally was willing to help the U.S. any further. Clifford returned to Washington with "nagging, not-to-be-suppressed doubts" about the validity of the judgments that had put the U.S. into Indochina. Clifford began to pay closer attention at the White House briefings; his questions took on a sharper edge.

In November 1967 Johnson decided to replace Robert S. McNamara as Secretary of Defense, and offered the post to Clifford. The President also spoke vaguely of replacing Secretary of State Dean Rusk, and hinted that Clifford could have his choice. Clifford didn't want to go back into government on a full-time basis, and he talked with Symington. "I told him not to take Defense," Symington says. "The war was so far gone he couldn't win, only lose. 'It's a rat race,' I told him." If he could be Secretary of State, take it; otherwise stay in private life. At one point Clifford thought Johnson had passed over him for both positions; then in January, Johnson more or less ordered him to the Pentagon.

For the first time Clifford could immerse himself in the gush of information flowing to Washington about the war. In a sense, he told me, he was once more the trial lawyer—weighing evidence and facts, winnowing out the important points, asking questions to fill out holes in the stories, listening, listening, listening. His first Presidential directive gave Clifford an excellent framework for a thorough study of the war. The Joint Chiefs of Staff wanted slightly more than 200,000 men to add to the 525,-000 already authorized for Vietnam. The President told Clifford to chair a task force on how the "requirement" could be met. "We were not instructed to assess the need for substantial increases in men and matériel; we were to devise the means by which they could be provided," Clifford said.

Now Clifford the trial lawyer, asking hard questions and receiving fuzzy answers. Would 200,000 men do the job? No one knew. If not, how many more? No one knew. What would the enemy do? Respond with a build-up of his own. Would bombing stop the war, or reduce U.S. casualties? Doubtful. What would the troop build-up do to the U.S. economy? Force tax increases and wage and price controls and worsen the balance-of-payments deficit? Finally, how much longer would the U.S. bear the brunt of combat? No one knew.

By mid-March Clifford had concluded the United States should start winding down the war and get out of Vietnam. He argued, as he wrote later, "that the United States had entered Vietnam with a limited aim—to prevent its subjugation by the north and to enable the people of South Vietnam to determine their own future. I also argued that we had largely accomplished that objective. Nothing required us to remain until the north had been ejected from the south, and the Saigon government had been established in complete military control of all South Vietnam." The White House debate was intensive, and both the participants and the historians will long argue what precipitated Johnson's stunning March 31 announcement not to seek reelection and to order a partial bombing halt to spur peace talks. But Clifford had an overpowering advantage in the debates: he spoke not as a long-term doubter—something which had destroyed the effectiveness of George Ball when he was Under Secretary of State—but as a man who had spent his entire life giving coldly objective advice to clients. And as a man whose professional survival depended upon his ability to convince juries, and government officials, of the rightness of his position.

Now, again, Clifford the private citizen. To become Secretary of Defense, Clifford formally withdrew from his law practice—cashed in his shares to the other partners, sold what stocks he had in defense firms, and took his name out of the firm. Reentering the practice required, perhaps, most of the morning of January 21, 1969. When Clifford "went dove on Johnson," as Washington political shorthand put it, some said his days as a legal high-roller had ended. The military-industrial complex does not tolerate defectors; hence Clifford would spend his declining years writing wills, or handling real-estate transactions. No, no, that theory is all wrong. Clifford ended the war—or tried to, anyway—on direct orders of the military-industrial complex. Too much spending on popguns for the Vietnamese, and inexpensive helicopters. We must get back to ABMs and supersonic bombs and kick up those high-profit ICBMs and supersonic bombers because here are profits a man can *count*.

Demonology makes good reading. But Clifford's turnaround in March 1968 relates directly back to tactical rules of thumb he learned defending corporations in the 1930s in quiet, high-ceilinged courtrooms around Missouri, Kansas, and southern Illinois. Ultimately, every trial lawyer gets into a case that he realizes is impossible to put before a jury. Make the best deal possible and settle. The buoyancy of self-deception will float a lawyer through weeks of trial; in the end, however, the client suffers. A hard task for a lawyer, telling a client he is wrong and he must pay; you lose business, and friends. Fight the bastards to the wire. Principle of the thing. Damn the expense. No, no, you are going to be clobbered if you proceed. You might "win" in a technical sense, years from now, but by then you'll be a ruined man. My professional advice is to settle.

Such was the situation with client Lyndon Johnson. No man likes to be told that he has lost control of a situation, that his basic policy is wrong, that his closest advisers are near-sighted fools who are leading him into even deeper disaster. When angry with a man, Johnson often succumbed to rigid politeness, a mock formality that fooled no one. That is the way he treated

Clifford before and after the March 31 speech. Johnson is piqued with Clifford, one man said, not so much because Clifford caused him to switch, but because Washington *knew* Clifford was responsible for the switch. To Johnson's credit, let it be said, he followed Clifford's advice, then turned on him.

Clifford leaves one with the feeling that estrangement from Johnson is an acceptable price for putting into motion the events that lead to a wind-down of the war. Clifford says he "was told" the first draft of Johnson's memoirs "was pretty rough on me"; despite the invitation to the May 1971 dedication of the LBJ library in Austin, he knows the former President still considers him a Judas.

Clifford is a rich man. He is past the age for another Cabinet position, even if the Democrats win in 1972. He says his law business is better now than ever. The Vietnam War continues to be a passion—a quiet passion, most of the time, but still one which consumes twenty percent of his week, in speeches and private talks with Congressmen and Senators and various anti-war groups. In June 1971 Clifford threw down the gauntlet to the Nixon Administration on the prisoner-of-war issue, saying he had "information" the issue would be resolved within thirty days of the time the United States announced a firm timetable for troop withdrawal. He also lent his name to a national lawyers' protest against the war—perhaps the first time in his life that Clark Clifford had signed his name to a petition other than a pleading filed in court.

Why the activity? Why continue a law practice at a time when further earnings only complicate the work of inheritance tax attorneys? Why not slip quietly into the role of Elder Statesman?

In the instance of the Vietnam War, Clifford is fighting a snake he thought he had killed back in March 1968, when he argued down Lyndon Johnson on continued escalation. Now, three years later, the snake is alive again, and with new heads in

Cambodia and Laos. And Clifford is after the snake again, this time as a private citizen.

In the instance of retirement—this question Clifford sloughs off with boilerplate comments about loving-to-work, can't-retire, like-the-busy-life. But something that happened during our second interview, one morning in June, provided the answer.

The person who telephoned was apparently a United States Senator ("my dear friend," Clifford said in greeting him). For five minutes he grunted and said terse "ummm hmmmms," and then in a minute of concise advice told the man how to go about answering an attack. "Don't do it by yourself; if you must answer, bring in Senator —— and have him sign it, too. But it sounds as if the guy is only giving an opinion. Now, if factual errors were involved, I'd answer, but your philosophy and reasoning are on the public record. I wouldn't bring further attention to it by answering. Let it go; that's my advice." Clifford listened a few more minutes, said good-bye to "dear friend," and hung up.

Power. Clark Clifford likes having United States Senators ask him what they should do. One loses that habit soon in retirement. Clark Clifford would rather stay by the phone. Who knows, in 1973 a President might be calling again.

3

Arnold and Porter:
Silent, as in Fortas

Arnold and Porter is money-jangling proof that doing a little good can enable a Washington law firm to do extremely well. Arnold and Porter's founding partners are a classic case of New Dealism gone sour: reformers who defected to climb over the battlements and join the "economic royalists" they had fought so vigorously for FDR. Arnold and Porter boasts its coterie of blue-chip clients—Coca-Cola, Lever Brothers, and Allis Chalmers, for instance. Conspicuous among its clientele, also, are corporations whose chips are Las Vegas blue, not Wall Street blue: the conglomerates that pumped much hot air into the American economy during the 1960s with the funny-money notion that collecting businesses is as noble as building them.

Brash. The word says much about both aspects of Arnold and Porter and some of the corporations it represents in Washington. Up and up and up it went, especially during the 1960s, under the tender aegis of Lyndon B. Johnson, whose long-term friendship with members was symbiotic, both financially and politically, and also well-publicized. And now . . .

"Arnold and Porter." A young lawyer who works for $75 a week (one-third the salary of an Arnold and Porter secretary) in a foundation-supported public-interest law office said the words, and he held his nose, and he made a nasty face. He worked at Arnold and Porter as an associate, briefly, and he had been telling me life-on-the-inside stories, and his gesture summed up what he had been saying.

"What really gets me," he said, "is the hypocrisy. Now look, I don't hold any brief for Covington and Burling. They are a corporation law firm, and they represent as many real live bastards as Arnold and Porter. But they don't pretend to be anything else. God, there's nothing more sanctimonious than a 'liberal' who thinks that putting his name on a letterhead of a civil rights organization gives him the right to behave like a latter-day Jay Gould." The young man held his nose again. "Arnold and Porter. Ugh."

Arnold and Porter is having what you could call an "image problem" in Washington, chiefly (but not totally) because its name used to be Arnold, Fortas and Porter. Arnold and Porter (A&P, Washington Lawyers call it) basked in the glory Abe Fortas reflected from the Supreme Court; it now cannot escape his tarnish as well. That Fortas has been out of the firm since 1965 is no matter, for his two-decade association is not something easily purged from the public mind. To much of Washington, and especially young lawyers with consciences left tender by the performance-promise gap of the sixties, Fortas's acceptance of a $20,000 fee from the foundation of financier Louis Wolfson was no particular surprise; indeed, to some it epitomized Fortas. Within the bounds of the law, but at the outer edges of propriety. Not *wrong*, but not exactly right, either, but excusable because . . . oh, you know, you must remember, Abe Fortas was a truly good liberal lawyer. Think of all those civil rights cases. Gideon. The McCarthy era. Owen Lattimore. And you must remember that Louis Wolfson's $20,000 was to cover work in "human relations." Now what could be more noble?

Only, the old answers don't seem to work anymore, even though three years have passed since Fortas's disgrace and resignation from the Supreme Court. At the time, *The Washington Post* and some other newspapers reported that a "quiet revolt" of junior partners and young associates prevented Fortas from returning to his old firm. A senior man there, however, says this isn't exactly true. "It was a *mutual* agreement," he told me. "It was discussed, very quietly, and both Abe and the firm sort of let it slide." This partner, and other men in the firm, insist that the Fortas contretemps—one of the most tempestuous judicial scandals in American history—and its aftermath did not affect Arnold and Porter's caseload. All the business we can handle, and more; constant expansion of lawyers and office space; earnings continuing to increase; rising economic barometer sort of thing. Yet . . .

Whether Arnold and Porter *deserves* public opprobrium because of a former partner's activities is not really relevant. Like it or not, the Fortas episode brought the firm into the public spotlight, and it is a focal point for much of the contemporary debate in Washington on the role of lawyers vis-à-vis the Federal government. Secondly, Arnold and Porter has an internal challenge: whether a Washington law firm of quasi-political origins can transform itself into a conventional, institutionalized office, one dependent upon pure lawyering skills, not the legal-politico mix of its founding partners. Put more bluntly, can Arnold and Porter air out the aroma left by Abe Fortas? The firm has a formidable list of challenges:

■■ The name Arnold and Porter is not popular with a large part of the Federal bureaucracy. The firm has irritated a good number of people during its quarter-century in Washington—middle-echelon bureaucrats who don't like lawyers who go over their heads to the boss—and they are tired of it. Paul Porter, the surviving founding partner, is easing into retirement, and when he snorts these days, Congressmen and other public officials don't jump as high as they used to. Some of the comments one hears about Arnold and Porter in the regulatory agencies and Congressional committee offices can best be summarized as billingsgate.

■■ The Nixon Administration apparently believed all those stories about Arnold and Porter and Johnsonian crony-ism, and tried hard in its early months to smear mud on A&P's bright brass doorplate. The Justice Department convened a grand jury in Cleveland to investigate whether burglars had in fact stolen documents Arnold and Porter held for a client it defended in an antitrust action. Eventually, several past presidents of the American Bar Association wrote Attorney General John N. Mitchell a letter protesting that the probe smacked of political inquisition, or words to that effect, and that some of the questions asked by the prosecutor directing the grand jury had violated attorney-client confidenti-ality. The grand jury did not return any indictments. Arnold and Porter partners I interviewed would not discuss the case, even on an off-the-record basis. But as an outside attorney says, "The significance is that Mitchell declared open season on Arnold and Porter. It was the Nixon Administration's way of telling its people they weren't to do any goddamned favors for Arnold and Porter." The Nixon-Mitchell scare didn't deter Arnold and Porter from Democratic politics. For two years after the Johnson Administration ended, the firm donated legal services to the Democratic National Committee, charging only for out-of-pocket expenses. Three lawyers in the firm helped write the delegate-selection procedures approved for the 1972 convention.

Arnold and Porter has hired only one prestigious name since Abe Fortas's downfall, and he left in a year's time. Joseph Califano, President Johnson's chief adviser for domestic affairs, joined the firm as a partner soon after leaving the White House, under terms that brought him more than $100,000 a year. He resigned in June 1971 to become a name-partner in the firm headed by famed defense attorney Edward Bennett Williams. There were no hard feelings, and Califano didn't take any clients or lawyers with him. But he has told acquaintances he was "too much of my own man to be part of a hundred-man operation." Califano celebrated his fortieth birthday two weeks before leaving Arnold and Porter, which means he has a quarter of a century of high-level lawyering left in him. His White House experience grants Califano ex officio tenure in the Washington power structure; as counsel for the Democratic National Committee, he has a voice in national politics. When the Democrats return to power, as they ultimately must, Joe Califano can be a Cabinet officer. In sum, he stands to become the Clark Clifford of his generation, and Arnold and Porter couldn't hold him. Another resignation much discussed among Washington Lawyers was that of Victor H. Kramer, longtime trial attorney for the Justice Department's antitrust division, who then worked hard for a decade for Arnold and Porter on the other side of the counsel table. People who know about such things say that if you ever had to count Washington's antitrust attorneys on the fingers of one hand, you'd include Vic Kramer. Well, he took a year's leave to help found the Center for Law and Social Policy, a public-interest firm, and then sent word to Arnold and Porter he wasn't returning; finished, just like that, tossing over a $200,000-a-year partnership and casting his lot with those goddamned kids who are always yakking about consumerism and berating Washington Lawyers who "whore for the corporations" and things like that. Kramer says he decided to "retire" because he was tired of the grind of big-firm work, and A&P's pension plan made a change attractive. But his choice of jobs is roughly comparable to that of General William Westmoreland resigning as Chief of Staff to help Lin Piao run the Red Guard.

That old Arnold and Porter political magic doesn't seem to work as well now that Lyndon is back on the Pedernales and new insiders are boasting around town about the powerful people *they* know. (See chapter 6, "Mudge, Rose, Guthrie and Alexander: The Former Partner's Firm.") One minor example: Arnold and Porter worked frantically in late 1968 to get Johnson to approve allocation to Braniff International Airways of a new route to the South Pacific via Acapulco. He did, and A&P received $408,636 in legal fees for the year for this case and other work. The music from the inaugural balls had barely died away when President

Nixon reopened the Pacific cases and stripped Braniff of Hawaiian routes via Mexico. (Six months later, Arnold and Porter did win permission for Braniff to fly to Mexico from the U.S. mainland.)

These present tribulations aside, Arnold and Porter remains big in Washington Law because, if for no other reason, of the strong personalities of the founding partners and their ability to get things done within the Federal bureaucracy. Arnold, Fortas and Porter was one of the first post-New Deal law firms run by former government officials who realized their blend of insider's knowledge and legal expertise was a very marketable quality. Men such as Thomas G. Corcoran had pioneered the field as individual practitioners, but at the end of the Second World War a "national" law firm run by Democrats was a relative oddity in Washington. The founding partners took varied routes out of government.

As chief of the Justice Department's antitrust division, Thurman Arnold initiated the case which resulted in a court decree that the Pullman Company could not both manufacture and operate railroad sleeping cars. Get rid of one function or the other, the court said. Arnold resigned to become a judge of the Court of Appeals, and the Pullman case dragged on. It was still alive in July 1945, and eccentric railroad financier Robert Young persuaded Arnold to leave the bench and try to win control of the Pullman service for him. Arnold worked hard for six months, but he and Young lost to a consortium formed by rival railroads. Sorry about that, Arnold told Young, and decided that since he was in private practice he might as well stay there.

Concurrently, Abe Fortas, a longtime friend and former student of Arnold's at Yale, was ready to resign as Under Secretary of the Interior. Fortas, only 36 years old, ranked as one of the brightest latter-day New Dealers, an expert in such diverse areas as petroleum and power law and labor relations. But the postwar law boom was beginning in Washington, and already columnist Marquis Childs was lamenting that "the Washington law industry is taking on oppressive size." Too young for promotion to a Cabinet position, too poorly paid to truly enjoy Washington— why stay in government? And, when you leave, why not take something along with you?

Something like the government of Puerto Rico, a United States territory which was one of Fortas's responsibilities as Under Secretary of the Interior. In 1945 Rexford G. Tugwell, the Governor of Puerto Rico, had talked to Interior about hiring a Washington law firm to represent the territory before the courts and Federal administrative agencies. Fortas reacted indignantly. He wrote Tugwell:

> I believe that continuing representation of a government or a governmental agency by private attorneys is unsound and unwise. I know that, from time to time, governmental agencies must and should retain private counsel on specific matters in order to assist government counsel. But except for such specialized assistance, governments and governmental agencies should, in my opinion, be represented by lawyers who are public officials. In my opinion, it is neither seemly nor appropriate for government agencies to be represented by counsel who are not regularly constituted public officials.

Fortas added that such representation "is apt to lead to embarrassment, regardless of the unimpeachable character of the private attorneys who might be concerned. In the event that the private lawyers obtained law business from private sources which involved dealing with the government, it is obvious that the situation would be embarrassing for both the lawyers and the government."

Less than a month after he left the Interior Department, Fortas signed on to represent Puerto Rico for a retainer of $1,000 a month.

The third founding partner also brought rich governmental and political ties into the firm. Paul A. Porter was FCC chairman and head of the wartime Office of Price Administration, which gave him wide acquaintance throughout the bureaucracy. Later President Truman sent Porter to Greece as a special roaming ambassador. (Thurman Arnold credited Porter with ending the Soviet-fomented civil war there.)

Describing the firm's founding in a *Yale Law Journal* article in 1970, Fortas wrote:

> The time was propitious for law practice in the nation's capital. The nation's business was struggling under the mass of rules, regulations, and restrictions which World War II had spawned. New enterprises had arisen in great number. Washington know-how was in demand, and the proliferation of Washington law firms had not yet taken place. Lawyers who were veterans of the New Deal and government service were presumed to be qualified to find their way through the maze, to guide and assist companies that had unfamiliar problems.
>
> These were relatively simple days in terms of the individual lawyer's approach to the problems of his working life. The object was to make a living, in economic terms. The criterion that determined the lawyer's decision as to whether he would represent a client, with few exceptions, was entirely pragmatic: Was the prospective client's problem such that the law firm could advise and represent the client with a reasonable prospect that the firm could contribute

something of value for which payment could and would be received?

Arnold, Fortas and Porter settled comfortably into a courtly old townhouse on the corner of 19th and N Streets NW that was once the home of Theodore Roosevelt. The three partners and four associates fitted nicely there; within the first decade, however, the firm had grown to forty lawyers, and into four adjoining townhouses, and then catty-corner across the street into a rabbit warren of five *more* townhouses. Now, with seventy-plus lawyers, it has trouble finding enough messenger boys to carry papers around, and associates gripe about having to walk in the snow when a senior partner calls them over for a chat. The growth was steady: three men a year. One quantum jump in size came in 1960 when the Washington office of the New York firm of Paul, Weiss, Rifkind, Wharton & Garrison moved over en masse, led by Fortas's tax-lawyer wife, Carolyn Agger. (The firm's resident Washington partner, Randolph Paul, had died, and the nine other attorneys in the Washington office felt no strong ties to New York; Miss Agger is credited with persuading them to join her husband's firm.)

The founders had clearly definable functions. In addition to his considerable legal talents, the debonair Porter charmed corporate clients in from the executive suites and gave them a cigar and told them funny stories about Harry Truman and walked them over to the Metropolitan Club for a drink. Arnold, as a former judge, exuded prestige and authority; as a one-time trust-buster, he had the special expertise of the repentant, now that he was telling clients how to fight the laws he was once paid to enforce. Fortas was the legal strongman and resident S.O.B.— the partner who supervised the caseload and worked the hell out of junior partners and associates, a blend of teacher and tyrant who got things done, and cases won. One man who worked for

Fortas during the 1950s called him "a smart son of a bitch"; some others leave off the adjective.

At one point during the 1950s Thurman Arnold was ready to throw up his hands and holler halt, that the firm was getting so big he didn't know what was happening. Someone in an audience of Chicago student lawyers once asked Arnold what characteristics his firm looked for when hiring. He replied, "We want bright young men of top standing with ability to grasp complicated legal problems and write eloquently about them . . . who after three years of service, just about the time that their salaries were getting burdensome, would come into the office, smile and say good-bye, and then gradually disappear like the Cheshire cat in *Alice in Wonderland*, leaving the smile behind them."

As it grew into a major firm, Arnold, Fortas and Porter developed two rather incongruous reputations: as a very gutsy defender of civil liberties, in an era when Joe McCarthy cowed much of the nation into craven silence, the legal profession included; and as a hard-nosed office whose tactics on behalf of corporate clients at times looked as rough as those of the government witch-hunters.

From the distance of twenty years the civil liberties cases seem like excerpts from a Kafka anthology: The young woman who held a non-sensitive position in the Labor Department, fired as a "Communist" by a loyalty board that didn't even know the name of her accusers, but which willingly accepted the FBI's assurance they were "reliable." The same fate for a Yale professor who served the government as a nutrition consultant; no names, no recourse. Scientists fired from Fort Monmouth during a McCarthy probe, this time with an added horror: the government kept anonymous not only the informers, but also the names of the loyalty board members. "As the law stood at that time," Thurman Arnold later wrote, "there was no constitutional requirement based on due process giving an accused the

right to learn . . . what the offense of which he had been convicted was." Arnold, Fortas and Porter chased this cloud
through the courts for seven years before the government
blushed and gave the men their back pay. And Owen Lattimore,
the academic expert on China, hailed into court on the most
bizarre indictment since the Salem witch trials: perjury, for
denying to a Senate committee that he was a "follower of the
Communist line" and a "promoter of Communist interests."
Judge Luther Youngdahl, a former Republican Governor of
Minnesota, dismissed two sets of indictments before the government gave up and let Lattimore go free. In some of these cases
the firm received its out-of-pocket expenses; in others, it didn't.

And criminal cases. Monte W. Durham, an obscure house-
breaker, wandered into the office in 1953, sent there by a public
defender who wasn't sure the man was mentally competent to
understand the proceedings against him. Fortas argued that the
traditional know-right-from-wrong rule was obsolete in the light
of modern psychological knowledge, and he won: If a criminal
act was the result of mental disease, the defendant could be
acquitted on the ground of insanity. For the equally obscure
Clarence Gideon, the Florida ne'er-do-well, Fortas took a Supreme Court assignment and won the case establishing that defendants, even indigent ones, must have counsel at all stages of a
criminal proceeding, even if the state must hire one. The cops
and prosecutors still yell about this one as starting America
down the road to crime and anarchy; Senators hooted and
stormed at Fortas for hours over Gideon during his confirmation
hearing for the Supreme Court. The principle he argued then is
the same as that of the "security risk" cases of the 1950s: every
citizen is entitled to a tolerably fair trial, even if it inconveniences
the bureaucracy.

Some Washington Lawyers—even ones friendly toward Arnold, Fortas and Porter—point to what they consider holes in

the firm's civil liberties record. The firm had a knack for choosing cases certain to demand publicity. Gideon had features of a can't-lose case, because when the Chief Justice chooses one of the nation's most famed lawyers to represent a petty criminal in the Supreme Court, he obviously is preparing to write some new law and wants a solid brief on which to base an opinion he has already decided to write. (Even these critics are quick to concede, however, that Fortas and his firm did first-rate work on Gideon, and that any preconceived ideas Warren had about the decision, if any, should not detract from his performance as a lawyer.) And the firm's managing committee would not permit junior members, acting as public-interest lawyers, to file a stockholder suit against major corporations which discriminated against blacks in hiring for their Southern plants. No, no, this would never do, because some of *our* clients have Southern operations, and we can't establish a precedent that could be used against them. Conflict of interest, you know.

Some of these complaints are cheap shots; Joe McCarthy, for instance, has so receded in most memories that it's hard even for people around at the time to recollect why they took him so seriously. McCarthy. Oh, that guy; Herblock used to draw funny cartoons about him. Sort of fell apart and became a drunk, didn't he? Arnold, Fortas and Porter fought McCarthy when he was a real live ogre, once capable of terrorizing a small law firm, just as he did, to varying degrees, the State Department, the Army, and the White House.

During this period a Senator demanded of Paul Porter whether it was true Arnold, Fortas and Porter spent much of its time representing Communists and homosexuals. "That's right, Senator," riposted Porter. "What can we do for you?"

So much for one face of Arnold, Fortas and Porter. The help-the-downtrodden–white-hat–good-causes–civil-liberties law firm. The other face is a composite: a large, efficient law office, churning out the routine legal work which never comes to the public eye, men adept at the humdrum mundanities of regulatory practice. The high-level policy counseling that isn't exactly law. The cases where corporations crash against one another in fearsome economic battle. In sum, a Washington law office, and a damned good one—and one able to protect its clients when proceedings degenerate into a saloon brawl.

In the mid-1950s Arnold, Fortas and Porter represented a Miami entrepreneur named A. Frank Katzentine, who was among bidders for the license to operate the lucrative television Channel 10 there. The FCC had just ended a freeze on new licenses, and businessmen throughout the country were competing for entree into a lucrative industry. Pressures on the FCC were enormous, with applicants recruiting whatever political allies they could find to jog the regulatory process.

Katzentine's chief competitor for Channel 10 was Public Service Television, Inc., a subsidiary of National Airlines. Public Service got into deep trouble for giving favors to Commissioner Richard A. Mack, a Floridian, who was driven from the agency in disgrace. When a House investigative subcommittee looked into the Channel 10 case later, G. T. Baker, the National president, claimed, in effect, that any influence-seeking he did was to defend against Paul Porter's lobbying. As a former FCC chairman, Porter surely knew his way around this particular battlefield. Baker's complaints about his activities must be heard with the forewarning that Baker failed to win a license worth millions of dollars, and that he was sore. But despite Baker's bitterness, he did give glimpses of what Paul Porter can accomplish behind the scenes.

Baker charged that Katzentine "was exerting political influence in every way he and . . . Porter could muster." Baker charged that Porter and Katzentine used Senators Estes Kefauver, Spessard Holland, and George Smathers as veritable errand boys, "putting on the heat . . . with members of the FCC." Porter did such effective legwork in Washington, according to

Baker, that Katzentine "was bragging around Miami . . . that through the efforts of his friends, they would have Senator [Warren] Magnuson, chairman of the Senate Interstate and Foreign Commerce Committee, abolish the FCC if National got . . . Channel 10."

Baker was particularly angry about some language which he claimed Porter managed to have inserted in a 1956 report by the Senate commerce committee on TV licensing. In awarding TV channels, the Senate document said, the FCC "should be on guard against the intrusion of big business and absentee owners —such as film producers, *aviation carriers*, magazine publishers, insurance companies, or other large investors." As Baker translated this language, Porter was using a Senate committee—one with jurisdiction over FCC matters—to exert pressure for a client. Another interpretation is more charitable: that the amendment represented sound public policy, in that it prevented big business from dominating a new medium.

Baker also accused the Katzentine legal team of resorting to "blackmail" of Richard M. Nixon, then Vice President, and other Administration figures. Again, the episode in question is subject to more than one interpretation.

In the Porter-Katzentine version, Commissioner Mack had "committed" himself to vote for National, and there was evidence he had accepted loans and other favors from a National attorney, Thurman A. Whiteside. A memorandum written by Downey Rice, another of Katzentine's lawyers, tells what happened:

> Last Saturday I met with Paul Porter for several hours and we had a thorough discussion of the Channel 10 problem . . . It was generally agreed that the place to cry wolf was as high up in a circle of close Eisenhower associates as possible. It had occurred to Paul Porter to get to Nixon

[then Vice President] through having Eddie Rickenbacker [president of Eastern Airlines] contact [Attorney General] Bill Rogers in the [Justice] Department.

I agreed that Nixon was the right man, but thought we might get the story over more satisfactorily through Bob King, Nixon's administrative assistant, and a former [FBI] agent. I had done some work with Nixon, Flip Flanagan, and [FCC Commissioner] Bob Lee back in 1950, and felt that Nixon would give some weight to what I might have to say.

Rice met with King in Nixon's office. According to Rice's account, King worried about possible exposure of Republican influence-peddlers. "I think the fact that he was told that Smathers had the story had the effect of forcing some action. Obviously they [the Republicans] cannot afford to risk exposure by Democrats of an 'influence deal.' " But Rice found King totally unsympathetic toward Katzentine, because the Miamian "was not only a Democrat, but even worse, was a Kefauver Democrat." Rice continued:

The session was concluded with King candidly stating that it was a serious question; that he would present it to Nixon and he knew that Nixon would know what to do. My guess . . . is that Nixon will simply telephone his friend, Bob Lee, and tell him that there are some loaded rumors afloat, and that Lee would do well to carefully consider any action being taken by the commission with an eye to the probability that, if said action was questionable, *prompt, unfavorable publicity could be expected.*

Rice was so pleased with the meeting that he advised Porter to forget about contacting Senator Alexander Wiley, as had been discussed earlier. "Action by Nixon compared with action by Wiley would be like comparing an atomic cannon with a pop-gun," Rice said.

The Katzentine legal team later interpreted the visit as an attempt to alert the Administration to possible misconduct by one of its appointive officials—one made in good faith. Civic altruism, or blackmail? A house subcommittee that heard both sides of the story passed no judgment. And whether Nixon in fact warned Republican members of the FCC of what was happening is not a matter of record. If he did, they did not heed him, for the FCC awarded the Channel 10 license to the National Airlines subsidiary. After public disclosure of Commissioner Mack's misconduct, the courts forced a reopening of the case, and ultimately the political pressures canceled out one another: the Commission said that both Katzentine and National were guilty of misconduct, and gave the Channel 10 license to a third applicant who had not relied upon influence.

One reads this record, and asks, "Well, so what? Arnold, Fortas and Porter lost the case. Doesn't that prove they are not influential?" No, it doesn't. Some cursory details of the Channel 10 manueverings are in the record because a Republican member of the FCC was indicted at a time when the Democrats controlled Congress. To get to the Republicans, the Democrats had to brush against Porter—not enough to disturb him, you understand, but enough to jar loose the secret manipulating a Washington Lawyer normally keeps locked in his desk drawer, or in his head.

Secrecy, too, for something else that was very valuable to the firm through January 20, 1969: its relationship, via Abe Fortas, with Lyndon B. Johnson. The basic outline of Fortas's *political* connections with Johnson is well-established in the public record. Less conspicuous, however, are the Johnson friends—corporate and individual—who used the Fortas firm as their attorney during Johnson's reign as Senate majority leader, Vice President, and President.

Johnson met Fortas when he was a first-term Congressman hot after public power for his Texas district, and Fortas, as director of the Department of the Interior's division of electric power, was the man who could give it to him. Thus began one of the more fruitful friendships of American government. Johnson first drew upon it in 1948, when a Federal District judge in Texas ordered his name off the ballot after he had won the Democratic primary nomination for U.S. Senator by 87 votes. Johnson's opponent, former Governor Coke Stevenson, charged fraud, and the judge wanted hearings on returns from a bleak mesquite patch precinct of Jim Wells County in South Texas. Johnson hastily recruited Fortas, who persuaded Supreme Court Justice Hugo Black to set aside the Texas judge's order on grounds Federal courts lacked jurisdiction over state elections. For the next 17 years, until he put Fortas on the Supreme Court in 1965, Johnson seldom made a major move without consulting his trusted lawyer-friend. Even from the bench Fortas did odd jobs for Johnson: advising on Vietnam, writing the speech in which Johnson ordered Federal troops into Detroit during the August 1967 riots, helping the White House settle a steel price dispute. "Whenever you put a man on the Supreme Court," Harry Truman once said, "he ceases to be your friend." Not so for Fortas and Johnson. For the record, Fortas found it politic after his nomination for the bench to soft-pedal his ties with the President. "There are two things which have been vastly exaggerated with respect to me," he told his confirmation hearing. "One is the extent to which I am a Presidential adviser, and the other is the extent to which I am a proficient violinist. I am a very poor violinist, but very enthusiastic, and my relations with the President have been exaggerated out of all connection with reality." Fortas has consistently refused to answer any specific questions about his relationship with President Johnson. "I think that it is my duty to observe certain limits, and one of those limits is any conversations . . . that I may have had with the President," he said in 1968, while still on the Court.

One Johnson friend who found Fortas's talents of use was Troy V. Post, a quiet Dallas multimillionaire who doesn't like to see his name in the newspapers. Post was a substantial millionaire by the mid-1950s through insurance and banking interests, but he wanted more, and he hit upon a very important idea: most insurance companies invest their premium income in stocks and bonds of other companies and are content to draw dividends. Why not use the premiums to buy outright control of other companies, Post asked, and pyramid a conglomerate empire? He tested his idea with a young Dallas electrical manufacturer named James Ling and by 1962 had started Ling-Temco-Vought on a dizzying rise through the financial world. Both Post and Ling are friends of Lyndon Johnson, through whom they came to know and trust Abe Fortas. In 1962 Fortas helped Post put together a conglomerate holding company, the Greatamerica Corporation. The incorporation papers, filed in Nevada on April 27, 1962, list Fortas as vice president, general counsel, and director of Greatamerica. Post put his insurance companies under the Greatamerica umbrella; he later used it as a vehicle to purchase Braniff International Airlines and the National Car Rental System. Fortas also went onto the Braniff board, and Arnold, Fortas and Porter did the airline's Washington work.

Fortas also handled occasional Washington business for Ling-Temco-Vought and subsidiaries. In at least one instance he cited Ling's financial support of the Democratic Party as a reason for favorable treatment of the company. The Securities and Exchange Commission was investigating a Ling subsidiary called Electro-Science Shares, Inc. According to investigative journalists Andrew Kopkind and James Ridgeway, Fortas told SEC

Chairman William Carey, "Hands off." Carey, furious, is said to have refused, and threatened to complain to President Kennedy if he heard anything further from Fortas.

Arnold and Porter continued its tight association with Braniff, Post, and Ling after Fortas went on the Supreme Court in 1965. Paul Porter replaced Fortas on the Braniff board. Another senior partner, Dennis G. Lyons, was elected to a Braniff directorship in April 1966. Both men held nominal amounts of Braniff stock. Braniff paid Arnold and Porter legal fees of $306,520 in 1970. Paul Porter also took Fortas's old seat on the Greatamerica board. Post finally sold control of Greatamerica to Ling in 1968 for almost half a billion dollars.

A single case illustrates Arnold and Porter's value to Ling-Temco-Vought, Inc. In late 1968 LTV began an attempt to acquire Jones & Laughlin Steel Corporation. The Justice Department was dubious. LTV was the nation's fourteenth largest industrial corporation, encompassing eighty separate companies with annual sales (in 1968) of $2.75 billion. J&L, the nation's sixth largest steel corporation, had sales of more than $900 million. The basic investigation was done in the waning days of the Johnson Administration, and the case was passed on with no recommendation.

On March 23, 1969, the Nixon Administration sued to halt the merger on grounds LTV was a "potential" competitor of Jones & Laughlin. Actually, knowing a suit was coming, Arnold and Porter had been negotiating for a consent decree for several months. Three days after filing of the suit, Arnold and Porter got what it wanted: an order permitting LTV to acquire up to eighty-one percent of Jones & Laughlin's common stock and hold it until the antitrust case was thrashed out. The agreement permitted LTV to file a consolidated income-tax return with J&L, giving LTV a tax saving estimated at $25 million. (A corporation can file a consolidated tax return only if it owns more than eighty percent of the voting stock of another company.) LTV eventually settled the case by disposing of Braniff and another subsidiary, the Okonite Company.

Through one favorable decision by the Johnson Administration, Fortas managed to benefit two clients simultaneously. Phillips Petroleum Company retained Arnold, Fortas and Porter to obtain changes in oil import quota regulations so that it could construct a mammoth petrochemical complex in Puerto Rico. A barrel of crude oil costs $2 when imported from the Middle East or Latin America, $3.75 when purchased domestically. The domestic oil producers obtained the import quota system in 1959 to assure themselves a market for their oil. Fortas convinced Interior Secretary Stewart Udall that Phillips deserved a boost in its existing quota so that it could use Venezuelan oil at the Puerto Rican facility. The extension enabled Phillips to cut its costs by $1.75 for each barrel processed—an economic boost both for Phillips and for Puerto Rico. A Fortas admirer says of his work, "Import 'tickets' aren't handed out like subway transfers; Fortas had to put on a good argument, and Udall bought it."

"When I was with Arnold, Fortas and Porter," a lawyer told me, "I could do the vast majority of the corporate stuff in good faith. I'm not anti-business, and even if I were, most of the cases involved one corporation fighting another. Who got screwed was academic; if you lost a case, you didn't feel like the world was coming to an end, or that the country was any worse off for it. But let me tell you something. The biggest damned mistake the office did was to get involved in the cigarette case. This is one where the public *was hurt; this wasn't just a business fight. I once did a rough head count and based on what people said to me, or indicated to me, more than one guy left the office over four years because of that case. It's the kind of thing that starts you thinking."*

The cigarette case. A political fight that shows the Washington Lawyer at his tactical best—and his social worst. Manuever the fight into a friendly forum, and warn away friends who don't want to get showered with unsightly blood, and bring in as many allies as you can. If it is politic to yield on a minor point or two, dictate the terms of your "surrender" so that it can be put to advantage.

The cigarette case began in early 1964 when the Public Health Service issued its famed report on the causal connection between smoking and bad health. The Federal Trade Commission, with uncharacteristic boldness, proposed rules requiring that tobacco companies put health warnings both on cigarette packages and in advertising. The tobacco industry mobilized under former Senator Earle C. Clements, a Tennessee Democrat who runs the Tobacco Institute, the lobby group. Washington Lawyers for the big tobacco companies formed a tight coalition to help him; prominent in its direction was Abe Fortas, who worked for Philip Morris. But to avoid embarrassing President Johnson, Fortas stayed in the shadows; Paul Porter made whatever public appearances were necessary. Fortas's strategy had three parts:

■■ *Get the issue away from the FTC and into Congress, where the industry has more influence.* Representative Oren Harris (D., Ark.), then chairman of the House Interstate and Foreign Commerce Committee, accommodated Fortas by writing Rand Dixon, the FTC chairman, and ordering him to take no action until Congress had a chance to "consider legislation" on the health warning issue. Dixon, who was occasionally brave but never foolhardy, backed away in a hurry.

■■ *Placate the public with a "self-regulation code."* Arnold, Fortas and Porter wrote one for the industry and presented it to Congress with great self-congratulatory flourishes. Robert B. Meyner, the former New Jersey governor, signed on as "code administrator," thereby giving authority to "self-regulation."

■■ *Accept a weak-worded health warning on packages.* People won't read it anyway, and it could help in defending legal actions brought by survivors of persons killed by cigarettes. ("Hell, lady, it says right there on the package the things could kill you; why didn't your husband read the warning before he upped and died on you?") In return for this "concession," refuse to give up advertising, especially the TV stuff aimed at the kids who are tomorrow's market.

The Fortas campaign worked. His firm's lawyers helped write testimony, and they marched witnesses through the hearings, and they stayed close around executive sessions to make sure dissidents didn't tamper with the script. The one concession, insisted upon by Senator Maurine Neuberger (whose husband had died of lung cancer), was that the ban against the FTC acting in the area last only for four years, not permanently as the cigarette manufacturers wanted.

A lawyer who now works elsewhere in Washington says he once very gently tried to draw Fortas into a discussion of the merits of smoking. "He looked at me blankly—not coldly, but like he didn't understand me—and he said, 'That isn't the point. Philip Morris is a client. You don't walk away from a client who is in trouble.' "

A law firm which invests in stocks of its clients runs subtle and varied risks. Erwin O. Smigel, in a study of Wall Street lawyers completed during the 1950s, found that most firms avoided such investments because they might "warp the lawyer's judgments." Smigel said this policy protected the lawyer "from accusations that he is seeking to serve his own interest rather than that of the clients . . ." In recent years many firms have abandoned such restrictive investment policies, and routinely accept stock options as partial or complete payment for legal services. But the risks cited by Smigel more than a decade ago remain valid.

Arnold and Porter does not have a rule against investing in client firms; further, lawyers assigned to cases are not always aware of the full ownership of client corporations. The result, inevitably, is the potential for grave embarrassment.

In the 1960s, Unimed, Inc., an amalgamation of small drug firms based in Morristown, New Jersey, got FDA permission to market a drug called Serc, an anti-vertigo medicine for persons suffering from Ménière's syndrome. Serc had been discovered in the 1940s, but no one tried to market it for two decades, apparently because of its dubious commercial value. But Unimed purchased the formula and pushed Serc as its major product. The FDA approved its sale November 11, 1966, with strongly worded label warnings on possible side effects. But W. Donald Gray, who directed many drug investigations for the House Interstate and Foreign Commerce Committee, discounts the importance of labeling. "A drug company's concern is 'get it on the market,' " Gray told me. "Doctors don't read the labels; the companies let the detail men sell it any way they want to; and the physician is so inundated with drugs he can't possibly check all of them."

According to Gray, Unimed's promotion of Serc smacked of a stock speculation. Only 300,000 persons in the United States are afflicted with Ménière's syndrome, and only 30,000 of them to the extent that Serc could benefit them. Yet the drug industry's *Pink Sheet*, a trade bulletin, quoted a Unimed official as saying Unimed would earn $7 million a year from the drug. "It's impossible," says Gray. "Divide 30,000 into seven million in profits and see for yourself. But this sort of statement would help the price of the stock." When Unimed asked FDA permission to sell Serc, its stock shot from $4 per share to $19; the FDA approval sent it to $88.

FDA evaluators, meanwhile, within a year found "serious discrepancies" in test data which a Unimed consultant, Dr. Joseph Elia, had submitted in support of Serc's efficacy. FDA called Dr. Elia in for conference, and Stuart Land, of Arnold and Porter, who had been representing Unimed, came with him. Dr. Elia admitted sloppy testing procedures, but Land argued that they weren't serious enough to warrant decertification of Serc. Dr. Herbert L. Ley, Jr., yielded to Land's pleas and decided to take no action.

Several months later, however, Gray learned of the affair. When Representative L. H. Fountain asked FDA for comment, FDA hurriedly changed its mind and ordered hearings to determine whether Serc should be taken off the shelves. Ley cited "defective" and "inadequate" testing procedures.

Unimed immediately began pulling whatever strings it could find. Martin Sweig, later convicted for criminal misuse of his position as administrative assistant to Speaker John McCormack, made several calls to the subcommittee. So did Nathan Voloshen, who pleaded guilty to being Sweig's partner in influence-peddling. Voloshen told Congressman Fountain he was an "old friend of the Speaker's" and plied him with "new evidence" on Serc's efficacy. Fountain told Voloshen, in effect, "Show it to the FDA, not to us."

Land of Arnold and Porter had no connection with the Sweig-Voloshen contacts, but he was most unhappy at the Fountain subcommittee's efforts in reopening a matter he thought he had already won. He encountered Donald Gray at a pre-hearing conference. "He was nasty," Gray says of Land; "he wanted to know why we were 'so interested in persecuting his client.' He changed his tune later."

Land's embarrassment resulted from a story on the front page of *The Washington Post* on October 21, 1969. *The Post*, in checking SEC records of companies for which Voloshen had done legwork in Congress, discovered he held options to buy 4,000 shares of Unimed at a reduced rate. Also on the option list, *The Post* story said, was the law firm of Arnold and Porter— 5,000 shares, at $12 per share. A firm spokesman told *The Post* Arnold and Porter had received the options from an Alabama broker who had actively promoted Unimed and said they were "in lieu of a fee."

Unbeknownst to *The Post*, the Serc decertification hearing was then in its second month. For the FDA's purposes, other names on the list were more significant than those of Voloshen and Arnold and Porter. Dr. Elia and five other physicians had sworn to the efficacy of Serc. According to SEC records, all but one of the doctors held long-term options to buy Unimed stock at reduced rates. FDA officials asked, somewhat irritably, what objectivity could be expected of a researcher who would profit from submitting favorable reports. According to Gray, the disclosures stunned Land. "He told me he had never heard of this." As soon as testimony ended, Land hand-delivered a letter to the FDA:

> Please take note that all appearances previously entered by Arnold and Porter, and all members and associates thereof, as counsel for . . . Unimed, Inc., are hereby withdrawn.

Land refused to discuss the proceeding. Another Unimed attorney, arguing for a delay in the case several days after Land's withdrawal, told the hearing, "As I understand it, the company did not change its counsel. They were quite happy about Mr. Land's presentation. Mr. Land withdrew for reasons of his own."

Land's embarrassment in the Unimed case should not detract from his reputation as a skilled drug attorney; indeed, people who practice at the FDA rank him among the top half-dozen specialists in Washington. He is particularly adept at the private bargaining with FDA officials that comprises an estimated ninety-five percent of a drug practice. In one instance, Land succeeded in keeping a product on the market even though its certification relied upon data the FDA called "phony."

Chesebrough-Pond's, Inc., a longtime cosmetics manufacturer, moved into the drug field in the 1960s with a sustained-release aspirin called Measurin. Such drugs are valuable to arthritis sufferers, who obtain relief during an eight- or twelve-hour period as the aspirin is slowly released into their systems. Initially, FDA was dubious about certifying Measurin, but Fortas wrote a letter threatening to sue unless the drug was admitted to the market immediately. FDA yielded, and Measurin proved immediately popular.

But Chesebrough-Pond's didn't like claims of Measurin's chief competitor, Relay, produced by Vicks. Land protested to the FDA in November 1965 that Vicks was making twelve-hour claims for Relay, whereas the FDA had restricted Chesebrough-Pond's to eight-hour claims. Land demanded an audience for high Chesebrough-Pond's officers with Deputy FDA Commissioner Winton B. Rankin.

Rankin was ready. He noted that Measurin's certification depended upon research documentation by Dr. Leo Cass, proprietor of a group called "Cass Research Associates." According to a memo Rankin wrote after the meeting, "We advised the visitors that the investigations we have made at Long Island Hospital show that the bulk of the clinical studies by Cass Research Associates which furnished the bulk of the efficacy data in their NDA [new drug applications] are phony . . ." Donald Gray of the Fountain subcommittee is more explicit; he reports that Cass stated many patients "felt no pain" after taking Measurin. "Cass was right," Gray states. "They didn't feel any pain because they had been dead for years—he used names off tombstones."

Since Dr. Cass's reports were the only "scientific evidence" that got Measurin onto the market, FDA could have ordered the product off the shelves. Nothing in the record hints that anyone at Arnold, Fortas and Porter was aware of the flimsiness of the claims made for Measurin. Nonetheless, Stuart Land tried to make the most of a bad situation. Land offered a compromise: Leave Measurin alone, he said, and Chesebrough-Pond's would delete Dr. Cass's challenged claims from future advertising and hurry along new supporting research on Measurin's efficacy. The FDA agreed—because, as Commissioner James L. Goddard has stated, "I felt that firms should not be punished when they are entrapped by false research data provided them when they went out and sought good data." Besides, he said, repeating one of Land's contentions, Measurin was nothing more than ordinary aspirin, and no one could be harmed by it. The advertising claims about "delayed-action relief" remain on the label.

An FDA attorney who is a veteran of dozens of such labeling negotiations told me Land's accomplishment was not overly unique. "You have to be reasonable," he said. "FDA's function is not harassment of drug companies. Why punish a manufacturer for something like this, when there is no possibility of harm to the public, and he was hoodwinked by shoddy research?"

In this instance, however, the FDA's willingness "to be reasonable" went a step further with Land. Concurrent with the negotiations at FDA, the Federal Trade Commission was conducting an independent study of Measurin's advertising. When FDA heard of this probe, M. L. Yakowitz, a case supervisor, suggested in a memo that Deputy Commissioner Rankin "may wish to phone or write Land and warn against further use of any promotional material that mentions Cass. I will be glad to provide any assistance you desire," Yakowitz wrote. Rankin agreed, advising Yakowitz to inform Land "we are obligated to tell FTC about the developments bearing on the Measurin ad." Congressional investigator Don Gray said, "It seems strange to me" that

FDA officials should be giving private attorneys advice on how to cope with an FTC investigation. Yakowitz disagreed. The purpose, he said, was to make sure Chesebrough-Pond's realized it was under FTC jurisdiction for advertising of non-prescription, over-the-counter drug products.

Paul Porter became close to Representative Wright Patman (D., Tex.) during the war because OPA legislation had to clear Patman's committee. Porter didn't forget the friendship. One day in the late 1960s he called Patman and announced, "Wright, I want to talk to you about this holding-company legislation." "Yes, Paul," Patman replied sweetly, "I understand there's something in it for you."

Drugs. Cigarette advertising. Corporate mergers. Aviation. "I suppose," an Arnold and Porter partner told me, "we practice everywhere in town except the Department of Agriculture." And with nigh-dazzling success. If existing laws or policies kept an Arnold, Fortas and Porter client from doing something . . . well, *change* the law or policy. "Much is said about 'influence' in this town," the partner continued. "Well, that well might be, sometimes, for some lawyers. But you've got to recognize that one function of a law firm is to find logical reasons for government to do something."

■■   In April 1964 the Supreme Court ruled for the Justice Department in an antitrust suit attacking the merger of the First National Bank & Trust Company and the Security Trust Company, both of Lexington, Kentucky. The Court ordered the banks to draft a divestiture agreement. Right away, however, the banks hired Arnold, Fortas and Porter to promote legislation in Congress which would nullify the Supreme Court decision and permit the merger to stay in effect. Gravice

Kincaid, president of Central Bank & Trust Company, a smaller Lexington bank which competed with the merged banks, said the local U.S. District Court had been unable to obtain the stipulated divestiture agreement.

. . . because the counsel employed by this bank [Arnold, Fortas and Porter] . . . has been able to have this bill breeze along through the Senate pretty good, without even a vote roll call, and now they are trying to railroad it through the House. And the directors say, "We are not going to do anything. We have this all taken care of in Washington. We are just going to drag our feet . . ."

The legislation passed. The merger (and those of banks in five other cities) remained in effect.

■▌ In 1965 Fortas negotiated a unique FTC consent decree permitting his client, Federated Department Stores, to acquire Bullock's, the big West Coast chain. Federated is the fourth largest chain in the country, with sales near $1 billion a year (its keystone stores are Abraham & Straus and Bloomingdale's). Bullock's was considerably smaller—seventeenth in rank, with sales of slightly more than $200 million—but was rapidly expanding in the lucrative Southwestern markets. The FTC decision is a masterpiece of something or other; lawyers who have studied the case haven't decided exactly what. It approved Federated's acquisition of Bullock's but said FTC approval would be required for any other purchases during the next five years. Commissioner A. Everette MacIntyre didn't like either the decision or the way Fortas went about negotiating it:

. . . the crucial decisions were made in the course of and pursuant to oral presentations to the commissioners by respondents on an off-the-record basis. A vital part of the decision-making process in that proceeding, as a practical matter, was simply unreviewable . . . Moreover, while the Commission agreed to listen to an informal presentation by Federated, it refused over my objection to extend a similar opportunity to one of the parties most directly concerned, the chief executive of Bullock's, the acquired concern, who opposed the merger . . .

What arguments did Fortas use to win a highly unorthodox consent decree? The public record is blank, for his presentation to the FTC was in executive session. But for the firm's purposes, what is important is that he won the case for Federated. Fortas's private bargaining has been criticized as an abuse of the regulatory process; Ralph Nader's Center for the Study of Responsive Law, in its 1971 critique of antitrust enforcement, noted that Fortas was a "Lyndon Johnson intimate," and concluded: "Given the general reputation of the FTC . . . a political deal was widely assumed by the agency staff and Washington lawyers." A Fortas defender could justifiably ask, "If the FTC agrees to discuss a case in private, should a lawyer demand an open hearing? Closed door meetings, as is true of many human activities, require two parties."

Six years later, Federated remains a contented client. During the two hours I was in a senior partner's office one afternoon in May 1971 he interrupted our interview four times to make or receive calls to clear up a detail of another minor antitrust action involving Federated. He ultimately resolved the issue by dictating a paragraph acceptable to the FTC man on the other end of the wire. "That," the Arnold and Porter partner said, "is how you practice law in Washington."

And that is how Arnold and Porter intends to continue practicing law—by maintaining its winner's reputation. Sit in the
Arnold and Porter townhouse offices long enough, and with a
sufficient variety of partners, and you sense two attitudes: an
uptightness because of what one man euphemistically called "the
Fortas thing"; and frustration over whether a subtle change of
direction is going to correct a very uneasy situation.

Until 1968 Arnold and Porter hired its new people almost
entirely from government service. The policy gave the firm instant expertise (and high-level contacts) in virtually every phase
of Federal practice. Milton Freeman, who directs the firm's securities work, was one of the first persons hired by the SEC
when it was formed in 1934. Mitchell Rogovin was general
counsel for IRS; he is the lead tax man. William D. Rogers,
former administrator of the Alliance for Progress, is useful on
Latin-American work—particularly Braniff's far-flung activities.
William Henry, also a former FCC chairman, has replaced the
aging Paul Porter as the broadcast specialist. According to bio-
graphical sketches in *Martindale and Hubbell,* twenty-one of
thirty-four partners listed are veterans of government service,
ranging from assistant special counsel to President Johnson to a
staff job on the House select subcommittee on education.

Murray V. Bring, a younger partner (he joined the firm in
1965 at age thirty) who is chairman of the management committee, maintains Arnold and Porter is now hiring more lawyers
directly from law schools. "When you bring in someone with a
lot of experience, and insert him laterally into a highly structured organization," Bring told me, "he jumps ahead of a lot of
people. In terms of career advancement this sort of thing can
hurt feelings and disrupt an office." At one time, partners en-
couraged new graduates to spend several years in government
before coming to Arnold and Porter. This is no longer done.

Partially as a result of pressures by younger men, Arnold and

Porter has extended and formalized its *pro bono* program (i.e., public-interest work for non-paying or low-paying clients). A partner is assigned full time as director of the program for a year and has authority to call upon the full resources of the firm. During 1970 all but six of the sixty-five lawyers then in the firm did *pro bono* work, at a cost (in time and out-of-pocket expenses) estimated at $500,000. Arnold and Porter policy is to devote at least fifteen percent of the firm's time to such work. (See chapter 10, "The New Washington Lawyers: Balancing the Scales.") In addition to salving consciences of partners already in the firm, the *pro bono* program is intended to make Arnold and Porter more palatable to new law school graduates.

Another partner maintains that Arnold and Porter's "institutionalization" has reduced its image as a "political firm." This man states, "A lot of people have the idea that Washington lawyering—especially Arnold and Porter lawyering—is wheeling and dealing. This does go on, but is really a misconception of what law is all about. The typical Washington Lawyer is a professional—a lawyer who spends his time doing lawyer's work. True, our specialty is the Federal government. We offer this as a service; we know our business. We keep track of decisions and orders and the way policy is going so we can advise our clients. I know of no instance where the firm has engaged in something that is not a straight legal function.

"Because of our connections with the Kennedy-Johnson Administration, and our carry-over influence with people still in the government, we might get some business we might not have received otherwise. But the connections have no bearing on the outcome of the cases.

"I'll admit we might be beneficiaries of some client's misconception that we do have inside power. Many clients have come to us because they thought we were close to an administration. We educate them to the fact that that is not really relevant. Most stay. Nor does our Democratic identification hurt now that the Republicans are in power. There has been no change whatsoever in our growth or income pattern.

"Once a firm gets to be well established and institutionalized, proficiency is the thing that attracts clients—the notion that this firm can handle matters competently and effectively, regardless of the politics of the Administration."

When Arnold, Fortas and Porter was first formed, the partners drifted into a little custom. Each Monday noon a secretary would go out for sandwiches, and every lawyer in the office, partners and associates, would gather in a garden courtyard and talk about their cases and socialize and linger over second cups of coffee until two p.m. Then everyone would go back to work. These were pleasant moments, for Paul Porter is a genuinely charming man, and Thurman Arnold was a storyteller who has made many a Georgetown drawing room explode with laughter, and Abe Fortas, despite his acerbic treatment of young associates, was a man of sophisticated wit.

The garden is no longer big enough to hold even a small percentage of Arnold and Porter's lawyers. For a while everyone spent Monday noon in a closed dining room of the International Club, a hundred feet or so south of the townhouse office complex. But something was missing. "Frankly," one partner told me, "they got to be like Rotary Club meetings—too damned many people around to talk business, or even to do any informal socializing. I stopped going." When the International Club moved in 1969, and the Communications Club took its old quarters, the meetings continued there for a while. Then the Communications Club folded, and no one at Arnold and Porter had any ideas on where to go.

4

Tommy the Cork Corcoran:
The Lawyer as Acrobat

One day not too many months ago, Thomas G. Corcoran, the mahogany-tanned, white-thatched Irishman who practices his own variety of Washington Law at a brisk canter, swept into the office of a thirty-five-year-old Congressional staff member, plopped his briefcase onto the desk, and flicked immaculate cuffs to the proper angle, wrist and ankle, as he settled into the visitor's chair. Huff-huff-huff and a smile, and pat-pat-pat go Tommy the Cork's feet, and he is comfortable, and now Tommy the Cork is talking. One thing that he always remembers about Franklin D. Roosevelt, he tells the younger man, is that . . . and a few minutes later . . . as Harold Ickes used to say . . . and then Henry Wallace, and then John Nance Garner, and then . . .

*And then something damnably embarrassing happened to the
Congressional aide, a polite Virginian who believes in listening
to his elders even if he isn't paying any attention to them. After
fifteen minutes of Corcoran's New Deal ramblings his head
nodded, and he aroused with a jerk and the knowledge that he
had dozed off. Gone to sleep on Tommy the Cork. God. Igno-
miny. He glanced furtively across the desk, mind racing for an
excuse. Hangover. Sick child. Insomnia.*

*No matter. "Corcoran hadn't even noticed," the guy told me.
"He was still chattering away about the New Deal. Hell, how do
you go about telling the man that I'm not impressed by how
close he was to FDR? That doesn't mean a goddamned thing to
me in 1970."*

Thomas G. Corcoran is the prototype of a legend most Washington Lawyers wish they could expunge from the public's con-
ception of government. He is a lawyer who does not practice
law—although of course his firm is equipped to do conventional
legal work. He is an insider who has said publicly that his utility
to a client derives from his ability to find out things a few hours
earlier than other people. He is a man who has dealt with the
Federal government for more than thirty years on public-policy
issues, yet has left a minimal public trace. The back room, not
the courtroom or hearing room, is Tommy Corcoran's haunt. He
is regularly blessed with that newspaper sobriquet, "politically
influential," yet he never appears on lists of campaign workers
or contributors. He is at Congress regularly—"almost as much
as the Speaker of the House," one man says—yet seldom does
he find it necessary to register as a lobbyist. He is one of the few
surviving FDR intimates, yet he is happy partying with Nixon
intimates in the Watergate high-rise apartment complex along
the Potomac in Foggy Bottom (often as the escort of Mrs.
Claire Chennault, a very charming, and very conservative, Republican).

"How does Tommy Corcoran do it?" a Washington Lawyer repeated what I had asked him. "A better question, I think, is, '*Does* Tommy Corcoran do it?'"

One would think so, if for no other reason than because corporations keep hiring him as their Man in Washington. Pan American World Airways paid him a retainer of $30,000 a year, although he never appeared on its behalf in a formal proceeding at the Civil Aeronautics Board (Steptoe and Johnson, a conventional firm that does conventional aviation work, received fees from Pan Am ranging from $55,601 to $80,752 during the 1960s). So, too, does Tennessee Gas Transmission Company, the pipeline company, although the Federal Power Commission doesn't permit the firm to classify his fees as ordinary business expenses. So, too, does United Fruit Company, which counts on Corcoran to maintain close liaison with the State Department officers responsible for Latin-American nations in which it operates. So, too, does El Paso Natural Gas Company, which as of this writing is relying upon Corcoran for legislation exempting gas pipeline and production companies from antitrust laws on certain joint ventures.

Exactly *what* Corcoran does for these clients—and, more importantly, *how* he does it—is what Tommy-watchers can't decide, for he is at once extroverted and secretive. Corcoran once insisted, in public and with a straight face, that he keeps very scanty records of how he spends his time, and for whom. No appointments book, no list of visitors to his office, no social engagement calendar, no record of long-distance calls, no time sheets of hours allocated to clients (the accounting backbone of most law offices). "I move too fast to be able to keep a diary," Corcoran claimed. "I can remember, when I go, the fact that I travel on an airplane." Anyway, Corcoran maintained, he prefers to charge on a retainer basis. "We can't work on a time-sheet basis in my office for any purpose."

Furtiveness is a key element of the Corcoran mystique. Sure, he is a charming, ruddy Irishman, so gregarious that Franklin D. Roosevelt guffawed once at a party and called him Tommy the Cork; most people, the older pols, anyway, enjoyed having him around; and he has private-line access to much of the Congressional leadership. Mrs. Chennault made sure he met all those interesting Republicans who moved into the Miami Beach-elegant Watergate apartment complex when the Nixon Administration came to town. Quite a transition, from playing the accordion for FDR to playing the piano for Martha Mitchell and Spiro T. Agnew, but Tommy the Cork is an adaptable fellow. But also a distinct caveat: fun in public, but business in private.

A man who worked for three United States Senators over a period of twelve years, and thus knows about such things, remembers occasions when Corcoran came around to talk to his boss about campaign contributions. That is what he *thinks*, at least, and was told by at least one of the Senators. Anything Corcoran had to say on the subject was for the Senators' ears only. No law prohibits a Washington Lawyer from contributing money to a politician, and no one has ever accused Corcoran of demanding a quid pro quo. But several political basics exist in Washington. One of them is that businessmen do not like to waste their money. If a contribution can keep a . . . well, a *philosophical friend* in office, give him the money, and don't waste it on people who are going to make trouble for your industry. Another basic is that few businessmen have sense enough to tell friend from foe in Washington without consulting an expert; hence the utility of a Washington Lawyer. Yet another basic is that politicians, in Congress and elsewhere, always welcome the sight of campaign money. There is nothing illegal about any of these things—yet they are done in the privacy of an office, not on the front steps of the Capitol.

And privacy is a Corcoran characteristic. Says another Congressional assistant: "Tommy doesn't like to mess around with staff people. He'll wait an extra day or two, if it's necessary, to go directly to the Senator. It's part of his mystique, and I used to get the idea he wasn't keen about letting too many people know exactly what he was doing."

And another man, this one formerly very high in the Internal Revenue Service in the 1960s: "Tommy might have clout in some places in Washington, but the bells started ringing when he walked into IRS. Whether he likes it or not, his 'political' reputation walks around with him, and the career people are wary of him and maybe even resent him a little bit. I've been told he's a damned smart lawyer, and maybe he is, in his special fields. But I never saw any evidence that he knew all that much about tax law. Oh, he could set up the high-level conferences, and get his clients in to see the people they wanted to see. But when the technical stuff started, he'd fade in a hurry, and anybody who was really up on tax law knew right away he wasn't an expert. I don't mean to knock Tommy by saying that, either; taxes are a tough field, and not many generalists know all the answers."

How does Tommy Corcoran do it?

In the late 1960s a tool and die company found itself in grave trouble on a Pentagon contract for barrels. Because of defective welds, the company was threatened with default on the contract and heavy penalties. The Defense Department had a clear-cut case against the company. Covington and Burling, its regular counsel, did what it could through normal channels, and got nowhere. Finally, Edward Burling, a C&B senior partner, and also a major shareholder in the company, recommended that it seek the aid of Tom Corcoran. C&B regularly refers "ticklish" matters to Corcoran.

Officers of the company spent slightly less than an hour detailing the problem to Corcoran. He listened intently and asked a question from time to time. When they finished, he picked up his office phone and asked for a number at the Pentagon. Should we leave? someone asked. No, stay where you are, Corcoran replied. He spoke briefly with someone at the Pentagon, giving cursory details on the company's problem. Then he hung up and announced, "It's settled, your problems are over."

The officers left the office with very warm feelings about Tom Corcoran. Then a few days later Burling received Corcoran's bill. It was for $10,000. The company was outraged—not so much at the amount of the fee (which was modest compared to what the contract default would have cost) as by Corcoran's arrogance. As one of the men involved complained later, "He made no pretense of doing anything other than that one phone call. If only he had stalled around for a day or two. The impression was that he was putting the company on notice that he could get things done."

Arrogance. Whether it is deliberate or otherwise, the word says much about Tommy the Cork. A lawyer recollects watching Corcoran at the U.S. Supreme Court one morning, sitting in the front row as Edward Bennett Williams argued a case. "Tom wrote a note and beckoned to a page to come get it and take it up to Justice ——, who was sitting on the bench," the lawyer said. "Justice —— read it, and looked down at Tom and smiled and nodded. I don't have the slightest idea what it was all about, but it was damned effective, to get that sort of attention from a Justice in open court. People remember things like that. It does a lot for a man's reputation if he wants to be considered influential in Washington."

So, too, did the appointment of Corcoran's brother and sometime law partner, Howard, to the U.S. District Court in Washington shortly after Johnson's accession to the Presidency. Tom Corcoran had been friendly with Joseph Kennedy, father of the slain President, since the days when they worked together to create the Securities and Exchange Commission. Yet Corcoran never was in the JFK inner circle. Even during the Kennedy Presidency, a life-sized oil portrait of Lyndon Johnson dominated the reception room at Corcoran's office. "There were damned few of those around Washington at the time," another Washington Lawyer remembers. Many lawyers blinked with surprise when Johnson submitted Howard Corcoran's name for the Federal bench. At a Senate Judiciary Committee confirmation hearing someone asked casually how much trial experience the brother had had. "Zero," he replied. There was an embarrassed hush; the nomination went through anyway. A Tommy-watcher told me, "This appointment was Johnson's endorsement of Tom. It was tantamount to a testimonial."

But Tommy Corcoran is a man who believes in the future. Today's President is tomorrow's ex-politician. So after 1965 Corcoran's bustling figure was frequently seen darting into Vice President Hubert H. Humphrey's suite in the Executive Office Building adjacent to the White House. What did they talk about? Did Humphrey ask Corcoran to drop by for a chat, or vice versa? Who knows? But a man working on the White House staff at the time recollects, "The visits were so frequent that it was damned obvious—to us, anyway—that Tom got along with Humphrey. I know *I* would have remembered that fact had Humphrey ever gotten to be President."

Formally, Tommy the Cork is but one member of a law firm named Corcoran, Foley, Youngman and Rowe. Nineteen members, two other lawyers of counsel, an intricate mosaic of legal backgrounds drawn from scattered power pockets throughout the Federal government.

Edward H. Foley was in government from 1932 until 1953, the last five years as Under Secretary of the Treasury. Political? Enough so to be general chairman of the Kennedy-Johnson inaugural committee in 1961. James H. Rowe, one of Lyndon Johnson's to-the-well friends, has had an insider's role in every

Democratic Presidential campaign since 1940. Along the way: secretary to Justice Holmes; Reconstruction Finance Corporation; Labor Department; Public Works Administration; the SEC; administrative assistant to Roosevelt 1938–41; special assistant to Attorney General Francis Biddle during the war; counsel to the Senate Majority Policy Committee in 1956–57, when LBJ was majority leader. (The other name-partner, William S. Youngman, one-time general counsel of the Federal Power Commission, is deceased.)

On down the roster. Robert Amory, Jr., deputy director, intelligence (DDI) of the CIA 1953–62, third most important job in the agency, the government's chief gazer into the crystal ball. Why an ex-spook? Amory is as secretive as is Corcoran, but a man once in the firm says, "Bob does the international stuff, especially for our oil and pipeline people. Just what, I don't know, for he doesn't talk much."

For daily Congressional work, the firm has both Democratic and Republican branches: Donald J. Cronin was right-hand man to the powerful Senator Lister Hill (D., Ala.) until Hill retired. Very often these days, Senators and their staff members receive phone calls that begin, "You might remember that I used to be with Lister Hill. I'm wearing a new hat now. I'm with Tommy Corcoran, and I'm calling about . . ." Republicans, meanwhile, get their you-remember-me calls from Clyde L. Flynn, Jr., counsel to Senator Everett Dirksen until the Senate minority leader's death in 1969.

In the spring I called Corcoran's office and told a secretary what I was doing, and asked for an appointment. I'll get back to you. She didn't. I called again. I'll get back to you. She didn't. I called again. Mr. Corcoran says he is too busy and good luck.

By June my Corcoran file contained a stack of interview notes and other material several inches thick, so I wrote him a letter.

"Candidly," I said, "writing a book on Washington Lawyers without mentioning Tommy the Cork would be akin to writing a book on the contemporary Presidency without mentioning Richard M. Nixon." Again, I asked for an interview.

Two weeks, no response. Calls on successive days. No luck. Busy. Leave your number. We'll get back. He finally did.

I can't give you an interview; there is too much pressure from the bar about lawyers and publicity. The partners feel the same way. I have too many wars without fighting an internal war with the bar.

I started to tell Corcoran that I had spoken to more than fifty lawyers and that none had refused an interview outright, and that we could talk on an off-the-record basis if he desired. I got the distinct impression he wasn't listening to me. Thanks for the note, good luck on your book, so long now.

So long, Tommy.

A reputation for being important is a self-propelling asset when a man reaches—or starts at—a certain level in Washington Law. Thomas Gardiner Corcoran, born four days after Christmas in 1900 in Pawtucket, Rhode Island, was a moderately wealthy man when he came to Washington in 1932 as a lawyer for the Reconstruction Finance Corporation in the waning Hoover months, on loan from his Wall Street law firm. Later, when the Democrats arrived, and his former Harvard law professor, Felix Frankfurter, began recruiting brains for the New Deal, Corcoran was one of the few ideologically acceptable people around with an insider's knowledge of the stock market. During the next eight years Corcoran's formal rank never changed; he never commanded a limousine or a carpeted office; his salary stalled at a paltry $10,000 a year. But when Corcoran left government in 1940, he was a personal extension of Franklin D. Roosevelt: legislative draftsman and strategist, speechwriter, lobbyist, talent scout, intelligence operative, political agent (and

atchet man), lightning rod for White House critics, court enter-
ainer. Seldom has any White House agent accumulated so much
delegated power—and used it so shrewdly and so ruthlessly.
Whatever Roosevelt wanted, Corcoran got—or tried to, anyway, and tough luck to any important people who got in his
way. Any account of what Corcoran did during those years
would quickly become a history of the first two Roosevelt Administrations. But divide his work roughly into two periods:

■■   From 1933 to 1936, working with Harvard classmate
      Ben Cohen, Corcoran drafted the three basic laws
      under which Wall Street still operates: the Securities
      Act of 1933, the Securities Exchange Act of 1934, and
      the Public Utility Holding Company Act of 1935. Big
      finance fought all three bills, but the Corcoran-Cohen
      team got them through Congress with skillful testimony,
      and the Supreme Court let them stand—indeed, the
      only early major legislation of the New Deal not killed
      by the Court.

■■   For the next five years Corcoran was a White House
      agent-without-portfolio, working directly under FDR
      and authorized to act in his name. Every President
      needs a resident bastard, a pragmatist capable of work-
      ing in the lower sewers of politics and government, if
      necessary, to move things along. Corcoran once de-
      scribed his role: "There isn't enough time to explain
      everything to everyone, to cajole everyone, to persuade
      everyone, to make everyone see why it has to be done
      one way rather than another. If a President tried to do
      this, he would have no time left for anything else. So he
      must deceive, misrepresent, leave false impressions—
      even, sometimes, lie—and trust to charm, loyalty, and
      the result to make up for it . . . A great man cannot be a
      good man."

The willingness to bully people, and to invoke the President's name, was one Corcoran tool. Another, perhaps even more important, was a careful seeding of the Federal government wit men loyal both to FDR *and* the positions Tommy Corcora advocated within the Administration. *U.S. News* (now *U.S News & World Report*) in a somewhat awed appraisal of Corco ran just before he left government, credited him with selectin four Supreme Court Justices, numerous U.S. attorneys in ke cities, and heads and key officials in enough agencies to make u a company of infantry:

> It was Corcoran who successfully urged the Supreme Court appointment of Stanley Reed, his nominal boss at the RFC. Corcoran influence dominated in the selection of William O. Douglas to fill a second Court vacancy. When Justice Brandeis resigned . . . Tom had an opportunity to repay an old debt by pulling successfully for the selection of Professor Frankfurter . . .
>
> In his latest maneuver . . . Tom Corcoran sold the idea of elevating Frank Murphy from the Attorney Generalship to the Court and raising his close friend, Robert H. Jackson, from the Solicitorship to the Attorney Generalship . . .

Corcoran preferred putting young men into key governmen agencies because they were less inclined to be swayed by senti ment or financial ties. Corcoran could command their loyalty He expected, and received, a daily flow of intelligence reports o what was happening in every nook and cranny of government The best-informed man in government, they called Tommy Cor coran, even more so than FDR.

Political hatchet men are notoriously poor insurance risks, an for Corcoran, the actuarial tables ran out with FDR's Court packing scheme of 1937 and the subsequent disastrous attemp to purge Senators who opposed the plan. Democratic politician who didn't dare criticize Roosevelt seized upon Corcoran as a symbol of Administration perfidy and arm-twisting, and roasted him with hot-air oratory. Postmaster James Farley didn't like Corcoran; neither, for that matter, did Mrs. Roosevelt. And here are hints that sometimes Tommy Corcoran pushed the President just a little too often and a little too vigorously for FDR's comfort. The crowning insult came when Tommy Corcoran, who prided himself on getting jobs for other people, couldn't get the one he wanted for himself.

The job was that of Solicitor General, a position even more prestigious in some eyes than that of Attorney General. The Solicitor General is the lawyer for the Federal government. He argues for the government in the Supreme Court, he decides which cases are to be appealed, which are to be dropped; he has vast influence over lawyers in other government departments with whom his office deals on a daily basis.

Corcoran asked for the position, and the Administration, as is customary, surveyed members of the Supreme Court to see if the appointment was acceptable. Four Justices said yes, four Justices said no. Corcoran's old friend and mentor Justice Frankfurter abstained. Corcoran, shocked, went to him and asked why. What Frankfurter replied is not recorded in history, but another Washington Lawyer who was friendly with both men (he studied under Frankfurter and worked under Corcoran in government) states, "The friendship between the two men ended —*snap*—just like that. Tommy would never say why. My own guess? Oh, Tommy at that time was pretty damned arrogant, and I suspect Mr. Frankfurter felt the power was going to his head."

In 1939, when Tommy Corcoran realized power was eroding from beneath him and flowing to Harry Hopkins, a new Roosevelt favorite, an attorney friend quoted him as saying:

"I'm getting out, Sam, but not for long. I want to make on
million dollars, in one year, that's all. Then I'm coming back t
the government for the rest of my life."

In 1941, less than a year after leaving the White House, Cor
coran encountered the friend again. "Say, Sam," he said, "I'v
got to raise the price or shorten the time."

Corcoran stepped from the White House into so thriving a law
business that for many months he didn't even bother to open a
office or list a business phone. To do so, he told people, would b
a nuisance. Anyone who really mattered could eventually find
him; anyone who couldn't wasn't the sort of insider-client h
wanted, anyway. A resentful rival viewed the lack of accommo
dations from a slightly different perspective. He told journalis
Andreas Spenser, "He practices law right out of his hat. Doesn'
need an office. He just uses the offices of all those boys he go
jobs in government. Hangs out first in one air-cooled Federa
building and then another, calling up people and quoting the
President. How is *that* practicing law?"

Then the man added, undoubtedly a bit jealously, "But h
sure does get results."

Corcoran never made good his stated intention of returning to
government after a year and a million dollars, although he di
occasionally wave a letter which he said was from Roosevelt
asking him to become Assistant Secretary of the Navy. During
the war FDR asked him to come into the Justice Department
Solicitor General or nothing, Corcoran said, and the matter
dropped. A political realist, Corcoran realized why Roosevelt
had let him leave government, and any hard feelings he might
have harbored toward the President he kept tightly within himself, even among friends. Besides, a reputation as the President's
one-time man was invaluable to a lawyer starting a practice in
booming wartime Washington. Corcoran maintained a brief as-

ociation with two former lawyers from the FCC, then jumped
into general practice with profitable vigor.

Corcoran's first major client was Henry J. Kaiser, the West
Coast builder who had helped construct the Boulder, Shasta,
and Bonneville dams, and who now opted for a share of the war
business. Corcoran opened the right doors for him: at the RFC,
where he arranged for meetings with Jesse Jones, his one-time
nominal superior; at the Justice and War departments; at the
Federal Reserve Board, where chairman Marriner Eccles knew
Kaiser from his own days as a construction executive in Utah;
even at the White House. Kaiser and Corcoran spent a busy six
weeks, and the results justified the energy consumed: an RFC
loan of $9,250,000 to build a magnesium plant, title to which
would revert to Kaiser at a nominal sum after hostilities ceased,
and $646 million in contracts at shipbuilding yards Kaiser
would build on the West Coast with government assistance. For
his efforts as a door-opener, Corcoran received a reported fee of
a quarter of a million dollars, and he continued to do Washington work for Kaiser throughout the war. He also received another bonus of inestimable value. The *Washington Times-Herald*
published a photograph showing Kaiser chatting amiably with
William Knudsen, the head of the War Production Board, to
illustrate a glowing feature story on Corcoran. The caption
noted that Corcoran represented Kaiser in Washington. Now
Kaiser's stature in American industry, and his presence in Washington, were news, and the press justifiably treated the visit as
such. But in a city of Washington's keen political sensitivities,
the picture said much more: "This is the sort of entree Tom
Corcoran has in high-level government; hire him as your lawyer
and you, too, can walk right into Knudsen's office and ask for
big defense contracts." A reputation for being important, for
having access to powerful men—once the idea is in people's
minds—remains there, and sustains itself, and grows.

The Kaiser representation alone was enough to give Corcoran rookie-of-the-year honors in Washington Law. Several other cases solidified his reputation for adroit reliance upon his old government contacts. Corcoran's brother, David, an officer of Sidney Ross & Company, part of the far-flung drug empire of Sterling Products Company, was one person who sought help. The Ross firm had subsidiary and related companies in Latin America, England, and Germany, and the Justice Department's antitrust division had grave questions about some of its overseas dealings. One point offered in Dave Corcoran's defense (in addition to a general denial that he, Sterling, or the Ross company had violated the law) was that as special counsel for the Chinese government he had resorted to shortcuts in finding supplies of drugs for the beleaguered Chiang Kai-shek. Therefore, the Corcorans argued, the Justice Department shouldn't bother them with questions about "who has been getting together with whom." According to Norman M. Littell, an assistant attorney general at the time, the Justice Department's antitrust division accumulated more than 30,000 documents detailing Sterling links with I. G. Farbenindustrie, a German drug company, in violation of the law. When war began, Littell told a Senate committee, Sterling took over I. G. Farbenindustrie's South American markets, and "in many cases the funds of this business were diverted from the German agents to spread German propaganda." According to Littell, the antitrust division pushed for criminal proceedings before a grand jury. Corcoran, however, persuaded Attorney General Biddle to settle the case via a civil consent decree—one day after Biddle took office. Littell commented that settlement of the case "without submission of all the evidence to a grand jury marks the lowest point in the history of the Department of Justice since the Harding Administration." Representative Lawrence Smith (R., Wis.) tried to foment a Congressional probe of the settlement, saying, "it is common gossip in govern-

nent circles that the long arm of Tommy Corcoran reaches into
nany agencies; that he has placed many men in important posi-
ions and they in turn are amenable to his influences." Nothing
esulted from Smith's demands.

(The work for Sterling began an on-again-off-again represen-
ation of the drug industry that continued for more than three
lecades. For the Pharmaceutical Manufacturers Association,
Corcoran tried—but failed—to emasculate the tough drug-la-
)eling bill Senator Estes Kefauver (D., Tenn.) pushed through
Congress in 1962. More often he succeeded. In 1963 Senator
Philip A. Hart (D., Mich.) wanted authority from the antitrust
,ubcommittee to issue subpoenas forcing drug manufacturers to
estify. Hart needed the officials, and documents from their files,
for a probe of apparent price-fixing in Latin America by U.S.
irms. According to Senate staffers who worked on drug matters,
Corcoran's persuaded Senator Russell Long (D., La.), a long-
:ime political friend and legislative buddy, to join with commit-
:ee Republicans to kill Hart's motion—and with it, the South
American probe.)

Corcoran's major wartime client was Chiang Kai-shek.
Chiang's brother-in-law, T. V. Soong, formed China Defense
Supplies to funnel Lend-Lease aid into China, both for the Na-
tionalist government and for the American-supported air force
headed by Major General Claire Chennault. Soong's operating
partner was a shrewd, charming Pole named Ludwig (Lulu)
Rajchman, a one-time League of Nations diplomat who arrived
in Washington in 1940 as a war refugee. *The Reporter*'s classic
study of the China Lobby says both Soong and Rajchman "had a
highly developed genius for understanding how the disparate
parts of a complicated structure like a government bureaucracy
fit together. They soon saw that official Washington was a jungle
of departments, often with overlapping functions and the usual
hostility toward one another. The best way to get something

done was to collect influential friends who would circumvent or overwhelm opposition."

Soong and Rajchman recruited Tommy Corcoran as counsel for China Defense Supplies; as its director they installed Corcoran's friend (and later law partner) William S. Youngman, Jr., who had been general counsel of the Federal Power Commission. Corcoran's brother Dave also went on the payroll. Rajchman managed to charm many New Dealers into believing there could be a "New Deal" even in China once the war ended and men like Soong came into power. Corcoran's network of friends proved invaluable in whisking China aid through the bureaucracy. Because she was in the forefront of the war against Japan, China basked in the warm glow of public and White House sympathy and admiration, which made things easier. By the time the Second World War ended, $3.5 to $5 billion in aid had flowed through China Defense Supplies.

Corcoran's visible connections with the China Lobby ceased after the war. One friendship resulting from it continues, however. When Corcoran's wife Margaret died in 1957 at age 44, he became the constant companion of General Chennault's widow, Anna.

"It hurts to be dropped as Tommy was dropped [by FDR], especially in Washington. And he can't prove he still has power except by fees . . . He wanted to be Solicitor General of the United States. Now he's only getting rich."
—*former FDR aide Jonathan Daniels, in* Frontier on the Potomac.

Joseph L. Rauh, Jr., the labor–civil-rights lawyer, came to the New Deal from Harvard and spent several happy years working under Thomas G. Corcoran—preparing testimony for Congress, writing legislation, doing routine administrative chores in the

Federal agencies. He found Corcoran's jauntiness exhilarating, and he shared Corcoran's zest for causes. That was almost forty years ago. Now Rauh sat quietly in the Federal City Club and swished around a glass of bourbon and ice and reminisced about his erstwhile crusader friend.

"Corcoran's case is particularly sad," Joe Rauh told me, "because he spent his youth slaying dragons. I considered myself lucky to carry his briefcase. Then he had his seventieth birthday party, and he got up to make a speech, and one of the first things he said was, 'One of the greatest things in my life is that I represent the largest pipeline company in the world and the biggest . . .' and on and on and on. I almost got sick. I looked across at Wayne Morse, and he was shaking his head and looking sad.

"I understand Tommy. He has to be the best. When he was in the government he had to be the best government lawyer there was, get more accomplished than anyone else. The same now that he's with the corporations. He wants to be the richest, and the most influential, the most highly regarded.

"How does he hang on, what is his source of power, why is he influential? God only knows, but he is."

On the rare occasions when Corcoran has lost his veil of secrecy, what was seen of him proved to be what legend leads the public to expect: a man not averse to jogging along the governmental process through personal contacts and entreaties, and one whom officials receive with uneven degrees of enthusiasm and credibility. Corcoran sees nothing unusual about the fact that he so seldom appears as an attorney-of-record or makes his arguments in a public forum. His most important ongoing client has long been Tennessee Gas Transmission Company. Discussing his work for Tennessee Gas, Corcoran once said, "I am the supervising lawyer in Washington and I sit in on the important hearings. I consult with these people [the hearing lawyers] but you simply cannot be in charge of all these things

[and] sit the interminable days in hearings. We always have a case or two before the Federal Power Commission. I don't think the sun ever sets on us."

Corcoran's stratagems as a "supervisor" are best revealed in an FPC case in 1959.

A Tennessee Gas subsidiary, the Midwestern Gas Transmission Company, needed FPC permission for a 500-mile pipeline between Emerson, Manitoba, and Marshfield, Wisconsin. Midwestern would obtain gas for the system from Trans-Canada, Ltd. The FPC certificate had to be obtained by November 1, 1959; otherwise, Trans-Canada could terminate the contract and renegotiate it at a higher cost. Hence Midwestern wanted a fast decision from the FPC.

Midwestern also wanted the FPC to permit it to earn seven percent on gas sold through the pipeline, arguing that this rate of return was necessary to make the project economically feasible. The FPC staff, however, recommended a return of only six and one-half percent. The rate was the only real issue during arguments before the Commission on October 20, 1959, since no one opposed construction of the pipeline. Corcoran attended with Midwestern President N. W. Freeman but was not the attorney-of-record. Lawyer Harry S. Littman presented the company's case. Corcoran's contribution was to suggest that the FPC go ahead with the construction certificate, in view of the November 1 contract deadline, and decide the rate of return later.

At an FPC executive session three days later—October 23, a Friday—two members endorsed Corcoran's idea, two others leaned toward the staff six and one-half percent recommendation. Chairman Jerome Kuykendall suggested that a draft opinion embodying the staff recommendation be written—not as a decision, but for discussion.

Word of the deadlock leaked to Midwestern officials over the weekend. By Sunday, Gardiner Symonds, board chairman of Tennessee Gas, was worried. He called Freeman, the Midwestern president, and told him to instruct Tommy Corcoran to "call on each of the Commissioners personally" the next day and relay two messages in his name:

- That if the FPC did not act by the November deadline, Midwestern could not build the pipeline except at a "rise in the price of gas that would make the gas almost unmarketable."

- That he doubted financing could be found for the $50 million of securities needed for construction until the seven percent return was authorized.

Corcoran managed to see Chairman Kuykendall and two other Commissioners within a few hours' time on Monday. Commissioner William R. Connole wasn't happy being pressured by Tommy the Cork. Connole said Corcoran arrived late in the day and "asked my secretary for permission to see me. He had no appointment and had asked for none. He had not told me or my office that he was coming, nor did he state to my secretary the purpose of his visit."

Connole immediately went on guard, for he well knew the stories about Tommy Corcoran and closed doors. "Since I knew that there was pending before us a proceeding in which one of the firms with which he was associated was involved, I went to the door of my private office and, in the presence of others, cautioned him courteously but unmistakably that I did not intend to discuss the issues in that case . . . I then invited him to enter." Corcoran stayed only a few minutes, and Connole said he didn't try to discuss the merits of Midwestern's case—only the need for a fast decision. He also said the warning was reflexive—not because he was apprehensive but "I wanted to be sure . . . I didn't have grounds for apprehension."

The second Commissioner, Arthur Kline, was also wary of

Corcoran but saw him anyway. What Corcoran did not know was that for a time Kline had instructed his secretary not to make any appointments for Corcoran or put through his phone calls. "I told her that I didn't want to see him anymore. I felt he was perhaps going outside of the record in some of these cases, and I just felt it was better not to talk to him anymore . . ."

Chairman Kuykendall said the visit irked him, too, because Corcoran and Symonds had pestered him with off-the-record visits during the previous year. One day they came to his office and began "telling about how they were all ready to go and they had their pipe and they had their labor, and that every day of delay is costing money and so forth and . . . I told them, 'All right, I knew all about that, anyway,' and I said, "Don't go any further. Don't discuss anything about this case.' "

In addition to the visit, Corcoran also telephoned Kuykendall, and this time he did mention the seven percent return. Kuykendall told a House investigative subcommittee he considered this call both "improper" and "unnecessary."

The FPC met again on Friday, October 30, and decided to leave the rate of return open, just as Tommy Corcoran had asked. Midwestern received the construction certificate on October 31, less than twenty-four hours before the contract expiration deadline. Corcoran had done his work well.

Or had he? Each Commissioner questioned by the House Interstate and Foreign Commerce Committee denied that the visits had anything to do with their final decision. But they were distinctly uneasy about the Corcoran visits. No regulator wanted to be caught in a repeat of the Sherman Adams/Bernard Goldfine scandals, and Kuykendall claimed later he and other commissioners debated reporting Corcoran's visits immediately to the Commerce Committee staff. They decided against doing so.

"If it were publicized," Kuykendall said, "I know I would have been pictured as pulling the lowest kind of political trick, due to the fact that Mr. Corcoran is a well-known, well-identified Democrat and former Democratic official. If I, as a Republican, had made an exposé of this, why, it would have looked like I was just gunning for him because he was prominent in his political party."

Shortly after the decision, however, *Oildom*, an obscure industry publication, reported Corcoran's visits and linked them with the favorable ruling for Midwestern. Kuykendall immediately took copies of the article to the subcommittee and gave a full report on what Corcoran had done. Pressured by Republican members, the investigative subcommittee held eleven days of hearings on *ex parte* contacts at the FPC. Corcoran was treated gently. Commission members were brought in for hours of intensive interrogation by the subcommittee staff before their public testimony, and they had to turn over their private appointment books for inspection. No such indignities for Corcoran: he was not even questioned until a few days before the hearings opened, and then only briefly, and no effort was made to obtain a record of his appointments. Corcoran's two days of testimony, once he got to the witness stand, are useful only because of the rare glimpse it provides of Tommy Corcoran on the prowl. Corcoran never flinched; indeed, many times he threw interrogators' accusations back at them, often with beguiling politeness, often with subtle sarcasm.

Corcoran maintained there was nothing secretive about his contacts. "I walked down the corridors of that Commission— and I have always walked down the corridors of the Commission —in broad daylight with a brass band behind me," Corcoran said. And he implied that the *ex parte* visits were actually a gesture of good will toward Congress. Corcoran's reasoning: "I have always felt that since, after all, the Commission was an arm of Congress—and I am sure that Congress in passing the Federal Power Act meant it should get gas to people who wanted it

and not find ways to not get gas to people . . . through indecision
—it was perfectly appropriate for me [to see] what I could do
to expedite these things." And he entered a broad denial of any
unethical conduct.

"There is a great deal of subjectiveness to anybody's definition of what propriety and impropriety is," Corcoran said. "I
prefer always to follow my own conscience in what I consider
appropriate or inappropriate, but always to know I am standing
on the hard rock of what is written as legal and as illegal in
determining my conduct." (Translated: Let your conscience be
your guide, but also read the law books.)

Corcoran conceded, "it is very, very hard to determine what
the bounds of propriety are"; doing so, he said, "has some of the
connotations of trying to decide how many angels can dance on
the head of a pin." Any conversation with a Commissioner relates back to a statement of fact. "You cannot say, 'Mr. Commissioner, I hope you will expedite that XYZ situation which I
cannot identify to you by name.' " So long as agency staff members are permitted to talk to Commissioners, Corcoran argued,
private lawyers should have the same privilege.

Corcoran was a wiggly witness, one difficult to pin to the mat.
When Representative John B. Bennett (R., Mich.) tried to elicit
just what Corcoran told the Commissioners that they hadn't already heard in the public hearing, he lapsed into long soliloquies
about Midwestern's determination to give gas service to the
Upper Pennisula of Michigan, when "nobody ever offered to do
it for you before." This parry was supposed to embarrass Bennett, who represented a Michigan district. But Bennett was
tenacious, and occasionally he got hold of Corcoran. Hadn't Symonds already given a full presentation to FPC in his formal,
public testimony? What points did Corcoran make that Symonds
did not state?

"He had made most of them, I am sure," Corcoran replied.

"What hadn't he said?" asked Bennett.

"I don't know," Corcoran said.

"Well," continued Bennett, "have you followed this policy of going to the Commissioners, as you did in this case, in all of the cases that you have tried before the Federal Power Commission? Do you always go back and talk to them privately to be sure they understand what your law firm tried to put across, three or four months after argument and trial?"

Corcoran filibustered away a direct answer, saying he had replied to the question "about nineteen times."

"In nineteen different ways," retorted Bennett. And then Corcoran managed to maneuver Bennett onto the defensive, blandly mentioning that the Congressman was among the persons who had written letters to the FPC supporting the pipeline. Corcoran waved a copy of Bennett's letters, photostated from FPC files by an employee of Tennessee Gas Transmission. Why was this done? Bennett demanded.

"You were part of our support," Corcoran replied, innocently. Perhaps, he suggested, "it was with *your* help" that the FPC approved Midwestern's application. And he thanked Bennett for "your *ex parte*, very desirable, and very proper and very welcome help in an *ex parte* communication to the Commission." The frustrated Bennett finally had to let Corcoran go.

Symonds, the Tennessee Gas Transmission president, said his only disappointment with Corcoran's work was that "he spoke much more softly than I would have spoken" in asking for the seven percent return. Bennett was curious about what Symonds really expected from Corcoran. "Unless you felt that Mr. Corcoran would seduce them by giving them your message or unless he threatened them in some way, what could possibly be the object of having him make these private contacts for you?" he asked.

"He was in Washington," Symonds replied. "It was one final

plea, that is all there was to it. He knows them better, but I don't think he has any particular amount of influence more than I.

"After all," Symonds continued, "I have the weight of the company which I represent behind me . . . I don't think I would use the word 'influence.' . . . Perhaps begging is a means of influencing. It certainly isn't a very dignified means of influence, but it is what we have done for these long years."

The Democratic majority accepted Corcoran's contention that the contacts were "in conformity with law and were entirely proper," and that "all members of the pipeline industry regulated by the FPC were constantly in *ex parte* contact with the Commission." No parties opposed the construction, the subcommittee said, and in such instances "the formalities of the courtroom will serve no purpose except to delay the administrative decision at the expense of the public interest."

The Republicans disagreed, charging in a minority report that the handling of Corcoran was "the most shocking political whitewash to come out of a Congressional committee in many years." The report said:

> The majority and its staff have sought to exonerate one of Washington's best-known influence peddlers . . .
>
> The record speaks for itself. His conduct is typical of many other "off-the-record" contact people which this subcommittee's investigations have revealed during the past four years.

When President Roosevelt visited Texas in 1937 he invited newly elected Congressman Lyndon B. Johnson to ride along on his train. He interrupted his farewell to scribble something on a piece of paper. "Here's a telephone number," the President told Johnson. "When you get to Washington, call it and ask for Tom. Tell him what we've talked about." Johnson did as he was told,

and the number turned out to be an unlisted White House line.
Tom, of course, was Corcoran, and the men were on the phone
together regularly from then until January 20, 1969. Johnson
was Corcoran's kind of man. As Corcoran once remarked, "The
Boss met Lyndon in Galveston and invited him to ride across the
state in his train. That was all it took—one train ride. Lyndon
was an operator." Corcoran can spot operators. After all . . .

In 1970, as part of his continuing inquiry into utility expendi-
tures, Senator Lee Metcalf (D., Mont.) sent Western Electric a
simple one-paragraph letter asking how much money the company spent on advertising and public relations. Western Electric
is the wholly owned manufacturing and supply subsidiary of
American Telephone & Telegraph Company. Since AT&T is
Western's only customer, Metcalf was curious about why the
company found it necessary to advertise its wares. No American
citizen can go out and buy a Bell telephone; you rent them from
the phone company.

Several days later, Metcalf received a phone call from James
Rowe of the Corcoran firm. Metcalf's administrative assistant,
Vic Reinemer, told me, "Jim is originally from Montana, and he
is friendly with Lee, who is part of his 'beat' for AT&T. Bell has
the Congress divided up among all sorts of lawyers. Southerners
work on Southerners, and that sort of thing. Anyway, Jim is our
man, or vice versa. Rowe said he just wanted to know what Lee
was up to with the query, and whether he was starting 'anything
major' with the phone company.

"Lee told him no, that he was just putting together some facts
and figures. Later Jim came in with a Western Electric vice
president who came especially from New York with the data.
They made a formal presentation of this one-page document and
told the Senator how happy Western Electric was to comply with
his request.

"It was all very silly. This is the kind of query a file clerk could have answered. But Rowe and Western Electric put on a big show. I don't have the slightest idea what AT&T pays Rowe,* but things like that come right out of utility bills—that is, the consumer's pocket."

Lawyering, or softening? Just what is it that Corcoran and his firm do to command their rank in Washington Law? What transpires between a law firm and a corporation is generally conceded to be none of an outsider's business; because of the bar's self-written ban on discussion of client-attorney relations, seldom can the work performed be subjected to objective scrutiny. In some areas, however, the public has a direct financial interest. If a utility, for instance, pays unnecessary legal fees, the consumer pays the cost, in fractions of cents added to utility bills. In one instance the Corcoran firm was subjected to such scrutiny. The finding: whatever Corcoran does, it isn't lawyering.

The question arose when the FPC staff challenged Tennessee Gas Transmission for listing, as ordinary business expenses, fees of $60,444 paid to the Corcoran firm and $15,000 to the Chicago firm of Arvey, Hodes and Mantynband. (The latter was run by Jake Arvey, the pre-Daley Democratic boss of Chicago.) Under FPC procedures, legal fees that actually benefit rate-payers can be charged to rate-payers; otherwise, they become an ordinary corporate expense that is borne by shareholders. The FPC staff maintained that Tennessee "has failed to meet the burden of explaining and supporting the nature and character of the services performed; that accordingly, it is impossible to form

* Sixty thousand dollars a year, according to the annual reports AT&T files with the Federal Communications Commission. However, AT&T also maintains a Washington legal staff befitting the world's largest corporation, and the Corcoran firm does not appear as attorney-of-record in any recent interstate rate cases, the phone company's major concern with the FCC. The AT&T annual reports do not reflect exactly what the Corcoran firm does for the company.

a conclusion as to whether such fees represent proper charges against the rate-payers." The payments were made on billings that "merely showed the name of the law firm and the amount of the bill, with no description of the services performed." Tennessee challenged the staff, and at a hearing a company official offered this description of the firms' work:

"Each of these firms continually renders advice on administrative matters, both on their own initiative as well as at the request of the company. These firms determine the individuals to whom inquiries with respect to such matters should be addressed, and arrange for and participate in meetings in connection therewith when such procedure is deemed advisable.

"When either of them encounters any situation which they believe would affect the company's welfare, they immediately advise the company and recommend a course of action to be pursued . . .

"In addition to the many other legal services rendered by T. G. Corcoran [they were not specified], he keeps the company advised on all governmental developments, be they legislative, administrative or judicial on both national and state levels.

"It is my opinion and that of the management that the legal services rendered by these firms are well worth the fees we are paying them."

The FPC hearing examiner, Joseph Zwerdling, did not agree that the fees were a worthwhile expenditure. "The real issue here," he wrote, "is whether these services are of the character which may properly be charged against the Tennessee rate-payers, or whether they are of such nature that the Tennessee stockholders should more properly bear the cost."

Even though Tennessee was told the staff intended to challenge the charges, the company's explanation of them "was of such vague and general character that it is not possible to determine here whether these charges are of the type which may be properly passed on to the rate-payer." The FPC followed his recommendation and disallowed the fees. And buried deep in the footnotes of Zwerdling's report is a commentary on Washington Law, Corcoran-style:

> Official notice may be taken of the fact that Tennessee is represented in all certificate and rate proceedings before this commission by competent counsel, not including either the Arvey firm or the Corcoran firm.
>
> The legal services rendered by these two firms thus admittedly relate to matters of an entirely different character —but that precise character can only be the subject of guess and speculation, so far as the record made here is concerned.

So grow reputations. Indeed, such is Corcoran's image in the bureaucracy that many Federal officials reflexively think "politics" when he appears in a case. In 1968 Burlington Mills, the world's largest textile corporation, with annual sales well above $1 billion, was bargaining with FTC officials over guidelines for future acquisitions. The case dragged for months without decision. Then Herbert Bergson, a Washington Lawyer renowned as an antitrust specialist, appeared at a conference flanked by Corcoran and James Rowe, *Fortune* Magazine, commenting on this case later, called it a "notable instance of Washington lawyers practicing their profession without using words at all, much less writing briefs . . ." *Fortune* quoted an FTC official's reaction:

> Bergson made his argument for more than an hour. . . . Neither Corcoran nor Rowe said a single word throughout the hearing. But there they were. L. B. J. was still President. Rowe was one of his closest advisors . . . You had to feel their presence was a signal of some kind.

The official said he thought Bergson had hired Corcoran and Rowe to exploit their political clout. He was wrong. In fact, Corcoran and Rowe had worked for Burlington Mills for years, and they had hired Bergson because of *his* special expertise. As Rowe told interviewers from Ralph Nader's antitrust study group later, "The case had been kicking around the Commission for a number of years and it was looking like we were going to get the business from the staff. We felt the staff wanted a complaint, so we brought in Bergson and talked to the Commissioners." Eventually the case was resolved on terms favorable to Burlington Mills.

James F. Doherty, while a staff member of the House Banking and Currency Committee, once worked on banking legislation in which a Corcoran client had an interest. Several times that year the phone rang and Corcoran would come onto the line and then apologize and say that he had actually been trying to locate Doherty's brother, William, who is president of the AFL-CIO's American Institute for Free Labor Development.

The first few times Doherty accepted Corcoran's explanation. Then he noticed something consistent: After each apology Corcoran, without a pause, would continue, "But while we're on the phone . . ." and go into an enthusiastic discussion of the merits of his client's case.

"I got the idea," Doherty told me, "that he was emphasizing his friendship with my brother in the thought that it would affect what I was doing in the committee. You know, it was amusing for a while. Eventually, though, it wasn't."

5

Ruling the Regulators:
Just Who's Doing What to Whom?

"Tommy Austern," the Washington Lawyer told me, "now, that's the fellow who knows the inside of how to practice before the regulatory agencies. Tommy keeps the bastards at bay for all of us. Tommy walks into an agency with a meat cleaver in his briefcase and chops the hell out of any nincompoop who gets in his way." Pause. The Washington Lawyer is thinking. "I started to say Tommy has forgotten more regulatory law than most of us will ever know, but that isn't correct. He never forgot any of it—he still knows it all."

H. Thomas Austern. The most senior active partner in Covington and Burling. A legal switch-hitter who is at once (a) the guru of the specialists in food-and-drug law, a code in which qualifying phrases dangle even from the exceptions; (b) an antitrust practitioner of such oomph that the FTC members before whom he appears have been known to pant after him for favors at the White House; (c) a legislative strategist who can carry through on that old chestnut, "If you don't like the law, change it" (Austern does); and (d) the most potent single voice in Covington and Burling, the chief justice of Washington's largest firm.

H. Thomas Austern. To know him isn't necessarily to love him. "Tommy Austern is a living refutation of the theory about there being courtroom lawyers and backroom lawyers," says a man who used to be at Covington and Burling. "He is a nasty, rude little man who insults his clients and everybody else. He has made it purely on performance. He is clearly the number-one food-and-drug lawyer in the world." To Ralph Nader, Austern is a ranking institutional evil in Washington—a man whose tactics and influence have afflicted the public weal at the FDA, at the FTC, veritably at any office he enters; defender of the cigarette menace and fancifully labeled food cans; backslapper and patron of more regulatory officials than even the President; manipulator of the bar associations; a one-man personification of what is bad about Washington Lawyers. Other consumerists have much the same attitude. They say, in many places and in many ways, *Shame on you, H. Thomas Austern; you don't give a damn about the public, only your evil, conniving corporate clients.*

Tommy Austern waved me into his office at Covington and Burling late on a Saturday, a day I had chosen over Sunday, when he would also be working. According to the sign-in book in the lobby, Tommy Austern had been in the office since eight-forty a.m. There he sat on a sunny June Saturday afternoon, sixty-six years old and in his fortieth year of Washington practice, coatless and tie askew, behind a desk heaped with briefs and file folders and mail he would eventually answer that day, dictating revisions to a speech he would deliver to an industry group the next week, arguing mildly with a statuesque blonde secretary over whether he stumbled on the word "despot" in the text, and refusing to change the line (she ignored him and edited it anyway). Grumbling, to open our conversation, that Covington and Burling's retrench-at-65 rule was forcing him into quasi-retirement.

Austern doesn't think much more of the regulatory agencies than does his arch-adversary Nader, but for very different reasons. Listen to him for several hours, and read his speeches and bar and trade journal articles, and the frustration and outrage are overwhelming; not simply because the agencies are failures, but because they are . . . well, a pain in Tommy Austern's *arse* (his pronunciation and emphasis), among other things. Tommy Austern guards the pass for the corporations, beating back the goddamned bureaucrats single-handedly with his briefcase, wishing to hell they would go away and let business do business; he believes in the industries he represents, he does, and he thinks they have vastly more collective sense than chemists and bacteriologists and nutritionists and economists and accountants, words that drip from his pen with the sarcastic precision of FDR's famous Martin-Barton-and-Fish speech at the Teamsters' convention in 1944. So the corporate lawyers dominate the regulatory agencies, uh? Har. My friend, you haven't seen the other side of the picture, and the troubles *we* have with those . . . with those . . . you know what I mean, you've seen them.

Winton B. Rankin dealt frequently with Austern while Deputy Commissioner of the Food and Drug Administration. During a chat one afternoon I casually asked him for an appraisal of

Austern. "Tom Austern," he replied, "is a man of very definite opinions. You never have any problem figuring out where he stands on an issue."

This chapter concerns the Washington Lawyers who practice before the Federal regulatory agencies, and their part in making the agencies one of the more miserable failures of American government. At the outset, however, several frames of reference, for the regulatory agencies, more so than any other part of Washington, are neither what they are supposed nor appear to be. They are connoisseurs of trivia; where else in the civilized world, one ponders, would grown men, and well-paid ones, quarrel furiously for twelve years over whether a foodstuff must contain eighty-seven or ninety percent peanuts before warranting the label "peanut butter"? Or where a Federal Trade Commission official would press a false-labeling charge against a small Georgia manufacturer who had used the name Red Fox on denim overalls for almost thirty years, on the grounds they contained no red fox fur? (Philip Elman, who managed to get away from the FTC before he went batty, commented on the Red Fox case, "Fortunately for the manufacturers of such products as Old Grand-Dad and Sunshine Biscuits . . . the Commission dropped the matter when Congressional intervention was threatened.")

For decades Americans had a curious tendency to believe that if something existed, it worked. We are no longer so naive, thanks to such diverse failures as the telephone company and the national security "experts" who got us into Vietnam. But Consciousness II mythologies—fostered by the apparently unperishable liberal faith in the efficacy of government—are not easily erased.

The Food and Drug Administration enforced the Pure Food and Drug Act; ergo, our foods and drugs are pure, because the

Federal government said so. And if the FDA occasionally slips, and some citizen dies from a dose of spoiled catsup, *reform* the FDA.

Freight companies didn't cheat the small merchant or farmer because the Interstate Commerce Commission hires wise lawyers and economists to *regulate* rates and services. Only the *Chicago Tribune* and mossback Midwestern Republicans could carp.

The broadcast companies performed in the public interest because the Federal Communications Commission *licensed* them; the airways are public property and must be used for the benefit of everyone, and furthermore . . .

These "truths" were transmitted to us in civics and government classes, to our accreting comfort, for very specific reasons. An agency that spends its time on bureaucratic make-work, emitting great whoops and hollers about protecting the public interest, creates an ongoing sideshow that distracts the citizen's attention. Soon he forgets (if he ever knew) the agencies were created to do more important stuff. Such as preventing monopolistic control of the economy. And ensuring that a modern industrial society maintain such fundamental services as passenger trains. And guaranteeing that the contents and label of a can bear a reasonable resemblance, one to the other. And protecting the consumer's interests when a pipeline company and a gas utility engage in clamorous battle over the wellhead price of natural gas.*

That these functions are not performed is partially due to the skills of some Washington Lawyers; not totally, mind you, for he is but a foot soldier, or perhaps a battalion commander, for the

---

* Rail and truck freight rates would drop by as much as twenty percent if surface transportation were freed from ICC regulation, according to a Brookings Institution study published in September 1971. The study, by Thomas Moore, an economics professor at Michigan State University, estimated total savings to shippers would range from $3.4 billion to $5.6 billion annually.

Corporate State. There is blame to spread on the souls of everyone. The Congress, for permitting a perversion of laws passed as declarations of national policy. The public, for being so gullible that it cannot separate sham from reality. The educators, who because they *wanted* to believe, believed, and forced us to do the same. The regulators themselves, for their acquiescent role in a process which makes a mockery of democracy.

Because the regulatory agencies serve business, the corporations long ago abandoned attempts to dismantle them. Business's public denunciations of the "Federal bureaucracry" delude the naive citizen into believing the agencies are actually doing their work. In 1892, just before he left a Chicago law practice to become Attorney General in President Cleveland's second administration, Richard Olney was asked by a railroad client to do what he could when he reached Washington to abolish the ICC. The agency was only in its fifth year, but the pragmatic Olney realized its utility to railroads. He wrote his client, the Chicago, Burlington & Quincy Railroad:

> My impression would be that looking at the matter from a railroad point of view exclusively it would not be a wise thing to undertake . . . The attempt would not be likely to succeed; if it did not succeed, and were made on the ground of the inefficiency and uselessness of the commission, the result would very probably be giving it the power it now lacks. The commission, as its functions have been limited by the courts, is, or can be made, of great use to the railroads. It satisfies the popular clamor for a government supervision of railroads, at the same time that that supervision is almost entirely nominal. Further, the older a commission gets to be, the more inclined it will be found to take the business and railroad view of things. It thus becomes a sort of barrier between the railroad corporations and the people and a

sort of protection against hasty and crude legislation hostile to railroad interests . . . *The part of wisdom is not to destroy the commission, but to utilize it.*

Olney's prediction has stood the test of seven decades, and it is painfully descriptive of today's regulatory agencies. Business has quickly doused most flashes of regulatory courage.

The corporations faced their severest test when the regulatory agencies proliferated during the New Deal. The agencies began to make decisions administratively, rather than acting through conventional court action. In one landmark case the FTC took jurisdiction over major steel and cement price-fixing cases on the grounds that its "administrative quasi-judicial remedies" would be faster and more effective than a Justice Department antitrust proceeding. The FTC won, whereupon business launched a frontal attack on administrative law as "the root of all the trouble stirred up by the Federal regulatory commissions."

But adhering strictly to Olney's Law, business did not move for abolition of the agencies. Its strategy was more subtle, more conniving, more effective. Bind the regulatory bureaucracy in a spider web of restrictive procedural rules and guidelines, and require that they be followed meticulously. Technicalities are the stuff of which defensive law is made; each increase in the number of rules and the steps in the administrative processes means a quantum increase in the corporate lawyer's chance of success.

The business onslaught against administrative law began in earnest in the late 1930s and, in the words of a study by the House Select Committee on Small Business, "spread to many fronts. With the passage of time, the representatives of regulated industries enlisted the aid of their attorneys to help them carry on the fight . . . Some of the attorneys . . . utilized their positions as members of highly respected bar associations to push the fight against administrative law in the bar associations. Carefully and painstakingly they argued their case against administrative law. The administrative law process was damned as un-American." Because of the war, the Administrative Procedure Act, their goal, did not get through Congress until 1946. But the end result was exactly what the corporations wanted. *The New York Times* reported shortly after its passage:

> Utility, rail and numerous other industries . . . are celebrating the recent passage of the Administrative Procedure Act . . . When the bill . . . became law last month, corporation counsel and company officials looked back on more than ten years of continuous effort . . . to remove the 'onerous' problems that beset companies appearing before these agencies. . . . Passage of the bill was considered a major victory for the American Bar Association, sponsor for the measure.

The Administrative Procedure Act, in effect, transformed each regulatory agency into a mini-court, most of which decided cases on an ad hoc basis, rather than in accordance with any broad policy goals. Judge Henry J. Friendly, among other critics, cites unpredictability as a major flaw. "Lack of definite standards creates a void into which attempt to influence are bound to rush," Friendly wrote in a 1962 critique, "legal vacuums are quite like physical ones in that respect. Although pressure produces diffuse decisions, it is likewise true that . . . pressure from one party in a case, or even a reasonable fear of it, arising from experience, will produce pressure from others." Unsurprisingly, Friendly noted, the two Commissions most subjected to industry pressures—the FCC and the CAB—are those "which have conspicuously failed to define the standards governing their decisions."

H. Thomas Austern has been in the midst of this administrative tangle since 1931, when he joined Covington and Burling and became general counsel for the National Canners Association. Austern's career is a microcosm of what is good and bad about administrative law—of how a skillful Washington Lawyer can guide the regulatory process to the benefit of corporate clients and reap economic victory even at the price of personal and professional frustration.

The canned food industry supports token Federal regulation as a means of keeping customer confidence. In 1930 the National Canners Association helped the FDA compile so-called "standards-of-identity" that had to be met before foods could be marketed under certain names—applesauce, for example, had to contain a set minimum percentage of apples. The standard-of-identity did help the consumer, because it halted the sale of high-grade garbage produced by fly-by-night canners and processors. But the canners were not completely altruistic. They were confident their Washington Lawyers could coax the FDA into writing the sort of standards desired by the industry. And they needed the standard-of-identity to defeat even stricter regulation—quality labeling.

Quality labeling was the brainchild of Rexford Tugwell, who was in charge of FDA as an Assistant Secretary of Agriculture in the early New Deal.* Tugwell thought standard-of-identity was a sham, for it did not tell the consumer what *grade* of food was inside a can. There are good green beans, and tolerable green beans, and the price difference can be considerable. Tugwell proposed, among other things, that all food products be labeled Grade A, B, C, or D, so that consumers could buy on the basis of quality, rather than by brand name. Then as now, products from the same cannery go to many different distributors. The brand label that goes on a can, not the food that goes inside

* FDA is now under the Department of Health, Education, and Welfare.

it, determines the price. If the quality was clearly marked, the housewife could ignore the brand names and buy on the basis of quality.

Austern rallied opposition when Tugwell's proposal went before Congress. At one meeting of the National Canners Association, Austern declaimed:

"Every canner should leave this meeting ready to sell the idea to other canners and to his representative in Congress that this bill should not be permitted to pass. Don't try to do this by writing letters. It is a selling job that you have on your hands. You must go out and talk to people."

The canners succeeded in beating Tugwell's bill. The President's Commission on Food Marketing estimated in 1966 that lack of quality labeling adds twenty percent to what the housewife pays for canned foods at the supermarket—the difference between what she pays for brand-name products and what she *could* pay for the same food marketed under a private non-brand label.

Austern thinks it rank nonsense to credit—or blame—him for the fact that quality labeling has never passed Congress. He says he is simply a lawyer who from time to time has presented a client's argument on an issue. If "consumer advocates" had the better case, and the support of the American people, Congress would listen to them. Even an amateur political scientist can find a basic flaw in Austern's argument: the average citizen has not the slightest idea why cans don't bear quality labels, or even that they are possible.

No, forget quality labeling. Austern would rather complain about the horrid, protracted legal battles he has been forced to fight under the standard-of-identity system. Poor Tommy. The FDA doesn't always do what the canners want. The FDA has taken standard-of-identity far beyond the canners' original scheme. Canners cannot produce something labeled simply "canned peaches." There are sliced peaches and peach halves, sliced peaches in heavy syrup, and sliced peaches in light syrup, and on and on and on and on, each variety with a separate standard, laboriously debated between government and industry, frequently with resort to the courts.

Angry Tommy. So long as a foodstuff meets the minimum standard, why meddle in business decisions? Tomato puree, for instance. There are three ways to make the stuff—either from whole tomatoes, or from the bits and pieces left over from the extraction of tomato juice, or from the skin, core, and juices left from the preparation of whole tomatoes. In each instance, the tomatoes (or the pieces of them) are put through a machine called a cyclone, which removes the skins, seeds, and hard fibers, leaving juice and flesh which is concentrated as puree. The end product is the same "chemically and botanically," and costs exactly the same, according to Austern. Yet the FDA ruled that puree not made from whole tomatoes had to be labeled "Made From Residual Tomato Material From Canning," or "Made From Residual Tomato Material From Partial Extraction Of Juice."

Austern argued for the canners that the labels were "commercially derogatory" and did nothing for the consumer. Why harass industry? He lost. Thereafter FDA had the authority to force canners to describe manufacturing processes, and Austern fumed for years in bar and trade association journals. His case:

An economic judgment remains one, no matter how much technical clothing it wears. How to determine the fat or moisture content of cheese, or the specific gravity of tomato puree, are technical questions. Where to put the permissible level of moisture or what label name to prescribe for a product, or whether a cheaper ingredient may be substituted for a more expensive one, are questions largely answered by economic judgments. With all deference, one need not be a chemist or bacteriologist, and might even be a lawyer, in order to exercise judgment as to what will "promote honesty and fair dealing in the interest of consumers." It is because they are not objective technical questions, but rather issues as imponderable as any in the field of government, that their resolution is often difficult.

Let's pause a minute. *Is* the FDA wasting the taxpayers' money and needlessly frustrating an industry? Austern can pluck out an isolated case—tomato puree, for example—and make the FDA look silly. The FDA, in retaliation, can pick *its* horrible examples of industry's willingness to stall and haggle and prolong a routine administrative process for seemingly endless years. The product in question was peanut butter. Austern guided a task force of a dozen industry lawyers who worked on the case, on and off, for more than a decade. Austern represented Proctor & Gamble, which produces Jif brand peanut butter. Closely aligned with him were Vincent Kleinfeld, for the Peanut Butter Manufacturers Association and the Corn Products Company, manufacturer of the Skippy brand; and Earl Spiker, for Swift & Company's Peter Pan. The Peanut Butter Case—both the FDA and the lawyers still speak of it in capital letters—produced hearing and other records of sufficient volume to fill a small room and occupied literally scores of thousands of man-hours of time.

When peanut butter was first produced, beginning around 1890, it consisted of ninety-five percent ground peanuts, the remainder salt and sugar. The "old-fashioned" peanut butter had distinct disadvantages: it stuck to the roof of your mouth; it got grainy in a hurry; it was oily; it didn't store well on store shelves; it wouldn't spread easily. So the manufacturers began tinkering with the recipe. They added more and more dextrose

and other artificial sweeteners, and they found that hydrogenated (solid) oils helped the sticky-mouth problem by forming a
film between the peanut butter and the palate. The "stabilized"
peanut butter eventually pushed the "old-fashioned" variety off
the market.

But was it really peanut butter? The FDA, in tests in the late
1950s, found that manufacturers were lacing the product with
from twenty to twenty-five percent hydrogenated oils—lard, to
be specific. Chemists knew this was far more than necessary. The
FDA asked the industry to help write a standard-of-identity for
peanut butter. The Peanut Butter Manufacturers Association
refused, opposing a standard in any form. Now let us go to a
timetable that shows how a skilled Washington Lawyer can use
the industry-written Administrative Procedure Act to a client's
advantage:

■■ July 2, 1959. FDA Commissioner formally proposes,
    via publication in *The Federal Register*, a standard-of-
    identity for peanut butter calling for ninety-five percent
    peanut content. As required by law, he invites com-
    ments.

■■ November 28, 1961. FDA, after two years of talks with
    industry, publishes order setting peanut level at ninety
    percent.

■■ February 1, 1962. FDA decides industry objections
    warrant further study, and stays effective date of new
    standard. Industry proposes eighty-seven percent stan-
    dard.

■■ November 10, 1964. FDA publishes slightly revised
    standard, still at ninety percent level, and again invites
    comments.

■■ July 8, 1965. After studying volumes of industry and
    consumer comment, FDA sticks with ninety percent.

■■ September 4, 1965. FDA receives formal request for

public hearings from industry and sets one beginning October 18, 1965. Effective date of order stayed again.

■■ November 1, 1965. After two postponements, public hearing begins, to run until March 15, 1966.

■■ December 6, 1967. FDA publishes proposed findings of fact and standard (still at ninety percent) and invites comments.

■■ July 24, 1968. FDA publishes final order, ninety percent standard.

■■ November 7, 1968. Order stayed pending industry appeal to courts.

■■ May 14, 1970. U.S. Court of Appeals for Third Circuit affirms FDA order. Stay remains in effect pending further appeal.

■■ December 14, 1970. U.S. Supreme Court declines to review case.

■■ March 3, 1971. FDA publishes notice making ninety percent standard effective in thirty days.

"The best you can say for this case is that it was a comedy of errors," remarks Ben Gutterman, the FDA official responsible for its prosecution. "We were using the ninety percent figure; the industry was arguing for eighty-seven percent. If we had said eighty-seven, they would have said eighty-three; if we said eighty-three, they'd have gone to eighty. They were saying, 'nutritionally, it is the same; price-wise, it is the same.' We were asking, 'But when does it stop being peanut butter?' That's what it was all about. We weren't saying it was a bad product, only that it was not what the consumer expected to find under that name. Does she expect to buy peanut butter, or a mixture of lard and peanuts, with maybe some turnip greens ground up in there besides? If that is what the manufacturer wants, let him produce it, but under that name.

"Why all the delays? You've got to take time to examine all

the comments the industry was making, and to evaluate their tests. There was a lot of lab work, to see what the various oil and sweetener combinations really meant. You don't get instant scientific decisions, you know. I remember a case involving frozen cherry pies where the lab work alone took one and one-half years. You finish *your* tests, and then the other side takes the information and runs *its* tests.

"Also, every person involved in a proceeding isn't always ready to go at the crack of the gun. FDA was working on other things, too, so what takes priority—canned dried peas, salmon, cosmetics, or peanut butter? The lawyers are busy in different agency hearings. Okay, you say you take a club and hit him on the head so he'll be here. He's being hit on the head elsewhere, too."

Still, Gutterman says wistfully, "It did drag on for a little while."

Why were the peanut butter companies willing to invest so much money in the case? Winton B. Rankin, who was Deputy FDA Commissioner much of the time the case was being heard, says, "Economics. There's enough of a price differential between raw peanuts and hydrogenated oil to make a difference. After all, you are talking about almost half a billion pounds of peanuts a year. Even if you shave the costs only two or three percent, the saving to the manufacturer is tremendous."

Rankin is quietly disgusted with the way Washington Lawyers go into administrative proceedings such as the peanut case. "Your attorneys have helped make a mockery of the procedures for setting food standards," he told a food industry group in Los Angeles in 1969. "How?" I asked Rankin. "Attorneys treat them like adversary proceedings," he said. "Attorneys go to some length to discredit scientific witnesses. That's not good. Scientists are not willing to put up with that for long, and you find them trying to avoid FDA work. There is endless repetition of testimony, witnesses saying the same thing over and over. When several industry lawyers are involved, they won't get together and let one of them do the cross-examining. Everyone has to speak. They'll ask for a recess of weeks to study documents that are put into evidence, even though the documents were available in advance . . . And appeals to the courts at every stage: you set a hearing date, they ask a postponement, you deny it, they go to court. They seldom win, but everything stops while it is argued. They try to put in superfluous testimony, the examiner says no, off they go to court again."

Austern does not apologize for actively challenging FDA and for turning the administrative proceedings into evidentiary trial-type hearings. Austern calls the process "legislation by litigation," and said, "I firmly believe that it is in the public interest. I do so not because it may provide work for food lawyers, or afford judicial review, but because of my abiding conviction that he who regulates ought to appear publicly if there is a challenge, and put on the table, subject to cross-examination, the facts on which he grounds his proposal." A full hearing is necessary at the FDA level, Austern maintains, because judicial review, even though provided for in the Administrative Procedure Act, "is largely a phantom. In my own experience, there are few courts that will second-guess the FDA, which has the reputation of protecting the consumer, the aged, the infirm, the ignorant, and the nursing infant."*

In 1965 Austern was representing Abbott Laboratories of Chicago, which got into trouble because of an alleged mix-up of labels on bottles of saline and dextrose solutions it sold to hospitals. Don Gray of the House Commerce Committee staff went to North Chicago, Illinois, to serve a subpoena on an Abbott lawyer.

* The last few phrases reflect Austern's penchant for sarcasm, not his true opinion of the FDA.

"You must be joking," the man told Gray. *"We are repre-sented by Mr. Austern."*

Gray assured the lawyer he was in fact not joking, and the only question was whether he could have copies made of the subpoenaed documents, or take the originals back to Washing-ton for study.

"I can't make that decision without consulting Mr. Austern," the lawyer said. *Call him. "I'd prefer to speak to him in person on such an important matter."* The flight from Washington to Chicago takes less than two hours; tell him to come on out. *"Mr. Austern prefers not to fly."* He may be afraid of flying, but I'm not. A plane is leaving at 3:30 p.m.; if you don't have an answer by 2 p.m., I'm taking the originals. Gray got the copies. There are *places where the mention of Austern's name doesn't do magic. Not many, though.*

Relations between some Washington Lawyers and officials of the regulatory agencies can be so intimate they embarrass an onlooker. The lawyers and the regulators work together, in a tight, impenetrable community where an outsider can't under-stand the language, much less why things are done the way they are. The lawyers and the regulators play together, at trade asso-ciation meetings, over lunch, on the golf courses around Wash-ington. They frequently swap jobs, the regulator moving to the private bar, the Washington Lawyer moving into the Commis-sion on a "public service" leave of absence from his firm. The story is told of the lawyer who enjoyed a three-martini lunch during a hearing before the Interstate Commerce Commission. When time came for the proceeding to resume, he instinctively sat down in the hearing examiner's chair and gaveled for order. Someone had to remind the poor fellow he had resigned two years previously and belonged at the counsel table on behalf of a trucking firm.

The turnover at Federal agencies is brisk. Paul Rand Dixon once estimated that the FTC hired 750 attorneys during his first five years as FTC chairman, just to maintain a 400-man level. The SEC loses about 75 of its 380 attorneys each year to private practice; the FPC, 10 of 70; the FCC, 35 of 200; the CAB, 20 of 80. Most go into private practice in Washington. The IRS requires that new hires agree to remain in government for four years; perhaps ninety percent leave after fulfilling that requirement. Government attorneys generally start at the GS-11 level, at slightly more than $11,000 a year. The going rate in private practice is from $14,000 to $17,500, depending upon the firm and the graduate's background.

In a report on regulatory agencies prepared for President-elect Kennedy in December 1960, former SEC and CAB Chairman James M. Landis conceded that direct contacts by industry representatives "of necessity . . . are frequently productive of intelligent ideas," while contacts with the general public "are rare and generally unproductive of anything except complaint." But Landis continued, "Irrespective of absence of social contacts and the acceptance of undue hospitality, it is the daily machine-gun-like impact on both agency and its staff of industry representation that makes for industry orientation on the part of many honest and capable agency members as well as agency staffs."

A lawyer who had a thriving practice before the Civil Aeronautics Board casually remarked to me during an interview that he took CAB staff officials to lunch at the nearby Washington Hilton Hotel at least twice weekly. "I'm telling you this," he said, "because many people have a misconception about agency contacts. I don't see anything wrong with it, personally. I'm dealing with career government officials who make more than $20,000 a year. You aren't going to 'buy' one of these men with a bourbon on the rocks and a minute steak. It's a matter of convenience for both of us. It adds ninety minutes to my working day, because we can get in a business conversation. I rotate it enough that I don't take out the same man more than once monthly or so. Now tell me the truth: Do you think I am doing anything unethical?"

I didn't attempt to answer the question. But a former FCC official, speaking from what he saw while in government, opined, "Forget the ethics; that isn't relevant. If you start taking food from someone, what you think of him is going to be colored. You are in the inferior position, and he gets that little thin edge over you, psychologically. It's not worth it. I'll eat with anyone, but I'll take my own check."

The socializing can go far beyond casual lunches. The Motor Carrier Lawyers Association is composed of attorneys who represent trucking lines before the Interstate Commerce Commission and the state regulatory agencies. Its record—no better or worse than that of any of a score of Washington-based professional groups—is acutely illustrative of how a Washington Lawyer can curry the friendship of the persons who regulate the industry.

The MCLA's 1969 convention in San Juan, Puerto Rico, spilled over to a five-day junket to the swank Tryall Golf and Beach Club in Sandy Bay, Jamaica. David A. Sutherland, a transportation law specialist in the Washington office of Morgan, Lewis and Bockius, a major Philadelphia firm, coordinated the trip. Six other lawyers (five of them with wives) and a trucking official made the trip; so, too, did James C. Cheseldine, the ICC's chief hearing examiner, and his wife; and Jerry E. Laughlin, another ICC executive, and Mrs. Laughlin.

This friendly little group first convened for post-convention golfing fêtes after an MCLA meeting in Dallas in the mid-1960s, and Cheseldine sees nothing wrong with the fellowship. "We have our wives with us. They go shopping and we play golf,"

Cheseldine says. "If you will look at the spread, it is all over the country and there is no one law firm. I don't see how anybody can infer partiality, because the record down at the Commission, I think, speaks for itself. We don't have any complaints about it."

Someone else heard complaints, however. Robert W. Lishman was chief counsel to a special investigations subcommittee of the House Interstate and Foreign Commerce Committee until his death in December 1970. Lishman stated that lawyers who practice before the ICC "who have made confidential complaints to the subcommittee have pleaded with us not to divulge their names, because they would lose their means of livelihood, and would never be able to appear successfully before the Commission if it were known by the Commission that they had made the complaints." The protests, according to Lishman, extended far beyond the golf tête-à-têtes.

Cheseldine heatedly asserted to a House investigative committee that he paid his own bills on the golf junket, and the portion of his Puerto Rican hotel bill not covered by his $27 per diem allowance from the government. (The week-long stay at the Tryall Club with the ICC lawyers cost Cheseldine and his wife another $496.55.) However, Congressional investigators found MCLA correspondence in which Cheseldine is quoted as asking whether the lawyers' group "would pick up the difference between their per diem and the hotel rate." William J. Lippmann, a Washington officer of the MCLA, replied that "we certainly would." But Lippmann groused privately at Cheseldine's request, writing to Joseph E. Ludden, counsel for a trucking firm in La Crosse, Wisconsin, and an MCLA officer:

I feel that Ches must know that the others have paid for or offered to pay their hotel bill and will probably be disposed to do the same. On the other hand, I am reluctant to ask for the money or to suggest that he should pay. It is a delicate matter and we should give it some thought before we proceed. Your thoughts on the matter are respectfully solicited.

Cheseldine pleaded general ignorance of making such a request of the MCLA, although he did say the lawyers "knew that we were on a limited per diem, going to pretty expensive hotels, and that we were paying our wives' expenses." And, he added, he paid the difference between the per diem and the actual bill from his own pocket. At the lawyers' 1968 convention in Detroit, however, Cheseldine was given a $60-per-day suite for $14, with the MCLA paying the balance of $45.50 per day. "Didn't you think that $14 was pretty low for a sitting room and a bedroom in the best hotel in town?" the Commerce Committee's Robert Lishman asked Cheseldine, who replied, "I thought it was low, but I had no idea it was that price." Cheseldine said an MCLA member told him "not to worry about the price," because the association received a group discount. "If the hotel was getting $60," Cheseldine says, ". . . I have been just ignorant." The MCLA paid bills for a total of six ICC officials at the Detroit convention. The hotel bills for four days amounted to $714.98; additionally, each of the officials received a desk pen set valued at slightly less than $10. H. Neil Garson, the ICC secretary, another of the guests, also insisted that he did not realize the MCLA was giving him a $60 suite for $14.50.*

Accepting such favors is legal. The ICC act permits Commissioners and staff members to accept "bona fide reimbursement for actual expenses for travel and such necessary subsistence . . .

---

* Garson resigned from the ICC when the House subcommittee charged he had accepted reimbursement from both the government and trade groups for convention trips and falsified check stubs in an attempt to hide the situation.

for which no government payment or reimbursement is made when attending industry meetings and conventions." They may not accept payment for speeches at the meetings, nor for "excessive personal living expenses, gifts, entertainment, or other personal benefits." Codes governing other regulatory agencies contain roughly the same language. There are variations. FCC members may not accept payment for writing, which the prolific Commissioner Nicholas Johnson estimates costs him $15,000 a year.

But William L. Carey, the former chairman of the SEC, says a Commissioner's problem of industry contacts goes much deeper than whether to accept lunch or other entertainment. "It rests basically on the question of personal security," Carey states. "Do they [the Commissioners] want to be liked? Or do they seek power? Do they look for a further career in the Administration? And what are they going to do when they leave? Do they plan to work for the industry?" Commissioners who inspire to a Federal judgeship "may not feel free with counsel who are powerful lobbyists, or with their clients who exert a wide influence. Some of the Washington Lawyers have developed a remarkably subtle method of exposing the source of their power without threatening to exercise it." A Commissioner who isn't concerned with his future job sleeps better at night. At his confirmation hearing for the FCC in 1961, Newton Minow was asked, "Just what makes you think that you are qualified to be chairman of the FCC?"

"Two things," Minow replied. "First, I'm not looking for a job in the communications business; and second, I don't want to be reappointed."

The ICC statute on future employment illustrates the general conflict-of-interest standard: "If a member or employee of the commission *entertains a proposal* for future employment by any person subject to regulation by the commission or by associations or representatives of such persons, such member or employee shall refrain from participating in the decision or disposition of any matter in which such person, association or representative is known to have a direct substantial interest, both during such negotiation and, if such employment is accepted, until he severs his connection with the commission."

The words "entertains a proposal" are sufficiently broad to permit an industry and a staff member (or Commissioner) to toss hints back and forth without ever committing themselves either to offer or acceptance of a specific position. A former agency attorney says the vagueness essential to this sort of bargaining-in-the-dark can backfire: "I had a friend who was assigned to a case involving ——. Their attorney peppered him with remarks like 'We sure think you are doing a fine job over here, and our president especially has been keeping an eye on you,' and 'Have you ever given any thought as to how long you intend to remain with the Commission?' These might have been very innocent—my friend thought they were implicit offers of a job. Although he wasn't asked to do so—and in fact the facts in the case warranted his so doing—he acted in a way that really benefited ——. A few weeks later, when he asked whether he might come around to talk about 'some ideas he had for the future' the attorney gave him a lunch and the brush-off, in that order. I think that any agency employee who tries to court favor puts himself into a real bad light. I mean, if you'll whore for someone else while working for the government, could a law firm trust you to work for it? Hell, if I was the kind of guy who would try to rig a case—I'm not, and make sure you get that down—I'd much prefer to leave my contact in place. I mean, really, if you have someone working for you on the inside, you are stupid to bring him into your own office, where he's just another attorney. Now, you understand I am speaking in theoretical terms . . ."

Representative Richard L. Ottinger, while in Congress, complained that the "close relationship between the ICC and the railroads is far more than a matter of philosophical affinity. It is a *working* economic and personal relationship, which frequently involves the most insidious possible influence by an industry upon an agency holding the public trust. ICC Commissioners, hearing examiners, and key staff personnel shuttle between employment with the government and the railroads in a never-ending symbiotic cycle." Ottinger was particularly upset by the case of former Commission Chairman William H. Tucker. After resigning, Tucker "served nine months in the 'purgatory' of his law firm, Maguire & Tucker," then became vice president for New England operations of the Penn Central. Ottinger found it of interest that Maguire & Tucker's office is in suite 815 of the office building at 2000 L Street NW in Washington—hard by the Penn Central Washington offices in suite 819.

A key aide to Tucker followed the same route. Gavin W. O'Brien, Jr., joined the ICC in 1961 as a legal assistant and was assigned to Tucker's office in 1965. When he resigned in 1967, he entered private practice with Maguire & Tucker. Similarly, Tucker's press agent, Joseph R. Ewing, who joined the ICC in 1961 as an information officer, eventually gravitated to Penn Central's Washington staff, via the United States Chamber of Commerce.

What do the ICC-industry ties mean to the consumer? In 1968 the commerce committees of both the House and the Senate asked the ICC for a study of the costs of intercity rail passenger service. In due course, such a report was submitted. The author, however, was not the ICC, nor even the Department of Transportation, which financed it. The report came from the Montclair, New Jersey, think-tank firm of Wyre, Dick and Company—a very reputable consulting firm, but one which is not only a member of the Association of American Railroads, but also is retained by two of the railroads covered by the cost study.

Ken Cox, who served on the FCC staff for more than a decade before appointment as a Commissioner, believes a staff attorney would be foolish to cater to industry in hopes of obtaining a plush job in private practice. Nonetheless, Cox says, "I've seen a couple of instances where I really wondered at some things a [staff] fellow was doing." But Cox—who is now in private communications practice—does not think lower-level staff people, the men likely to be naive enough to do favors for industry in return for a career boost, have enough power to really affect policy. "If you are friendly with them, they'll return your calls immediately, rather than forty-eight hours later, and they'll give you fast information when you go see them. That's the way it was when I worked on the staff, that's the way it is now." At noontime, restaurants around the FCC (the Black Horse Tavern, on 20th Street, is a favorite) draw a generous sprinkling of FCC and industry lawyers. "You don't have to be important at the FCC to get a luncheon invitation. But this is important for a lawyer, for he'll be treated politely when he comes around next week on business."

Tommy Austern had heard all the stories about industry influence on the regulatory agencies. He should have, for he is the subject of many of them. Whatever Tommy wants, the saying goes, Tommy gets. But Austern sniffs, and with some justification. Washington being the political pit that it is, any man of prominence who walks anywhere near the fringe of impropriety is eventually dragged before a Congressional subcommittee or other inquisitory body. Four decades Tommy Austern has been at it, and his feathers are unruffled by official hands. Austern thinks the public overlooks an agency practice even more insidious than *ex parte* contacts by private lawyers—that is *ex parte* contacts by agency lawyers.

What is called the "Plotkin Amendment" to the Federal Administrative Procedure Act was passed in the early 1950s because of the vigorous advocacy of a man named Harry Plotkin —then assistant general counsel of the Federal Communications Commission, now a senior partner in Arent, Fox, Kintner, Plotkin and Kahn. Ken Cox, the former FCC Commissioner, states, "Harry was a hard regulator. The Commissioners would come into an executive session, after the public hearings, with their minds made up to give 'Old Joe' a license for a TV station. Harry would tear it all up. He would point out how horrible the applicant was, and lay out the facts and figures. What he would be saying, in effect, was that the Commission was silly even to consider the applicant. Time and time again he completely turned the Commission around, and 'Old Joe' wouldn't get the license.

"The communications bar hated Harry's guts, and eventually they got him. The National Association of Broadcasters and the bar associations got Congress to put a provision into the Administrative Procedure Act that said the staff was separated from the Commission when it was considering adjudicatory matters. This means, in English, that they couldn't be in the room during deliberations. Silly rule, of course, for the Commission needs legal and engineering advice when it is deciding cases."

Austern heartily approved of the Plotkin Amendment because it was "supposed to cure the evils of having agency prosecutors talk *ex parte* with those who write the agency opinions or who reside in the ivory tower of legal secretaries to Commission members." But regardless of what the law says, Austern maintains, it is not followed. He quotes with approval Judge Henry Friendly's quip that "a good subject for a seminar paper would be 'The Influence of the Car Pool on Administrative Adjudication.' " Friendly suggested the paper might also include the cocktail party and the Thursday night poker games. Austern adds, "Those who have seen some agencies in action would also want to include the morning and afternoon cafeteria coffee breaks." He continues: "I am not suggesting venality, but merely the enthusiastic dedication of people working to a common end in the same agency who may forget the psychological impropriety of pushing their legal theories or their view of the facts or their feeling about the nasty respondent outside the record in a more congenial atmosphere. No ethical lawyer would discuss his pending cases even when lunching with the friendly judge."

Strict separation of the investigatory and adjudicatory roles is essential, Austern argues, because no man or group of men should be able to serve as de facto prosecutor, judge, and jury. He told a New York University Law School audience group in 1970:

"Only the most credulous and naive would believe that commissioners, board members, or even single administrators actually adjudicate cases. How could they perform, without massive delegation to their staffs, the job of investigating violations, initiating action, holding a hearing, and ultimately deciding whether there has been, on the particular facts, a violation of law or of their regulations."

The public clucks over agency lawyers and officials who rely upon their insider's edge to get business when they go into private practice. From Austern's side of the hearing room, the view is a bit different. During public hearings, the parties face a supposedly impartial hearing examiner. But as Austern has pointed out, "Not infrequently, the examiner is a former lawyer in the agency's general counsel's office. If so, he will know the controlling statute and have a good working background in the field. Yet it is not overly invidious to suggest that he may be agency-oriented. If he is, agency counsel and agency witnesses often have an easier road than the lawyers who are there trying to challenge the proposed rulemaking. Whether you credit them, or lay it to sour grapes, many private practitioners still insist that there are few rulemaking hearings in which the burden does not fall harder upon the objector."

But one watches the regulatory commissions and asks, Does it really matter? The personal bias of Commissioners and "policies" developed at the staff level on critical issues can determine the outcome of a case, regardless of the factual evidence accumulated at a public hearing. In many instances, the hearing is an expensive sham. The public is given the illusion of fairness. Industry is permitted to present its case, as are opposing parties. But the decision does not necessarily derive from the formal record taken in accordance with law.

An example: From October 6 through 19, 1968, ICC hearing examiner W. Wallace Wilhite conducted hearings on a petition by the Chicago, Burlington & Quincy Railroad Company to discontinue two trains between Omaha, Nebraska, and Billings, Montana. Whilhite held sessions in nine cities along the route to elicit testimony from citizens and from union and state and local officials. When he finished, he gave the transcripts and exhibits to Robert T. Wright, an attorney-adviser in the ICC's opinion section, who had been assigned by Commissioner Kenneth Tuggle to write the order and opinion.

Attorney Wright didn't even glance at the material before he knew what his "decision" would be, for as he said later, "I knew what Tuggle wanted"—to drop the trains. He had done a number of other reports for Tuggle, and "we think a lot alike." Wright said he based the decision strictly on the basis of the railroad's original application and supporting documents, and that he placed little or no weight on testimony or evidence presented by citizen protestants.

Two somewhat surprised Congressional investigators to whom Wright made these admissions said it appeared he could write an opinion regardless of what appeared in the record. Wright agreed, saying it was "simply a matter of what evidence you want to place the weight on."

Rail passengers are given a modicum of protection by the bias of another Commissioner, John W. Bush, who Wright said was "known to favor keeping trains on."

Wright also said that based upon his "years of experience in handling these matters . . . no weight can be given to protestant testimony," and that "all railroad testimony and evidence [in his opinion] is good and unquestionable, and all protestant submissions are not worthy of consideration." Wright had worked for government bureaus for thirty-five years.

Another example: For two years in the late 1950s a Civil Aeronautics Board hearing examiner received testimony on applications for air routes in the upper Middle West, the so-called *Seven States Area Investigation*. The complexity of *Seven States* was outweighed only by its profitability for the lawyers involved, one of whom told me, "You know, I put a daughter through two years of college on my share of that hearing." The examiner heard sworn testimony from 194 witnesses, who submitted more than one thousand exhibits, many of them encyclopedic in girth, with enough fold-out charts to paper every office at the CAB. The examiner's report alone was 684 pages. The airlines commented on his findings in twenty-one hours and thirty-five minutes of oral arguments (presented to the full board over four days) and in written submissions that formed a stack five and one-half feet tall. Louis J. Hector, a CAB member at the time, says he and his colleagues did not even attempt to examine the record before making a decision. "They worked mainly from briefs and from their *memory* of the long oral arguments," Hector says.

In this case the formal bar on staff attorneys having contact with examiners and board members made madness of the proceedings. For two years the examiner did not have any communication with the board to whom he was to report. He was bound to make his report on the basis of what he heard, *not* the predilections of the majority of the board. In *Seven States*, Hector wrote in the *Yale Law Journal*:

The board had, in its own thinking, come around to the conclusion that any town which had a reasonable chance of producing five passengers a day should have a chance to see if it could do so, and if it could, then it should have an airline. The hearing examiner did not know this, because he is independent, and the board could not talk to him. So he spent two years hearing evidence and turning out a 500-page opinion. It came up to the board, and the board's first reaction was, "This wasn't what we had in mind at all. We were thinking of a much more extensive route pattern."

So the CAB threw out the hearing examiner's report and wrote its own decision, which the airlines promptly appealed to the courts, thereby renewing the weary process of taking testimony.

Most industry lawyers—including Austern—don't feel the courts are capable of monitoring agency processes. The courts are loath to overturn an agency's interpretation of its controlling statute; the courts are not physically able to read the massive formal record that accompanies each appeal; the courts are convinced that agencies have "expertise." And, further, as Austern told a group of food-law specialists in 1969:

Somehow during the course of almost every judicial hearing, someone mentions "cancer." The judge then remembers his mother-in-law who, at the age of 108, died of cancer. He grabs his belly, and flying out of court goes that purveyor of those noxious, contaminated, filthy, unsafe, hazardous and defiled foods. If the product also happens to contain a chemical, that even more promptly ends the court argument.

Austern's laments about the plight of the corporations must not be taken too seriously. A skilled Washington Lawyer need not accept an unfavorable staff-level decision. He can undercut the bureaucracy by appealing to a higher official within the agency, by invoking Congressional pressure, by going to a friendly court. Procedural haggling and delays can benefit a corporation even in a case that is ultimately lost, for each day a questioned product remains on the market means extra profits. The FDA's effort to ban the controversial drug Panalba is a classic study of how a Washington Lawyer can orchestrate a fight against a regulatory agency.

In 1962 Congress tightened drug-licensing laws to require, for the first time, that pharmaceuticals must be effective as well as safe. Manufacturers of drugs already on the market were required to appraise their products and submit proof of their efficacy. The FDA recruited the National Academy of Sciences–National Research Council to review the test data and pass on the effectiveness of the drugs. The FDA deliberately went to this outside source to ensure "objectivity, expertise [and] authority," in the words of FDA Commissioner Herbert D. Ley.

One of the drugs reviewed was Panalba, produced by the Upjohn Company. Panalba is a mixture of two antibiotics—tetracycline and novobiocin—that Upjohn promoted to the medical profession as a general-purpose antibiotic better than tetracycline. But the National Academy of Sciences panel questioned the use of novobiocin because of "a high incidence [up to twenty percent] of adverse reactions, the most common of which are skin rashes and other manifestations of allergy. Another group of patients experienced a transient injury to the liver which may contribute to death in seriously ill patients . . . People who take novobiocin rapidly get drug resistant germs; these develop because the germs acquire an ability to survive in the presence of the antibiotic." The panel recommended that Panalba be discontinued.

Ley agreed. On December 24, 1968, FDA published in *The Federal Register* a notice declaring that Panalba was ineffective as a fixed dosage combination, and giving Upjohn thirty days to submit additional information if it desired to keep the drug on the market.

Enter now Stanley Temko, a senior partner in Covington and Burling, and a lawyer ranked among the top half-dozen drug practitioners in Washington. Immediately after the FDA order, he obtained an extension of the thirty-day limit to present evidence of Panalba's efficacy. Several months passed, and Upjohn did nothing. On April 30 Ley proposed that Upjohn send "Dear Doctor" letters citing the National Academy of Science warning on novobiocin, that all existing Panalba stocks be decertified, making their sale illegal, and be recalled by May 31, and that further certification be discontinued.

Ley acknowledged that "it may well be expected that these actions on our part will be regarded as controversial, but primarily from the safety standpoint we believe the actions taken are necessary. It must be recognized that if the firms involved do not voluntarily recall the outstanding stocks from the market, it will be necessary for FDA to issue appropriate publicity and institute a campaign of legal actions to effect the removal of the goods from the market."

Ley never mailed the memo. Instead, on May 1, 1969, he received a delegation of Upjohn officials—and lawyer Stanley Temko—who vehemently protested the stop order. Temko called the action "terribly extreme. We have not anticipated your drastic and shocking call for cut-off by May 31," he said, and claimed that combinations such as Panalba "are important products for the practice of medicine." Temko argued that "the limitations of the use of Panalba have been well known to doctors," and that "if there was a large incidence of side effects the drug wouldn't be as widely used." Temko also complained that "it seems to us that you [the FDA] are going harder and faster than in any other actions I have seen you take."

Ley didn't flinch. He told Temko that FDA could not "justify the continued marketing of Panalba," and that if Upjohn chose to contest the ban, FDA would "use other avenues at hand, including cancellation of certificates, multiple seizures, and the like." Ley gave Upjohn four days to decide.

Temko put the time to use. Earlier, he and Upjohn officials had asked help from Representative Garry Brown, a Republican whose district includes Kalamazoo, Michigan, the Upjohn home. FDA staff people, meanwhile, leaked details of the controversy to two Congressional subcommittees,* which promptly announced plans for public inquiries.

"I decided I had about as much chance as the proverbial snowball of getting anyone's ear at FDA," Brown said later. "By any stretch of the imagination I couldn't see anyone there being impressed with a 'fair play–due process' argument while a political holocaust was raging around them." So he took a delegation

---

* The intergovernmental relations subcommittee of the House Committee on Government Operations, and the monopoly subcommittee of the Senate Select Committee on Small Business, both constant critics of FDA and the drug industry.

of Upjohn representatives—including Stanley Temko—to John G. Veneman, the Under Secretary of the Department of Health, Education, and Welfare, of which FDA is a branch. By Brown's account, all he asked was a "fair and impartial hearing" for Upjohn before any action on Panalba.

Temko won. Veneman instructed Ley to "consider a resolution of the Panalba matter" by doing exactly what Temko had advocated: Withhold any Panalba publicity, including the "proposed warning to doctors about its hazards," resume certification pending a hearing, and grant Upjohn a hearing on the merits.

Ley protested. In a memo he shed the bureaucrat's caution and declared, "The basic question before us is whether the government is prepared to move promptly and effectively to stop the use of a hazardous drug when the available facts and the national drug law dictate such action. We believe that the facts show clearly that Panalba presents serious hazards to patients who take it which are not balanced by any benefit to be expected from the product . . . When the Food and Drug Administration certifies a stock of an antibiotic, it certifies that the drug is safe and effective when used as directed in its labeling. I cannot issue such a certificate for Panalba because I believe that the hazards from use of the product outweigh its potential benefits, i.e., that is not safe."

One factor Temko could not control was publicity. Ley noted in the same memo that the two Congressional committees "have shown great interest in the actions we are taking" as a result of the efficacy studies, and that they intended to ask him about Panalba and what was being done "to protect the public from questionable drugs." Ley did not object to further hearings on Panalba, but he felt sales should be suspended. Upjohn, he said, had known since the 1962 drug act "that it must show by sub-

stantial evidence that its products are effective. It has not done
so. It cannot claim surprise when the law finally is brought to
bear on Panalba almost seven years later, in 1969."

But Under Secretary Veneman ordered Ley to leave Panalba
on the market and to proceed with a formal hearing. This was
done on August 13. Temko submitted fifty-four pages of medical literature. But as Ley (the hearing officer) noted, "We were
not favored with an evaluation of the paper by the Upjohn medical staff or by any consultants that the company had employed.
No new significant evidence was found in them."

Oh, come, retorted Temko, doctors around the world had
prescribed 750 million doses of Panalba. "If this drug wasn't a
safe and effective product, it wouldn't have the record of acceptance and use over these past twelve years by . . . thousands
upon thousands of doctors." To which Ley responded, "But unless the physician who has used it has critically evaluated the
results, I am concerned that it is difficult for us, or for you, to
evaluate how well that drug has performed."

"Never in my practice before administrative agencies,"
Temko said, "have I seen a situation where such abrupt action
has been taken with respect to a company and its products . . ."

Temko realized the futility of winning a favorable decision
from Ley. Ley, after all, was on record against Panalba; to reverse himself now would be to confess error. Upjohn and Temko
had recruited Congressional help, from Representative Brown.
So, too, had FDA, by alerting the investigative subcommittees.
The National Academy of Sciences evidence weighed against
Panalba; Upjohn's evidence supported Panalba. Temko at one
point expressed "my chagrin that we are in an adversary position," and hoped "we can get this back into a give-and-take
status between the company and the FDA"—i.e., off-the-record
bargaining over the label.

This could not be done; hence one final legal spasm by Temko. Working through Congressman Brown's Kalamazoo law firm, Temko asked a U.S. District Court in Michigan for an injunction barring FDA from action against Panalba. In doing so, Temko exercised the lawyer's prerogative of finding a friendly forum. Upjohn is Kalamazoo's leading industry. And Judge Kent ruled as Temko expected. Complaining of the "specter of the heavy bureaucratic hand," Kent conceded that the law did not entitle Upjohn to an evidentiary hearing "as a matter of right"; nonetheless, he invoked other Federal procedural statutes to say it should receive one anyway.

The U.S. Supreme Court ultimately upheld FDA and barred Panalba from the market—something which was finally done in March 1970, seventeen months after FDA initiated action.

What did Upjohn gain from the delay?

According to figures given the Congressional subcommittees, Panalba sales reaped $1.5 million a month for Upjohn, about twelve percent of its domestic gross. Hence Upjohn received more than $25 million extra, even while fighting a losing cause. As Dr. Lester Breslow, president of the American Public Health Association, said in a November 1969 speech, "The administrative and judicial action to assure continuing sale was clearly designed to protect the interests of the drug manufacturer, not to avoid the hazard to patients taking the drug."

A prudent businessman recognizes the value of insurance— and in the regulatory agencies insurance equates with friendly Commissioners. Through trade associations and corporate clients, some Washington Lawyers try to push friendly candidates toward Commissions—not so much in expectation of specific favors as in anticipation of a "right" attitude on an ongoing basis. Miles Kirkpatrick, President Nixon's second appointee as

FTC chairman, spent his professional career representing defendants in antitrust actions, and certainly is aware of their position. So, too, for William J. Casey, member of a securities and tax law firm with offices in New York and Washington, named chairman of the SEC in 1971. (Casey also had the proper political credentials: he was a law partner of Leonard Hall, Republican national chairman during the Eisenhower Administration.) So, too, for Richard W. McLaren, who as a Chicago lawyer defended corporations in antitrust suits before his appointment as Assistant Attorney General in charge of the Justice Department's antitrust division.

So, too, for Peter B. Hutt, who as a Covington and Burling partner specialized in food-and-drug cases before his appointment as general counsel of the FDA in September 1971. Hutt's predecessor as counsel, William W. Goodrich, became president of the Institute of Shortening and Edible Oils, a trade association which Hutt listed as a former client. Hutt's appointment came over heated Congressional and consumer group protests. Representative Benjamin Rosenthal (D., N.Y.) conceded Hutt's professional qualifications, but said he "should not be appointed to a job of supervising his former clients. Every decision he makes is under a cloud," Rosenthal said. "It is time that we in Washington say that the in-and-out incestuousness between industry and the regulatory agencies has to end." And nutritionist Robert Choate said it was discouraging that "the FDA would choose its new general counsel from the very group of lawyers most adept at tying up FDA's regulatory processes." Hutt promised the Senate subcommittee for consumers that he would disqualify himself in cases on which he had been consulted as an attorney.*

---

* Covington and Burling had mixed emotions about the appointment. Although noting the benefits of having an "understanding" lawyer in the position, one partner there noted, "Peter is so damned fine a lawyer that

Such appointments are not accidental. The White House assistant in charge of coordinating appointments—Charles Colson, in the instance of the Nixon Administration—routinely canvasses the Washington Lawyers who practice before agencies for nominees. Recommendations are seldom publicized—or even admitted—for to do so could embarrass nominees who are rejected. There is another factor, as expressed to me by a former official of the Grocery Manufacturers of America in a non-attributable interview: "Why should we be so dumb as to announce in advance that —— [and he named a Commissioner] is our man? Hell, you make him a marked man. You go around labeling a man as a friend, and he's going to have to vote against you to prove himself. You lose." But a letter from the Washington office of the Air Transport Association to member airlines indicates how the process works:

> From time to time rumors indicate anywhere from one to three vacancies on the Civil Aeronautics Board during the next six months. While these rumors cannot be definitely confirmed, it is my opinion that all hands should be alerted to these possible vacancies, with the idea of having suitable names submitted for membership on the board when and if vacancies occur. On our part, advance action is necessary in order that we may be in a position to back up our candidates at the earliest practicable date . . . It would be much appreciated if you would . . . advise me of your nominations and recommendations in order that we may present a united front.

The existence of this letter notwithstanding, Stuart Tipton, the

---

I wish he would stay in the firm. It's nonsense to think of any 'favoritism' benefiting us. What it means is that we are losing a very sharp food-law specialist."

Washington Lawyer who worked his way to the ATA presidency, insists that he "cannot remember any instance" where
the ATA board made a specific recommendation, although
"there may have been occasions when someone on the staff or
the president of the ATA has expressed a recommendation." But
he denies this is a general practice. Tipton's protest contains
more fuzz than substance. Grand juries and Congressional subcommittees being what they are, trade associations decades ago
learned to be wary of making some actions a matter of formal,
subpoenable record. Tipton sees no difference between industry
favoring candidates and the bar associations offering nomina-
tions for judicial vacancies. "I don't think recommendations of
that sort result in the appointee's having allegiance to anybody
except the proper functioning in his job," Tipton has said.

There is contradictory evidence. One well-documented case
of an industry favorite becoming a friendly regulator involved
James Bradshaw Mintener, who until the early 1950s was a
counsel for Pillsbury Mills in Minnesota. Then in 1952 Mintener helped in the "Minnesota Miracle" write-in vote that won
the state's Presidential primary for Eisenhower. This feat gave
him an unlimited blank draft at the White House. The FDA
Commissioner, Charles W. Crawford, died in office in 1954, and
HEW Secretary Oveta Culp Hobby was about to give the position to a political appointee. The drug industry didn't want to
risk having a maverick as a regulator, preferring a man of
proven complacency—like George P. Larrick, a non-scientist
who came up through the ranks as an inspector and administrator. When Mrs. Hobby's intention became known, according to
The Pink Sheet, the drug-industry trade sheet, "the regulated industries rallied in support of a 'non-political' FDA by making
their views known via letters, telegrams, telephone calls and personal visits . . . it took heroic efforts on the part of industry to

maintain the career tradition for the top spot. Brad Mintener, a longtime friend of President Eisenhower, went to the White House on the matter, and subsequently agreed to resign his post in industry to become Assistant HEW Secretary, thus insuring Larrick's appointment as FDA commissioner." Mintener's duties included "policy supervision" of FDA, and another trade publication said he would give industry "a supra-FDA office" to which it could bring complaints about meddling bureaucrats. This publication predicted, accurately, that he would be "especially valuable in supplementing the work of FDA's career officials." Commissioner Larrick also proved acceptable to the drug companies. *Drug Trade News* commented on June 29, 1959, that from the industry's point of view, his regime "can be characterized as one of sweetness and light, togetherness, of loving one's neighbor [i.e., Congress] as one's self." The Pharmaceutical Manufacturers Association gave Larrick a plaque in 1958 for "devoted service to the public welfare" and "understanding of mutual problems." The American Pharmaceutical Association, four years later, gave him an honorary membership and said his "constancy and judicious application of authority . . . earned the respect of pharmacists everywhere."

Lawyer Mintener stayed at HEW only two years, then resigned to open a Washington office specializing in food-and-drug law. His clients have included E. Fougera & Company, Inc., and Richardson-Merrill, Inc. For the latter, he handled a ticklish action against a product called Mer/29, an anticholesterol drug whose licensing proved to be based on false research data. Mintener helped Richardson-Merrill officials plead their case with Deputy FDA Commissioner John Harvey, and they emerged with a favorable settlement. After new research, MER/29 went back on the market.

Mintener also was appointed chairman of a special drugs subcommittee of an FDA citizens advisory committee. *Consumer Reports*, organ of Consumers Union, harshly evaluated the resultant report:

> Few documents in history purporting to review matters of serious public concern can have been so inauspiciously timed or so poorly conceived. The report failed to mention at all the big problem in drug testing—whether it is wise to allow the manufacturers to control the clinical testing of their own products.
>
> Aside from this, the report gave as its first and most urgent recommendation that the FDA take a more lenient attitude toward industry to the end that "mandated self-inspection and self-regulation" should eventually supersede control by regulatory investigation and legal enforcement. As one drug trade commentator put it, the pro-industry bias of the committee's report was so plain that even Congressmen out to pin something on the FDA or its Commissioner, George P. Larrick, could not use it for that purpose . . . It seems to CU that . . . the Congress might well investigate how a citizens committee happened to come out with so uncitizenlike a philosophy.

For purposes of historical perspective, the report was issued during the public furor over birth defects caused by the tranquilizer Thalidomide—a drug which stands as a prime example of the dangers of manufacturer-controlled testing of radically new pharmaceuticals.

A Commissioner who is indiscreet enough to be linked publicly—even if inaccurately—with a party to a proceeding can say farewell to any expected reciprocal favors. In 1968 Broadway-Hale Stores of Los Angeles, the nation's sixteenth largest department store chain, tried to acquire Neiman-Marcus, the

Texas chain. On December 17, 1968, the FTC voted 3–2 to deny the merger, the majority votes coming from Commissioners Philip Elman, Mary Gardiner Jones, and James Nicholson. A day later, however, Miss Jones said she wasn't so sure, and asked that her vote be withdrawn so the case could be given further study. Several weeks later she asked to be relieved of supervision of a staff study of the case. People around the Commission began to ask, "What's going on? What has Mary so nervous?"

One apparent reason was Tommy Austern, Broadway-Hale's counsel in the case. The Nixon Administration was about to take office, and the President would appoint a Republican to replace Rand Dixon as chairman. Mary Jones, as the only card-carrying Republican on the Commission, could expect prime considera-tion. And among her sponsors was Tommy Austern, whose rank in the antitrust bar demanded the respect of the Nixon Adminis-tration.

On January 23, three days after Nixon's inauguration, the Commission voted again and split 2–2, Miss Jones having left the meeting early to avoid participating. The tie had the net effect of vetoing the merger, but Broadway-Hale president Ed-ward Carter got busy before it was announced. He telephoned Chairman Dixon, who favored the merger, and asked that the matter be reconsidered. This time Miss Jones stayed to cast the deciding ballot permitting the merger. Chalk up a victory for Broadway-Hale and attorney Austern.

But not for Miss Jones. On February 5, 1969, *The Wall Street Journal* published details of Miss Jones's vote-switching, including her candid admission, "I flip-flopped all over the place and at one time I tried to duck." She also tacitly conceded that she had discussed her aspirations for the chairmanship with various Washington Lawyers who practice before the FTC and said, "Tommy has been helpful and encouraging."

What can a "friendly" regulatory Commissioner do for an

industry? And what involvement can a Washington Lawyer have in the favors? Archetypical of agency sensitivity for corporate interests was the Federal Power Commission's performance in the mid-1950s over regulation of the field price of natural gas. Tough regulators like veteran Commissioner Leland Olds* had long maintained that the FPC could not do an effective regulatory job without determining what was a "reasonable payment" to the producer at the point where natural gas enters the trunk pipelines. The gas industry is intricately rigged against the consumer. Because the pipeline companies own the production companies, they can "afford" to pay inflated prices for gas because (a) the payments go from one corporate pocket to another and (b) the consumer unwittingly pays any extra costs.

The Wisconsin Public Service Commission brought suit to force the FPC to regulate the wellhead price, and the U.S. Supreme Court ruled in 1955 that it must do so. Whereupon FPC Chairman Jerome K. Kuykendall—a former utilities lawyer appointed to the Commission by President Eisenhower—undertook a unique campaign to strip their agency of a power the court said it must exert. Kuykendall and three other industry-oriented Commissioners asked Congress to rewrite the Federal Power Act to deny the FPC any control over wellhead prices. Kuykendall recruited a task force of industry lawyers to write a bill palatable to the gas companies: Randall Le Boeuf, Jr., Washington Lawyer for Consolidated Edison Company of New York, representing gas distributors; William Tarver, a former FPC lawyer then working for a pipeline company; and David Searls, attorney for the production companies.

The FPC-industry collaboration came to light by accident when Representative Torbert Macdonald (D., Mass.) offhandedly asked Kuykendall why the FPC was sponsoring legisla-

---

* The Senate denied Olds's reappointment in 1949 because he had repeatedly offended the gas industry.

ion written without consultation with consumer groups, or even the mayors of some two hundred Eastern cities who had formally requested strict FPC regulation. No purpose would be served by talking with these citizens, Kuykendall said, "because I knew very well what their position was"—i.e., that the FPC should strive for low gas prices. "I got three extremely able men from . . . three segments of the industry, and I believe that among those the consumer interests were adequately represented."

Kuykendall was wrong. Each of the industry "segments" which he mentioned—gas producer, gas pipeline, and gas utility —simply passes costs on to the consumer—the individual homeowner or businessman who pays the monthly gas bill.

Austern is talkative and prolific, and in addition to an interview he gave me a stack of articles to read and return. Some Tommyisms:

Austern on pharmaceuticals. *"No drug is absolutely safe. If it were, it perhaps would not cure anything."*

Austern on consumerism. *"The collective noun 'consumer' has content but not specific identity. Its range covers all sections of the country, all economic levels, all tastes and preferences, and presumably all standards of cooking . . . Individual housewives are not qualified to answer for a nation of consumers . . . [Consumer witnesses often testify as if] the authority and discretion delegated to them to speak for all American women has apparently no bounds."*

Austern on federal antitrust activities. *"It may well be that legal judgment in this field of business regulation has ceased to be an intellectual process, and has become a matter of instinct. If this is true . . . both counseling and enforcement should be left to that long quiescent group of professional witch-finders who practiced before the courts in the 16th and 17th centuries. They*

*could pursue their profession unfettered by logic, unhampered
by definition, and unconfined by proof—as the Privy Council of
Scotland in 1632 said of one of them, their accusations were
'onlie conjecturall.'* "

Austern on Nader. *If any corporation is "dumb enough" to
take Nader seriously, Austern doesn't want him for a client. The
study group on antitrust law was comparable to "permitting law
students into an operating theater to critique open-heart surgery;
they'd be about as qualified there." Nader himself? "Fuck
him."*

Mudge, Rose, Guthrie and Alexander:
The Former Partner's Firm

Stuart Saunders was a desperate man the morning of June 8, 1970, as he faced directors of the Penn Central Company in the company's board room high atop the Suburban Station Building in downtown Philadelphia. For most of 1970 the railroad, of which he was board chairman, had careened toward what appeared to be certain financial disaster. On April 22 the line, the nation's largest, had reported a staggering first-quarter loss of $79 million, $30 million more than budgeted. A month later the company withdrew an offering of $100 million in debentures, proceeds of which were intended to float Penn Central through the crisis. Bankers wouldn't lend Penn Central money even at an interest rate of ten and one-half percent—the sort of no-confidence vote that told management the end was near. Penn Central needed an immediate, massive infusion of cash to stay live.

Stuart Saunders was a desperate man, but there was one more chance. Six days previously, a group of seventy-three banks headed by the blue-ribbon First National City Bank of New York had asked the Federal government to guarantee a $225-million loan to Penn Central.

Working closely with Penn Central on the deal, Saunders told the directors, was a lawyer named Randolph H. Guthrie, whom he identified as a member of "the Nixon firm" and as being "close to the White House." Guthrie would join the meeting later, Saunders said, but he had already been helpful in negotiations in Washington.

According to a company officer's notes,* Paul A. Gorman, the executive vice president, agreed with Saunders. Guthrie, Gorman noted, had "been influential" in Washington and also in coordinating the many banks involved in the bail-out attempt. Gorman was confident the line would receive at least $180 million for six months.

Guthrie entered the meeting a bit later, his first appearance ever before the Penn Central directors. He, too, was confident, according to the officer's notes, saying it was "probable" Penn Central would receive the $225 million and that the Federal Reserve Board had worked out an arrangement "satisfactory" with the government. He expected to hear final approval later that day, or the next.

And the notes quote Randolph Guthrie as saying Federal offi-

---

* The notes were taken by Bayard H. Roberts, then secretary of the railroad, and made available to me by a non-company source. Statements made at the directors' meetings that are quoted in this chapter came from Roberts's notes, unless otherwise noted.

:ials with whom he had talked about the $225 million bail-out 'now understand" the deep-rooted nature of the railroad's prob-em, and were ready to set about correcting them.

As it developed, the Penn Central did not receive the $225-million loan guarantee, a failure which on June 18 pushed the company over the brink into the largest bankruptcy in United States history. And Stuart Saunders, who had been so happy that the line had a lawyer whose friendships extended right into the office of the President of the United States, was dismissed before the June 8 meeting ended—victim of intensifying director hor-ror at the company's financial plight.

Resounding though it was, however, the Penn Central col-lapse is not central to our story, save for one element, the deep involvement of what Stuart Saunders called "the Nixon firm."

His reference was to a Wall Street law office now called Mudge, Rose, Guthrie and Alexander, which until the day after the 1968 Republican national convention was Nixon, Mudge, Rose, Guthrie, Alexander and Mitchell. The "Nixon" of that title, of course, is the President. The "Mitchell" is John M. Mitchell, Attorney General of the United States. And Nixon is unique as the first practicing lawyer since Abraham Lincoln to accede directly to the Presidency (although 23 of the 36 Presi-dents have been lawyers).

Because of this connection, Mudge Rose has become one of Washington's more conspicuous law offices. Before Mr. Nixon's election, Mudge Rose's sole outpost in Washington was a one-lawyer office maintained chiefly to give the New York partners a place to leave their briefcases and make phone calls while in the capital on business. As of this writing (June 1971), the office has eleven lawyers and is a striking example of what luck, pluck, hard work, and having a Former Partner in the White House can do for a law firm.

Mudge Rose's quantum jump up the Washington politico-legal power ladder has provoked antagonisms as well as new business. States a middle-echelon official at the Securities and Exchange Commission, "This might sound silly, and overly defensive, but I sort of bridle every time anyone calls from 'Mudge Rose,' because I know—and they know—the other names that used to be in the title. No one there has ever said a damned thing I could put my finger on, but the hint of superiority is there. That's all you need—a hint."

An investigator for Representative Wright Patman who encountered the Former Partner's firm on two occasions states, "Some of the people at Mudge Rose are gauche—they use the wrong forks at the table in their law business. When I hear Martha Mitchell, I think of the firm—loud, a little too obvious, not too wise, nouveau riche in power, and making the most of their White House tie."

And this story, from an official of the Federal Home Loan Bank Board, which charters savings and loan associations:

"I got a call from a young member of Mudge Rose's Washington office who needed charters for two S&L's in the South. He had never handled a proceeding at the home loan board, and asked, 'How do you go about it?' I told him what kind of paperwork was required, the information that should go on the documents, and how to process them through our office. These are routine—once you have done your first one, which can be a bitch. Just before he hung up, this young lawyer asked, 'By the way, what is the going rate for handling one of these applications?'

"I told him that lawyers typically charged $5,000 to $10,-000, depending upon the time required and the size of the S&L. 'We don't know about other lawyers,' this guy replied, 'but we're Mudge Rose, and we'll charge whatever we want—$50,000 if we want to.' "

Some friends of Mudge Rose partners claim they tried to keep the firm from embarrassing itself, with singular non-success. A Washington Lawyer who formerly practiced in New York states, "I had a long talk with Len Garment soon after the election, when the word got around that Mudge Rose was expanding its office here. 'There is nothing in the world you can gain by this,' I told him. 'You are going to attract a lot of political work, and a lot of political trouble. You know good and well the type of clients who are going to come to you. Len, for God's sake, be realistic and practical. What good reason could you give me for this sort of thing?' Garment couldn't say anything."

Immediately after Mr. Nixon's election, columnist Drew Pearson ticked off a list of the firm's clients, as if putting Mudge Rose on public notice that anything it did for them in Washington would be under extra-close scrutiny. *The Washington Post*, in a restrained but comprehensive post-inaugural survey of the firm, noted that it was the subject of "considerable public speculation and discussion." Even the Chesapeake & Potomac Telephone Company contributed to the firm's discomfort. Its 1969 directory, compiled far in advance, but published months after the GOP convention and Mr. Nixon's publicly announced resignation from the firm, carried the following line on page 389:

> Nixon Mudge Rose Guthrie Alexander
> & Mitchell lwyrs
> 1701 PaAvNW—298-5970

Despite its highly public existence, however, Mudge Rose has yet to be caught in a situation that caused anything more than fleeting embarrassment, either to the firm or to the Former Partner. Indeed, there is evidence its "connections" mean trouble, not cooperation, from the career bureaucracy, from Democrats who date back two administrations, and who delight in making life rough for Mudge Rose—delaying an application here, losing a filing there, bucking papers back for more information—the petty but possible harassment akin to grabbing a new kid's cap on the playground. A shadow "opposition government" exists within the bureaucracy, staff attorneys and assistant division chiefs and deputy administrators, a Civil Service old-boys'-club, ever ready to whisper information embarrassing to an administration with which it disagrees. Politics, mischief, altruism—the motive really isn't important. Every administration lives with the knowledge it can be clobbered by a brick thrown from its own backyard. Mudge Rose has been pelted with a few minor pebbles; the firm and the Administration live with the knowledge that one gross misstep could bring the fatal brick.

Randolph Guthrie is a heavy, slow-talking South Carolinian with more Dixie than Wall Street in his voice; close your eyes when he speaks, and envision magnolias and the lazy drift of a Southern summer; a transplanted good ol' country boy who would be at home as a judge in Caddo Parish, Louisiana, or at a bar association luncheon in Tallahassee, Florida. Seeming slowness and congeniality even with strangers—no, *especially* with strangers—are tactical mannerisms sons of the South have used for decades to beguile and disarm unwitting Northerners; a hint of the country yokel, no single word or inflection you can isolate, but a come-on-now-let's-talk-about-it camaraderie, golly-knows—but-we-know-how-it-is. Randolph Guthrie talks like this, and you must keep reminding yourself that he is an extraordinarily sharp and rich man who is a senior partner in a Wall Street law firm, and that when he turns his chair to a half right and walks four steps to the window he can look down on the New York Stock Exchange, both figuratively and literally.

Randolph Guthrie is glad to see me, yes he is, for he thinks that lawyers should talk to reporters, and to hell or thereabouts with the bar rules; if someone wants to know about his business, well, walk right in and ask about it, and he'll answer as best he can, within the bounds, of course, of client-lawyer confidentiality, but we all know that, now, don't we, and we can get along well together; now go ahead, young fellow, and ask your questions, and let me talk about them.

Randolph H. Guthrie is the partner with whom Nixon was the closest. The first name is that of the famed Virginia family, from which he is descended. A specialist in corporate law and international finance; a man who puts together eight-digit deals with less effort than most of us expend in paying the monthly utility bills. A lawyer by strictest definition only—actually, *the* dominant voice in almost every situation he touches.

A story—perhaps apocryphal—is told of the time Randolph Guthrie paid his first visit to a Midwestern company that was about to lose a take-over fight to a company he represented. "Gentlemen," Randolph Guthrie began, "you are about to be raped. Now, why don't you lay back and enjoy it?" That is the way, one is told, Randolph Guthrie earns $1,000 per working day, year in and year out. A tough man, a successful man, a man to attract a former Vice President seeking a retread of his morale and his spirit and his career. A man who talks politics but doesn't practice them.

"I'm beyond either of the parties, Democratic or Republican," Randolph Guthrie told me. "I'm like the old boy who said he didn't believe in segregation, and somebody asked, 'What the hell are you for—integration?' 'Nah,' he said, 'I'se for *slavery.*'"

I must have blinked, good ol' Southern boy pose and all, for Randolph Guthrie hastily added, "Now don't read that wrong —I just mean that I don't fit into any boundaries."

Later, after John Mitchell became a partner and the Mudge Rose partners gathered at the future Attorney General's home in Rye, New York, for a party, Richard Nixon would play organ-piano duets with Martha Mitchell, and sing a bit, and it is said he even laughed at a joke or two. But when Richard Nixon wanted hard-core advice on how Wall Street *really* worked, and *exactly* what he should do for this client, and *how* this point should be argued, Randolph Guthrie was the man to whom he turned. A senior-junior relationship, the old sarge showing the recruit how to keep the water out of his tent; Guthrie so confident, so competent, in his own field that he was one of the few men in Richard Nixon's world not reflexively deferential. Someone who, when discussing the Former Partner, could state without conscious condescension, "We practice good law here. We earned good livings before Nixon came here, we earn one now. We're not hungry." Ah, yes, young Nixon. Did quite well with the firm, then went on to other things, in Washington, I believe. And his tenure with the firm . . . ah, hem . . . no, no effect at all upon what is happening now, because of course Mudge Rose is not that sort of firm. "We are technicians," Randolph Guthrie said. "We are not in the business of affecting government. We work directly with the staff people, not at the high level—we're really not in that area.

"We are not ex-politicians, future politicians, or present politicians. We are caught up in something we never expected.

"We don't take clients who come to us because they have problems in Washington. On the other hand, for existing clients, we should proceed to do our best for them when they have problems. We lean over backwards to avoid getting into situations where we might be criticized. But we are in business.

"We do have some sensitivities to the situation; after all, the President and the Attorney General *did* come from our firm. But we are not going to withdraw from the practice of law. We are a hundred years old, after all.

"We are carrying on our profession in the same way as if Johnson or Kennedy was President. We are trying to pursue a sensible course and not get into any situation where any reasonable charge can be made against us for trying to make a political fix.

"It's not that we're so goddamned moral—we've got enough clients to get along without it. We have no economic pressures to take that kind of business."

That is Mudge Rose speaking for the record. Poke around in the bureaucracy for a few months, however, and you encounter several pictures of Mudge Rose. A Mudge Rose with elbows. A Mudge Rose to which the Former Partner won't always listen, drat him anyway. A Mudge Rose skilled in the toughness essential to prosperity in Wall Street, where multimillion-dollar deals bang around like so many boxcars in a Penn Central freight marshaling yard. A Mudge Rose that hears the unnerving sound of knives being whetted behind its back in the predominantly Democratic Civil Service.

Item: Soon after he became Attorney General, John Mitchell intervened in an attempt by Treasury Department attorneys to remove the tax exemption from state and municipal bonds, proposed as a part of the Tax Reform Act of 1969. One of these attorneys stated, "We were told to do nothing in this field without special consultation at the Assistant Secretary level. The Assistant Secretary, in turn, received his guidance from John Mitchell. And Mitchell was adamant: he wouldn't tolerate any changes. No one in Treasury dared to buck him, and the haven remained. This is the loophole, you understand, that permits people like Florabel Dodge [heiress to the auto fortune] to earn more than a million dollars a year in interest from bonds and not pay a cent in taxes." Mitchell's law specialty, as we have noted, was state and municipal bonds, the marketability of which depends largely on their tax exemption.

Item: Soon after its creation by Congress in June 1970, the United States Postal Service (successor agency to the old Post Office Department) set about marketing the first $250 million of the $10 billion in bonds it was authorized to sell. USPS intended to sell the bonds through private Wall Street houses. Even so, James Hargrove, a senior assistant postmaster general, was confident USPS could hire a law firm directly for legal work on the issue if it so desired—"one of the Wall Street legal firms that normally does such things for corporate and government clients. . . . We will obviously incur a fee of some significance, but not more than $5,000 or $10,000 for this particular purpose." Even if the Wall Street houses were permitted to choose the lawyers, Hargrove wrote in another memo in August 1970, "the issuer [USPS] would normally have a good deal to say about the counsel the underwriters selected, although the underwriters themselves engaged such counsel and pay their fees."

Nine months later, in May 1971, USPS permitted the leading underwriter firm, Salomon Brothers and Hutzler, to retain Mudge Rose for the work, at an anticipated fee of $100,000— or ten times the maximum estimated by USPS had USPS hired the counsel directly. Mudge Rose could expect much more. If it continued as counsel for the full $10 billion issue—normal practice for bonds issued by government agencies—its fees would total approximately $2,500,000.

Both the USPS and the underwriters stated that the outside bond houses, not the Nixon Administration, chose Mudge Rose. But a postal subcommittee headed by Representative Morris K. Udall, a testily partisan Arizona Democrat, but also a reformist, looked deeper. Udall was irked because one reason for creating the quasi-governmental USPS was to wrench the post office from politics; indeed, former chairmen of both the Democratic and Republican national committees had headed a citizens' lobby that got the reform legislation.

Udall surveyed the five bond houses handling the issue. "Only one of the five managers gave Mudge Rose as their first choice for bond counsel. This was the firm of Salomon Brothers and

Hutzler. One other firm listed Mudge Rose as its third choice while the remaining three did not mention the firm at all." Although Udall conceded Mudge Rose was well qualified, "there are a number of law firms equally qualified and willing to do the work, *much of which is* pro forma *and does not require unique expertise.*" Udall also found correspondence in which a vice president of Goldman Sachs, one of the bond firms, urged that USPS refer technical problems on the issue to Attorney General Mitchell. The vice president, Daniel W. Heffgren (a White House special assistant from 1969 through mid-1970) said of Mitchell, "my experience has indicated he has an understanding of this problem." Udall could find no further trace of Mitchell, and USPS denied having consulted him. Udall concluded, "The only possible connection Mr. Mitchell had with the bond issue would have been through his former association with Mudge, Rose, Guthrie and Alexander."

Summarizing this conglomeration of circumstances, Udall wrote in a formal report that Mudge Rose's selection "seems at best insensitive to appearances, and at worst, highly political," and "a mistake of a high magnitude." Udall said, "A law firm that formerly had as its senior partners the current President and Attorney General of the United States should have been excluded from consideration, if only for appearance's sake. . . . While there is no direct evidence linking the selection of the bond counsel to any political decisions of either the U.S. Postal Service or Salomon Brothers and Hutzler, there is a great deal of circumstantial evidence to indicate that improprieties did exist."

Item: In July 1968 (before Mr. Nixon was nominated for President) Liquidonics Industries, Inc., Westbury, New York, a small manufacturer of engineering apparatus, launched a takeover attempt at UMC Industries, Inc., St. Louis, whose products range from matches to vending machines and such defense gear as radar and navigational equipment, missile warheads and launchers, and various munitions. To outside appearances the take-over made as much sense as a Little League team challenging the Baltimore Orioles. UMC outearned Liquidonics about $22 million to $4 million; the companies' net worths, respectively, were $54.5 million and $6.1 million.

The disparity in sizes didn't deter Liquidonics, for borrowed money permitted many of the minnow-swallows-whale take-overs of the 1960s. Liquidonics president N. Norman Muller, after months of fruitless direct negotiations with UMC, and some financing scheming too complex for recitation here, decided he couldn't pull off the merger without substantial outside help, and began looking for it. One idea was to merge with a friendly larger company, and use the combined assets to grab control of UMC. Sometime in early 1969 he had conversations along this line with Studebaker-Worthington, Inc., successor firm to the old car company, now a manufacturer of automotive accessories.

Randolph Guthrie is board chairman of Studebaker-Worthington, a longtime Mudge Rose client, but he had no role in the merger discussions, and no deal was reached. So Muller changed course. He knew that Guthrie and Mudge Rose were U.S. representatives for Banque de Paris et des Pays-Bas (Suisse) S.A., in Geneva, and asked Guthrie if a loan might be arranged from that source to help the merger. The amount involved was $40 million, a transaction which Guthrie tersely summarized as follows: "A fellow here [Muller] wanted to borrow some money, and knew my relationship with the bank. The bank was willing to see him, so he went. In two days they discussed out the thing and made the loan."

The target company, UMC, now began squirming in earnest to avoid being gobbled up. One point seized upon by its attorneys was whether Liquidonics violated Regulations G, T, and U of the Securities and Exchange Act in using the borrowed funds to buy UMC stock. These regulations require that a company which borrows money to buy stock must satisfy the same eighty-percent margin requirement that covers other broker-customer dealings; i.e., the borrower must post eighty percent of the purchase price in order to borrow twenty percent. This Liquidonics had not done, and UMC complained vigorously to the Securities and Exchange Commission. The SEC official who handled the question was Patrick J. Griffin, Jr., chief of the Branch of Small Issues in the Division of Corporation Finance. Griffin discussed the complaint with James Sargent, a lawyer in the New York firm of Parr, Doherty, Polk & Sargent, which represented Liquidonics. Griffin reported what happened in a "memorandum of telephone conversation" dated February 12, 1969, less than a month after Mr. Nixon became President:

UMC has raised the question as to whether or not the two brokerage firms, who were acting as dealer-managers for Liquidonics in the tender offer, were not in violation of Regulations G, T or U with regard to arranging a loan with a foreign bank which was collateralized by stock where the loan exceeded 20% of the value of the stock. I conveyed this information to Mr. Sargent's secretary in his absence and he telephoned today and advised that the loan was arranged by a lawyer who was a former partner of President Nixon and the Attorney General and who is still in the name of the firm. He stated that *under the circumstances there was no violation of the law in the arranging of the loan*.

Mr. Sargent will send us a letter regarding the status of the loan under the Federal Reserve regulations and the legality thereof.

The loan was challenged neither by the SEC nor by the Federal Reserve Board.

I showed Griffin's memo to Randolph Guthrie. He didn't like

it, and he asked for a copy of it. ("Take me a picture of this," he told a secretary.) Then he talked about it. The Federal Reserve Board, he argued, "was never intended to cover loans made by European banks—that's a lot of crap. As a matter of fact, we consulted with the Federal Reserve Board before we made the loan. If it was not a first-class loan, we didn't want to make it. So I call up [the Fed] and find out—I tell them all the facts. 'Why are you calling me on this?' the man asked. Based on that conversation, and what we knew of the law, we gave the opinion the loan was all right."

Guthrie argues that the Fed could cover the use of foreign funds for stock purchases any time it wishes by extending the jurisdicitions of Regulations G, T, and U to American *citizens* rather than limiting them to American *banks*, the present limit. Of the Presidential name-dropping quoted in the memo, Guthrie exclaimed, "That's the sort of thing we keep running into."

The take-over ultimately aborted—Liquidonics could not raise long-term funding to cover the Swiss bank loan and suffered a loss of more than $16 million in a forced sale of the UMC stock it had purchased. After the debris was sorted out, UMC was found to be controlled by Overseas International Corporation, a Luxembourg subsidiary of the Banque de Paris et des Pays-Bas (Suisse). Randolph Guthrie and another Mudge Rose partner, H. Ridgely Bullock, became chairman and secretary, respectively, of UMC, acting on behalf of the European financiers.

To Guthrie the Liquidonics deal is routine financial business —a bit complicated, perhaps, to the eyes of laymen, but something that big-time law firms do frequently, and profitably. Mudge Rose was actively involved in the transaction for only three months, from January 1 through March 31, 1969, during which time it arranged the loan and prepared and consummated the tender offer through which Liquidonics bought UMC stock.

Its bill was $200,000, the sort of figure that explains why Mudge Rose is a very big and very rich law firm.

The chain of events which resulted in Mudge Rose's shedding its cherished anonymity began with Richard M. Nixon's humiliating defeat in the 1962 California gubernatorial election. Nixon wanted a place to rebuild his life and to make money while doing so. He found some peculiarly appealing qualities in New York; to Robert J. Donovan of the *Los Angeles Times* he described it as "very cold and very ruthless and very exciting, and therefore, an interesting place to live . . . The main thing, it is a place where you can't slow down—a fast track. Any person tends to vegetate unless he is moving on a fast track. New York is a very challenging place to live. You have to bone up to keep alive in the competition . . ."

Nixon told many friends of his discontent with California— after all, what affection can a politician have for a native state that gives him the terminal rejection of defeat?—and of his desire to seek personal regeneration in the East. One man who heard Nixon's plaint was Elmer H. Bobst, then in his late seventies, who had risen from a $3-a-week drugstore clerkship to be head of Warner-Lambert Pharmaceutical Company, and one of America's greater self-made fortunes. Bobst and Nixon met during the 1952 campaign and achieved instant sympatico. "We're all one big family," Mrs. Bobst has said of the relationship. The Nixon daughters call Bobst "Uncle Elmer," and the families spent Christmases together. For Nixon's professional purposes the relationship was useful because Warner-Lambert's legal counsel was the Wall Street law firm of Mudge, Stern, Baldwin and Todd. Bobst told the firm Nixon "was available." At about the same time, Donald M. Kendall, president of Pepsi Co., and also a longtime friend, offered Nixon a substantial annual retainer ($120,000 a year is one figure bandied about) to represent his corporation on the East Coast, should he settle there to practice law, and internationally. Pepsi-Cola was in the process of challenging Coca-Cola for what we could call the Soda Pop Leadership of the World, and a former Vice President of the United States is a good detail man for softening up potentates and premiers who can make it easy—or tough—for foreigners to operate. The "international" responsibility would also give Nixon a pretext to travel and maintain his contacts with world leaders. After several weeks of negotiations, Nixon and Mudge, Stern reached an agreement, and the new partner issued an announcement in writing from his suite at the Waldorf-Astoria Towers:

On June 1, 1963, I shall move my residence to New York City and shall become counsel to the firm of Mudge, Stern, Baldwin and Todd.

After I have met the six months' residence requirement of the New York law, I shall apply for admission to the New York bar. When admitted to the bar, I shall become a general partner in the firm.

Pending my admission to the New York bar, I shall engage principally in matters relating to the Washington and Paris offices of the firm.

Descended from a firm founded in 1869, Mudge, Stern was aged as well as venerable, a firm with an unexciting reputation among the lawyers in the twenty-odd "law factories" that service Wall Street and the major United States corporations based in New York. "The general feeling was that Mudge, Stern had too many old men in the office, partners who had been good in their day but who didn't pull their own weight," an outsider lawyer told me. "When an office is burdened with nonproductive partners who continue to draw a full share of the proceeds, new men are discouraged from joining. Lawyers certainly didn't talk about it as an exciting place to work." Another lawyer disagrees with this evaluation: "On the amount of work done, and general expertise, I'd have put it in the top ten in New York—maybe not on the same level as Cravath, Swaine; or Dewey, Ballantine, Bushby, Palmer & Wood; or Paul, Weiss, Rifkind, Wharton & Garrison; but at least in the same league. Why didn't it have a bigger reputation? So what? They didn't choose to practice that way."

Politically, the firm was a neuter. Randolph Guthrie, who joined the office in 1931, could think of only one partner who ever held a significant public office: Henry Root Stern, Jr., head of the State Board of Social Welfare under Governor Thomas E. Dewey. "This has never been a political firm," Guthrie told me. "Nixon said it himself, that he was coming to New York to practice law to 'bury the corpse.' When he joined the firm there was no expectation—by him or anyone else—that he would ever enter political life again." Had anyone asked, another man said after thinking a bit, most of the pre-Nixon partners would have described themselves as moderate to conservative Republicans. ("Which is not to say the office had no Democrats," he adds. "We just didn't think of each other in terms of party.")

Why, then, Nixon as senior partner? When he satisfied the six-month residency requirement in December and was sworn into the New York bar, the former Vice President's name immediately went to the head of the firm—Nixon, Mudge, Rose, Guthrie and Alexander (three deceased partners were dropped from the title). For someone going into a major Wall Street firm, Nixon's practical law experience was minimal: a small local practice in Whittier, California, from 1937 to 1942, a brief stint with the Office of Price Administration in 1942; an association with the Los Angeles firm of Adams, Duque and Hazeltine from January 21, 1961, when he left the Vice Presidency, until September 27, 1961, when he entered the California gubernatorial race. Why Nixon?

Money. A drawing card for new business. Celebrity appeal for corporate executives who delight in saying oh so casually, "As my lawyer Dick Nixon was telling me the other day at lunch . . ." Political appeal for businessmen who in their hearts *know* they will benefit from retaining a former Republican Presidential candidate. Derivative status for all persons connected with "the Nixon law firm."

Nixon performed as expected, and in flowed the clients: Mutual of New York. Eversharp-Schick. Matsui of Japan. Investors Diversified Services. Hornblower-Weeks. El Paso Natural Gas. Big clients, well-paying clients.

Mergers brought in even more business. In 1963 Mudge Rose absorbed Dorr, Hand, Whittaker & Watson, a Wall Street office that did a thriving railroad business. In 1964 it added Becker & Greenwald, Washington admiralty law specialists. In 1966 came Caldwell, Trimble, & Mitchell, also of Wall Street, which did a thriving—and extraordinarily technical—business of advising state and municipal governments on how to issue bonds. With the latter firms, whose clients included the State of New York, came a new partner and name for the firm title, John N. Mitchell.

Pleading client-attorney confidentiality, firm members decline to specify exactly how much law Richard Nixon practiced between late 1963 and his nomination in July 1968. He appeared in court in only one case: to argue, in the U.S. Supreme Court, an invasion-of-privacy suit against *Life* Magazine for publicizing a fictionalized play about a suburban Philadelphia family held hostage by escaped convicts. (After two rounds of oral arguments, Nixon's clients lost the key point in a 5–4 decision; *Life* then settled out of court.)

Nixon also got to Washington occasionally. His stature as a

former Vice President enabled Nixon to obtain briefings from old State Department friends before his foreign travels. He was especially interested in Taiwan, whose long time ruler, Chiang Kai-Shek, gave Mudge Rose client PepsiCola an exclusive franchise arrangement.

But Nixon did most of his work out of public view. Two young West Coast professors, Joel M. Fisher and William M. Treadwell, studied the firm for an academic project and concluded Nixon was the pacemaker. "He sets the tone and style," they wrote of Nixon, "and furnishes the central image, both within and without. Main directions are of his choosing. The others will follow his lead. He attracts a certain body of clientele, and his associates must render them the bulk of the necessary legal service they seek. Or, his partners bring in a type of business in which they specialize, and he must be the all-important generalist. He is a catalyst, in other words, melding together the disparate ambitions and conflicts of a variety of men, giving them order, cohesion and forward thrust."

During Nixon's four-plus years there, the firm expanded from fifty-seven lawyers to a hundred twenty. As a senior partner he earned around $150,000 a year, according to tax returns made available to Fletcher Knebel of *Look* Magazine during the 1968 campaign. Mudge Rose made Nixon a rich man. And Nixon made Mudge Rose a famous law firm.

Pleased as they were about the prospects of a partner becoming President of the United States, Nixon's return to politics put his colleagues in a dilemma. The day after the Republican National Convention nominated Nixon for the Presidency, his press people issued a formal announcement of his resignation from the law firm. What, if anything, should the firm do? According to Randolph Guthrie, "we talked a number of hours about what should be done. We finally decided to do it the routine way we do when anyone leaves the office: to put an advertisement in the [New York] *Law Journal*. Now, Nixon's nomination was no news to anyone. But let me give you an example. Just last week there was a formal notice in the *Journal* that Tom Dewey was dead, run by his firm. Now everyone knew Dewey is dead, but his firm followed the routine. After it happened [the Nixon ad], of course, everyone was saying how 'eager' we were to tell the world the President was our former partner. No matter what you do, you are criticized."

Considerable legal talent followed Nixon out of Mudge Rose. Mitchell ran the campaign, then became Attorney General. Leonard Garment coordinated media activities in the campaign, and Thomas W. Evans served as general counsel. Both subsequently took White House positions. Franklin B. Lincoln, Jr., was Nixon's liaison with the lame-duck Johnson Administration, while John Sears was the special emissary to Spiro T. Agnew; both took middle-echelon positions in the Administration. And corporate Washington—the lobbyists and trade associations and big business firms which are acutely dependent upon favorable government—eagerly sniffed around the Former Partner's firm, to see what sort of business it would be doing.

Case: The Johnson Administration spent its last days resolving heated competition for valuable trans-Pacific air routes, with each airline involved resorting to lawyers and lobbyists with political clout. In dizzying succession, the Civil Aeronautics Board overruled its own examiner's decision—one reached after three years of exhaustive study—only to be reversed in turn by Johnson, who as President has final authority over international routes. The scent of political pollution was heavy; Senator Robert P. Griffin (R., Mich.), for instance, charged in a floor speech that "cronyism" influenced Johnson's decision. Nixon reopened the proceedings.

Enter Eastern Airlines, which had profited handsomely under

the examiner's ruling, obtaining routes to the South Pacific via Hawaii, only to lose them under Johnson's reversal. Eastern had used no overtly political lawyers in the first part of the proceedings. Now, however, it asked Mudge Rose to help. Mudge Rose's new-business committee—the group of partners who must approve all new clients—rejected Eastern, telling the line, in effect, "We're not specialists in air route cases, and we have the idea you want us for another reason, and we're not that politically stupid."

Case: Within months after the election, Mudge Rose became bond counsel for the Virgin Islands, which came under "Republican control" by virtue of its dependence upon the Department of the Interior, and the District of Columbia mass transit authority, which recognizes the value of good relations with the White House. State agencies in New Jersey and Virginia, both of which elected new Republican governors, and in Kentucky, Wisconsin, and Nebraska, retained Mudge Rose for the first time. A House subcommittee staff spent weeks investigating rumors about the reason for Mudge Rose's sudden attractiveness. (The Congressional interest derived from the fact that Federal funds were involved in some of the state bond issues for which Mudge Rose was hired as counsel.) Mudge Rose pooh-poohed insinuations that politics was involved; the explanation, one man in the firm said, was that Mudge Rose was able to hire two crack bond lawyers from a competing New York office, Hawkins, Delafield and Wood. The House subcommittee gave up the chase without finding any evidence it cared to explore in public hearings.

Case: Between 1961 and 1967 El Paso Natural Gas paid Mudge Rose legal fees of $770,000, give or take a few thousand dollars, in part to fight a Justice Department antitrust suit against pricing policies which government lawyers alleged cost citizens unnecessary millions of dollars annually. In March 1969 the Justice Department announced that it would not appeal decisions it lost in the case in the lower courts. Mitchell scrupulously kept in the background. Solicitor General Erwin Griswold, a career government lawyer appointed during the Johnson Administration, said the Attorney General did not participate in the decision not to appeal, which he said was made before Nixon took office. But San Francisco attorney William Bennett, instrumental in starting the action while serving on the California Public Service Commission, and who continued to press it as an independent "consumer advocate," caustically attributed the Justice Department's attitude to El Paso Natural Gas's ties—via Mudge Rose—to the Nixon Administration.

Case: In June 1968 President Johnson recommended a broad reorganization of the Department of Health, Education, and Welfare, recommended by two former HEW secretaries, John W. Gardner and Wilbur J. Cohen. The shakeup would have removed the Food and Drug Administration from the direct control of the HEW secretary and put it under the Consumer Protection and Environmental Health Service. The hoped-for result would be greater FDA independence from the powerful, aggressive, drug-industry lawyers and lobbyists, and better protection for the public. One pharmaceutical executive who didn't like the change was "Uncle Elmer" Bobst, Nixon's close friend and law firm client. When *Chemical Week,* one of the McGraw-Hill publications, accused Uncle Elmer of lobbying against the change, he testily denied doing any such thing, saying that "any view" he would care to urge would be presented privately "to those in authority." But Bobst would neither confirm nor deny to *The Washington Post*'s Morton Mintz whether he had spoken directly to his one-time lawyer, the President, about the matter. (The reorganization did not go through.)

Item: Uncle Elmer's drug company threw another conflict-of-interest problem at the Administration in mid-1970 when it tried to merge with Parke-Davis & Company. Warner-Lambert had sales of $887.3 million in 1969; Parke-Davis, $273.5 million. Richard McLaren, the Assistant Attorney General in charge of the antitrust division, recommended action to stop the merger, for the resultant $1-billion firm would eliminate much horizontal competition in the drug field. Because of Mudge Rose's representation of Warner-Lambert, Attorney General Mitchell withdrew from any consideration of the case. His chief deputy, Richard Kleindienst, refused to approve any antitrust action, so angering McLaren that, according to Bobst and other competent sources, he threatened to resign. Because of McLaren's protests, and others by Representative Emanuel Celler (D., N.Y.), a monopoly watchdog via his House Judiciary Committee, the Justice Department finally agreed to buck the case to the Federal Trade Commission, which decided to challenge the merger. Once this was done, Celler backed down on his stated intention of subpoenaing Justice Department files telling why Kleindienst had refused to act. But as one government lawyer involved in the case states, "Celler could have looked for months and not found anything. I'm not saying politics was involved in this case, but if they were, they weren't the kind you would find on paper. The most you could do would be to hang Kleindienst for making, on his own, the kind of decision that would please Mitchell and Warner-Lambert. You never go wrong in government, or politics, by pleasing the boss."

Item: Soon after taking office, Mr. Nixon ordered a task force to study business taxes and appointed as its chairman a Mudge Rose partner, John Alexander. One recommended change was in the rules for depreciation of business equipment. The saving to American business was estimated at $3 billion per year. The Alexander task force said the Internal Revenue Code would have to be amended to permit the liberalized depreciation. There the matter rested until January 1971, when the Nixon Administration announced it intended to implement the new rules through administrative action, without going to Congress. An aide to Senator Edmund Muskie, who opposed the change, studied the situation and reported, "How can you charge 'favoritism' when Nixon in effect overruled the advice of his own law partner? Muskie is not going to put himself in the position of relying upon a Mudge Rose legal opinion* to fight a former Mudge Rose partner [Nixon]."

Mudge Rose and its predecessor firms have maintained offices in Washington since the early 1950s, according to Randolph Guthrie. His cited reasons are the same as any out-of-town firm with Washington representation: to cut commuting costs, to "provide us a place out of which to work while in Washington," and "to give Washington service to clients on routine problems. It's hard to do business without coming into contact with the government, you know, and a lot of this stuff is the one-phone-call routine you can handle better on the scene." Guthrie says the Washington branch is a convenient but not vital part of the Mudge Rose operation, and hints (without saying so directly) that the lawyers assigned there do rather humdrum work—running papers to Federal agencies for filing, doing legwork for the New York office, conducting general commercial intelligence at the agencies capable of affecting a Mudge Rose client.

Now, that matter of the President's name appearing in the Washington phone book as head of a law firm. In view of Mudge Rose's stated care in not capitalizing upon the Former Partner, can such a listing be accepted as a clerical slip?

"That phone book thing *was* an accident, and there was nothing devious about it," responds Randolph Guthrie. "Let me tell you why. We have a big estate and trust practice, and we deal with people who don't come into the office but once every ten years. Old ladies will come into the building [in New York] and

---

* Actually, of course, it was not a *Mudge Rose* legal opinion, but a legal opinion written by a Mudge Rose *partner* acting in a private capacity.

look for the previous firm name. They don't know our firm by the name of individual lawyers, the one who drew the papers, but by the firm itself, and that has changed many times over the years. Hell, we have a vault over at Irving Trust Company that is filled with wills. We probated one the other day that was written in 1910.

"What I'm trying to say is this: We have to keep all these old listings in the phone book so that people can find us. It's a very, very practical problem that we face all the time . . . Nixon's name was in there so people can find our firm. What is someone to do if he knows us as Nixon, and so forth? He's got to have some place to look." Guthrie said the firm keeps many of its prior names on the lobby directory—"Check on your way out; I wouldn't even guess at the ways we are listed"—and in the New York as well as Washington phone book.

I did check the lobby directory, and I found Mudge, Rose, Guthrie and Alexander; Mudge, Stern, Baldwin and Todd; Mudge, Stern, Williams and Tucker; and Baldwin, Todd, Harold, Rose, and Cooper (the latter being a firm merged into Mudge Rose in the mid-1950s). The 1969–70 Washington phone book—the one with the Nixon listing—contains also Mudge, Rose, Guthrie and Alexander and Mudge, Stern, Baldwin and Todd. The 1971–72 directory shows only Mudge, Rose, Guthrie and Alexander.

Which really isn't important. Washington *knows* Mudge Rose as "the Nixon firm" and behaves accordingly and for reasons more compelling than a line of agate type in the telephone book. Penn Central, for instance.

By the darkest interpretation, Penn Central's use of Randolph Guthrie in its bid for a $200-million bail-out loan from the Federal government was influence-seeking of the rankest sort. By the most charitable interpretation (that of Guthrie himself), Mudge Rose's involvement became a handicap for the railroad, but very probably saved the United States economy from collapse in June 1970. Versions of key events differ, as do accounts of Mudge Rose's exact role in the loan affair; Guthrie, for instance, challenges the accuracy of notes made of certain of his remarks to company board meetings. One fact is indelibly written on the records of bankruptcy court, however: Penn Central failed.

According to Guthrie, Mudge Rose and predecessor firms had represented the Pennsylvania and New York Central railroads "for a great many years" before they merged into the Penn Central, although not on a continuing basis. Both railroads maintained large staffs of house attorneys, but also relied upon outside firms for specialty work. David C. Bevan, Penn Central's chief financial officer, solicited Mudge Rose's advice initially on loans from the First Pennsylvania Banking & Trust Company, a Philadelphia bank, and from German financial sources. These loans were due heavy payments in the late spring of 1970, and Penn Central did not have the money to make them. "We happen to be a firm with expertise in the railroad finance field," Guthrie says. "We got into this situation on the $100-million refinancing issue, strictly a matter in which you represent a client in an underwriting. It was no different from hundreds of other issues we've handled."

The $100-million refinancing issue to which Guthrie referred was the proposed sale of debentures in that amount to meet payments on U.S. bank loans. Wall Street initially seemed receptive to the debentures. Then Penn Central announced its first-quarter loss figures—$79 million, rather than the $49 million projected in its budget—and investors cooled, refusing to buy the debentures even at a ten-and-one-half-percent yield.

As adviser on the bonds, Guthrie had taken a close look at Penn Central books, and what he saw frightened him. He concedes that at first he didn't realize the depth of Penn Central's

problems—that he thought it was simply one of liquidity (that
is, a temporary squeeze in cash flow). "That wasn't it," Guthrie
says now. "I gradually came to realize that they were not going
to have *any* money. The banks were not going to make the
loans. Normally a company can get extensions—but everyone
[the banks] was pulling the rug out from under the company."
Board chairman Stuart Saunders on May 19 told Secretary of
the Treasury David M. Kennedy of the tightening bind on his
company; that the debenture issue had failed; that if Penn Central did not receive money from some source—any source—it
would be driven into bankruptcy.

Blocked from further bank financing, Penn Central could
turn only to the Federal government. But under what authority?
Secretary Kennedy wanted to help Penn Central, but Guthrie
says he was "uncertain" as to what statutes to proceed under.
Guthrie helped steer Kennedy—and the government—toward
emergency loan guarantee provisions of the Defense Production
Act, intended to protect companies considered essential to the
national defense. Guthrie felt the act was "not as direct on this
situation as it might be, but adequate." Attorney General John
N. Mitchell took part in some of the early discussion, then di-
vorced himself from the loan issue, presumably to avoid any
conflict-of-interest problems. Convinced the Administration
could proceed under the Defense Production Act, Kennedy and
Transportation Secretary John Volpe began drafting two sets of
papers: for a $200-million loan guarantee for Penn Central, to
be made with existing Defense Department funds, and for legislation guaranteeing $750 million more in loans to railroads,
much of which would go to Penn Central.*

* The entire episode was laden with potential conflicts-of-interest. Secretary of Commerce Maurice H. Stans, whose department was involved in
the negotiations, held more than $300,000 in shares of Great Southwest
Corp., a Penn Central subsidiary. Apparently mindful of the political risks,
Stans deputized James Lynn, general counsel of the Commerce Department,

Steeped as he was in the workings of Wall Street, Guthrie was keenly aware of the consequences of a Penn Central bankruptcy. The company was a major American institution, vital to the transportation system. "You also have to think about the conditions existent at the time this was happening. The country was not doing too well economically. The whole commercial paper structure was at stake. Hit one part of it, and the whole thing can fold. This could have touched off a financial panic. I came here [to Wall Street] in 1931 and I saw what happened then. The economy is a complicated structure. You throw a spoke into it, and you have all sorts of consequences.

"The gravity of a bankruptcy depends on the steps you take to minimize the effect. If the Penn Central thing had blown into the open without any warning, there could have been a real panic. As it happened, the Federal Reserve Board had time and a fore-warning; they could take steps to ease the situation." (The Federal Reserve Board held extraordinary meetings with leading bankers the weekend of the bankruptcy and pledged them the credit necessary to get through the crisis.)

Guthrie's contact man at the White House was Peter M. Flanigan, a vice president of Dillon, Read, the investment house, until he resigned in 1968 to join the Nixon campaign. Flanigan, a seasoned Wall Streeter, shared Guthrie's fears about the impact a Penn Central failure would have upon a falling stock market. "The government was not anxious to have a company this size go into bankruptcy," Guthrie says.

Guthrie played a role—though not the major one—in the negotiations with Kennedy and Volpe over the bail-out loan. He

---

to act for him. Paul A. Gorman, first Penn Central president, then board chairman, was chairman of the Commerce Department's Industry Advisory Committee for Railroads, which helped draft the request for the $750-million loan from which his company would benefit. Gorman consulted other advisory committee members, who told him to proceed.

says his primary mission was convincing Washington that Penn Central's troubles were serious and not false distress cries intended to attract Federal money. "I communicated these problems to people in Washington—that deep difficulties were on the horizon, and that the Penn Central was not going to come out of them very easily. I gave them all of the facts. My function was to bring it to their [the government's] attention and let them do what they could.

"Saunders had already talked to Kennedy. All I did was talk to some of the people I knew. 'This is not a bluff,' I told them. 'This is for real. This is going to blow.' Now it's one thing for someone in the company to do this. He might be looking for cheap money. I had credibility."

Concurrently, however, Stuart Saunders was giving the Penn Central board another version of Guthrie's role, saying that he was "close to [the] White House" and had "been influential" in the negotiations. Guthrie flatly denies the implication inherent in Saunders' remarks made to the board meeting of June 8. "If I have any influence in Washington," he told me, "it's because I am not going to tell a lie. There is collateral confidence—they know me, and that they can believe what I tell them."

When word of Mudge Rose's involvement began to leak to the press in June, Penn Central management became skittish. At the June 18 meeting Director John M. Seabrook suggested putting Guthrie onto the board, quoting Guthrie as saying there would be "less political embarrassment" were this to be done. But director Robert S. Rausch said he was "dubious" about a directorship, for it would require listing Guthrie's fees in proxy statements for public scrutiny, giving ammunition to the "Democratic Congress." Director E. Clayton Gengras chimed in that he was "apprehensive politically" about Guthrie. The matter dropped.

Penn Central's concern over Guthrie's involvement was too

late. Representative Wright Patman, the Texas Populist-Democrat, had frowned on the loan from the outset, and as chairman of the House Banking and Currency Committee he could have made life miserable both for the railroad and for the Administration. Patman considered the guarantee a scheme to protect a bad bank loan. Board meeting notes show Patman's antagonism and the directors' reciprocal bitterness: Director Seabrook, for instance, quotes Patman as saying he was "sorry that Administration failed to go through [with the guarantee] because he wanted to knock hell out of it." Paul Gorman, the Penn Central head, said Patman and his staff were "all vindictive and not interested in helping; Patman couldn't care less whether Penn Central goes under or about the effect on the financial market."

Ironically, by mid-June Guthrie felt the government should not guarantee the loan. Penn Central's problems were so deep-rooted, so basic to the entire railroad industry, that stop-gap financing would not solve them. From the government's viewpoint, he said, "a key question was effectiveness—that is, if you got in, how could you get out later, without a constant drain? Penn Central couldn't tell how much was needed to bail out the company. It's like blackmail—if you start paying off, how will you ever stop?" Gurthrie said Penn Central was so far gone that it was "maybe better to let the whole thing collapse" so that a bankruptcy referee could start with a fresh slate.

These statements brought me up short. After all, I reminded Guthrie, the story was that he had actively sought the $200-million guarantee for Penn Central. What would he have done had he been the government official responsible for saying yes or no on the guarantee?

"I would have turned it down," Guthrie said without hesitation. "I didn't advise them [the railroad] to go after it; I told them the truth—that they were in a hell of a mess, and that two hundred million wasn't going to make that much difference."

A Patman staff member readily states that Congress was prepared to use Guthrie and Mudge Rose as whipping boys to stop the loan. The Penn Central board, according to this man, operated on a false assumption, which he summarized as follows:

"Everybody takes it for granted in Washington that you pull all the plugs you can, like Stuart Saunders did for years. They actually thought that putting Guthrie on the board would do the trick. They were pleased, telling Volpe about it. They really thought it was smart.

"Actually, using Guthrie down here was a grave mistake, because it gave Patman his necessary opening. This was an instance where we had them by the tail and there wasn't a thing they could do about it. It gave us an opportunity to kill the loan.

" 'Go ahead and grant the loan,' we told them [the Administration] in effect, 'then come up here next week and explain it.' This would have been a transaction without precedent. Not until too late did Penn Central realize the gravity of its mistake. By then, of course, the whole deal had collapsed."

Transportation Secretary Volpe was the first Administration official to realize—very belatedly—the gravity of Penn Central's political error. According to the Penn Central minutes, he claimed to be "thunderstruck" by Patman's opposition and demanded of Penn Central executives, "Who hired Guthrie? End it now with publicity." Volpe said he [i.e., the Administration] would support legislation for the second bail-out loan, the one for $750 million, "only if Guthrie [was] dismissed."

Volpe's statements were reported to the Penn Central board on Sunday afternoon, June 21, as the Administration neared a decision on whether to proceed with the loan. Guthrie resented the implication by Volpe that Penn Central employed him as a high-level influence-peddler. Notes taken at the meeting give this outline of what Guthrie said in his defense:

Took case as public effort . . . No fee arrangement. No fee paid. No effort to achieve special results from government . . . Mudge etc. not going after special interests. Might have turned [Penn Central] down had they not already been in.

(Guthrie disputes the accuracy of this passage. "I didn't take this case as a public effort," he told me. "That's a lot of crap. I took it because we represented these people. I would have been delighted if we had gotten the loan, but I was not upset they didn't." He also avows Mudge Rose neither expected nor received any financial benefit from the Penn Central work. "As a matter of fact," he said, "we probably lost $50,000. They still owe us that much, and I'm not confident of getting more than a few cents on the dollar, if anything, from the bankruptcy referee. Lawyer fees are pretty far down on the list of priorities.")

According to the notes, Guthrie told the board President Nixon made the final decision not to grant the loan guarantee. The meeting ended with the directors voting to file the bankruptcy petition.

So, too, ended Mudge Rose's involvement. At one point in July the Penn Central directors discussed retaining the firm to represent them and company officers in the bankruptcy proceedings. But Director Gengras, noting the firm's "apparent conflict in Washington," squashed the idea.

"In retrospect," said a Patman committee staff member, "Guthrie did Mudge Rose more good by keeping the government out of the loan than he would have by getting it for the railroad. I admit this. We'd have kicked their ass around for months, and this would have been the opening to really embarrass the Administration." Once the loan deal collapsed, Congressman Patman ordered his staff to keep the Former Partner's firm out of their investigation. Patman's control of the House

Banking and Currency Committee is shaky. He holds the chairmanship by virtue of the seniority system, but Democrats have voted with Republicans to override him in the past. In the instance of Penn Central, the GOP members told Patman, "One scent of partisan politics, and we'll gut you."

Hence Patman's reluctance to explore several interesting avenues, ones open only to someone with subpoena power. An example: The Patman committee, in a staff report published in early 1971, noted the director interlocks between Penn Central and Allegheny Corporation. Two mutual funds controlled by Allegheny—Investors Diversified Services and Investors Mutual, Inc.—sold a total of 489,000 shares of Penn Central stock between May 19 and May 27, 1970, their total holdings. Not until May 28 did Penn Central announce publicly that it was withdrawing its $100-million debenture offer and looking elsewhere for help. Noting these and other sales by banks and financial groups, the Patman report said they "conducted their massive sales of Penn Central stock on the basis of either great clairvoyance or inside information."

What Patman discreetly failed to mention—or to single out for further investigation of conflict-of-interest factors—was the fact that Mudge Rose for years had done legal work for Investors Diversified Services.

A Washington Lawyer—a Democrat not enraptured with Richard Nixon—says, "You've got to be careful not to assume too much cause and effect when you watch Mudge Rose and the President. Sure, they think alike, but what's so wrong about that? The President is business-oriented, so is the law firm. Hell, do you expect a horse to suddenly grow horns and start acting like a reindeer? You've got to remember that Nixon was elected on the Republican ticket." Says another, "Whatever success Mudge Rose has in Washington after 1972—or 1976—isn't going to depend upon whether Nixon is in the White House. A law firm eventually reaches what you could call the critical mass —the size where it can't help but keep growing. Besides, look at all those Mudge Rose lawyers who're in the Administration. The Washington office will pick up one or two of them after 1972. What this firm is is a new force in Washington Law."

Randolph Guthrie doesn't necessarily agree, or disagree. To him, Washington is "just another office," no different from that which Mudge Rose maintains in Paris. "I keep trying to tell you," he said, "we don't give a damn about the politics of things, we're *lawyers*."

7

The Invisible Brokers: The Lawyer as Magician

Congress is the police court of Washington Law. Despite the economic stakes for themselves and clients, few attorneys are really comfortable practicing there. Raffish, raucous, fawningly deferential to second-raters who are powerful for reasons other than ability, a place where favoritism and influence outweigh common sense and the common good—Congress makes the law, but doesn't live by the law. Physically, Congress and the Supreme Court are only a few hundred feet apart, separated by an expanse of lawn and First Street NE. Morally and professionally, however, Congress and the Supreme Court are at the poles of Washington Law.

To fault the Washington Lawyer as an *individual* for what is wrong with Congress is akin to blaming a single smoker for air pollution. But some Washington Lawyers are vital in the process through which Corporate America rules the United States; they contribute to the shortcomings of the system, and hence are accountable for their share of what is wrong with it. We all pay the price for manipulation of Congress, whether it be the $100,-000 subsidy for breeders of race horses, wangled by former Senator George Smathers, or the $30 million tax windfall for business, in the form of accelerated depreciation rules, which Covington and Burling helped ease out of Congressional purview in early 1971. Washington Lawyers will argue—and many did to me—that they go to Congress as *spokesmen* for powerful corporate interests, that their actual influence derives solely from economic prestige of the client. Further, anyone, individual or corporation, may exercise his First Amendment right "to petition the government for a redress of grievances." But as one Washington Lawyer told me, "Somehow, when I catch a cab and ride down to the Senate Office Building to talk to a Senator or a committee staff director, I don't really feel like I am practicing law."

The frequent shabbiness of Congress is reflected in the unwillingness of many Washington Lawyers to register as lobbyists, even on behalf of clients they happily represent elsewhere. Clark Clifford, for instance, has masterminded some of the legislative coups of the century, including the multimillion tax break for the du Pont empire discussed in chapter 2. Under law, anyone who seeks to influence the passage or defeat of any Federal legislation must register with the Clerk of the House of Representatives and the Secretary of the Senate. He must file quarterly reports detailing the interest represented and the amount of money spent. Clifford and other lawyers avoid registering in a perfectly legal manner: they sit in their offices two miles from

Congress and tell the client what sort of legislation is needed, and exactly how he should go about obtaining it. Then they shake his hand at the door and send him a bill. Clifford is careful never to approach a Congressman face to face on behalf of a specific client. And even such an experienced legal warhorse as H. Thomas Austern, with Covington and Burling since 1931, states, "To the best of my recollection I have never talked, alone, to a Congressman or Senator about pending legislation. On the two or three occasions during the last thirty years when I was asked by a client to accompany him on such a visit, it was to state my views on some legal issue involved. Even my appearances at public Congressional hearings have been infrequent."

Charles D. Ablard, experienced in both government and private practice, considers the reluctance to register an anomaly. "The same lawyers would never consider taking the same approach to the courts and counsel the client as to how to enter a plea and then send him off to the courthouse to follow instructions," Ablard wrote in a 1970 law review article. "Yet the strange stigma that some seemingly sophisticated members of the bar attach to lobbying leads them to send a client into a forum at least as confusing to the uninitiated as the courts." Ablard's argument, however, has a major flaw: Even if Clifford won't go personally with a client, he ensures that another lawyer does. Corporations are not friendless waifs when they petition Congress for favors.

Ablard has lobbied for interests ranging from the Post Office Department, the Magazine Publishers Association, the American Society of Magazine Editors, and the U.S. Information Agency. And he argues that a combination lawyer-lobbyist is vastly more valuable on the Hill than a non-lawyer-lobbyist. "He is trained to interpret laws and provide legal analysis for his client," Ablard has written. "One who can interpret and analyze existing laws can also analyze the need for remedial legislation and the specifics for achieving it. In addition, the lawyer is trained as a skillful gatherer and interpreter of facts. And facts, properly presented and carefully analyzed, provide the rationale for most legislation, the cynics notwithstanding."

The astute lawyer-lobbyist involves himself in a bill from the time it is drafted, through the committee hearings and floor debate and final conference. As little as possible is left to chance. The lawyer plants questions with friendly members if he wants to bring out a point at hearings. He carefully rehearses his witnesses. Rodney N. Markley, Jr., Ford Motor Company's resident lawyer-lobbyist, is famed for the hot-box training he gives Ford witnesses the night before they testify. Markley puts the witness in a chair in Ford's Shoreham Hotel suite and asks him the nastiest questions conceivable for hours. Get rid of the temper before the man goes to the Senate, Markley reasons; give him the chance to think of answers to anything that can be thrown at him, and in advance.

The lawyer's work does not end with the public hearings; now is the time for him to go behind the closed doors with friendly members and staff aides. As Ablard states, "Writing the report that creates the legislative history is often the most important part of the lawyer's role, for it prepares the basis for the later interpretation of his bill by the courts and the agencies which administer it. It can also set to rest certain arguments that the committee has considered, rejected and may not wish to hear again in future deliberations on related subjects."

Under the American Bar Association's Code of Professional Responsibility, rainmaking is unethical. Disciplinary Rule 9–101 (C) provides: "A lawyer shall not state or imply that he is able to influence *improperly or upon irrelevant grounds* any tribunal, legislative body, or public official." [Emphasis added.]

Improperly or upon irrelevant grounds. So says the bar. Ah, yes, the American Bar Association. So much to say about the

Supreme Court of the United States, on the one side of First Street, so little to say about Washington Lawyers who practice in Congress, on the other. Anyway, the rule exists, and you just read it.

The Sugar Lawyers. Why do many attorneys redden and stutter when asked about their antipathy to practicing before Congress? The Sugar Lawyers. Start here. Congress is a muddy swirl of special-interest groups, but ones which seldom compete directly one with the other for largesse from the Federal treasury. Not so the Sugar Lawyers. One pile of money, many supplicants, and each with his own connections and techniques.

The sugar subsidy is one of those quiet little spigots of Federal money that contribute to our tax bills but not to our well-being. Since 1931 the Department of Agriculture has paid foreign sugar producers the difference between the world market price and the U.S. domestic price on sugar imported into the United States. The stated aim is to protect U.S. producers from cheap imports. The cost to consumers is considerable; because of the subsidy, we pay almost twice as much as necessary for sugar. In 1970, for instance, the world price was 3.8 cents per pound. Honduras, a typical producing nation, received 4 cents per pound on sales to Canada, 5 cents from the United Kingdom, 6.8 cents from the United States, which took two-thirds of its crop. The subsidy made up the difference. With 20-odd countries sharing this bonanza, the sugar subsidy bill the past decade ranged from $250 million to $350 million. Indeed, Washington Lawyers for many of these nations admitted that the U.S. subsidy was the only thing that made their crops profitable—that sales elsewhere were at a loss.

The sugar subsidy survives because of a peculiar coterie of supporters. Most prominent are Congressmen from the twenty-four states that produce sugar beets. As is the case with the rest of U.S. agriculture, large agribusiness corporations dominate sugar production. But there are enough patch-sized farms to entitle 28,000 farmers to call themselves "sugar producers," and their claimed work force of 150,000 persons—low-paid stoop labor—must be protected from "price-cutting foreign competition." Or so the story goes, anyway. Another subsidy supporter is a seven-company group of brokers which controls virtually one hundred percent of the raw sugar imported into America— the Czarnikow-Rionda Company; M. Golodetz and Company; Christman Associates; Farr, Whitlock, Dixon and Company; Cargill, Inc., and Lamborn and Company. (Cargill, Inc., is a politically ecumenical Minnesota-based corporation whose lawyers have included Mudge, Rose, Guthrie and Alexander, President Nixon's old firm, and Max M. Kampelman, longtime aide and political friend of Senator Hubert H. Humphrey.) Quotas are assigned to sugar-producing nations every three or four years via extensions and amendments of the Sugar Act. And each renewal of the Sugar Act is a signal for frenzied activity for the Washington Lawyers hired to get as much of Uncle Sam's sugar subsidy as they can for their foreign clients.

The uncrowned Sugar Kings are Arthur L. Quinn and Arthur Lee Quinn, a father-son team who are partners in the firm of Dawson, Quinn, Riddell, Taylor and Davis. They are registered as agents for Ecuador, Panama, the West Indies, and British Honduras, for which they receive a total of $88,000 a year. The younger Quinn used to be an attorney in the office of general counsel of the Agriculture Department. Representative Charles M. Teague (R., Calif.), second ranking Republican on the House Agriculture Committee, treats him on a first-name basis during hearings, even in public. ("Arthur Lee, tell me . . .") Unlike many of the Sugar Lawyers, the Quinns give a detailed account of their activities in statements filed with the Justice Department. A sampling:

- Throwing a cocktail party at the junior Quinn's home for the managing director of a Guyana sugar producer, attended by the Ambassador and officials of the State Department and the World Bank.

- Attending a luncheon for the Hawaiian Sugar Planters Association honoring the chairman of the West Indies Sugar Association, a client. There they socialized with such people as Representative Thomas G. Abernethy (D., Miss.), an Agriculture Committee member; three officials of the Agriculture Department's sugar division; and a tropical products specialist for the State Department.

- Hosting a luncheon at the International Club, a chromy but comfortable lobbyist hangout, to honor the managing director of Tate and Lyle, Ltd., a vast British firm that has sugar properties in British Honduras. Tom Murphy, who heads the Agriculture Department's sugar division, was on the guest list.

- Escorting Sir Sydney Gaine, of Brooker, McConnell, Ltd., a Guyanian producer, around official Washington, and arranging meetings with such persons as Murphy and Representative W. R. Poage (D., Tex.), Agriculture Committee chairman. After the formal office visits the Quinns arranged a formal dinner in Sir Sydney's honor at the International Club; Poage attended.

- Attending meetings at the World Bank, the Agriculture Department, and the State Department, and cocktail parties honoring such diverse persons as the Prime Minister of Jamaica and the U.S. Ambassador-designate to Barbados.

Another lawyer-lobbyist who knows his way around the House Agriculture Committee is Harold D. Cooley, who was its chairman for sixteen years until his defeat in a North Carolina

Democratic primary in 1966. A life-size full-color portrait of
Cooley looms over the committee hearing room; most of the
present staff got their jobs from him. Before the 1971 hearings
Cooley wrote to Samuel Edward Peal, the Liberian Ambassador
in Washington, to explain what he intended to do for his $10,-
000 retainer (plus $1,000 a month) as Liberia's sugar lobbyist.
"The obtaining of a sugar quota for your country will be quite
difficult, but I have reason to believe that we will be successful in
our efforts . . . I am, of course, acquainted with all of the important persons who will be involved in both the preparation and
passage of the legislation." Cooley was also confident of a personal audience with Congressman Poage, his successor as chairman. Cooley wrote Peal: "While I realize that the chairman
cannot possibly confer with all petitioners personally, I am certain that I shall have an opportunity to meet with him and to
discuss our problems."

When Cooley tugged the strings, however, nothing happened.
He requested a quota of 50,000 tons for Liberia, which had
never been covered by the program. The committee gave him
nothing. For Thailand (which paid $10,000, plus a guarantee of
$5,000 upon enactment of the bill) Cooley succeeded only in
preserving the previous quota of 18,681 tons; he had asked an
increase to 100,000 tons, citing Thailand's role in the Vietnam
war as one reason.

One Congressional staff member suggested that the committee
—and especially Poage—"bent over backwards to avoid showing any favoritism for Cooley." When chairman, Cooley preferred to deal with the sugar lobbyists in the privacy of his office,
and some of his decisions on the valuable quotas, stated charita-
bly, were highly subjective, if not outright mystifying. Douglass
Cater, in his 1964 book, *Power in Washington*, likened Cooley's
conduct with the lawyer-lobbyists to that of a king, and stated,
"It was a widely accepted belief that he was being paid off. The

whole process had the appearance of an open scandal." Suggests the Congressional aide, 'Liberia thought it was pulling a coup by hiring Cooley. Actually, I think Liberia hurt itself." Nonetheless the foreign embassies continually search for men whose past positions suggest clout. Some people who worked the sugar beat in 1971:

- Former Senator Thomas H. Kuchel, whose firm received $2,400 a month and boosted Colombia's quota from 60,880 tons to 72,650 tons. Kuchel, a California Republican, used to be minority whip in the Senate. His firm charged the Colombians $200 per hour for Kuchel's time, $100 per hour for other members.

- Sheldon Z. Kaplan, formerly a staff member of the House Foreign Affairs Committee, who got previously excluded Paraguay a 15,079-ton quota. Kaplan received a modest $500 per month.

- Thomas Hale Boggs, Jr., son of House Majority Leader Hale Boggs of Louisiana, for the Central American Sugar Council (which appears for Costa Rica, El Salvador, Guatemala, Honduras, and Nicaragua). Boggs's firm received $50,000; the 240,195-ton quota he received was virtually the same as in the old act.

- W. DeVier Pierson, who handled sugar matters for the Administration (among many other things) while a special counsel to President Johnson. Mauritius paid Pierson's firm of Sharon, Pierson and Semmes $25,000; he succeeded in getting its quota boosted from 18,681 tons to 30,000 tons.

- Former Representative Charles H. Brown (D., Mo.), now a law partner of former Senator George A. Smathers (D., Fla.), worked hard for the Fiji Islands. Representative Thomas G. Abernethy (D., Miss.), third-ranking Democrat on the Committee, gushingly welcomed "our old friend Charlie Brown" to the hearings. Brown received $2,000 a month plus expenses, and the Fiji Islands kept their previous quota of 44,719 tons.

A Washington Lawyer does minimal public work on a sugar case. The Agriculture Committee limits testimony to fifteen minutes for each country (plus whatever questions members might have, which are general and minimal). The formal statements filed with the Committee contain economic data on each country's sugar industry—statistical and factual stuff routinely available through any ministry of agriculture.

So what do the Sugar Lawyers do to command such handsome fees?

Walter S. Surrey, formerly a Marshall Plan attorney, and Monroe Karasik, a State Department legal counsel, left government in 1950 and formed a law partnership. An early client was the Dominican Republic. In 1954 the firm signed two separate agreements: one provided a flat fee of $95,000, which was reported to the Justice Department under the Foreign Agents Registration Act; the other, unreported, called for a bonus of $1 per ton "for each ton over and above the present quota of 30,000 tons up to a quota of 100,000 tons, and 50 cents per ton for every ton over and above 100,000 tons." In return, Surrey and Karasik agreed to "devote its entire energies to securing a larger U.S. import quota for Dominican sugar . . . In carrying out this responsibility our primary activity will naturally be related to working with the Senate and the House of Representatives, concentrating on the appropriate commitees in each House . . . as well as on the key Senators and Congressmen, and staffs, who will be involved in considering this legislative program." Surrey and Karasik also promised contacts with the Agriculture and State departments; the Foreign Operations Administration, the aid agency; and the executive offices of the President.

Specifically, what did the firm do for the Dominicans?

On January 28, 1956, while visiting in Ciudad Trujillo, the Dominican capital, Monroe Karasik wrote a memorandum to Jesus Maria Troncoso, head of the Dominican sugar commission. "Through channels of personal obligation," Karasik said, "we have made contact with a powerful law firm in the Senator's home state." Karasik, who did not name the Senator in the memo, continued:

> The senior member of the firm is the executive officer of the Senator's political machine. The second partner is the son of the Senator's first campaign manager; there are very close family connections between this man and the Senator. The third partner is the private confidential attorney of the Senator; he handles important confidential matters for the Senator's machine.
>
> All three propose to call upon the Senator on Monday, January 30, to engage his sympathy for the position of the Dominican Republic with respect to sugar legislation. They will represent themselves as being interested purely because of their very close ties of friendship and business with my firm. Each of the three will adopt a different approach to arouse the Senator's sympathy.
>
> They ask for a retainer fee of $2,500. In addition, they ask a fee of $5,000 if the Dominican allocation under the legislation as finally enacted is no less than that under the present House version of HR 7030 [the Sugar Act extension]. If the Dominican allocation does turn out to be less than this, but is of a size which my firm in its sole judgment considers to be a satisfactory figure, the contingent fee to be paid would be only $2,500.
>
> We believe that these lawyers can be effective in advancing the interests of the Dominican Republic and we accord-

ingly recommend that the retainer fee be paid, and the contingency fee be agreed, all as outlined above.

The Karasik memo came to light in roundabout fashion. Assassins killed the Dominican dictator Rafael Trujillo in 1961, and literally bales of material from his government's private archives passed to the Central Intelligence Agency. Some of the papers dealt with Trujillo's foreign representatives. The Dominican records also showed that on March 31, 1956, while visiting in Ciudad Trujillo, Surrey received $3,500 in Dominican currency "to cover emergency expenses in the city of Washington." In addition to $29,934 for out-of-pocket expenses during 1956, Surrey and Karasik got another $13,010.63 "for special expenses not specified," to quote a Dominican government document. The CIA gave one set of the documents to the FBI for investigation; another went to the Senate Foreign Relations Committee, which used them as the basis for an extensive inquiry into activities of foreign agents. Lawyers Karasik and Surrey were called before an executive session of the Committee on March 13, 1966, for questions about their work for the Dominicans.

Both lawyers denied remembering why the memorandum was written. They could recall neither the name of the Senator discussed, nor the law firm they used as a go-between. Senator Burton Hickenlooper listened with incredulity.

"I will say that it is unbelievable to me," Hickenlooper said. "It is difficult for me to understand that a man of your background and your experience in government and in private practice, attempting to handle important litigation and important affairs for clients, can't remember the details of a letter which has gone into so much detail and which is of such importance."

"That is correct," Karasik said.

"My disgust is complete and thorough," Hickenlooper said,

"and my contempt is utter in this case because it is beyond my belief that a man of this background and experience in writing a detailed letter of the intimate detail which this contains cannot remember a single thing about any of these people or anything of that kind."

Karasik tried to explain away the letter by saying he wrote it while in the Dominican Republic. "I think that when I went down there, I probably had a recommendation, but I am not—I think it was not a firm which I knew personally. I believe I would have characterized it differently if I had known that firm of my own knowledge."

"Is it possible," Senator Stuart Symington (D., Mo.) asked, "that the whole letter is inaccurate and you just dreamed this up in order to impress the client?"

"I don't think so, sir," replied Karasik.

Karasik wrote the memo on January 28. On February 3, the Dominicans gave him $2,500—the same amount as mentioned in the letter as a fee. Karasik admitted it was "unusual" that he received the $2,500 in cash, and again his memory failed him: He couldn't recall what he had done with the money—whether he spent it or turned it in to his law firm.

"Mr. Karasik," said Senator J. W. Fulbright (D., Ark.), "you don't really expect us to believe that, do you?"

"Yes, I do," said Karasik.

"I will disabuse your mind," said Hickenlooper. "I don't believe it."

Three months later a former partner of Surrey and Karasik offered a "clarification." Samuel Efron had resigned from the firm in 1956 to practice in New York. He gave the Committee the following story:

In early 1956 he contacted Bernard M. Fagelson, a partner in an Alexandria, Virginia, law firm with supposed entree to Senator Harry F. Byrd, Sr. (D., Va.), now deceased. Efron asked

Fagelson if his firm would help present the Dominican case to Byrd before the Senate Finance Committee (of which he was chairman) considered the sugar quotas. Fagelson agreed to "think about" the matter, whereupon Efron sent a skeletonized account of the contact to Karasik, who was then in Ciudad Trujillo. A few days later Fagelson declined, and the matter ended. Efron said he never told Karasik the identity of the firm he had approached.

The committee heard Efron with skepticism. "What could this firm do that your firm couldn't do?" Fulbright asked. What was needed, Efron replied, "was a firm which practiced in the jurisdiction of the chairman of the Committee, who could speak to the staff on better terms than obviously we can."

"So that in essence, then," Fulbright said, "Mr. Karasik specifically asked that you get a firm in Virginia close to Senator Byrd, is that correct?"

"That is right, sir," Efron said. He said he met Fagelson at a party, casually mentioned the Dominican case, and said he needed "access on a friendly basis with people in the Senate." Fagelson introduced him to Byrd's administrative assistant. Efron said he gave the aide background information. And he also termed Karasik's memorandum "a considerable exaggeration of any information with which I was familiar."

Lawyer Fagelson, after reading the memo, called it "absurd and ridiculous." He said that "by no stretch of the imagination could we be considered a 'powerful law firm,'" as Karasik described it. He ticked off the exaggerations: that his "personal obligation" to Efron consisted of casual social meetings; that his senior partner had "never been an executive in the Senator's organization"; that his father had "never managed the Senator's campaign," although he worked for him in a local election in 1924; that no one in the firm was Byrd's "private confidential secretary." Fagelson was exasperated and embarrassed. "I am not trying to be funny," he testified. "We are not even a poor man's description of this law firm." To Efron, the memo was a result of a chain of exaggerations: "I suppose that Mr. Fagelson . . . as is normal with lawyers, may have puffed a bit. I may have puffed a bit to Mr. Karasik; he may have puffed a bit to Troncoso [the Dominican sugar chief]; and Troncoso may have puffed a bit to his government."

"What good does Hill experience do for a Washington Lawyer? Well, let me give you one minor example. John Yingling used to be on the staff of the Senate Banking Committee. When he went into practice he got some good banking clients right away—the First National City Bank of New York, and Continental Illinois of Chicago, to name a couple.

"Yingling is a friendly fellow, and damned smart, and Congressmen respect him. He can walk into a House Banking Committee meeting and catch a member's eye, and give a little nod, and in a few minutes the member will excuse himself and go outside. You'll see him huddled in the hall with Yingling, listening.

"What members? Tom Ashley, of Ohio, and Robert Stephens, of Georgia. One a Northern pseudo-liberal, the other a Southern conservative. It doesn't make any difference to Yingling—he can play them all."

The speaker was a House committee counsel who doesn't particularly like Washington Lawyers—especially those who are former members or employees of Congress. "If you go to the Hill with the idea you are eventually going to work for industry and make a hundred grand a year," he said, "you are going to be nice to industry people when you deal with them. If not, you are going to do your job. The choice is that simple.

"The corporate lawyer goes around with the superior attitude that 'I made it in the private world—this other guy is just a bureaucrat, a government hack who hangs onto some piddling little Congressional job.'

"But it's a self-generating machine. The big firms, by their very nature, keep moving young people through government. And they and the industry groups really scout heavy for someone who knows his way around Congress."

Someone like George Smathers, a smashingly handsome Floridian who double-dated with John F. Kennedy when both men were gay-blade Senatorial bachelors, and who ensured that the entire town knew he dined frequently at the White House. Smathers was popular in Florida; he was guaranteed automatic reelection for as long as he cared to stay in the Senate. But in 1962 Smathers appraised the advantages of remaining in the Senate or becoming a full-time Washington Lawyer.

Even after his election, Smathers had retained ties with the Miami firm of Smathers, Thompson, Maxwell and Smathers, and some of his Senate work had benefited clients. As a member of the Senate Commerce Committee, Smathers played a key role in writing the Transportation Act of 1958, which gave railroads broad authority to drop unprofitable passenger trains and to increase certain categories of freight rates without obtaining permission of the Interstate Commerce Commission. The act extended government guarantees to some private bank loans made to railroads. One beneficiary of the act was the Seaboard Coast Line Railroad, which paid the Smathers firm a total of $97,100 the two years the legislation was before Congress. Smathers also put an amendment in the 1961 tax bill removing the ten percent excise tax from railroad, airline, and bus tickets, at a revenue cost of $300 million. Again, a boost for the Seaboard line, and also for Pan American World Airways, another client. Smathers periodically raised hell with the State Department when it helped obtain U.S. landing rights for foreign airlines; Pan Am didn't want the competition. And in 1960

Smathers made a floor speech lauding the sordid dictatorship of "President" Rafael Trujillo of the Dominican Republic. "We are always a little naive in thinking that because we have democracy in our own country," Smathers said, "and because of our love for humanity, people in other lands should have exactly the same type of government we have." What Smathers didn't mention in his speech was that his law firm represented the Dominican Republic steamship line. (When Trujillo was killed the next year, the new regime promptly fired the firm.)

There was much, much more. In 1968 the Treasury Department proposed removing a quirk in tax regulations which permitted appreciations in convertible stock to be taxed at capital gains rates, rather than at the higher rate applicable to dividends from common stock. The change threatened an ambitious refinancing plan then being developed by Winn-Dixie Stores, Inc., one of the South's largest grocery chains. As a member of the Senate Finance Committee, Smathers tried to kill the proposal; he failed, but he did manage to make the effective date January 10, 1969. Winn-Dixie had pushed through its refinancing plan only two weeks earlier—thereby getting in under the deadline, and saving its shareholders millions of dollars. What was not generally known at the time was that Smathers was the secret owner of two Winn-Dixie stores, purchased with little cash investment under terms which brought him an estimated half-million-dollar profit in a decade. And when Winn-Dixie put him on its board after he left the Senate, Smathers filed papers with the SEC listing ownership of Winn-Dixie stock valued at $400,000, much of it the convertible type which would have been affected by the Treasury regulation change he had opposed. *Newsday*, which explored this deal at length, quotes Winn-Dixie board chairman James Davis, "Smathers was the best goddamn senator we ever had here."

Another Florida company which Smathers aided while in the

Senate was Aerodex, Inc., of Miami, one of the nation's 100 largest defense contractors. Aerodex got in trouble with the Pentagon because of what the Air Force contended was "poor quality" work on an engine-overhauling contract. Smathers and other Congressmen came to Aerodex's defense, and managed to keep it from being put on a Pentagon blacklist. Two months after Smathers left the Senate, he joined Aerodex as a director. He was also permitted—according to SEC records—to purchase 20,000 shares of its stock for $1, although the market price was $21.75 a share. The difference: $435,000 of stock for $20,000. (Smathers quit the Aerodex board and sold back the stock for $1 in mid-1971, when a *Newsday* investigative team began looking into the relationship.)

Smathers said publicly as early as 1966 he intended to leave the Senate after his second term expired, in 1968. "I'm going to be a Clark Clifford," he said in 1966. "That's the life for me." And after only a few months of private practice he told a Miami reporter: "I've found the pastures outside are a lot greener than I had presumed. A fellow with my background can make more money in thirty days out here than he can in fifteen years as a Senator." But as a lawyer-lobbyist, he said, "you don't sneak around, playing the footpads. You know who can be helpful and you talk with them right out in the middle of Pennsylvania Avenue if that is convenient."

Smathers was certainly public in his representation of an outfit called "The American Horse Council, Inc.," formed to block passage of tax reform legislation which would close loopholes benefiting gentlemen farmers who purchased horses and orchards for tax purposes. The saving works two ways. Conventional businessmen deduct their expenses after sales, and pay taxes on the profits. Farmers, however, deduct the expenses as they occur, and are permitted to treat many sales—such as livestock—as capital gains, taxable at a lower rate than ordinary income. A person with a large nonfarm income can buy a horse or a grove of lemon trees, deduct their costs from his regular income to offset taxes, and then sell for a profit taxable as capital gains. Senator Lee Metcalf (D., Mont.) launched a campaign against the gimmick in 1968, asserting that doctors, movie stars and other persons with large personal incomes (including Governor Ronald Reagan of California) were abusing a plan originally designed to help the conventional, working farmer. Enter The American Horse Council, Inc., George A. Smathers, counsel, and formed by Ogden Phipps, chairman of the New York Jockey Club. The Council arranged audiences with various Congressional and Administration higher-ups, and then went right to the top. The Council's Washington newsletter for June-July 1969 featured a large front-page photograph taken in the Oval Room of the White House. Pictured are President Nixon, Smathers, Governor Louie B. Nunn of Kentucky; Ogden Phipps, the Council chairman; and Thruston B. Morton, former Republican national chairman. An accompanying story told of "two days of very fruitful meetings in Washington" and claimed "the President evidenced considerable interest in equine industry problems during the forty-minute meeting." The Administration changed its position and opposed the Metcalf amendment; ultimately the horsemen got what they wanted, and the loophole was left intact.

Another major Smathers client has been the Association of American Railroads, the industry's major trade and lobbying group. Because of Smathers' past Senatorial experience, he could be expected to help the railroads develop a coherent policy for solving the nation's transportation problems. His record, however, is of an entirely different nature. "My biggest disappointment with the AAR," says a Congressional aide involved in transportation matters, "is that it never tried to get legislation dealing with the basic problems afflicting the railroad industry.

The attitude from the late 1950s through the 1960s was that all they needed from government was tax breaks and permission to cut back on passenger service. The industry, which is to say, the AAR, never stopped to think about how it could save itself through any other means than gradual dismemberment. And I'll have to give Smathers a lot of the blame. Let me say it another way. The railroads were so screwed up that they needed much more than tax write-offs. But the AAR didn't concern itself with anything else."

The AAR's preoccupation with Federal doles and favors reached an apogee in 1971 with its intensive (and successful) campaign to have the government take over all rail passenger service, via a quasi-public corporation named Amtrak. The railroads also wanted appropriations to overcome past operating deficiencies, tax credits and exemptions, rapid tax write-offs on equipment, loan guarantees, low-interest government loans, and authority for automatic rate increases. The AAR created a front group entitled "America's Sound Transportation Review Organization." The cumbersome title produced the desired acronym—ASTRO—to fit the railroad's figurehead spokesman, Wally Schirra, the former astronaut. Smathers headed ASTRO and directed a nationwide network of railroad public relations men and legislative lobbyists intended to gain grassroots support for the bail-out. ASTRO internal documents list some of the other goals the railroads will be pursuing at the state and national level over the next few years, under Smathers's direction:

- "The Federal government should exempt rail transportation from state and local property taxation and reimburse the states for the revenue loss."

- "As a long-range program to assure an adequate supply of general purpose cars, the Congress should create a federally chartered non-profit corporation to acquire cars under government guaranteed loans."

■■ "The Congress should require that the states devote 10 percent of Federal highway trust funds to grade crossing projects."

Critics such as Senator Lee Metcalf (D., Mont.) suggest that since the Federal government is being called upon to subsidize the railroads with billions of dollars of loan guarantees, tax breaks, and other favors, Congress should take the next logical step and nationalize them outright. He estimated that ASTRO's package could cost taxpayers $36 billion during the 1970s—half again as much as the $21 billion which the National Association of Railroad Passengers, a consumer lobby group, estimates as the fair market value for existing railroads. (AAR's figure is $60 billion.) But Smathers and his railroad clients don't want nationalization: All they ask is that the government underwrite rail operations so that dividends can continue to flow to shareholders. And the fact that Smathers and the railroads succeeded in the first phase of the campaign—drastic curtailment of passenger service—illustrates the value of having a dashing former Senator as a Washington Lawyer.

Smathers is not the only Senator who chose to remain in Washington after leaving office. California Republican Thomas H. Kuchel, who served in the Senate from 1952 until his defeat in 1968, became the Washington representative of the Beverly Hills firm of Wyman, Bautzer, Finell, Rothman and Kuchel. The firm is headed by former Democratic national committeeman Eugene Wyman. Kuchel has done work for such diverse clients as the Association of Motion Picture and Television Producers; the City of Palm Springs, California; and a copyright law revision committee. And like many other former officeholders, Kuchel finds it hard to draw a line between politics and law. In September 1970, for instance, he endorsed the reelection candidacy of Governor Ronald Reagan, a longtime political adversary. Jess Unruh, the Democratic candidate, promptly charged,

"I suspect that the White House political arm-twisting bureau went to work on him [Kuchel]. The word went out that he had better support Ronald Reagan and Senator George Murphy—or else. After all, his law firm has some very big clients who do business with the government."

Earle C. Clements, former Democratic Senator from Kentucky, is a registered lobbyist for the Tobacco Institute, an industry lobby group, and four tobacco corporations: Brown & Williamson, Liggett & Myers, Inc., R. J. Reynolds, and Philip Morris. Working closely with him at the Tobacco Institute is Howard R. Kornegay, a North Carolina Democrat who was a member of the House Interstate and Foreign Commerce Committee during his four terms in Congress. Kornegay went on the tobacco lobby payroll to help emasculate legislation requiring strong health warnings on cigarette packages; he succeeded. Former Representative Walter E. Rogers (D., Tex.) lobbies for the Independent Natural Gas Association of America. Prentiss M. Brown, who was in the House and Senate as a Michigan Democrat from 1933 to 1946, stayed in town as a utility lawyer-lobbyist; his most active client is the General Public Utilities Corp. And so the list goes.

How effective are ex-Congressmen as lobbyists? Their value is grossly overestimated, in many opinions. "Give me a good staff man anytime," says an official of the Air Transport Association; "effective lobbying means that you have to immerse yourself in the details of legislation, the real dull routine. No Congressman ever did that while in office, because he didn't have the time. Also, Congressmen have little working contact with the bureaucracy, the agencies. A lobbyist can't just stay on the Hill when he is after legislation, he must also work with the people who will be enforcing the legislation. I've yet to run across a Senator or a Representative who had that sort of relationship with, say, the CAB or the FTC."

A former Senator who still lives in Washington, but in retirement, notes, "Lots of people wanted to rent my name, even after I was beaten. One man told me, 'We'll make you resident partner for our Washington office, and give you a couple of young lawyers to help you.' I asked him, 'But exactly what do you want from me? I haven't practiced law for more than twenty-five years.' He said, 'Oh, your advice, your knowledge.' Like hell he did. He wanted me to work my old liberal friends in the Senate. I declined. I don't want to practice that kind of law."

"You hear a lot about the 'old-school-tie' friendships in Congress," says the administrative assistant to a Western Senator, "but once a man is on the outside, the members don't feel quite the same about him. Why? Oh, I can see a couple of reasons. Politicians don't like being around losers. They see a guy who has been beaten, and it makes them uncomfortable. My boss will deliberately dodge ——, for instance, even though they served in the House together. And the second thing is that the member always feels the former member is trying to trade upon a past friendship—that if he hadn't been in Congress, he wouldn't be here.

"The only man who can really walk in here and find the door open is Paul Douglas [former Democratic Senator from Illinois]. Paul doesn't practice much, but he is careful who he represents. We know it, and anyone lucky enough to hire him automatically gets credibility. Only one time did he show up with someone who was . . . well, not really Paul's type. And Paul was honest about it. 'Look,' he said, 'this company wants so-and-so, and I'm not sure they have too good a case. But they are good people and I think they deserve a hearing.' They got that, but nothing else."

William L. Carey, SEC chairman from 1961 to 1963, tells a story that illustrates how access may make effective lawyer-lobbyists out of former Congressional aides. In 1963 Carey

worked hard for an amendment to the Securities and Exchange
Act, tightening reporting requirements for insurance companies.
The insurance industry had fought the legislation for years, but
now it seemed on the brink of passage. Carey negotiated an
apparently satisfactory compromise with Senator Willis Robert-
son (D., Va.), then chairman of the Senate Banking and
Currency Committee, which had jurisdiction over the bill. For
safety's sake, Carey decided to make one last round of Committee members, particularly one Senator who opposed the insurance
portion of the bill.

"Since the committee was meeting at ten o'clock," Carey said,
"I arranged to be in his office at eight-thirty that morning, but
when I arrived I found he had driven down with his former
administrative assistant, who was then a leading counsel of the
insurance industry. I said I might as well give up, but would like
a moment of his attention. I was received courteously, although
it was clear that I could not change the views which the Senator
had reached." (The insurance industry lost in the Senate, the
former aide's efforts notwithstanding.)

Doing a good job practicing before Congress can mean *avoiding* Congress. John H. Yingling, the bank lawyer-lobbyist we
met earlier, knows when to fight and when to sidestep. When
possible, he tries to keep his clients out of range of the irascible
Representative Wright Patman (D., Tex.), chairman of the
House Banking and Currency Committee. Patman is congeni-
tally hostile to bankers, and Yingling knows little can be gained
by serving up witnesses for him to torment with needling questions. Patman loves to preface "questions" with rambling de-
nunciatory obiter dicta on the evils of the financial community;
even if a banker witness has the right answer, and proves that
the premise of Patman's query is wrong, the damage is done—
immediately, to the banker's ego and temper; the next day, in
the newspaper headlines.

In 1969 the First National City Bank of New York purchased an insurance company and announced its intention of creating a bank holding company. Patman asked board chairman George Moore to explain the plan at public hearings, for he was writing holding-company legislation. Moore declined, pleading, among other things, lack of time. Soon thereafter, however, Yingling guided Moore on a tour of Washington newspaper offices and bureaus of leading national publications. Moore outlined the holding-company concept to business writers of such publications as *The Washington Post, The Evening Star, The New York Times, The Wall Street Journal,* and *Business Week.* Moore and Yingling didn't seek spot publicity. Their aim was to make friends with the reporters and writers who would be handling the holding-company story as the bill went through Patman's Committee and Congress. At their best, Congressional hearings are notoriously one-sided. No single day's proceeding gives both sides a chance to develop their cases. Both the press and Committee members slacken interest after the first few days, and especially when the subject matter is as technically arid as the banking code. Smart Washington Lawyers also realize the average Congressman relies upon the press for information on bills outside his immediate sphere of interest. Transcripts of committee hearings on bills, even major ones, often are not even printed until long after the measures have been voted upon. Hence Yingling's interest in ensuring that reporters had enough background to listen intelligently to anti-bank witnesses. A Patman Committee staff member credits Yingling with getting "an extraordinarily fair press" for the banking industry's position.

"If you really want to do a good job with Congressmen," says another House veteran, "find something that will make a Congressman look good. It's the ego factor. Congressmen, as politicians—hell, as humans—have this inner need to demonstrate they can accomplish. The smart Washington Lawyer, the man who wants to build a relationship that will last, finds some friendly guy and gives him a list of easy targets." Some examples? "Huh-uh," the man said. "My boss likes to trade credit for some things that originated with lawyers and trade groups. We all have our little secrets."

Jerry S. Cohen, longtime chief counsel and staff director of the Senate Antitrust and Monopoly subcommittee and now in private practice, agrees; indeed, he told me, "The secret to Clark Clifford's success is his ability to convince a Senator that 'It's to your advantage to do it this way'—which is to say, Clifford's way."* Cohen argues that Clifford and some other name Washington Lawyers are successful not because of influence, "but because they know how to play their act better than other people —they cannot convince a Senator if he disagrees with them." As a politician whose guiding instinct is survival, a Senator learns to rely upon advisers who "are not going to get him into trouble," to use Cohen's words. A Washington Lawyer who sells a Senator on a course of action that backfires can forget any future favors.

Max M. Kampelman, who was legislative counsel to Senator Hubert H. Humphrey (D., Minn.) from 1949 to 1955, and who continues as an intimate friend and political adviser, notes that "keeping a Senator out of trouble" is also a responsibility of persons connected with him in the public mind. Soon after going into private practice, Kampelman says, he was approached by three separate prospective clients: a trade association interested in getting legislation to tax farm cooperatives; a representative of Trujillo, the Dominican dictator; and a mining industry representative wanting an extension of the depletion allowance. Each of the prospects, it developed, was more interested in Humphrey than in Kampelman; the Dominican, for instance,

---

* Almost everyone who watches Clark Clifford picks out the "secret" of his success. The cited reasons were seldom the same one. That they were not, I ultimately concluded, is itself Clifford's secret.

wanted Kampelman to persuade Humphrey to visit the country as a guest and see for himself how the charges of tyrannical dictatorship were "exaggerated and even irrelevant." Kampelman declined all three approaches.

In a 1970 article in the *George Washington Law Review* Jerry Cohen called the Washington Lawyer a "contrived legend," and said his work in the Senate convinced him that the "alleged 'influence' on the legislative process of the 'select few' is mostly a myth." When influence is exerted, Cohen said, it comes from a powerful corporate client—not from the Washington Lawyer representing him. And other factors negate the importance of any single lawyer or law firm. As Cohen wrote:

Each Senator is a bundle of principles, areas of concern, viewpoints, fields of expertise and publicly stated positions. Based on past positions, votes and public utterances, he has projected an image which he values. That image is more important to him than the arguments of any and all Washington lawyers urging an inconsistent position. The head of the antitrust subcommittee [Senator Phillip Hart, when Cohen worked there] seldom can be expected to support exemptions from the antitrust laws. A free trader generally will not support greater import restrictions. On the other hand, little influence is needed to convince an oil-state Senator that oil quotas make good sense or a Western state Senator that water conservation legislation should be supported. These are facts of political life.

An example of the latter point: In the late 1960s Lloyd Cutler, counsel for the Automobile Manufacturers Association, wanted legislation exempting car makers from antitrust penalties if they met to discuss an industry-wide timetable for installing safety devices. Senator Hart is generally friendly to the auto

industry, for it dominates his state. But he is also a strong advocate of strict antitrust enforcement, so he refused Cutler's client's
request. Several weeks later, the bill appeared under spon-
sorship of Senator Russell Long (D., La.). In the same vein,
Senator Sam Ervin (D., N.C.) is noted among colleagues for
meticulously studying constituent mail before voting on any
major issue; if Carolinians oppose it, lawyer-lobbyists are wasting their time with him. But Senator John McClellan (D., Ark.)
reflexively favors any legislation benefiting the petroleum industry, and he is unfailingly hospitable to its representatives when
they want bills introduced or other errands performed.

On October 29, 1833, Senator Daniel Webster, that thunder-
ing tower of New England Puritanism, wrote a snippish letter to
Nicholas Biddle, the president of the Bank of the United States.
Webster had represented the bank as a lawyer before going to
Washington, and he had continued to pass along intelligence on
Federal activities concerning it. But now Webster was ag-
grieved. "Since I have arrived here," Webster wrote, "I have had
an application to be concerned, professionally, against the bank,
which I have declined, of course, although I believe my retainer
has not been renewed, or *refreshed* as usual. If it be wished that
my relation to the bank should be continued, it may be well to
send me the usual retainers."

To Webster's credit, he made no secret of his dual status as
legislator and bank lawyer, because he publicly (and successfully) represented the bank in forty-one cases argued before the
United States Supreme Court. But even full disclosure did not
satisfy the conscience of a contemporary, Representative John
Quincy Adams. In 1845 Adams was offered $5,000 to plead a
case in the Supreme Court. He declined, and wrote in his diary:
"It occurs to me that this double capacity of a counsellor in
courts of law and a member of a legislative body affords oppor-

tunity and temptation for contingent fees of very questionable moral purity. Of one such transaction I had knowledge last winter, which in my mind was tainted with the vilest corruption; and I have heard of others, which I shall not specify, because they are familiarly spoken of as in no wise exceptionable . . ."

Unfortunately for the cause of national ethics, Webster, not Adams, set the moral standard that Congress followed for the next 130-odd years. The era of the lawyer-Congressman apparently is ending, because of stringent new bar rules. But that it continued as long as it did warrants a brief look at an aberration of Washington Law. The conflict of interest in a Congressman's handling legislation benefiting private law clients is so gross, so obvious—*so basic*—it can be detected by a schoolboy. But not by every Congressman. Senator Joseph Weldon Bailey, a turn-of-the-century Texas Populist, when caught taking $225,000 in fees from an oilman, declared, "If my constituents want a man who is willing to go to the poorhouse in his old age in order to stay in the Senate during his middle age, they will have to find another Senator. I intend to make every dollar that I can honestly make, without neglecting or interfering with my public duty, and there is no other man in this country who would not do the same, if he has sense enough to keep a churchyard." Again: Senator John W. Bricker (R., Ohio) represented a natural gas company that lost an intricate pipeline case in the Supreme Court. Nonplused, Bricker pushed special legislation reversing the decision through the Senate Commerce Committee, of which he was chairman, without the formality of hearings. To the benefit of another client, the Pennsylvania Railroad, Brinker managed to stall the authorizing legislation for the St. Lawrence Seaway in the Commerce Committee for seven years, during which time the railroad paid Bricker's law firm $148,-000. (Bricker paid into the firm his entire Senate salary of $12,500 a year, and received $24,000.) When someone once asked Bricker about the ethics of these situations, he replied "Everyone knows I'm honest, so what's wrong with my being chairman of the Committee and receiving money from the law firm?" Besides, he said, he did no work directly for the railroad

Senator Everett Dirksen, while Republican leader of the Senate, continued close ties with the law firm of Davis, Morgan, and Witherell, in downstate Peoria, Ill. The town is not exactly a corporate crossroads, but an astounding number of national companies found their way to Ev's firm: Panhandle Eastern Pipe Line, Pabst Brewing, International Paper, Keystone Steel & Wire, National Lock, International Harvester, and scores of others—from the oil, gas, timber, mining, utilities, banking, insurance, and savings and loan industries. Dirksen consistently espoused their causes in the United States Senate. And Dirksen consistently refused to discuss his law practice, or to support limitations on outside activities of Congressmen, or public disclosure of outside income. "I've been on the platform before my constituents since 1926," he boomed in one Senate speech. "Any man, any citizen, could stand up and say, 'Dirksen, what do you own?' if he wanted to know, and he would have received an answer. But I am not going to see it done by compulsion."

Even as Congress discreetly averted its eyes from such goings-on, however, a firecracker string of scandals put the question before the public eyes repeatedly during the 1960s. In 1963 Representative Thomas F. Johnson (D., Md.) was convicted of taking money to help savings and loan firms which were under indictment for mail fraud. Johnson used his law practice as a conduit for the payments. He went to jail. So, too, did Robert G. (Bobby) Baker, secretary to the Democratic majority in the Senate, who used his law office to collect both campaign funds and other payments from lobbyists. Some of these payments were purportedly made for future legal services that Baker never performed. The voters disciplined two Senators: Edward V.

Long (D., Mo.), who received at least $48,000 in "referral fees" from a Teamsters Union lawyer, Morris Shenker, at the same time his subcommittee was conducting wiretap investigations potentially beneficial to imprisoned Teamsters president James R. Hoffa; and Thomas J. Dodd (D., Conn.), who took both legal and finder's fees from Connecticut insurance companies while leading a desultory probe of the insurance industry. Both men were defeated in their next reelection attempts. Senator Sam Ervin (D., N.C.) represented the Darrington Company, a North Carolina textile firm, in the appeal of a National Labor Relations Board ruling to the Supreme Court. He lost, and subsequently investigated NLRB procedures in hearings before his judiciary subcommittee on separation of powers.

The merits of any of these cases notwithstanding, their public notoriety supports the charge by a special committee on Congressional ethics of the Association of the Bar of the City of New York that "law practice has demonstrated a special potential for actual and alleged Congressional improprieties, and that law practices have played a disproportionate role in the history of Congressional scandals." The veteran political writer Fletcher Knebel stated the case with journalistic precision: "The legislator who accepts a $20,000 bribe for pressing a special-interest bill faces a prison term if caught, but the legislator who receives a $20,000 fee from a company whose interests he champions in the legislature faces no penalty. He is doing what comes naturally in American politics."

The New York Bar committee recommended that Congress adopt rules requiring that (1) Senators "totally refrain from any form of law practice" after election to their first full term, and Representatives their third term; (2) a Congressman's law partners not accept any cases which he could not accept; and (3) Congressmen not practice before Federal agencies or courts. Congress ignored the recommendations. After the Dodd affair, both houses established an ethics committee, but nothing was done to curb members' outside activities, nor to require any meaningful financial disclosure. Congress still operates under the quaint assumption that it is a gentlemen's club, and gentlemen, after all, can be trusted to do the proper thing. If citizens don't want their Congressman to practice law, they can tell him so, at the polls. The ballot box, unfortunately, doesn't give a citizen much recourse. Any Congressman with brains enough to run for office can fuzz up details of his practice; hence the public isn't sure exactly what, if anything, he is doing on the side. Longevity, one-party domination, and machine rule guarantee automatic reelection for perhaps sixty percent of the incumbents in any Congressional race; as the late Joe Pool (D., Tex.) used to jest, "The only way to beat an incumbent Southern Democrat is for him to be caught in bed with a live man or a dead woman."

Nonetheless the death knell has sounded for most Congressional law practices. In August 1969 the American Bar Association House of Delegates passed a new Code of Professional Responsibility which said, in part:

> A lawyer who assumes a judicial, legislative, or public executive or administrative post or office shall not permit his name to remain in the name of a law firm or to be used in professional notices of the firm during any significant period in which he is not actively and regularly practicing law as a member of the firm, and during such period other members of the firm shall not use his name in the firm name or in professional notices of the firm.

Standing alone, the ABA code is meaningless; as San Francisco attorney Melvin Belli has said, the ABA has less practical control over lawyers than does the Book-of-the-Month Club. The ABA has no authority or machinery to enforce codes of ethics on a national basis. But forty-one of fifty state bar groups did choose to include the section—Disciplinary Rule 102 (B)— in their codes of ethics. On the state level, bar codes are adopted by the Supreme Court, and any lawyer who practices is subject to them. Hence the new rule caused literally dozens of Congressmen-lawyers to withdraw from their firms during the two years after its enactment.

But not everyone. Robert Walters, investigative reporter for the Washington *Evening Star*, during a survey of Congress in April 1971, discovered two pockets of resistance: in Florida, where one Senator and five of twelve House members continued their affiliation with law firms, and in New York, with one Senator* and ten of forty-one Representatives continuing. Among them was Representative Emanuel Celler (D., N.Y.), the dean of the New York delegation and the chairman of the House Judiciary Committee. Celler is famed for his so-called "double door" practice. One of the glass doors leading to Celler's law office in Manhattan bears the legend "Weisman, Celler, Allan, Spett & Sheinberg"; the other door, "Weisman, Allan, Spett & Sheinberg." The duality, however, enables the "non-Celler" firm to accept Federal cases with which the Congressman prefers not

---

* The Senator, Jacob K. Javits, resigned from his firm of Javits, Trubin, Sillcocks, Edelman and Purcell five months later, saying "the practice of law and being a Senator, considering the enormous range of issues, has become increasingly difficult." Javits said the firm had a policy of not representing clients in matters involving the Federal government, to avoid any appearance of conflict of interest. In June 1971 a team of law students working under Ralph Nader charged, in a study of the First National City Bank of New York, that the bank made political contributions "in disguise" by retaining the Javits firm for real-estate transactions. Javits told *The New York Times* the suggestion that the legal fees represented political contributions was "deplorable, reckless, careless and entirely untrue."

to be associated. Celler has said repeatedly he does not share the income from the "non-Celler" firm, and that he considers his practice to be "active and regular" within the meaning of the ABA code. "In any event," he says, "my constituents must be the ultimate judges to the quality and character of my performance as a public official."

8

The Corridors of Congress:
Looking Down on Capitol Hill

"You are looking," the Washington Lawyer told me, "at one of the dumbest sons of bitches in Western civilization." He nodded across the Falstaff Room of the Sheraton-Carlton Hotel to a middle-aged man who smiled politely and then very deliberately returned his attention to another man at the table. But during the next half-hour I saw him glance back at our table, as if the Washington Lawyer was an unpleasant memory.

"This fellow," the Washington Lawyer was saying to me, with three-martini candor, "is in the —— business in Maryland. Three, four years ago, he came to me, on recommendation of a friend of mine in Baltimore, and said he needed some help in a bad way. He had been doing some odd-ball discounting to some customers and not to others, and the way he admitted it to me, it was a clear-cut violation of the Robinson-Patman act, because it was as discriminatory as hell. Apparently one of the unfavored customers had complained to his lawyer, who in turn had complained to the Federal Trade Commission. Trouble was coming; it was just a matter of time.

"Now, in a situation like this, the documents should tell the whole story, and I don't see any reason why a man should help the Federal government build a gallows for himself. At the same time, the bar rules are pretty simple: If I advise him to go burn everything, I can be disbarred for interfering with the processes of justice.

"So I take another route. I tell him just what I told you— without all his sales records, the FTC will have a hell of a time making a case. Oh, they could, but only by backtracking to customers. But I know the FTC is so short-handed they won't do that except in a major case. 'Do you *still* have any documents around that could hurt you?' I asked him. 'Some of this stuff must be getting pretty old, and most people turn over their records fairly *fast*.'

" 'Oh, no,' he said, 'I've got everything. My bookkeeper is meticulous.'

"I tried again. 'You know,' I said, 'there's no law that says how long you've got to keep stuff, so long as you have enough to substantiate your tax records. That must be quite a storage problem, maintaining all those old outdated files.'

"God, he didn't even blink. 'Oh, we have plenty of space,' he said. 'We just put it in crates and put it in the back of the warehouse. It's all right there.'

"I gave up. He was so damned dense he wasn't about to tumble to what I was saying and I didn't dare take it a step further and tell him to go home and have himself one hell of a big bonfire. I kind of like being a lawyer, you know. Just as I feared, the FTC subpoenaed enough to make a case, and it cost the poor bastard one hell of a lot of time and trouble. 'But why didn't you just *tell* me I should have cleaned out the files?' he kept asking me. I finally unloaded on him and gave him an informative little talk.

"He's still mad at me. He haggled over the bill, and he cussed me all over Washington and Baltimore. I don't give a damn, though; I still have my law license."

This chapter concerns some phases of Washington Law that aren't taught at the Harvard, Yale, or Nebraska law schools. Strategy, shortcuts, shrewdness—call it what you may, legal gamesmanship is an integral part of building and holding a Washington practice. Some Washington Lawyers gripe a lot about their out-of-Washington reputations as hustlers and fixers, as attorneys who win through wire-pulling, not the law. They'll gripe about this for half an hour, and then begin giving examples of what they do—examples that give the appearance, if not the reality, of . . . well, of *wire-pulling*. The myth of the Washington Lawyer is both self-created and self-nourished, and deep under the *pro forma* denials one gets the idea most lawyers wouldn't have it any different at all. Law is one profession where you are acclaimed because you can make the routine look miraculous; if the client doesn't know any better, that's his expense. Showmanship is essential. Listen to an antitrust specialist:

"A businessman from Keokuk will come into the office with the FTC breathing down his neck and ask for help. I must sympathize with him. At the proper time, I'll sigh and say, 'Well, it will take some effort, but I think I can make them hold off for a year, or possibly two, before any final action is taken.'

"I'll then call someone at the FTC staff level with whom I deal every week and say, 'Charlie, this is Joe. I'm going to be handling this Acme case, and there's a lot of work to be done.' Charlie knows me, and he knows that I am a serious lawyer, and he takes off the pressure. We have a reasonable time to prepare an answer and to go through the preliminary maneuvering. Sure enough, the year slips by, or even two years, and the client is happy. This gives him time to clean up the practices the FTC was after in the first place, and he escapes with a consent decree that forbids him to do what he has stopped doing. He goes to his state manufacturers association convention and tells all his business buddies about what a hot-shot law firm we are, and how we can 'handle those goddamned bureaucrats,' and there is a tremendous—and profitable—multiplier effect.

"Now there is one danger: when you ask a regulatory agency for a delay of this sort, you'd better not come up with sand when the day of reckoning arrives. Do this a couple of times, and you lose your credibility, and you'll have the devil's own time with the bureaucracy, for they don't like to be hoodwinked."

Because it sounds nice to say so, Washington Lawyers talk frequently and fervently about how they like to resolve cases in a hurry. Less cost to the client, administrative efficiency for government, prompt resolution of public-policy questions . . .

Lawyers say these things so often they begin to take them seriously—but not enough so, of course, to practice them. In some cases, delay is as important as victory. Profits continue while a proceeding drags. So does the lawyer's bill. When they become old and mellow, lawyers will even brag in public about how they've led the government in circles. Bruce Bromley was an active antitrust attorney in Washington and New York before and after serving on the New York Court of Appeals bench. He was astoundingly candid in a 1958 talk to a conference at Stanford Law School: "I was born, I think, to be a procrastinator," Bromley said. "I quickly realized in my early days at the bar that I could take the simplest antitrust case that [the Justice Depart-

ment] could think of and protract it for the defense almost to
infinity." In one of his early cases Bromley defended an antitrust
action against Famous Players–Lasky Corporation, a theatrical
and movie booking company, for block sales of motion pictures.
Famous Players said to exhibitors, in effect, "If you want a license to exhibit one hundred four pictures we are going to make
next year, you must take them all, or you cannot have any."

Bromley boasted, "That proceeding lasted fourteen years.
The record was nearly 50,000 pages, and there were thousands
of exhibits. I was on the road for four years almost without
interruption, sitting in sixty-two cities . . . We won that case, and
as you know, my firm's meter was running all the time—every
month for fourteen years. The president of that company was a
good friend of mine, and the company was very prosperous. He
was accustomed to road show productions of the most lavish
nature and feature pictures that cost a million dollars or more.
He saw nothing at all untoward in this young lawyer of his
making a road show production out of his lawsuit."

Bromley also defended United States Gypsum against an antitrust suit filed in 1940. Thurman Arnold, then the Assistant
Attorney General for antitrust matters, knew Bromley's skill at
muddling a case and sought to expedite the suit by convening a
special three-judge court. He told Bromley, "I'll fix your kite, my
friend." Bromley laughs. "The case lasted eighteen years. That
three-judge court was a lawyer's paradise. We had discovery of
hundreds of documents. There were six sets of defendants and
six lawyers. The proof of the government, which took nearly a
year, consisted in large part of comments or admissions of co-
conspirators. At the trial a document would be offered in evidence and then handed to each defense counsel, who would take
five or ten minutes to read it. Each one would then get up and
object." The presiding judge wanted a good record, "so he made
each attorney state very carefully the grounds for each objec-

tion. Then he would state his ground when he came to rule . . . This served as a sort of inspiration to his brethren, and they finally got in the habit. The one on his left would concur and state what he thought was the ground. Once in a while the fellow on the right would dissent, and of course he had to state his ground . . . We went on for months and months and months . . ." Lamentably for Bromley and other chronic procrastinators, tightened procedural rules now make it more difficult—but not impossible—to stall an antitrust proceeding.

The deliberate withholding or destruction of evidence—as alluded to in the opening of this chapter—is business of another sort. The subject must be raised obliquely, for the question implies, "Do you violate the law and the canons of ethics in your practice?" The answers, when not firmly negative, were also oblique. Several Washington Lawyers cited trade gossip about cases where documents were withheld or destroyed. (Both firms named emphatically denied such a thing, and one pointed to a publicized but negative grand jury investigation as "proof" of innocence.) But a partner in one of the larger firms did spell out what he called "obvious advice" which is frequently given to clients.

"There's no reason in the world to write, and retain, detailed memoranda on everything a business does internally. Before you put something on paper, think about how it would sound in court. If you wouldn't care to explain it from the witness stand, don't write it." This lawyer said he regularly helps corporate clients develop a "records retention program," something he calls "basic preventive maintenance." Corporate officers and house counsel are told, in so many words, what type of material is helpful to the Justice Department's antitrust division, and how to avoid accumulating it. "Companies put too damned much information in the minutes of directors' meetings," the lawyer said. "We found one corporation that kept almost a verbatim transcript of what everyone said. The *reason* a decision is made can be even more incriminating than the *fact* that a decision was made, and there's no use preserving it in black and white. The decision and the vote, who made and seconded the resolution, that's all you really need. Anything else is dangerous chitchat. Besides, you cut down on the stenographic bills."

Public-policy decisions are inherently political, and hence subjective. A regulatory official must answer to Congress as well as to his conscience. According to the statutes and the civics textbooks, the regulatory agencies are independent both of Congress and the Executive. They set their own policies, and hire their own personnel, and make their decisions on the facts. A Commissioner may not be removed except for gross misconduct; hence he won't write opinions intended to please the White House. Independent. Certainly. Congress said so. Except . . .

The Bureau of the Budget, an arm of the White House, approves each agency's requests for appropriations and legislation, a non-statutory screening which began in the mid-1930s, and which has never been challenged. And Congress decides how much to appropriate to an agency. Independent. Certainly. So long as the agency pleases both Congress and the Executive . . .

To the Washington Lawyer, this control-by-pursestring is important because it means a regulatory official must answer to Congress as well as to his conscience. A chairman of the Federal Communications Commission will not offend either Senator John Pastore (D., R.I.) or Representative Harley O. Staggers (D., W.Va.), both chairmen of committees that oversee FCC matters. Nor will the FTC violate the sensitivities of Representative Joe L. Evins (D., Tenn.), chairman of the House Small Business Committee. Recruit any of these men as an ally, and the agency *must* give your client attention. "Sure, it's cheating when you get one of Evins's staff people to make a call to the FTC for you," a lawyer told me. "But if it's going to gain my client some time or relief, you're damned right I'll do it." Timing is important. Several weeks before an agency chairman is due to testify before the appropriations subcommittee which will determine his allowance for the coming year, the staff scours the files for any outstanding Congressional mail. The chairman is given a background memorandum on the status of whatever matter has excited the Congressmen's interest. "This does not necessarily mean that action will be taken immediately, or that it will be favorable," one lawyer states. "But it does mean some guy has to pull the case out of a file, and look at it, and think about it. This alone can move him along. Also, the agency people are human. If they can bend things a bit, and make a Congressman happy, they'll do it, especially in a borderline case." Agencies learn to prepare for a deluge of Congressional mail during late January and early February, the weeks before appropriations hearings open.

Once a regulatory agency launches a formal proceeding, its decisions supposedly must be made on a formal, sworn record. A lawyer who makes an *ex parte* approach to a Commission risks severe disciplinary action (although there are few recorded instances in which anyone has actually been punished). But there are ways around the rule.

"Use the press," says a lawyer who is a transportation specialist. "Everybody at the ICC, for instance, reads *Railway Age*. Plant a story there, and the right people see it." Most Washington agencies circulate a daily "clip sheet" of news stories dealing with their activities or publics. "You know that the traffic column of the *Journal of Commerce* always goes onto the ICC sheet, so that's a primary target," this lawyer said. "Steve Aug of the Washington *Evening Star* is also key here, because anything he writes is circulated. Aug is good, and he is reliable, and he has good sources. I know because I am one of them. So if I want someone on the ICC to see a story, I leak something to Aug.

Getting a story on the clip sheet is a very nice way to affect agency policy." And Aug, as a journalist, is happy to receive leads on legitimate news stories from the attorney.

This lawyer, understandably, wants to remain friends with Aug, so he would give no examples of stories he planted personally. But he did point to a case where, he maintained, an Aug story played a purpose. An ICC hearing examiner was charged with accepting favors from industry, and the Civil Service Commission scheduled hearings on whether he should be disciplined. Someone involved in his defense leaked a story that one of the ICC Commissioners pressing the charges had also accepted industry largesse, thereby cutting the ground from under the case against the examiner. For Aug's purposes, the leak was a perfectly legitimate news story.

A tax lawyer finds another use for the press. He subscribes to dozens of periodicals, chiefly trade association journals, and also rents a United Press International wire that transmits Washington news. The lawyer's secretary spends several hours daily clipping items from the periodicals and the ticker copy and mailing them to persons named in the stories with a printed card that says, in effect, "I thought you might be interested in reading the attached. Best wishes." The lawyer says, "When I worked on the Hill I learned that Congressmen like to read things about themselves, and most keep scrapbooks of a sort. Some of these guys I won't see for months at a time, but every week or so they are reminded of my existence. I figure the postage costs several hundred bucks a year, but it's inexpensive for the return I receive."

Representative Wilbur Mills (D., Ark.), who has much to say about tax legislation because of his chairmanship of the House Ways and Means Committee, gets considerable attention. Rodney Markley, Jr., Ford Motor Company's resident political agent, can get his boss, President Henry Ford II, an audience with Mills with a single phone call. John L. Wheeler, Sears,

Roebuck and Co.'s vice president for governmental relations, a Harvard Law School classmate of Mills, occasionally gets Mills free rides on Sears's corporate jet to meet speaking engagements. (Return favors are neither asked nor expected, both men told Shirley Elder of the Washington *Evening Star* in June 1971. Wheeler said if a Sears plane is making a trip, "friends traveling in the same direction are given a lift if requested.")

A Washington Lawyer is a corporation's "man in Washington" in the broadest sense, and he must constantly look beyond the case at hand if he does his job properly. In the spring of 1970, American Telephone & Telegraph Company was asking the FCC to permit an increase in its authorized rate of return on interstate long-distance calls, the only phone service under Federal jurisdiction. Bell's strategy was to use these higher returns as an arguing point in obtaining increases in local and intrastate rates from the state regulatory agencies. Gordon MacDougall, a Washington utilities specialist who is also a special assistant Pennsylvania attorney general, was well aware of Bell's intentions, and he dropped into the FCC one day as a conference was ending to see how things were going. MacDougall casually mentioned to an AT&T attorney that he was considering intervening in the FCC case on behalf of Pennsylvania so that phone subscribers there could be protected from a possible major increase in their bills. "When I got back to the office two hours later, Governor [Milton] Shapp had already called. The Bell lawyer had telephoned AT&T headquarters in New York, who in turn contacted their lobbyist in Harrisburg, a vice president of Pennsylvania Bell, who went to the Governor. Shapp told me to check with him before doing anything in the case. Shapp certainly isn't any friend of the telephone company, but he didn't want to stir up a fight unnecessarily. I'm not surprised at *what* AT&T did, but I am at the speed with which they acted."

MacDougall a year later had the chance for gamesmanship of

his own. In May 1971 he was in Philadelphia arguing against discontinuance of a bus the Penn Central Company had substituted for rail service on one of its routes. The railroad attorney remarked that a case then pending before an ICC hearing examiner in St. Paul, Minnesota, had parallel features to the Philadelphia proceedings (which were before a Federal judge handling the Penn Central bankruptcy) and could be binding.

"When I returned to Washington I went immediately to the ICC and began asking about the St. Paul case," MacDougall told me. "An attorney I knew put me into contact with the right office, and I obtained a quick rundown on the facts. I learned that the chief opposition was being presented by the State of Montana, since the discontinuance involved service to that state.

"Now what they do out there in St. Paul is going to affect me in Philadelphia, so I have an interest in making sure they present as good a case as possible, because if they lose, my client [the State of Pennsylvania] is hurt."

MacDougall called another acquaintance on the staff of Senator Lee Metcalf (D., Mont.) who in turn telephoned the Montana Public Service Commission and spoke with the lawyer assigned to the case. MacDougall knew of a U.S. Supreme Court case which referred tangentially to buses substituting for trains —the obscure legal footnote likely to be overlooked by someone not totally steeped in transportation law. As MacDougall had expected (and feared) the Montana lawyer was young and inexperienced, and did not know of the Supreme Court case. MacDougall managed to give him a telephone crash course in how to argue the matter.

MacDougall told of this incident matter-of-factly, for to him it was a routine happening. He adds, "This illustrates the value of working from Washington—to be able to walk into the ICC and have someone give you the facts on some abstruse proceeding in St. Paul, Minnesota; to be able to pick up the phone and have a

Senate staff member, a friend, put you with the right person in a
state two-thirds the way across the continent. Now if you had
been trying this sort of thing by phone from Houston or Chicago, it would have been *possible*, but also very time-consuming
—you wouldn't know the people, they might not be willing to
drop everything and walk down the hall to the office of the right
guy. But they do know me, and they'll help me. This is part of a
Washington practice—to work with other lawyers so they don't
innocently screw up my cases."

MacDougall does this in highly informal fashion. The industry lawyers, conversely, have the resources and the manpower to
make their corporate clients instantly aware of what is happening in Washington. The Washington Lawyer is a key figure in
most of these intelligence bulletins. Arent, Fox, Kintner, Plotkin
and Kahn, whose eighty-five lawyers make it the second largest
firm in the city, practices chiefly before the regulatory agencies,
and its clients are inundated with a steady flow of bulletins and
newsletters. "We put out perhaps fifty newsletters a year for the
Motor and Equipment Manufacturers Association alone," says
Earl W. Kintner, the former FTC chairman and general counsel
who is the guiding spirit in the firm. "We are always developing
memoranda on trade regulations, tax matters, wage and hours
law, and so forth. I was a bug on education in government; I am
a bug on education as a lawyer." Harry Plotkin, the firm's communications specialist, has his own chain of publications about
what's current at the FCC. Cable TV entrepreneurs, for example, receive a weekly memorandum on developments in Federal
law. "Plotkin keeps up with what is happening in the industry, and makes sure that his client does, too," says another lawyer. The Washington counsel of the Association of American
Railroads draws upon a national network of attorneys for news
of decisions and pending cases that might affect lines elsewhere,
and issues a weekly private letter to members. "This isn't

unique," says Gordon MacDougall, the private transportation attorney. "Any trade association attorney worth his weight watches the national situation and has people contact him immediately when a case is breaking." But private practitioners such as MacDougall are at a disadvantage: "Lawyers as a group are not nearly so well-organized as the trade associations. There is much jealousy—for instance, out-of-town lawyers sometimes just don't like Washington Lawyers, because we can do things they can't do."

"The nicest thing about Washington practice," a regulatory specialist said, "is that you don't have to meet your clients. Do your business by phone and relax." He paused and gestured across his Ring Building office toward chairs and end tables and a couch littered with tan file folders and stacks of briefs and week-old copies of *The New York Times* and the *Congressional Record*. "If your office is messy, who cares? The Government Printing Office and the electric company are the biggest industries in town—there's no one here to bother you.

"When you work in New York, you're always being called in for conferences and meetings with the client. You call an attorney in Washington, and he's working in his office, and you can get through to him.

"One advantage of this separation is that you can control the client better—make certain decisions on your own, whereas if you were in the same town, you could consult him. Here you tend to go ahead and do it, and inform him later. It's more of an independent role than when you are the house counsel and the president or vice president is in the same building and even on the same floor and you keep meeting him at the water cooler. From the lawyer's standpoint, it gives you more of a sense of power. Also, the client is not likely to override you by dealing directly with the adversary party."

Clients, of course, are somewhat basic to a law practice. Once a lawyer has them, geographical separation *is* a blessing. "I handle twice as many clients here as I could in Chicago," says one lawyer, "simply because I don't have to waste time in damned fool meetings." Says Mortimer M. Caplin, Commissioner of Internal Revenue between 1961 and 1964 and now head of a thriving tax firm:

"I saw the same thing happen many times when I practiced in New York. At nine o'clock you'd get a phone call from a client who had a big merger going that had to be consummated in a hurry. You'd get all the troops working on how to do it through issuance of debentures, his plan.

"At ten-thirty the phone would ring again. The plan changed. Now they're going to do it with preferred stock. You blow the whistle and the troops march in another direction.

"At four o'clock, guess what? The phone rings again. Now it's an all-cash deal, so you start over again. That makes for a lot of wasted motion. Now the beauty of being in Washington is that before they pick up that long-distance phone, they have played around with all the alternatives. You are handed a problem that has already been screened."

"Yeah, that's all very good," retorts another attorney. "It's fine when you do business over the phone. It's faster, and you don't go through all this Mickey Mouse ritual of shaking hands all over the office. But there does come a time when you've got to see the client face to face. I was out of Washington eighty-seven nights last year, and I'm not what you would call a hot-shot lawyer." Max M. Kampelman, who *is* a hot-shot lawyer, ticked off some calendar items. "This week, I had two business dinners; one night I flew to New York to meet with clients from Milan to discuss a problem. One of my partners flew on to Los Angeles with them later the same night. Next week I've got to fly to Minneapolis for a shareholders and directors meeting for one client, then back to Wilmington the next day for the same thing for another client. You get around." Kampelman adds, "The two handiest things in my office are the phone and the Teletype machine." Covington and Burling partners do so much flitting around the country that one secretary is detailed permanently as an in-house travel agent.

Washington is not a bright-lights town, to the lasting relief of men who practice law there. "Feed 'em, do some boozing in the hotel bar, and put them to bed by midnight—and only once or twice a year per client, if you are lucky," says a younger partner in Arent Kintner. "Anyone from out of town who's been in Washington twice knows that this isn't exactly the Sodom and Gomorrah of the Western world, so they don't expect it. Not from us, anyway. You might see some classic hangovers, but I've never had to rescue anyone from the vice squad. Not yet, anyway." Says another, "If a client starts dropping those broad hints about 'entertainment' or 'some fun,' I'll hoke up some story about having to be home early and turn him loose with one of our young bachelors. Both of them are on their own thereafter, and I don't want to know what happens." An older man, who began practicing in Washington during the frenetic war years, says Washington Law hasn't always been that innocent. "Many a lasting client-lawyer relationship," he says, "was cemented during the course of a wild evening in Baltimore. But most of that was nonsense related to lobbying, not strictly law." And another: "You start handling clients on that basis, and you're little better than a pimp, and thought of as such." And another: "Human nature being what it is, there'll always be phone numbers with women on the other end of the line, and many law firms in this town that deal with out-of-town clients have a few of them stuck around someplace. Unofficially, of course, but they're there. Still, this *is* something you'll find in lobbying more than in straight lawyering."

Travel and entertaining aside, geographical separation poses an even more direct problem: How does the Washington Lawyer obtain enough business to open an office, if the vast majority of his clients are based out of town?

The easiest—and hence most common—way is to join an established firm, which counts on the new lawyer's prestige to bring in enough money to warrant a hefty first-year salary. Joseph Califano, of the Johnson White House, by reliable report, had the pleasant challenge of choosing from half a dozen six-figure offers before going to Arnold and Porter. Califano's colleague, Harry McPherson, does quite well at Verner, Liipfert, Bernard & McPherson. So, too, does former SEC Chairman Manuel F. Cohen, at Wilmer, Cutler and Pickering.

But for the lawyer who decides to open his own office and start a fresh practice, life can be dull—and impecunious. "There is a notion," a former Kennedy White House staff member told me, "that all you need to make a fortune in Washington Law is two years in a well-publicized government job, and a desk. Well, it doesn't work. You remember —— [he named a former assistant secretary of an executive department who shall remain anonymous]. He had it all tapped out. He left government after five years, and he was going to make it big. Well, he opened an office, and he sat, and he sat, and no one came. Would you believe that within nine months he had totally exhausted his savings, just to meet office expenses, and had handled exactly two clients? He's back in —— now, and I get a bitter letter occasionally. The trouble is, people think you leave government and clients are going to storm your office. That isn't so. You are a fool to go it on your own without finding a client whose retainer at least meets your overhead. Hell, let's be realistic. If you have the basic monthly nut—the rent, the phone bill, your secretary's salary—you can go a long time, because you are going to have a little money stuck away. But walking in cold—uh-uh, don't do it."

Earl W. Kintner found problems of an unexpected sort when he went into private practice in 1961. Kintner declined several Wall Street offers because he wanted to stay in Washington and work with a small firm. He went into an office then named Berg, Fox and Arent. Right away, two bad breaks.

"*The Wall Street Journal* ran a story saying I couldn't practice before the FTC because of a conflict-of-interest situation, since I was a former chairman. Well, that wasn't true, so I went to see someone at the *Journal* and protested. Right away they ran yet a second story saying the same thing, wrong all over again. Mind you, this was at a time when I was trying to build a practice. It hurt.

"Then a rumor got around town that the Justice Department was actively investigating me because of some 'conflict of interest.' It was untrue, and I knew who started it—someone who saw me as a competitor in antitrust and FTC law. Everywhere I went, this rumor kept bobbing up. It was deadly. I finally went over to the Justice Department and saw Lee Loevinger, who ran the antitrust division. Lee was an old friend of mine; when I was [FTC] chairman, he introduced me a couple of times when I made speeches in Milwaukee. I laid it out straight for him. 'Lee, I want to find out what's happening down here. *Am* I under investigation?'

"Lee picked up the phone and called whoever headed the criminal division at the time and asked the same question. The guy said, 'There's nothing happening, but if he wants to come down and confess anything, let him do so.' That was it—I knew it, but I wanted to clear the air.

"Then Lee did something that shows what a real man he is. He knew how the rumors had hurt me, and he knew they had to be squashed. Twice in the next few months he made speeches to Federal bar groups, and each time he deliberately brought up my name. I was an officer of the groups, so he could do it naturally. He would say, '. . . and if I had an antitrust problem in Washington, I would hire Earl Kintner.' That is the sort of endorsement that clears the air."

Indeed it did. When Kintner when into Berg, Fox and Arent in 1961, it had nine lawyers. "I brought over two more from the FTC. Now [June 1971] we are up to eighty-five, which makes us the second largest in the city."

Kintner's performance as FTC chairman illustrates how a Federal official can *build* a practice without *soliciting* a practice, and in good faith. Kintner has long had a thesis that "the overwhelming majority of businessmen will make every effort to comply with the law *if they understand it*. Enlightened self-interest requires no less. Further, such understanding is necessary if economic democracy is to continue to be a viable means of allocating goods and resources in our society." As FTC chairman, Kintner made some 250 speeches, twenty-five hour-long telecasts, and fifty to sixty radio shows, all on the functioning of the FTC. "I'm a great believer in education," Kintner says. "Tell the businessman how and why government does the things it does, and he'll cooperate. I do the same thing now, only for specific groups, rather than for business as a whole." One profitable by-product of Kintner's public appearances was an accretion of good will among small businessmen and trade associations he now represents. Kintner lists more than twenty trade groups among his clients, many of which first met him across a speaker's podium. "Sure, it was helpful," a member of the firm says, "but most of them came in so long after Earl left the FTC that I don't think you could ever prove any connection."

A firm that is built around a name-partner has a distinct advantage in attracting new business, for corporation presidents sleep a little better at night knowing that a Clark Clifford or a Mortimer Caplin or an Earl Kintner or a Lloyd Cutler is protecting their interest in Washington. The clock and human limitations being what they are, however, none of these men is going to give his undivided attention to any single client, much less to all of them. I asked a series of name-partners exactly how much individual attention they could give clients. The answers fell into a soon predictable pattern: overall supervision of *everything*, with delegation of the details, and final say on major decisions. As Mortimer Caplin puts it: "Any lawyer can come up with a list of alternative actions. What the client wants from me, as a tax specialist, is a recommendation of which to follow." Caplin implies, without actually saying, that a junior member of his firm will do the routine work of compiling the alternatives. In other name-partner firms, the process is not nearly so open. Libel laws dictate a retreat to anonymity in the following:

"—— has two duties in our firm. When a prospective client walks in the door, —— must convince him that no other law office in Washington can do him a bit of good, only us. And then he must persuade the client that of all the lawyers in our firm, Joe Blank is the man best suited to handle the case. Clients, of course, want the 'name lawyer' to handle the case, and it's politic for the lead partner to appear occasionally. But the client must be made to realize that the daily work will be done by someone else. That sometimes takes a lot of selling, and —— is good at it."

The more realistic corporate executives realize a Paul Porter or a Clark Clifford doesn't spend his Saturday afternoons in the library, researching fine points of the law. But protocol demands that the name-partner make certain appearances. Says a Covington and Burling partner: "Lots of times, when we go in to report to a corporation president, the senior man on the account does the presentation. What he knows he might have picked up in a one-hour briefing. If a particularly detailed question is asked, he can give a general answer, and then say, 'Mr. Jones, would you care to add anything further?' Jones will say, 'That pretty well covers it, I think. Just let me add . . .' and he'll proceed to put it all out. I don't think we are fooling anyone, nor are we trying to. Our associates pretty well understand they are there as ob-

servers, but that they should cut in, very discreetly, if any misin-
formation is passed. Why do the corporations want our senior
man present? Oh, when you're paying the kind of money they
do, I guess they just expect it."

(Corporations also desire something they can hold in their
hand and weigh. H. Thomas Austern, the Covington and Burling senior partner, states, "In these days when every other type
of professional report, good or poor, is dressed up in a lovely
ringed and colored plastic binder, some people still are prone to
judge legal performance quantitatively by verbal volume. Thirty
years ago two of us answered a difficult and intricate legal problem by concisely writing: 'Gentlemen, after examining the statute in your state, all analogous statutes, and all of the cases, we
have concluded that what you want to do is lawful.' That client
was not happy; he went down to Wall Street, got the same opinion backed by thirty turgid typewritten pages, and felt much
more comfortable.")

Lawyers with less ex officio prestige—the staff attorneys, the
deputy bureau chiefs, the sword-carriers of the Civil Service—go
into private life with no assurance of a living, much less riches.
Bar canons forbid them to advertise, or to solicit business, other
than to distribute professional announcements that they are in
practice, and to put their names in the yellow pages of the phone
book. One young (under-thirty) lawyer who spent five years
with the FCC told me, "You really feel lost. I dropped a lot of
hints when I was at the FCC, just letting broadcasters know I
was going on my own. None of them picked them up. So what
do you do? You *could* go to the conventions and shake hands
and meet people, but if you aren't making any money, how can
you afford Chicago or Los Angeles? Referrals from other lawyers are a help; but these tend to be old dogs that the guy dumps
because they smell. Anyway, you can't make it representing a
dozen or so one-lung radio stations that pay a thou a year.

You've got to find that unusual client who needs something special—maybe a guy with no money but with a special problem. A lot of guys like me are shooting craps—you get behind the letterhead and the secretary, and we don't have a damned thing. But the chances of the big payoff make this better than accepting what you know you can get from the government." (He let me take the $4.12 luncheon check.)

One form of legalized solicitation is a listing in such law directories as *Martindale and Hubbell* and *The Attorneys' Register*. But as is noted by Professor Monroe Freedman of George Washington University Law School, "Not every attorney is permitted to advertise his professional autobiography, prestigious associations, and important clients in *Martindale and Hubbell*. One must await an invitation from the publisher to apply for an 'a' rating, which can be achieved only upon submission of favorable references from sixteen judges and/or attorneys who have already received an 'a' rating."

The Attorneys' Register, which is approved by the American Bar Association, contains paid advertisements listing the attorney's name and qualifications. A soliciting brochure lists "important corporations which . . . have requested, and will receive, a copy of our current edition . . . for use when seeking qualified . . . counsel . . . The primary purpose of *The Attorneys' Register* is to continue to be a valuable forwarding medium aimed at securing SUBSTANTIAL legal business for our listees and to assist them in making profitable and ethical contact with other members of the legal community." *The Attorneys' Register*, according to the brochure, "has been distributed free to . . . a careful selection of banks and trust companies, important industrial corporations, insurance companies, financing institutions, and the like, who are believed to be prolific forwarders of SUBSTANTIAL legal matters."

States Professor Freedman, "This is the way solicitation is

done by attorneys who represent corporations and wealthy people . . . Ambulance chasing may be in bad odor, but corporation chasing carries an ABA seal of approval."

Judge Learned Hand, surely not a man to panic at legalistic language, threw up his hands at the tax code. The words of such an act, he wrote, "merely dance before my eyes in a meaningless procession: cross-reference to cross-reference, exception upon exception—couched in abstract terms that offer no handle to seize hold of . . . [They] leave in my mind only a confused sense of some vitally important, but successfully concealed, purpose, which it is my duty to extract, but which is within my power, if at all, only after the most inordinate expenditure of time."

Which is good for the tax lawyers, who are busy even if prematurely gray. Tax law is an interesting specialty for Washington Lawyers for several reasons. Success in a proceeding is immediately convertible into dollars in the client's pocket. No need to await several years' workings of a new law or regulatory agency ruling; once Internal Revenue Service decides an issue, hard dollars are in hand. The game is played with relatively fair dice. If Congress ever succeeds in destroying the Republic, whoring for special interests in the tax field will be high on the list of reasons. But once a law is written, a tax attorney is reasonably certain he can proceed on the merits of his case, without reliance on influence.

The tax bar is the most closely knit of any in Washington; virtually a hundred percent of the private practitioners are alumni of the Treasury Department and/or the Justice Department's tax division. Hence tax lawyers work on a track uncluttered with amateurs, which makes their work easier and safer. A code convoluted enough to stagger such a jurist as Judge Hand quickly frightens casual practitioners back to their own area of the law. And, finally, tax law is a field in which the Washington

Lawyer can choose from a vast variety of forums, ranging from the informal office conference to a full-blown court proceeding, or even to Congress.

Given the proper resources—i.e., a rich enough client—a good tax lawyer won't stop until he has exhausted all avenues, including special-interest legislation from Congress. A rather peculiar last-minute addition to the Tax Reform Act of 1969 tells much about how a skilled Washington Lawyer handles a tax problem. The amendment itself was given only cursory notice even by the petroleum trade journals, and none by the daily press. Before this century ends, however, it stands to save the shale oil industry a billion dollars or more in taxes. And the shale oil companies worked fifteen years to get the loophole they wanted.

Beginning in 1954, the Treasury Department, with minimal but confusing guidance from Congress, tried to write depletion allowance schedules covering the recovery of oil from shale rock. The key issue was at what stage of the process the fifteen percent allowance should be computed: when the shale was still rock, or when the petroleum had been extracted. The difference was $1 per barrel compared with $2.40 per barrel; with several trillion barrels of oil reserves locked in domestic shale, industry had a most recognizable economic stake in getting as liberal a rule as possible. In regulations issued in 1968, Treasury interpreted a 1960 act as saying heat-treating of minerals was not to be considered mining, for purposes of computing depletion; the industry interpretation was just the opposite.

Enter Michael Duncan, tax specialist in the firm of Cleary, Gottlieb, Steen and Hamilton, which has offices both in New York and in Washington.* Duncan represented The Oil Shale Corporation (TOSCO), a pioneer oil shale developer. Duncan's

---

* Washington partners testily note their office is not a *branch* but a co-equal wing of the firm.

first call, when he began arguing for revision of the rules, was to Thomas F. Field, who specialized in petroleum affairs in the tax legislative counsel's office at Internal Revenue Service. Duncan had worked on the issue on and off for several years, but Field was a logical first stop for him for other reasons, as well. Field was the line attorney responsible for depletion matters, and a Washington Lawyer who knows his protocol starts at the bottom. Also, Duncan had been Field's office mate when both men worked for the Justice Department earlier in the 1960s, and a Washington Lawyer prefers to deal with an acquaintance. Field sees nothing wrong with this. "Any decent official tries to treat everyone even-handedly," he told me, "but you can relax more with someone you know, and he'll go away with a better feel for what you are thinking."

Duncan got nowhere with Field. "I told him I didn't really see how we could turn the statute around," Field says. "The question was unusually complex, for it involved four or five branches of law—tax, mining, accounting, minerals, and so forth. But we felt we were right." Duncan politely disagreed, then and now. "The discretionary nature of the law troubled some of the IRS officials," he told me. "One of them used to say that tampering with the regulations was like feeding an alligator—offer one finger, and you lose three or four; and that if you 'give' something to one special-interest group, along comes another wanting special treatment."

Duncan next went to Jerome Kurtz, the tax legislative counsel, bringing along a TOSCO vice president and a briefcase of statistics and legal memoranda. Again, nothing. So a slight escalation. The Nixon Administration was about to take office, and both IRS and the private tax bar realized that Congress would deal with some form of tax reform during the 1969 session. Duncan put together an ad hoc coalition of special-interest lobbies—featuring the American Mining Congress and the American Petroleum Institute—and generated enough pressure to force Treasury to withdraw the regulations "for further study." In early 1969, right after the change in Administrations, Duncan politely asked Field if IRS intended to switch. At this time the Treasury Department didn't have a new Assistant Secretary for tax matters, nor was there a tax legislative counsel. "Just me and Secretary [David] Kennedy," says Field, "and I certainly didn't intend to call him on a highly technical question his first month in office." Whereupon Duncan turned to Congress—first telling Field exactly what he intended to ask on behalf of TOSCO. That he did so is standard operating procedure for a Washington Lawyer; let your adversary in government know what you want, so that he can find as much common ground as possible; the other points, conceivably, are negotiable.

Duncan testified before the House Ways and Means Committee in the spring of 1969, simply putting a prepared statement into the record with a few brief introductory remarks. (Rule: The Washington Lawyer isn't paid to make speeches, but to produce results. The hearings dragged for months, and Duncan saw no point in wasting twenty valuable minutes of Committee time by reading the statement aloud.) To Duncan's surprise, the Ways and Means bill did not include his shale oil amendment. Why it did not remains a matter of controversy. Duncan insists the amendment was approved by routine Committee vote and dropped from the final report because of apparent clerical error. Field, however, states his Committee sources said the amendment simply did not have any support; there is no significant shale oil production, and the members didn't want to worry about what was then a moot point.

The bill thus went to the House floor without any mention of shale oil. It also went under a so-called "closed rule" from the House Rules Committee, which prohibits any amendments being offered from the floor. Many members protested having to vote up or down on such sweeping legislation without a chance to offer changes. Unfortunately for "representative democracy," that is the way the House of Representatives operates, and some Congressmen would just as soon be protected from the people. Representative Tip O'Neill (D., Mass.), for instance, said the closed rule prevented tinkering with a bill written by experts: if amendments were permitted, he argued, "we would be deluged with vans bringing in all the lobbyists from all over the United States who were working on this legislation."

Of the myriad lobbyists and lawyers working on the Tax Reform Act—the House hearings alone fill fourteen volumes—only one managed to breach the closed rule: Michael Duncan, on behalf of TOSCO.

On August 6, 1969, as debate opened on the bill, Ways and Means Committee Chairman Wilbur Mills had the bill temporarily recommitted to committee for the stated purpose of correcting typographical errors in complex tables showing tax liabilities for different income brackets. When the bill returned to the floor the same day, however, Duncan's oil shale amendment came with it—the only special-interest amendment permitted. Mills made a cursory explanation of the amendment, but without shedding any light on its economic significance: "At the present time the depletion allowance is applicable to the value of the rock itself—which has very little if any value. As a result, the industry will never develop unless we change the cutoff point . . . so oil taken from oil shale will get more nearly the same percentage depletion allowance as oil produced from a well. As a result, this bill extends the point at which percentage depletion is computed in the case of oil shale to after extraction from the ground, through crushing, loading into the retort, and retorting, but not to hydrogenation, or any refining process or any other process subsequent to retorting."

Got that? Apparently the House of Representatives understood every word of Mills's explanation, for not a question was raised. The amendment was adopted along with the tax reform package without floor discussion.

"Once Mike got it into the bill on the House side," Field relates, "he was in; he knew he had it made in the Senate, with Wallace Bennett (R., Utah) and Clifford Hansen (R., Wyo.), both from mining states, and both on the Senate Finance Committee." Treasury tried hard, with Assistant Secretary Edwin S. Cohen arguing eloquently against creation of what he termed a "loophole" at a final session of the Finance Committee. He managed to cut the vote to 8–7, but remarked to Field after his defeat, "It'll never come out of the statute." Comments Field, "He's right—it's engraved on stone."

How did you do it? I asked Duncan. How did you manage to persuade Mills to recommit the bill and insert your amendment? Duncan invoked a modified version of client-attorney confidentiality but made these points: He won the case on its merits. Shale oil is sold in direct competition with petroleum, but with fifteen percent rather than twenty-two percent. The fifteen percent had been applied on the rock, the twenty-two percent on oil. "This was manifestly unfair." Also, Duncan says, "There was substantial sentiment in his [Mills's] Committee to the effect we were being screwed." Beyond that, Duncan smiles and says, in a variety of ways, no further comment.

What is the potential value of the amendment to the oil shale industry? States Field, "The answer is that better than two trillion barrels of oil are out there in the shale, a 100- to 400-year supply of petroleum for the entire United States. The cost to the Treasury Department in lost revenues will be staggering. How much? Who knows? But you are talking in terms of billions of dollars."

Mortimer M. Caplin, who was Commissioner of Internal Revenue before starting a now thriving tax practice in 1964, has stated, "The fact that the national office of the Internal Revenue

Service is situated in Washington is undeniably the single most important influence upon the nature of the Washington tax lawyer's practice. Physical proximity to the national office permits rapid transmission of information, personal discussions, readily scheduled conferences and all of the other obvious advantages for any case in which timing is an important factor." Not every case results in a multibillion-dollar saving for a client, such as Mike Duncan gained for the shale oil industry. But Caplin says the same principles apply in any tax proceeding: Know the people with whom you are dealing, and how they should be approached; develop an "early warning sensitivity to changes that may be taking place" in tax policy; and, when possible, "limit the issues in contention to those that absolutely must be passed upon."

Most of the Washington Lawyer's tax work is done in face-to-face conferences with IRS officials, ranging from agent level up to (albeit rarely) the Commissioner of Internal Revenue. Each official has varying authority to settle a dispute; the lawyer must know this authority, and what higher officials must be satisfied. Caplin has suggested that basic human psychology must be used; the IRS official is just as anxious to settle the case as is the taxpayer, and the lawyer should always keep this fact in mind: "In helping the official solve his problems," he told a Florida tax conference in 1969, "a taxpayer's representative will be going a long way toward solving his own. Table-pounding and a loud voice may sometimes impress a client. It is needless to note that such conduct represents only a minus quantity before the IRS."

As a man who has sat on both sides of the Commissioner's desk during tax disputes, Caplin says it is important for a lawyer to know what *not* to do in dealing with IRS. High on his list is the Washington Lawyer who insists on arranging a personal audience for his client with the Commissioner of Internal Revenue.

"I used to waste hours meeting with people as a courtesy,

even when I wasn't going to make the decision in a case," Caplin told me. "Sophisticated corporation executives know this, but you still find lawyers who'll trot them in. Ninety-five percent of the decisions in IRS are made below the level of Presidential appointees, so they could better spend their time with the staff."

The fact that the person requesting the interview was a former government official was nigh automatic entry into his office, Caplin says. "It's a combination of camaraderie and courtesy. You find time for a former official. If a man who used to be Assistant Secretary of the Navy called you, for instance, you felt he would not bother you unless he was serious." But oftentimes, Caplin said, the lawyer would go through a desultory recitation of his case and leave a memo for the IRS staff to study. "All he wanted was to give the client a chance to sit in the same room with me, for whatever it was worth." Eventually, he says, "over-handling" can damage a tax case, for IRS becomes irritated at the maneuvering and subconsciously stiffens.

Caplin says he was somewhat surprised at the gingerly manner in which most Congressmen approached his office (a feeling not universal among his staff people). He attributes their wariness to the tax-fix scandals of the late Truman Administration, when grand juries and Congressional committees scoured IRS for irregularities. There are exceptions. Soon after Caplin took office, a newly elected Representative called his secretary and demanded, "Will you have the Commissioner come to my office right away?" Caplin: "He wanted to discuss some constituent's problem. I ignored him." Conversely, Senator Robert Kerr (D., Okla.) who as chairman of the Senate Finance Committee most likely could have persuaded Caplin to tap-dance on Pennsylvania Avenue, used an entirely different approach. "He would call and ask, 'May I come by and see you sometime tomorrow?' Right away I'd make plans to go to *his* office as soon as possible." Caplin states, "I never turned down a request for a Congressman to see someone, but sometimes I'd reply, 'Sure, I'll see him, but why?' What they do a lot of times is pass on a constituent, just to get them out of their hair. They know I can't—or wouldn't—do anything for them, but the constituent is satisfied he had a hearing. Part of the job of being Commissioner, I suppose."

Caplin's point: A Washington Lawyer is foolish to bother the Commissioner of Internal Revenue unless he is trying to obtain a ruling on a truly momentous tax question.

For adept orchestration of Congressional pressure, former and present IRS staff members point with awe toward an extraordinarily shrewd lawyer named Claude Maer. Maer is a "Washington Lawyer" only part of the month; most of the time he spends in Denver, as a partner in the firm of Holland and Hart. But twice monthly Maer flies into town on behalf of such clients as the Portland Cement Association, the cement lobby, and the Cattlemen's Association, a trade group formed in and run from his office for the convenience of rancher-clients. The profitability of both the cement and cattle industries relates directly to maintenance of tax breaks. Maer's ongoing assignment is to keep existing loopholes open and to search for new ones. Maer establishes quarters in the Washington Hotel, across 15th Street NW from the Treasury Department, and goes to work.

"Claude's forte is the Congressional letter," states a former IRS staff man. "He will come into your office and discuss letters that Representatives and Senators will be sending later in the week. He asks how they should be written to evoke the desired reply.

" 'I am going to protest this and this and ask for that and that,' he'll say. I would respond, 'If you ask for X, we don't have that information. But we can offer you this about Y.' The purpose is to make sure that something exists before a Senator asks for it, so that he doesn't look like a boob."

Once Maer determines what Treasury wants, he writes a draft

letter and seeks out a Senator who will have it typed on official stationery and mailed under the Senator's signature. Senator Russell Long frequently obliges him; so did Senator Everett M. Dirksen before his death. Says the IRS man, "If the Senator is a straight-shooter, he will say to Maer, 'You write a letter to me on this,' and then he'll compose his own version, based upon what Maer supplies. But often as not, Maer's draft comes right into the office."

Maer's system isn't perfect, Congressional mail-handling procedures being what they are. IRS remembers one letter he addressed to Senator Fred Harris of Oklahoma asking for help in a tax problem involving the cement industry. Maer's letter also invited the Senator to visit a cement plant in Ada, Oklahoma, and noted that plant managers have broad discretion on allocating campaign contributions. Someone on Harris's staff simply attached a routing slip to Maer's letter and forwarded it to Treasury "for appropriate comment."

When Maer is working on a specific tax case, he will use a single Senator or Representative to obtain information or a policy statement from IRS. When his client's problem is broad-gauged, he will generate letters from up to a dozen Congressmen. The technique is of questionable effectiveness. A former IRS official told me, "When seven or eight letters arrive from the Hill, the first thing an assistant secretary asks is, 'Who's stirring up mail on this subject?' We know it isn't spontaneous. The benefit to the lawyer is that it does make us take a close look at the problem."

Thomas F. Field, who dealt frequently with Maer while in the IRS tax legislative counsel's office, sees nothing underhanded about his method of operation. "He was always completely candid about what he was doing, using the Congressional mail and that sort of thing. It is no more clandestine than anybody with an immigration problem asking a Congressman for a private bill. What he wanted was a change in the rules. He asked if you, as a line attorney, could change them. If the Treasury Department was in error, with a regulation or with draft legislation, I would recommend to my superior that he change the rule. This happened in one out of twenty cases. But in the other nineteen, you listen to the lawyer—and maybe a vice president he has brought along—and you can only say, 'I'm really not convinced by this. I will write up this conversation very carefully, but I think we must face up to the fact that the rule will not be changed.' " The lawyer can continue to press his case with the tax legislative counsel, the Commissioner of Internal Revenue, even the Secretary of the Treasury, if he has sufficient clout to arrange an audience. That failing, he looks to the Congress.

An example: In the late 1960s, during drafting of what became the Tax Reform Act of 1969, the Treasury Department wanted oil companies to submit certain financial information on the so-called Form O, a widely used business reporting form. The oil companies knew Treasury intended to use the data to attack the depletion allowance. Predictably, Representative George Mahon, (D., Tex.), an industry friend who chairs the House Appropriations Committee, wrote a politely stiff letter to Treasury several days before he opened hearings on its budget request. Form O was not used. Says a former IRS staff member:

"The purpose of these letters is not to obtain information, but to pressure the Treasury Department. The real cruncher comes when you have two or three of these letters outstanding. You are David Kennedy or John Connally arguing for an increase in the national debt limit, and you get into that little back room where the Senate Finance Committee meets for executive sessions. It's small, and it's right behind the podium of the main Committee hearing room, and when fifteen Senators go in there, with the Committee staff and other interested parties, it's a real smoke-filled room.

"It's at that point where Senator Dirksen, for example, would have a letter outstanding. 'Mr. Secretary, I'm very sympathetic about the point you make on the national debt, but before we get into this, have you made any progress in solving that Portland Cement matter?' The day before a Senate Finance Committee executive session is when the legal staff at Treasury puts together background papers on as many as seventy-five letters that might have been received; even if you want to say no to a request—*know* you should say no to a request—it's wise to say yes."

9

Mr. Cutler, Meet Mr. Nader: Making It Personal

Lloyd N. Cutler was uncomfortable even discussing The Nader Problem. God, how Cutler has suffered these past few years, since Nader began tormenting him publicly as the personification of the powerful Washington Lawyers who manipulate the Federal government for corporate clients. People cluck sympathetically at Cutler at cocktail parties, and at bar functions men are always coming over and saying, in effect, *Damn that Nader, I think it's just awful* . . . Reminding him. Wherever Cutler goes, he feels Nader's teeth nipping at his ankles, little sharp bites, but incessant bites, until he might want to turn and KICK. Around and around swirl Lloyd Cutler's hands, stopping

so his fingertips can tap-tap-tap on the table in the main dining
room of the Metropolitan Club, now moving again, rubbing,
clinching, interlocking. Midday on a sleepy summer Saturday,
and the Metropolitan Club is so relaxed with itself, and the
world outside, that even the bright sunlight gushing in from
three sides of the room can't rouse any life. Only five other men
in a room that can seat more than two hundred. Mumble-mum-
ble-humm-mumble, and, once or twice, the muted clink-clank of
silver against good china.

Lloyd Cutler sighed and chewed a piece of his minute steak.
The Nader Problem, Cutler says, must be put into proper perspective. And he told me some instances where he worked for
good causes, noble causes, but as a *lawyer*, not as a public
polemicist. Sitting around his swimming pool one afternoon with
John Gardner, the former HEW Secretary and philanthropoid,
he wrote a court petition challenging the murky system of rais-
ing money for national political campaigns. "If there's any corruption in government," Cutler said, "it's right there. I know it,
and I'm prepared to lay it out if necessary." Cutler's suit,
brought in the name of Common Cause, the citizen lobby group
run by Gardner, is going to step on a lot of important pocket-
books, political and corporate. Cutler isn't worried, he says;
clean up the elections, and you go a long way toward cleaning up
political America—think of it, to have a Congress and a President not caught on the fishhooks of special interest. And Lyndon
Johnson's Commission on Violence, which Cutler directed. A
scholarly, dispassionate study which showed the 1968-sickness
(Bob Kennedy, Martin Luther King, Chicago) was the norm for
America, not a deviation. Brave man, Cutler, to put his name on
a document challenging The King's Wisdom. Johnson disowned
the Commission—off the record, of course—three months after
establishing it because it wouldn't condemn TV as responsible
for what Daley's cops did in Chicago; disowned it, and a White

House aide leaked a story to Drew Pearson that Cutler "went soft" on TV because he represents CBS. (An untruth. Cutler first declined to serve on the Commission because of CBS. When Johnson insisted, he filed formal notice he would abstain from any Commission work on TV. A man who served as personal assistant to Dr. Milton Eisenhower, the chairman, says, "Cutler was scrupulous about it, too; he kept away from TV altogether.")

Sighhhhh. Then Nader. What *can* be done about him? A lawyer who didn't get his way in the auto cases, and isn't man enough to take a licking without whining, the way a good lawyer is supposed to do. No understanding whatsoever of the adversary system, which is my God after all what law is about, American style. It is disappointing, Cutler wrote Senator Abraham Ribicoff in 1969, "that Mr. Nader, a lawyer himself with no lack of ability in a stand-up fight, would stoop to conquer." Now let's give Nader credit for doing good things, because things *are* wrong in the country. And a smart publicist, too. He took Lloyd Cutler, and used him to personalize the fight against auto safety defects, and auto air pollution. A very unlawyerly thing to do. And then Cutler began to give me his side of the auto cases . . .

"He told you that! Whee! That is vintage Lloyd Cutler. I mean, that's rich!" Ralph Nader stomped his foot on the floor in glee, and Ralph Nader laughed again. "Well, let me tell you this . . ."

We were sitting in a third-floor hideaway Nader has behind an unmarked door in a commercial building in northwest downtown Washington, a block from Arnold and Porter's townhouse office. Nader, the man who became a Movement. Short hair, black suit, black shoes; put Ralph Nader in some decent socks that don't fall over his ankles, and you could pawn him off as an FBI agent. Until he starts talking, that is, for Hoover's men aren't as messianic even about commies and hippies as Nader is about his demons. Cigarettes, rotten meat, shoddy procedures in the Federal bureaucracy, weak-sister antitrust enforcement, the continuing auto safety/pollution mess. Nader has come a long way since 1965 and *Unsafe at Any Speed.* But not far enough. The pattern became familiar: Nader would expose an evil of industry and/or the bureaucracy, and seek redress in Congress or at the regulatory agencies. Good publicity, promises of action, floor speeches, a flurry of hearings and reports . . . grinding down to nothing, or near it.

Why? The Washington Lawyers, that's why. The sleek, well-paid guys who yawn and wait, and as soon as the tumult dies down go into the offices of . . . understanding Senators and thwart Nader and the public. The Washington Lawyers. Okay, baby, you do the front work for the corporations and take their money, so let's put you to use in another way. General Motors, as an impersonal corporation, is beyond embarrassment. So, too, is the Automobile Manufacturers Association. So let's humanize the situation. Lloyd Cutler is someone you can see, someone you can touch, and not just a symbol on the stock market ticker tape.

In September 1969 the Justice Department announced it intended to accept a consent decree closing an antitrust action against the Automobile Manufacturers Association and the Big Four member companies—General Motors, Ford, Chrysler, and American Motors. The suit, filed in the last days of the Johnson Administration, accused the AMA and the companies of deliberately suppressing development and introduction of pollution-prevention devices for sixteen years, even as the country slowly smothered in auto-produced smog. At midday on October 9, fifteen students from the George Washington University Law School walked over to Farragut Square in downtown Washington to picket the office of Wilmer, Cutler and Pickering, in which Lloyd Cutler is a senior partner, to protest the consent decree.

In terms of noise, the protest was quiet. The students sang no songs, they shouted no slogans. But they did carry some rather rude placards, "Smog Control Demands Legal Ethics Not Legal Retainers," and "Lloyd Cutler Plus General Motors Equals Smog," and "Deadly Pollutants Are Overcome by Lawyers' Ethics, Not Lawyers' Retainers." And they handed passersby a resolution demanding that Wilmer, Cutler and Pickering persuade the AMA to accept a court trial of the case; if the AMA declined, the firm should resign as its attorney.

Cutler let some of the students into his ninth-floor office to receive the petition, and oh, he was mad; a *New York Times* reporter who went upstairs with the group wrote that his "hands trembled" as he accused the students of "trying to drive lawyers away." Cutler says he was angered because of the failure to do the first thing lawyers should do in considering any problem, i.e., acquaint themselves with the facts, analyze the issues, and consider the remedies. Cutler told me, "The picketing students had not read any of the court papers such as the government's complaint and the consent decree; they did not know that numerous governmental and other bodies had filed objections and suggestions regarding the consent decree with the court to consider in deciding whether to enter the decree; and they did not realize that they could do so themselves." After an hour or so, when the noontime crowds began to recede, the students returned to the George Washington campus.

And Cutler, in white-heat anger, distributed perhaps the first press release ever issued by a Washington law firm:

> Today's picket line is a prime example of McCarthyism —1950 style. The late Senator from Wisconsin also believed he had a divine monopoly on knowing where the

public interest lies. His zeal led him, as it now leads Mr. Nader, to assail his fellow lawyers for defending the targets of his attacks. We defended some of Senator McCarthy's victims. In appropriate cases, we intend to continue defending clients who are attacked by Mr. Nader.

Mr. Nader and the lawyers in this firm share membership in a great profession. We happen to be opponents in a controversy now pending in a court of law. The public interest is best served when all sides of such a controversy have the benefit of skilled advocacy; all sides in his case are receiving it. The Department of Justice and counsel for the automotive industry are urging to the court that their position serves the public interest because it will achieve more rapid future progress in reducing air pollution; Mr. Nader and counsel for other interests are urging a different course. Lawyers owe their profession of the duty of trying to resolve such issues in a court of law—not on the city streets.

Mr. Nader's zeal for the public interest as he sees it ought not to lead him to try to prevent or intimidate the representation of opposing views. We regret that he disdains a basic premise of our constitutional system—that where the public interest truly lies can best be determined by the presentation of opposing views in the proper forum.

Low-keyed though it was, the demonstration hit Washington Lawyers where it hurts—in their respectability. *Aha, so those are the guys who screw up the ecology, right up there in that office building, eh? Shame, shame. Lloyd Cutler, the good liberal, eh?* Nothing like this had ever happened before in Washington Law —*ever*, and oh, but the tremors. "All around Washington that afternoon," a lawyer in another firm told me two years later, "people were asking, 'Well, when does our turn come? Should we adopt a contingency plan for repelling boarders?' "

Regardless of the merits of the attack on Cutler, the students succeeded in dramatizing a question that Washington Lawyers —and those elsewhere—had previously discussed only in the most theoretical terms: What is the lawyer's responsibility to society, as opposed to his responsibility to an individual client? If a case contains a major public-policy issue, should the lawyer let it be resolved in an open forum—or negotiate a settlement that leaves the questions unanswered? At what point does personal conscience require a lawyer to throw up his hands and say, "Enough! What you have done is such an affront to the public that I want no part of you." The lawyers, of course, have a swift answer: Every party in court, even the most bestial child-murderer, deserves good representation. If lawyers accept clients on the basis of popularity, many people will go unrepresented. As Cutler told a Senate subcommittee in 1969, "unpopular individuals and institutions" have varied "according to the fashion of the times from Communist conspirators, foreign agitators and security risks to the military-industrial complex, Wall Street and Detroit."

This answer, however, does not necessarily relate to the question being asked by Nader and others. Louis D. Brandeis said it well in 1905, thirty years before going on the Supreme Court:

> . . . The leaders of the bar have, with a few exceptions, not only failed to take part in constructive legislation designed to solve in the public interest our great social, economic and industrial problems; but they have failed likewise to oppose legislation prompted by selfish interests. They have often gone further in disregard of the common weal. They have often advocated, as lawyers, legislative measures which as citizens they could not approve, and have endeavored to justify themselves by a false analogy. *They have erroneously assumed that the rule of ethics to be*

applied to a lawyer's advocacy is the same where he acts for private interests against the public, as it is in litigation between private individuals.

Brandeis's charge was safely non-specific—the sort of thing you could say in a law school classroom, or an ABA convention, without offending anyone. Cluck-cluck-cluck, he certainly can't be talking about *my* firm, because we represent only the better corporations. The innovation in the Nader/student attack on Cutler is that they picked out a specific lawyer and said, *Look at him, here he is, he is a guy who is doing the things we're mad about.*

An influential Washington Lawyer decides early in his career whether he wants fame as well as clout. For men such as Clark Clifford, whose careers are quasi-public, the decision is out of their hands. For Thomas G. Corcoran, the goal was non-specific glory—be friendly with journalists, but don't talk about your own cases, only about things that make you look good. (Corcoran loves whispering into the ear of columnist Joseph Alsop, whom he met as a distant FDR cousin and fervent China lobbyist.) Covington and Burling partners opt for total anonymity. The name men at Arnold, Fortas and Palmer were as shy and unassuming as a . . . well, a 19-year-old starlet at a Riviera film festival.

Lloyd Cutler, prior to the 1969 Nader confrontation, was powerful but deliberately quiet. The bare outline of his early career is that of scores of Washington Lawyers: Yale Law School, a brief stint with Cravath, Swaine and Moore, the New York super-factory; wartime service in Washington with the Lend-Lease agency; a partnership with Oscar Cox, the general counsel of Lend-Lease (now deceased). In 1962 Cutler and Cox reached a friendly disagreement over the future of the firm, both on size and responsibilities to be given junior members. Cox wanted to freeze at under twenty lawyers; Cutler wanted to keep growing. So Cutler and seven other lawyers left and joined with ten lawyers from the firm of Wilmer and Broun which for practical purposes was the Washington branch of Cravath, Swaine and Moore. (Wilmer, Cutler and Pickering now serves as the Washington office of Cravath, Swaine and Moore; the two firms even share the same address and phone number in the Washington telephone directory.)

Growth, which Cutler wanted, was swift; as of mid-1971 the firm had sixty lawyers; Cutler expects it to level at a hundred during the decade. The firm is truly "national" in character. A background sheet prepared for job applicants says the firm has clients, both large and small, in "most" major industrial, retail, financial, transportation, and communications fields. Corporate clients, the background sheet relates, include manufacturers of industrial and consumer products such as aerospace equipment, automobiles and automotive supplies, aluminum, business machines, cement, chemicals, computers, electronic products, housing, machinery, nickel, paper, petroleum, pharmaceuticals, and steel. Other clients include retail merchandising chains, domestic and foreign commercial and investment banks, financial service companies, newspaper and magazine publishers, a trunk airline, mutual funds, trade associations, railroads, a commercial radio and television network, and radio and television stations. The firm is also Washington counsel for a number of universities, foundations, and nonprofit research organizations. It also acts as Washington correspondent for several law firms in New York, Boston, San Francisco, Los Angeles, and other cities either "on a continuing basis or for specific projects." In sum, most of the capitalistic endeavors practiced in the United States. Indeed, Cutler told me, one reason he expects his firm to stop growing at the hundred-lawyer level is that it will have exhausted categories of potential clients. A firm that attempts to represent more than one corporation in a given field encounters conflict-of-interest problems, and Cutler feels his office is near the limit.

"One remarkable quality about Lloyd," remarks another Washington Lawyer, "is his ability to produce a legal memorandum justifying what his client wants done. Even persons favorably inclined toward your client are more comfortable if you give them something real heavy and legal-looking to stand on." Two 1971 cases illustrate the point:

▮▮ Cutler defended the Columbia Broadcasting System against an attempted citation for contempt brought by the powerful Representative Harley Staggers (D., W. Va.), chairman of the House Interstate and Foreign Commerce Committee, for its refusal to produce unused film made in preparation of a documentary on Pentagon public relations. Cutler wrote a freedom-of-the-press brief which was given to every member of the House. "There were lots of people who didn't want to vote against Staggers, but Cutler's brief gave them an out, and they took it," says a Congressional aide involved in the dispute. The House voted against the contempt citation—the only time such a committee recommendation has been rejected.

▮▮ Cutler did not fare so well with his memo-writing in another case, but only because he was checkmated by two aroused Congressmen. The case was the proposed merger of American Airlines, a Cutler client, with the smaller Western Airlines. The problem was to bypass antitrust objections which the Justice Department was almost certain to raise when the Civil Aeronautics Board considered the case. Cutler's solution was to fall back on language of the 1966 act which created the Department of Transportation (DOT). One of the law's purposes was "to assure the coordinated, effective administration of the transportation programs of the Federal government." Cutler wrote an eight-page memorandum arguing that DOT—not the Justice Department—should prepare and present a unified government position on the merger. Previously, any affected department could have presented independent recommendations. Cutler and the American board chairman, George Spater, used the memo as a talking point in visits with high Nixon Administration officials, trying to win support for their position, and to take the case away from the critical eye of Richard McLaren, the assistant attorney general for antitrust matters. Lee M. Hydeman, counsel for Continental Airlines, which opposed the merger, heard of the Cutler Memo, and objected strenuously, both to its content and the manner in which it was being used. Hydeman forced American to put the memo into the formal CAB hearing record, and he attacked the private contacts because they provided "no opportunity to cross-examine." Representative Emanuel Celler (D., N.Y.) and Senator Phillip Hart (D., Mich.), both antitrust watchdogs, "raised hell at Justice," according to a party in the case, and forced release of a McLaren brief critical of the merger. Cutler's "unified position" argument was rejected by the Administration, and the merger ultimately came to naught.

Cutler moved into the upper strata of Washington Law concurrent with his break from the Cox firm. The drug industry gave him the lead role in a fight against regulatory legislation pushed by Senator Estes Kefauver (D., Tenn.) in the early 1960s. Kefauver compiled a damning dossier on the industry in well-publicized hearings. Some of the drug companies gouged on prices, with markups of more than one thousand percent on vital, life-giving pharmaceuticals. They advertised extravagantly, with the twenty-two largest firms spending an average of twenty-four percent of their gross income on ads and other promotion. They earned exorbitant profits—Carter Products, 38.2 percent on invested capital after taxes; American Home Products, 33.5 percent; Smith, Kline & French, 33.1 percent. A conservative faction in the PMA didn't take Kefauver seriously, because his probes historically resulted in more publicity than legislation, and the White House wasn't backing him. Cutler, however, sensed danger. He and Edward H. Foley, one of Tommy Corcoran's partners, told the PMA that an industry confronted with a public demand for regulatory controls could elect either to fight to the bitter end, or to recognize that there were some abuses and cooperate in seeking constructive legislation, as the securities industry had done when the SEC was proposed in 1933. "We advocated the latter course," Cutler says. But Congressional people involved in the drug legislation put another interpretation on Cutler's strategy: Public outrage was at the point where events could get out of control, and the industry should play along with Kefauver and accept minor changes; total resistance could result in total disaster. Whatever the analysis, Cutler had the support of John T. Connor, president of Merck, Sharpe & Dohme, and the PMA chairman, Eugene N. Beesley, head of Eli Lilly & Company, both of which came out of the Kefauver hearings unscathed.

Cutler and Foley (later joined by Corcoran) jousted with Kefauver for more than eighteen months as separate bills went through Congress. At one stage, Kefauver managed to get a strong bill—one calling for compulsory cross-licensing and tolerably truthful advertising—out of his monopoly subcommittee. Whereupon Senator James Eastland (D., Miss.), chairman of the parent Senate Judiciary Committee, called a closed meeting from which he excluded Kefauver and his staff, and permitted Cutler, Foley, and Marshall Hornblower, Cutler's law partner, to rewrite the Kefauver bill. HEW representatives were present for the Administration. Cutler says the bill that resulted was "substantially" one which the Kennedy Administration preferred over the Kefauver version; Kefauver, however, regrouped and won on the Senate floor, restoring much of the bite to the bill.

For the fight in the House of Representatives, the PMA bloc added two former Congressmen turned Washington Lawyers: Harry L. Towe, general counsel for *Medical Economics*, a major professional journal; and Joseph P. O'Hara, one-time second-ranking Republican on the House Commerce Committee, which heard the legislation. According to Richard Harris's definitive account of the drug legislation effort (in *The Real Voice*, Macmillan, New York, 1964), Cutler got overconfident during House hearings. He simply passed out copies of a fifty-page substitute for Kefauver's bill—basically, what had come out of the Eastland committee—and asked that it be adopted in toto. House members didn't have time to study the bill in detail. What Cutler should have done, an unnamed drug lobbyist told Harris, was to dole out separate amendments and revise the Senate bill piecemeal. So again, a torrid floor fight, with the drug industry winning some rounds and losing others, with O'Hara and Towe exercising their privileges as former members to lobby on the House floor right up to the vote. When reformists led by Representatives John Dingell (D., Mich.) and John Blatnik (D., Minn.) succeeded in restoring the bill to what Kefauver wanted, Senate staff member John Blair glanced across the gallery to see the reaction of the PMA team. At the final vote, he told Richard Harris, "They looked like statues on Easter Island."

Cutler was suddenly a very hot lawyer—one trusted with the delicate political assignments that, in Washington, equate with power. Attorney General Robert F. Kennedy and Louis Oberdorfer, Kennedy's assistant for tax matters (and now a Wilmer, Cutler and Pickering partner) brought Cutler into the prisoners-for-drugs swap of Bay of Pigs survivors in 1962. Cutler arranged for member companies of the Pharmaceutical Manufacturers Association to donate drugs with a retail value of $53 million, which Premier Fidel Castro demanded for the captives. Cutler's role was negotiation of two agreements between the PMA and the Federal government: clearance from the Justice Department for forty-odd companies to work together without fear of subsequent antitrust or other action, and an Internal Revenue Service ruling on tax deductions for the donated drugs. Next, Cutler helped the Justice Department dispose of the U.S. government's controlling share in General Aniline & Film, the German firm seized early in the Second World War. Because of the emotional residue of the war, the General Aniline deal had literally dozens of political booby traps: Cutler helped Justice settle several stockholder suits which gave the U.S. a marketable clear title to the company and then complete the public sale. Lloyd Cutler on the Supreme Court, replacing Justice Tom Clark; Lloyd Cutler in the Commerce Department as deputy to his old friend Secretary John Connor early in the Johnson Administration; Lloyd Cutler as Deputy Attorney General when Nicholas Katzenbach moved to State as backup man for the wearying Secretary Dean Rusk. These were the stories that wafted around Washington in those years (although Cutler insisted he never heard any of them save the Commerce position, which Johnson withdrew after a leak). None of the high-level jobs ever materialized. Cutler sat in his office above Farragut Square and watched his income soar over the $100,000 mark and was a happy man.

Then along came Ralph Nader.

"In fairness to Cutler," one man told me, "you've got to remember that he got into this mess after it was already a mess. Otherwise the entire thing would have gone differently." The "mess" was the 1966 fight over auto safety legislation.

The automobile industry, through a specially created committee of manufacturers and dealers, retained Cutler's firm in 1965 for advice on how to go about repealing the ten percent Federal excise tax on autos. Although Cutler describes his role as "quite limited," the tax was cut to seven percent with good prospects of phased abolition; then the Vietnam War, and its massive revenue demands, intervened. The auto industry, meanwhile, had encountered a more serious problem—the public furor over safety, stirred by Nader's exposés. General Motors, stupidly, hired a private detective to investigate Nader's private life. Nader worked as a consultant to Senator Abe Ribicoff's investigative subcommittee, which was preparing auto safety legislation. Caught red-handed, GM management was summoned before Ribicoff to explain itself. GM compounded its blunder by hurriedly retaining Theodore Sorensen, John Kennedy's longtime aide, who had just left the Johnson White House to practice law in New York. Several Senators felt—and so stated at the time—that GM's choice of Sorensen was exquisite bad taste, that his identification with the recently slain President overshadowed his abilities as a lawyer. GM's next decision showed more sense. It and the Automobile Manufacturers Association hired Lloyd Cutler to help stave off apparently unavoidable disaster. Lloyd Cutler, the fix-up man. Nader's hard exposé of auto defects had struck a responsive chord among citizens restive over the mechanical lemons produced by Detroit. Congress heard what the country was saying and nervously dampened its lips and readied itself for a workout on the car makers. The private eye snafu made Congress even madder; after all, Nader was one of its own, if only as a temporary consultant.

Listen to Nader and Cutler talk about what happened next, and one wonders if they're even discussing the same Congress, much less the same issue. First Cutler:

The auto companies were unique in American industry as a business virtually immune from Federal regulation. Their managers and owners attributed industry growth to freedom as much as they did to their own wisdom, and they considered Washington to be infested by demagogues and dolts. Cutler argued that demagogues are effective only when they tell the public what it wants to hear—and the masses were very much aroused on auto safety. And he gave two reasons for acceptance of a system of mandatory standards:

■■ Many safety improvements that increase costs and prices (e.g., seat belts) are what economists call "externalities"—something which most consumers will not pay for if you give them a choice. The manufacturer who innovates a safety improvement at increased cost may lose in the market, rather than gain.

■■ The antitrust laws limit the ability of manufacturers to agree to adopt a new device. Accordingly, mandatory government standards based on "reasonable criteria" are the only solution.

Initially, the AMA's safety administrative committee decided to ask Congress that the industry should be permitted to develop voluntary safety standards. But Rodney N. Markley, Jr., Ford Motor Company's Washington representative, agreed with Cutler, for he knew that the Senate—and the public—wouldn't stand for voluntarism, the industry's recent record being what it was. "In the face of current public attitudes, I knew that it wouldn't go," Markley told Booton Herndon, a friendly biographer of Henry Ford II. In meetings with Ford, Markley urged that the company (and industry) face reality. Herndon tells Markley's reasons:

Because of the changing public attitude, the automobile industry must accept some safety regulations. *For sound, competitive business reasons, he advised, standards must be set by the Federal government so that one company could not undercut the other*. Rather than protesting against all regulation, the industry should draw up a model bill that would establish a sympathetic climate and set forth a preliminary approach.

With the support of Henry Ford, Cutler managed to swing over the industry. Cutler stayed close with the committee in writing the legislation, and he was satisfied with the outcome—both with the requirements and the timetable set for their implementation.

That is Cutler's version, and Nader snorts at it, and the reasons he does so are at the crux of his bitter quarrel with Cutler over the responsibilities of an attorney to the public. "Cutler's special task from the beginning was to prevent the law from including criminal penalties for willful and knowing violations that would endanger human life," Nader said.

"Early on, Cutler was willing to accept criminal penalties. Then the manufacturers hauled him out to Detroit and gave him the word. They weren't *about* to risk a criminal section. Everybody knows the only deterrent to that sort of thing is jail. Cutler was arguing that criminal sanctions shouldn't be in such a bill because 'willfully and knowingly' is a hard thing to prove. He was saying a criminal penalty would be punitive and difficult to enforce because it would be hard to single out the real responsible violator, and that his respectable auto clients wouldn't violate the law, anyway. Well, this is a double standard. Arsonists and murderers are hard to single out, too, but we still have laws against arson and murder, and we punish the violators who are found.

"The law must pinpoint responsibility within a corporation to a *person*. Time and again, you have corporations pleading that 'top management' didn't know what was happening, and that the underlings were 'following orders and long-established policies.' Remember the electric price-fixing cases?"

Cutler, in rebuttal, denies that criminal penalties were ever a priority item for the industry, although it "did and does" oppose them. Further, he notes, criminal sanctions were never in the auto safety bill—neither in the original Johnson Administration submission, nor in the versions reported from the House and Senate committees that considered the legislation. When Nader succeeded in getting a criminal penalty amendment introduced in both chambers, Cutler states,* "it was fully debated and roundly defeated, by 62–14, in the Senate and 120–15 in the House. The majorities were not made up of any conservative coalition. Many of the liberals voting in each chamber voted against Mr. Nader's idea."

"Oh, nonsense," Nader replies. "You know, and I know, and certainly Lloyd Cutler knows that the time to work on a bill is *before* it is introduced, and that is what he did. The criminal sanctions weren't in the Administration's bill because Cutler got them out at the drafting stage. As I was saying, you have to listen between the lines when Lloyd Cutler is talking, because he can slip right by you." Oh, come, Cutler retorts, who is slipping by whom? "I had nothing to do with the drafting of the Administration's bill," he told me. "My work on the legislation did not begin until after the Administration's bill had been introduced and the industry had testified in the Senate hearings."

Soon after their clash over the auto safety bill, Nader encountered Cutler one evening at a party at the home of Chalmers Roberts, the veteran Washington Post *reporter. Nader says, "Cutler told me, 'Ralph, you should look into the reform of criminal laws in the District of Columbia. That is an area that needs a lot of work.' I replied, 'Oh, Lloyd, that would be too easy. All you'd have to do is remove the penalties for crime.' I don't think he liked it."*

* In a 1967 letter to *New Republic*, responding to Nader's charges on the criminal sanctions section.

Given Cutler's continuing representation of the AMA, and Nader's role as a consumer ombudsman in the auto industry and elsewhere, a further clash between the two attorneys was inevitable. Nader attacked Cutler frequently in national publications, both in interviews and in signed articles. In *New Republic* he accused Cutler of advocating a "double standard that is rapidly being institutionalized for corporate and individual crime." In *Playboy* he charged that "Congress caved in to Cutler" and that Cutler "lost little sleep" over his role in shaping the bill. Cutler fumed but said little publicly, occasionally writing a rebuttal letter to an editor. At one point he suggested that Nader read the section of the bar canon pertaining to one attorney criticizing another. Nader laughed and continued. And, inevitably, they clashed again in an open forum. This time the issue was industry responsibility for auto pollution, in a Justice Department antitrust case that had its genesis with Nader.

In 1964, while gathering material for *Unsafe at Any Speed*, Nader learned of a 1955 cross-licensing agreement among auto manufacturers which restrained the development and installation of antipollution exhaust devices. He complained to William Orrick, then the Assistant Attorney General in charge in the antitrust division, charging outright that "domestic automobile and truck manufacturers have been engaged in a concentrated effort not to compete with one another to improve automotive . . . pollution controls." Orrick ordered a staff investigation, which accumulated enough hard evidence to warrant convening a grand jury in Los Angeles. Orrick's successor, Donald Turner, wrote Attorney General Nicholas Katzenbach on May 12, 1966, that "if the grand jury investigation discloses an absence of justification for the agreement not to compete, *as seems quite likely, the agreement would be so plainly unlawful as to warrant a criminal proceeding.*" The grand jury worked from June 1966 until December 1967 and uncovered hundreds of internal industry documents that spelled out the discussions in minute detail. A summary written by the antitrust division attorney directing the grand jury investigation stated:

> The cross-licensing agreement was merely a vehicle to accomplish the non-competitive and delaying activities of the signatories . . . The evidence adduced before the grand jury clearly developed that the signatories to the cross-licensing agreement had the following understandings and agreements . . . : (a) not to publicize competitively any solution to the motor vehicle air pollution problem; (b) to adopt a uniform date for announcement of the discovery of any air pollution control device; and (c) to install devices only on an agreed date.

According to an AMA memo, the industry was aware as early as 1954 that "very serious legal problems might be involved in the cooperative acceptance and review of devices." The documents obtained by the grand jury contained many references to discussions of agreements to keep pollution gear off the market. For instance, when Chrysler developed a new exhaust system, its assistant chief engineer said it probably wouldn't be marketed because "if this was done Chrysler would be severely chastised by the rest of the industry . . . [because] the AMA agreement says that no one company will gain any competitive advantage because of smog," and that "Ford and GM were calling the shots." Nader has told the story in many forums of a conversation Kenneth Hahn, the Los Angeles smog prevention official, had in Detroit with a senior official of a Big Four company. When Hahn asked for introduction of pollution-suppression devices the official asked, "Well, Mr. Hahn, will that device sell more cars?"

"No," replied Hahn.

"Will it look prettier? Will it give us more horsepower? If not, we are not interested."

Further, when public and official pressure mounted for new exhaust devices, especially in suffocating Southern California, the AMA lied about when they could be ready.

Three of the four attorneys working on the case recommended that the Justice Department bring both civil and criminal antitrust actions, and that the auto manufacturers and the AMA be indicted for a Sherman Act conspiracy in restraint of trade. The attorneys also urged that eleven individuals be indicted, including officials of both the AMA and the Big Four auto companies. But Turner and his top assistant, Edwin Zimmerman, after studying the case, recommended against indictments. Ramsey Clark, by then Attorney General, agreed.

In doing so, the Justice Department accepted an argument which Lloyd Cutler and other AMA representatives pushed in a series of conferences with Turner.* The auto companies had no intent to violate the law. The Justice Department had never brought a criminal action in a case involving the exchange of licensing data—"product-fixing, rather than price-fixing." Cutler's argument—and the department's own analysis—convinced Turner. And by late 1967, when the department finally decided against criminal indictments, Turner had also had enough of Nader's complaints that he was a patsy for the auto industry and lawyer Cutler. Turner wrote Nader:

> . . . the joint research venture among the auto companies, though in my view unlawful . . . was not in the category of *'per se'* offenses and . . . most of the alleged

* Cutler objects to characterizations of these meetings as "private," preferring to call them "the normal conferences between lawyers in the Department and lawyers for companies under antitrust investigation." He says they were "private" only in the same sense that Ralph Nader's original meetings with William Orrick on the same subject were "private."

restricted agreements were arguably ancillary to the joint undertaking. I will not pretend that a reasonable man, *particularly if he had a more evangelical approach* to antitrust than I have, could not have decided differently . . .

The Los Angeles grand jury did not agree, and the foreman advised Samuel Flatow, the Justice Department lawyer directing its work, that the majority wanted to return indictments anyway, and Washington be hanged. The grand jury could have done so on its own volition, but apparently was unaware of this authority, according to the Nader antitrust study. When Flatow told the foreman the Department had instructed him not to ask for an indictment, the grand jury did not push further.

Cutler next tried to halt the Department from filing a civil suit. He argued with Turner and other antitrust officers for most of 1968. What he said is basic to an understanding of his deep feelings in the confrontation with Nader. After listening to Cutler talk about the antitrust case at length, and reading some things he has written about it, I am convinced that (a) he sincerely believed the auto industry was innocent of wrongdoing, civil or criminal; and (b) therefore as a lawyer he had no qualms whatsoever about making the best deal possible for them. He put the industry position into one concise sentence in court: "It is the first case involving a costly technological development for which individual consumers are unwilling to pay if they have a choice, and which as an economic and competitive matter can only be installed on a substantially uniform basis . . . under [a] mandatory regulatory system which did not exist when this cooperative program began." According to Cutler, the auto industry, through exhaustive surveys, concluded that most motorists wouldn't even use safety gear such as seat belts, which gave them immediate and *personal* protection. Despite public concern about auto pollution, the industry concluded that the vast majority of citizens would not pay the $50 to $100 extra for pollution gear. A manufacturer who introduced such equipment might be applauded for social conscience—and suffer economically. The cross-licensing agreement was intended to permit all companies to bring pollution devices—and standardized ones— to the market simultaneously.

So goes Cutler's argument—one which is accepted, in fact, by many eminent economists. I disagree with it. The American economy supposedly is competitive; conceivably American Motors and Chrysler, given brave enough management, could have used pollution-free cars as a marketing gimmick to wrest a larger share of the market from the mammoth GM and Ford. Conceivably there *are* enough American citizens with the social commitment to cause them to spend $100 extra for a car—if the manufacturers had given them a choice. Conceivably the pollution scare beginning early in the 1960s, when Los Angeles realized its variety of civilization faced imminent doom, could have forced the industry into proceeding faster, even unilaterally. Cutler's argument satisfies Cutler, however, and that it does explains the depth of his personal feelings about what Nader has done to him in public.

By late 1968 the Justice Department had written a draft complaint citing the 1954 cross-licensing agreement as a restraint-of-trade scheme, and charging the companies with agreeing in 1961, 1962, and 1964 to delay the introduction of pollution-control equipment. The auto firms, led by Cutler and Ross Malone, the GM general counsel, took their fight to Ramsey Clark. The bargaining was tough. Interviewers from Nader's antitrust study project quote Clark as saying:

"Industry fought that tooth and nail. We had three separate meetings on it. Tom Mann [the longtime Johnson friend who then was president of the AMA] still won't talk to me because he thought we had no moral right to bring the case. Cutler was at the meetings, as was Ross Malone. It seemed that he was sent to make an *ad hominem* appeal."*

By late 1968 Cutler realized the Justice Department intended to go ahead with the suit. Contrary to reports circulated at the time, Cutler denies that he or anyone else† in the AMA appealed to the White House to block it. Cutler told me that "contrary to popular opinion," the White House (at least during his years in Washington) has kept away from antitrust cases because of the potential for political scandal. Responding to a Justice Department offer, Cutler, Mann, and other AMA representatives began bargaining for a consent decree even before the suit was formally filed (ultimately, on January 10, 1969, eleven days before the Johnson Administration left office). Cutler says the Justice Department even offered to negotiate a "pre-filing" consent decree to be filed along with the complaint, but he "declined for lack of time." He did write Zimmerman, however, telling him the AMA wanted a consent decree. Zimmerman replied Justice was willing to negotiate "an acceptable decree." Cutler cites this correspondence as evidence that the idea of a consent decree had its genesis with the Johnson Administration, and was not a whitewash arranged through the pro-business Nixon Administration.

Once the Nixon Administration took office, negotiations for a consent decree intensified. For Nader, who had nurtured the action by now for more than five years, Cutler's activities were disquietening. As he was to complain later to Richard W. McLaren, then the Assistant Attorney General for the antitrust division, "The process of secret *ex parte* type negotiations with

---

* Cutler told me Clark denied, to him, making any such statement. The Nader team says he did make it. Clark did not respond to my query.

† Thomas Mann, the AMA president, served the Johnson Administration as Ambassador to Mexico and Assistant Secretary of State for inter-American affairs; a former mayor of Laredo, Texas, he was a close and longtime friend of the President.

representatives of corporate defendants, in particular Lloyd Cutler, counsel for AMA, discourages confidence in antitrust enforcement and facilitates sloppy or political decision-making. When decisions can be made without prior citizen access or without criteria publicly displayed on which such decisions are rendered or without adequate explanation, abuses, distortions, and laceration of the public interest can occur with greater frequency than would be the case otherwise."

The negotiations succeeded. The Justice Department announced filing of a proposed consent decree on September 11, 1969, with an accompanying press release in the name of Attorney General John N. Mitchell, saying it "represents strong Federal action to encourage widespread competitive research and marketing of more effective auto antipollution devices." The judgment contained these major provisions:

■■ The auto manufacturers were prohibited from restraining in any way the individual decision of each company as to the date it would install emission-control devices, and restricting publicity about research and development in the field.

■■ The manufacturers were required to withdraw from the 1955 cross-licensing agreement, to grant royalty-free licenses on auto emission-control devices; to stop exchanging confidential research data, or patent rights; and to halt requiring outside inventors to license patents to all manufacturers.

■■ The manufacturers and the AMA had to stop submitting joint statements to governmental agencies concerned with pollution-control standards.

The net thrust of the decree was "Don't do it again," and the AMA and the manufacturers made no specific admission they had done anything illegal. (An important reservation, as we shall see.) Indeed, the AMA, in its press release on the decree, acknowledged the junking of the 1955 cross-licensing agreement, but nonetheless claimed, "the program substantially aided in providing workable and effective emission-control devices throughout the nation much earlier than would have been possible without the cooperative program."

To Nader, the most grievous flaw of the decree was that it permitted the AMA and the Big Four to avoid public trial. Nader considered this bad for two reasons.

After years of jousting with corporations, Nader realized their dread of adverse publicity—that the most effective way of halting pollution is to point an accusing finger at specific companies and individuals. By one Federal estimate, property damage from corrosive pollutants costs the public $13 billion annually; half of this is attributable to motor vehicles. Nader blames it directly on the "auto industry's intransigence to innovation over the past generation." As he wrote to McLaren of the antitrust division after the decree was announced, "Can anyone deny the need and benefit for the public to learn about the nature and depth of this colossal corporate crime? The citizens of this country, who are the customers of this industry, have a right to know the extent to which the auto companies are deliberately responsible for the enormous health, economic and aesthetic damages caused by the internal combustion engine. One of the purposes of a public trial is deterrence; the [antitrust] division has chosen to lose a grand opportunity to bring these companies and their harmful practices into the public arena of a courtroom. . . . [A] public trial would at the least have shown that such corporate officials are holding far greater power over citizens . . . than they can exercise responsibly or even legally."

The consent decree, by law, could not be considered *prima facie* evidence of a past conspiracy by litigants who claimed injury from the conspiracy. Los Angeles County already had filed a $100-million treble-damage suit against the manufacturers. As Nader notes, "the practical effect of this provision is that . . . plaintiffs would have to duplicate the investigative process which took the [Justice] Department several years and several hundred thousands of dollars even with its extraordinary discovery powers." The decree also put the all-important grand jury testimony beyond the reach of private litigants.

Cutler says he would not consent to inclusion of an admission of guilt in the decree because "the defendants in this case believe they did not violate the antitrust laws." If such an admission had been required as the price of an agreement, he said, there would have been no decree, and "the case would have to go to trial." The last statement points up the importance the industry attached to damage suits looming over them. And Cutler also scoffed at Nader's complaint that settling the case without a trial would harm plaintiffs. He said the prospective litigants included "several of the leading and richest states in this country, very ably represented by their own attorneys general and by skilled practice . . . counsel."

A whirlwind publicity campaign by Nader prompted twenty-one public and private parties and more than fifty Congressmen to file petitions asking permission to intervene in the proceedings and modify the decree. But U.S. District Court Judge Jesse W. Curtis denied their request, and on November 7, 1969, the parties gathered in a Los Angeles courtroom to end the case.

Cutler came into court with head high, stating again, for the record, his insistence that the industry he represented had done nothing out of the ordinary. Less than a hundred words deep into his summation he declared, "It is the first case I am aware of that has ever been brought against an industry for cooperation in the exchange of technology in order to solve a public health problem." He repeated the industry claim that "our conduct has furthered and not retarded the public interest in controlling air pollution," and challenged critics to continue the fight in another forum if they wished. "Whether we are right on this issue of past violation, as we firmly believe, or whether our opponents are right is a matter for another day."

To critics of the settlement, Cutler also points to something Judge Curtis said in court in accepting the decree:

"The thing that amazes me is that all of the opponents seem to assume with such assurance that if this case were tried the government would win. Now there are many knowledgeable people who disagree with this.

"It would seem to me it would be tragic if this court would refuse to sign the decree and compel the government to go to trial only to lose the case, which would mean that the benefits of this decree, which are great, would be lost to the entire country forever, and it would help the treble damage claimants not a whit."

The Nader-Cutler dispute must not be oversimplified into a good guy/bad guy confrontation—which is, unfortunately, the position of many of Nader's young fire-bellies. To some of the legal militants the fact that Cutler *does* involve himself in public-interest work (the Violence Commission and Common Cause, to name two of many) is dismissed as further evidence of perfidy. By demonological interpretation, Cutler works on "good causes" to gain protective coloration and access to that part of liberal Washington that whoops and hollers at the sight of an unmasked corporation lawyer. Nonsense. As a longtime student of Robber Barons and their accomplices, I admit I sniffed suspiciously at Cutler for several weeks, searching for confirmation of the Nader thesis. The evidence does not exist. I argue with many of the things Cutler does for his clients; but I cannot shake the hard core of his sincerity. Cutler has more faith than most of us in the public spirit of corporate moguls. He thinks he can cajole these people, and pat them on the back, and lead them to good citizenship (i.e., building safe cars that don't emit deadly gunk). In short, he still believes much of what he was taught at Yale Law School.

All things considered, I suppose this is beneficial. Let us not be naive about the reality of corporate power. Muckrakers, trustbusters, New Dealers, and other reformers have assaulted the corporations relentlessly throughout this century, and yet their economic power is even greater now than it was in 1900. Cutler is a broker; when he talks to business clients about "discerning where the public interest lies," he has credibility. And to the corporations, he is a palatable alternative to Nader.

Which is why, of course, society sorely needs a Nader (or, more accurately, a regiment or so of Naders). Nader tailgated the auto industry on safety and pollution until it veritably pleaded for surcease. By dint of incredible energy Nader has usurped the muckraking role in society once performed by the press. In terms of access to public officials, argues Jerry S. Cohen, longtime Senate aide now in private practice, Nader is the most influential of Washington Lawyers; his phone calls are returned; he receives audience upon request; Congressional committees are happy to put him on the witness list; the newspapers print his frequent press releases.

Yet during the auto case Nader came to realize that a single "public-interest" representative, regardless of his energy or public constituency, cannot match the ongoing representation the Washington Lawyers give the corporations. What is needed, Nader decided, is a *corps* of such "public-interest lawyers," men able to follow a case for year after dreary year as it proceeds through the regulatory agencies, the Congress, the courts, the executive branch bureaucracy. But how does the public obtain such permanent representation?

Through the creation of a new species of Washington Lawyer —one which is rapidly becoming, in its own way, every bit as powerful as the Cliffords and the Corcorans and the Cutlers and the Covington and Burlings. Let us now see how the scales are being balanced in Washington Law.

10

The New Washington Lawyers: Balancing the Scales

One morning in the winter of 1971, after several weeks of interviews, I jotted a list of concurrent activities of attorneys working in what is broadly called "public-interest law." The list speaks for itself:

■■ Richard Copaken, a young associate at Covington and Burling, was fighting to stop the United States Navy from using the Puerto Rican island of Culebra as a naval and air gunnery firing range. Aligned against Copaken was not only the Defense Department but the administration of Governor Luis Ferré. C&B's investment, in time, travel, and other expenses, was by then well over $100,000, and when I talked to Copaken six months later, Culebra still kept him busy. "We'll get 'em," he told me, and launched into a detailed explanation of a campaign he was waging in both houses of Congress to force the Navy to stop raining ordnance on Culebra by June 30, 1975.

Benny Kass, whose office could be lost in the C&B reception room, was challenging airline advertising practices in a case at the Civil Aeronautics Board. "American Airlines advertised a $110 Monday–Thursday round-trip fare from Washington to the West Coast for a wife traveling with a husband. In very small type—so small you had to *look* for it, really—American said the rate was subject to CAB approval. American sold 4,000 tickets, one of them to me, before the CAB disapproved the rate. We had already planned the trip, so if we wanted to take it, we had to cough up more money. I socked them for deceptive advertising." (He lost, but thinks American reads ad copy more carefully as a result of his action.)

William Dobrivir, who spent eight years at Covington and Burling before leaving to work in Robert F. Kennedy's tragically abbreviated Presidential campaign, was in the first stages of a landmark case on the way most D.C. savings and loan associations handle insurance and tax escrows. At one time a homeowner received interest on the escrow money until it was forwarded to the insurance company and tax collector. Then the companies quietly discontinued the interest. "It's an outrage," Dobrivir told me. "There are tens of millions of dollars involved in the District of Columbia alone. I filed the suit here, but before it's over, it'll cover every jurisdiction in the nation."

■ Bruce Montgomery, director of the *pro bono* program at Arnold and Porter, was preparing for Interior Department hearings on the pipeline oil companies' plan to build across the Alaskan tundra to speed exploitation of the North Slope reserves. Arnold and Porter represented an Indian tribe that feared the line would decimate its lands. "Come back in a few days," Montgomery said, "and I'll introduce you to an Indian chief who is coming down to testify." Although I have never met an Indian chief, I declined. But Montgomery went ahead with a press conference in the Arnold and Porter office which got the chief's picture in *The Washington Post*, along with a friendly story.

■ Charles Halpern, director of the foundation-supported Center for Law and Social Policy, also prepared for the pipeline hearings, and with an especially keen enthusiasm. The Center's original injunction had halted construction on the line and forced the Federal government into new hearings. Concurrently, Center lawyers readied scientific testimony for hearings at the Environmental Protection Agency on limitations on the use of DDT and other insecticides—hearings they had forced the government to conduct through prolonged court proceedings.

■ Joseph L. Rauh, Jr., who practiced public-interest law before anyone thought of calling it that, kept the pressure on the Labor Department and the Senate Labor and Public Welfare Committee for their probes of the murders of mine union leader Joseph Yablonski and his wife and daughter. Soon Rauh was to announce formation of an ongoing legal action team to help dissidents in the strife-torn United Mine Workers of America. All this, of course, without fee, for Joe Rauh works at least as much time for other people as he does for himself.

As these examples indicate, a very noisy revolution is under way in Washington Law. It is free-form, fought on many fronts by many types of lawyers with many goals. But a common factor is present: a determination to bring life into the adversary system by becoming the second party to proceedings before the regulatory agencies and in the courts. The corporate lawyers long ruled Washington because they seldom encountered any meaningful opposition. The industries they represent dominate the regulatory agencies and have inordinate influence in Congress and the Executive. The New Washington Lawyers, instead of trying to destroy the adversary system, are out to make it work. And, collectively, they are the most exciting bunch of people unleashed in and on the Federal bureaucracy since the New Deal.

Ralph Nader is responsible for the revolution. "I have never said the corporations shouldn't be entitled to retain their Lloyd Cutlers and their Clark Cliffords," Nader told me. "The whole thrust of my argument is that there must be lawyers on both sides of a hearing room. The corporate lawyers must be constantly challenged and counterbalanced by the *pro bono* lawyers. That's what it's all about."

Nader's influence is felt at two levels of the New Washington Law. First, he is attracting literally scores of new law graduates to Washington, kids who sniff at the $15,000 a year associateships in the big firms to do public-interest law. Second, he is forcing the major firms into *pro bono* work in what could be called destructive self-defense: new graduates won't go to firms without public-interest programs, and much of the work done under that banner further radicalizes the men doing it. Where does it all end? Not even Nader knows.

A handful of the newcomers make the Nader team, to work at his Center for the Study of Responsive Law or one of a half-dozen satellite groups. Nader pays them $40 to $60 a week and is as demanding an overseer as the training masters at Covington and Burling and Arnold and Porter. But one seldom hears complaints—only continuing enthusiasm for working on a "Nader's Raider" task force study of Federal antitrust enforcement, or the highway lobby, or the meat industry, or Union Carbide, or a dozen others. When persuasion and publicity fail, Nader litigates, which means even more work.

For youngsters for whom Nader can't find room, there are a dozen-odd other public-interest law centers scattered in the antique old townhouses west of Dupont Circle in downtown Washington—the Citizen's Advocate Center, whose practice is chiefly local, run by Edgar Cahn; the Washington Research Project; the Center for Law and Social Policy. And there are a handful of fee-charging individuals and firms that do public-interest work primarily or exclusively—Berlin, Roisman, and Kessler; Dowdey, Levy and Cohen; and Asher and Schneiderman.

The format of the Center for Law and Social Policy is illustrative of what the public-interest firms are trying to accomplish. The center has a core of staff attorneys who work closely with resident students in a practice "addressed primarily to federal decision-making and federal policy . . . to insure that important issues of public policy are fully aired and are given due consideration by the federal administrative agencies." As the center states in a fund-raising prospectus:

Although the power of the administrative agencies has grown since the New Deal, there has been increasing recognition that the agencies have not fully lived up to their mandate to serve the "public interest." The work of the federal agencies is demanding and complex, and their decisions are in many instances strongly influenced by the advocacy of the Washington law firms which represent corporations and other private clients with a large financial stake in the actions of such agencies.

In a key decision in 1966, Warren Burger, then a judge of the Court of Civil Appeals in Washington (now Chief Justice of the United States) underscored the need for public-interest advocacy in regulatory agency proceedings. In a case involving the FCC, Judge Burger said the "theory that the commission can always effectively represent the listener interests . . . is no longer a valid assumption." Burger thereby opened the door for outside parties. But no one stepped forward, for no one was prepared to do so. As Charles Halpern, a onetime Arnold and Porter associate who now directs the center, states, "Few attorneys familiar with administrative practice were in a position to serve unrepresented citizen groups. Members of the Washington bar active in administrative practice and skilled in dealing with the Federal government are rarely available to serve clients who lack substantial financial resources."

Halpern and a friend, Bruce J. Terris, worked for eighteen months drafting a format for an organization to fill the gap. They toured the foundations and eventually came up with funding,* and opened in August 1969. The Center concentrates on environmental protection, consumer affairs, and health problems of the poor. In selecting cases, it follows these criteria:

▮▮ An important public interest is involved, and the individuals and groups do not have the financial resources or sufficient pecuniary interest to retain and compensate competent counsel;

---

* The New World Foundation, the Stern Family Fund, the Meyer Foundation, the Ford Foundation, the Rockefeller Brothers Fund and the Norton Simon Foundation.

▐▌ No other legal institution is likely to provide representation, and the subject matter is one in which the Center staff is competent;

▐▌ The area of law has not been adequately explored, there are opportunities for legal innovation, and students associated with the Center are likely to benefit.

Even with these limitations the Center has found much to do. It is representing Nader in a suit seeking to compel the Department of Transportation to reopen an investigation into 200,000 General Motors trucks equipped with wheels which are alleged to be potentially dangerously defective. It is suing WNBC-TV of New York for Friends of the Earth (FOE) for fair-time commercials to answer auto commercials that downplay pollution. It intervened in Food and Drug Administration proceedings on new-drug testing and enforcement of legislation requiring hazardous and ineffective drugs to be taken off the market.

The drawback to public-interest law is basic: a lack of money. Enthusiastic though they may be, the centers work with one eye on the calendar, the other on the bank balance. During its first year, before the foundation money arrived, the Center for Law and Social Policy had an "office" in the kitchen of the apartment of a staff lawyer. The Center now rents a ramshackle townhouse which is functional if not comfortable, teeming with energetic youngsters with Pancho Villa mustaches and briefcases. Funding is in hand through the end of 1973. After that? Hopefully, more foundation money. But the strictures on foundation activities contained in the Tax Reform Act of 1969 have yet to be formally defined by IRS guidelines; if IRS goes the wrong way, the Center (and its companion groups) could be out of business overnight. Foundation interest in any given area is notoriously short-lived, for a basic principle of the men who run them is to create "self-sustaining" organizations that can pay their own bills after three or five years. "Foundation funding is a sometime thing," says Monroe Freedman, the George Washington University law professor who took a year's leave to start the Stern Community Law Firm, restricted to D.C. affairs. "Right now public-interest law is fashionable. Five years from now, the thing might be to put money into groups of scientists to solve environmental problems. Unless public-interest law is put on a self-sustaining basis, it will not survive." And foundations can be fussy benefactors. The Ford Foundation has already intruded in management of the Center for Law and Social Policy.* Bruce Terris, who conceived the Center with Halpern, is also Democratic chairman for the District of Columbia. Ford "suggested" he give up either politics or the Center. He dropped the latter, and is now in private practice in association with Philip Elman, the former FTC member.

But the flow of kids continues—the law review editors in mod clothes who chide at white-shirt classmates who go to Covington and Burling (*"pro malo"* law, the Naderists call it) and who will work around the clock—twice, thrice—if Ralph Nader wants a brief in a hurry. "Gee, I don't have the slightest idea how long it will continue," Nader told me. "I see problems occasionally. When a man gets into his late twenties, and the family starts, he feels the money pressure. But the new ones are always there."

When the big-firm recruiters toured the name law schools beginning in the late 1960s, they encountered a recurrent phenomenon. Ho-hum indifference. No one wanted to listen to them. "Interviews" turned into angry confrontations, with students haranguing dignified lawyers on "responsibilities to society" and "whorish corporate attorneys." Who wants your money? the students asked. I want to do something more impor-

---

* Ford was nervous because of language in the Tax Reform Act of 1969 severely restricting use of foundation monies for political purposes.

tant in life than work for General Motors or United States Steel.

The recruiters were philosophical, if stunned. "We had no trouble in finding enough good people to fill the slots we had vacant," a Covington and Burling partner told me. He paused. "But I must admit we did miss getting some people we wanted. You'd find someone with good grades and an outstanding law review record, but his attitude would be so fouled up you could get nowhere with him." One result of this experience was a decision by the major Washington firms to expand and (in some cases) to publicize their *pro bono* programs. (Not every firm believes in *pro bono* work, by that or any other name. I asked a man formerly with Corcoran, Foley, Rowe and Youngman what public-interest work this firm did when he was there. He thought a moment and replied, "Tommy Corcoran used to be nice to Lyndon Johnson.")

Pushed by activist young associates, Arnold and Porter's management committee decreed that as a matter of formal policy the firm would devote fifteen percent of its time to *pro bono* work. Arnold and Porter assigned a partner as full-time supervisor of the program, with authority to draw upon the full resources of the firm. One figure I saw listed Arnold and Porter's *pro bono* outlay, in manpower and non-reimbursed expenses, at $500,000 for 1970. Wilmer, Cutler and Pickering computes that thirteen percent of the firm time went for public-interest/*pro bono* work during 1970. Mortimer Caplin, of Caplin and Drysdale, says his firm invested "a couple of thousand hours" for nonpaying or low-paying clients during writing of the Tax Reform Act of 1969.

Most of this work, however, is done in the name of individual lawyers, not of the firm. There is a reason. "Any time an office has more than one lawyer in it, you have two opinions on a subject," states a partner at Hogan and Hartson. A background sheet on Wilmer, Cutler and Pickering's *pro bono* program explains:

> The firm's 57 lawyers have individual and sometimes widely differing views on public questions. It is our shared belief that individual lawyers with the firm should be free, consistent with the Code of Professional Responsibility, to pursue their own personal and professional goals. Rather than attempting to achieve a unified "position" on any particular matter, the members of this firm encourage each individual to take whatever public position on issues of public concern he feels appropriate.

A sampling of Wilmer, Cutler and Pickering cases: Contesting unreasonably high utility charges to the poor, especially in the South and Appalachia. Helping organize a nonprofit corporation to build low-income housing in Mississippi. Challenging early voter registration cutoff dates before Texas primary elections. Assisting the G.I. Office, a center for servicemen complaining of military abuses, and the Vietnam Moratorium Committee and the New Mobilization to End the War in Vietnam, the anti-war groups. Combating freeways planned to cut through a scenic park in Memphis, Tennessee, and New Orleans's Vieux Carré. The firm can also mobilize manpower for an emergency: in April and May 1968, ninety percent of the lawyers in the firm helped represent persons arrested during the riots following the murder of the Rev. Dr. Martin Luther King; later, a partner chaired a D.C. committee that revised police, court, and jail procedures during situations that result in mass arrests. And Cutler has been a guiding force in the Lawyers' Committee for Civil Rights Under Law, virtually the only surviving white-dominated group pressing for desegregation.

Law activists deride the *pro bono* programs. One morning

while awaiting an appointment at the George Washington Law School I talked with two guys at the coffee machine, and we got onto *pro bono*. "Pure bullshit," one of them said. "Public relations," said the other. "You ever hear of them going after anybody with money, the big corporations?" Yes, as a matter of fact. Arnold and Porter is helping Nader in a suit to require General Motors to recall trucks whose wheels allegedly have the disquietening habit of breaking apart. Some Arnold and Porter clients protested vigorously that the firm would help the demon Nader do anything whatsoever, but the firm persevered. And Benny Kass, who practices all alone, without foundation money or visible sympathy for Washington Lawyers, told me, "Unhappily, a measure of sincerity in 1970 is how much money you are paying for something. Covington and Burling had paid $100,-000 on the Culebra case the last time I checked. Now, that means something."

But the *pro bono* programs have inherent defects. The large firms are limited in the type of actions they can bring, lest they are caught in a conflict-of-interest problem with existing clients. For instance, airline business is spread evenly across Washington Law. A Benny Kass was required to sue American Airlines for allegedly deceptive advertising. When student activists wanted to sue District of Columbia banks for alleged violations of usury laws, the big firms politely told them to go away; any firm with a D.C. bank for a client—or possibly *any* bank—would have a conflict of interest. There are anomalies. Louis Oberdorfer was national co-chairman of the Lawyers' Committee for Civil Rights Under Law at the same time that his firm, Wilmer, Cutler and Pickering, represented Crown-Zellerbach, which was being sued for employment discrimination under the Civil Rights Act. (The case ended with Crown-Zellerbach signing a consent decree.)

Even more serious a threat to *pro bono* work are the internal pressures from within a firm. When Richard Copaken began representing residents of Culebra he asked other public-interest lawyers for advice. "Get all the publicity you can," he was told. One lawyer suggested that he demand equal TV time to counter Navy recruiting advertising—for each "Join the Navy and see the world" spot, he should demand one saying, "Join the Navy and bomb the people of Culebra." The lawyer told Copaken publicity was always vital on a public-policy case being fought in the political forum of Congress. Copaken liked the idea, but told the other lawyer a few days later: "The firm wouldn't let me do it. We represent a network, and such a suit might embarrass it." Again, a Covington and Burling partner who formerly held a high Department of Defense position subtly suggested that Copaken go easy on the suit. Copaken refused.*

Lawyers' reflexive clubbiness is another inhibiting factor in *pro bono* work. In December 1971 the directors of the Washington branch of the American Civil Liberties Union were debating how much, if any, assistance the ACLU should give to attorney Phillip Hirschkop, who had been cited for contempt of court for his conduct of the defense of anti-war activists. The District of Columbia Bar Association, through its grievance committee, concurrently was initiating its own disciplinary proceedings. Hirschkop's attorney, Monroe Freedman, wanted ACLU support in a court action enjoining the bar committee from acting. But two lawyers on the ACLU board argued against involving the ACLU in the case. One of them—David B. Isbell, of Covington and Burling—noted that Edmund L. Jones, a leading partner in Hogan and Hartson, another big firm, was chairman of the grievance committee, and that any suit would have to

---

* Copaken did not tell me of these incidents, which I learned from sources outside the firm. Covington and Burling is so chary of publicity, even on *pro bono* activities, that Copaken would not discuss his relations with the firm, even as they related to the Culebra case.

name him as a defendant. According to two persons at the meeting, Isbell noted that Hogan and Hartson handles fifteen to twenty cases a year for the ACLU, and that a suit against Jones could so "embarrass" the firm it would withdraw from further *pro bono* work. Isbell was outvoted. The ACLU decided to aid Hirschkop.

The big firms also must be careful that their *pro bono* programs don't bog down with what Ernest Jennes of Covington and Burling calls "cook's law"—petty civil cases for a partner's domestic servants. When a young lawyer is on loan to Neighborhood Legal Services, the OEO-funded group that runs storefront law offices in urban ghettos, he takes any client who walks in. But the big firms prefer that he not bring trivial cases back to the office when his assignment ends. As one lawyer states, "It's not a matter of class distinction, but of common sense. We'd prefer to take a case that would change a basic procedure of government rather than haggle over the usury involved in a single installment purchase. You could work your ass off the rest of the century on these nickle-and-dime cases."

What motivates men to choose public-interest law? There is no "typical" public-interest lawyer, just as there is no typical Washington Lawyer. But after several months of interviews I picked out some people who represent different sectors of the public-interest movement: a law professor, a young attorney, a middle-aged man who left an established firm, and a one-time government attorney and regulator who, having watched the Washington Lawyers for thirty years, decided not to become one.

The first question John Banzhaf asked his unfair trade practices class at George Washington University Law School was why they were taking the course. "Most said 'to find out how to protect the consumer.' I told them, 'Okay, go ahead, I'm giving each of you two weeks to find an unfair trade practice in the District of Columbia, and to think of a way to stop it.' 'How do we tell whether something is unfair or not?' a student asked. 'Use your conscience,' I told them. After a couple of weeks the reports began to come in. They were all over the ball park— auto sales practices, gasoline octane ratings, credit practices. One youngster had a number of cans supposedly containing sixteen ounces of string beans. He poured out the water in which they were packed, and the true weights ranged from six to twelve ounces. I divided the class into teams of five students each. The teams researched their cases and filed actions in the courts and with the regulatory agencies."

The results surprised even Banzhaf. The FTC had charged Campbell Soup with putting marbles into bowls to support vegetables and make the soup look richer on camera than it actually was. Under a proposed settlement, Campbell would not have to admit any wrongdoing, only to stop marbling its soup. A Banzhaf group calling itself SOUP (Students Opposing Unfair Practices) argued that Campbell should have to inform customers they had been deceived. The FTC rejected SOUP's novel argument by a 4–1 vote but said such ads might be appropriate in some situations. SOUP tried again a year later with Firestone tires; this time the FTC gave the students legal standing in the case, and the FTC order pending as of this writing would force Firestone to admit the use of misleading and deceptive language. Another group, PUMP (Protesting Unfair Marketing Practices) helped persuade the FTC to require oil companies to post the minimum octane ratings of gasoline on pumps at service stations they own or lease. CRASH (Citizens to Reduce Airline Smoking Hazards) tried (and failed) to have the CAB ban smoking on commercial airlines; it is now appealing in the courts. NOSE

(Neighbors Opposing Smelly Emissions) joined a citizens' fight against a rendering plant on the Georgetown waterfront. FATS (Fight to Advertise the Truth about Saturates) did just that, at the FDA and the FTC. SMASH (Students Mobilizing on Auto Safety Hazards) offered the National Highway Safety Bureau a proposed safety standard on auto bumpers.

The acronyms are no accident, for Banzhaf runs the only law course in the nation where writing press releases is part of the syllabus. Banzhaf considers the general public the students' "clients" and thinks publicity is necessary to let them know what's being done on their behalf. The media love the acronyms, and their constant use keeps the Banzhaf groups in the public consciousness.

Banzhaf is peculiarly suited to direct-action law because of a landmark FCC suit he initiated and won soon after his graduation from Columbia Law School in 1965. Banzhaf, a non-smoker, was irritated with cigarette commercials on WCBS-TV in New York and asked the station for time to rebut them under the FCC's fairness doctrine. The station refused, and Banzhaf next went to the FCC. The Commission handled the matter very quietly, not even inviting comment from the station. And to the surprise of everyone—especially the broadcast and tobacco industries—it ordered WCBS-TV to give free time to anti-smoking ads. "A real blockbuster of a decision in the form of a three-page letter to a single station," Banzhaf says. "I am sure to this day they [the FCC] did not recognize the magnitude of what they were doing."

Banzhaf read a *New York Times* account of the decision late one Friday night while riding the subway from his office to his home in the Bronx. Banzhaf realized the tobacco-broadcasting axis would challenge the adverse ruling. By law, FCC rulings may be appealed to any U.S. Circuit Court in the nation. "I was afraid they would go to some remote court, say in San Francisco, to make it harder for me, or look for a 'best-deal' court, where they could rely upon a friendly judge," Banzhaf said. The court where the first appeal is filed assumes jurisdiction over all future proceedings in the case, hence timing is important. "I figured I would beat them and put it in the Court of Appeals in Washington, which is historically favorable to consumer arguments, and prone to uphold regulatory agency rulings."

But how do you appeal a favorable decision? Banzhaf switched to a downtown train and read *The Times* story as he rode back to his office. He found one point which was enough to get him into court. Although he did not ask for *equal* time, only proportionate time, the FCC ruling lectured him at length for confusing equal time with fair time. Banzhaf typed out an appeal, flew to Washington early the next morning, a Saturday, and was lucky enough to find a clerk on duty at the Court of Appeals to accept his filing.

Just as he anticipated, the tobacco companies filed their appeal several days later in the Court of Appeals in Richmond, Virginia, home of several cigarette firms ("real Marlboro country," Banzhaf calls it) and then tried to have Banzhaf's petition dismissed. One company argued that Banzhaf won the race-to-the-courthouse because he "was running before the gun sounded." Court procedural rules required that a copy of the decision at issue be attached to the appeal—which Banzhaf did not do, of course, for he had only *The Times* clipping when he filed his first papers. But the FCC frequently announces decisions via press releases and does not issue a formal opinion for days. Banzhaf contended—successfully—that since the law requires appeal to be filed within sixty days, he should not be required to wait for the formal opinion.

Other gamesmanship helped Banzhaf. The Tobacco Institute's brief covered twenty pages and cited forty precedent cases.

Court rules gave Banzhaf five days to reply. "Normal professional courtesy is that the other side will agree to give you more time when the pleadings are so complex. I called Arnold and Porter and asked for an extension, and they told me, 'Hell, no.' I could have gone to the judge and asked for an extension, but this would have tipped them to how vulnerable I was to a war of attrition, and I would have faced a blitz of paper throughout the suit. So I worked virtually around the clock for five days and came up with a forty-page reply that had twice as many citations as they did. I researched it and typed it myself, and ran off twenty copies, one for each opposing party. Even the mailing took a couple of hours. But it worked—I never got the paper blitz."

Banzhaf quit his law job at this point. "I knew I had to work full time. You don't take a chance with a $100-million decision. If this had been a decision benefiting a corporation, a dozen law firms would have been defending it. But I was pretty much on my own. The FCC lawyer was working on three major constitutional cases in the Supreme Court simultaneously, and any one of them was a full-time job. So he couldn't take the lead."

Branzhaf won. The appeals court upheld the FCC, and the Supreme Court refused to review it further. Thereafter TV stations had to give one anti-smoking ad for every three cigarette ads. "That's $175 million of free time," Banzhaf says. And Banzhaf feels the dramatic effectiveness of the anti-ads so cowed the cigarette companies that they did not protest too vigorously when Congress finally banned all TV and radio smoking commercials effective January 1, 1971. "They were being clobbered," Banzhaff says.

The cigarette victory ultimately brought Banzhaf to Washington and the GWU Law School. Knowing the FCC didn't have the manpower to monitor TV tobacco ads, he created Action for Smoking and Health (ASH) as a permanent smoking watchdog agency. And he discarded conventional law teaching methods, where students spend dreary hours in the library memorizing appellate decisions. Banzhaf decided on the go-do-it approach.

"The danger in public-interest law is that you can become a Don Quixote, because you are up against some pretty big windmills," Banzhaf says. "If you go at them head-on, you get sucked into the blades. So you look for a windmill with a loose stone very near the bottom, one that if dislodged makes the whole thing come tumbling down. Techniques for doing this are very different from what you are taught at law schools—hell, most of them are interested only in teaching one businessman how to sue another, or to defend a client who is sued.

"My idea as a teacher is to show the students that *it can be done*, just as I proved in the cigarette advertising case.

"You'd think that with as many lawyers as there are in the country there would be no public-interest problems whatsoever. Most people come out of law school fairly idealistic, and they know what's wrong with society. Why don't they do something? Because they think it *cannot* be done. They slough it off. Tell a man a hundred times he can do something, he won't believe you; show him once, and he is convinced.

"Listen, I've turned out more than a hundred twenty students, and they're spread around. One day something is going to bug each one of these guys, and he is going to remember what he did in law school. You get a couple of hundred lawyers doing this, and you are going to have a legal revolution in this country."

Banzhaf is not a universally popular man. He is outspoken, and many of his GWU colleagues think him a bit cocky, and they did not care for his implied criticisms of their teaching methods. His activities also offended a number of prominent Washington Lawyers who are GWU alumni; the way the story got to Banzhaf, they told GWU they'd be most happy if Banzhaf were elsewhere, and they might withhold further contributions until the campus was rid of him. In the spring of 1971 the law faculty voted 18–13 to deny Banzhaf tenure. More than eight hundred students signed protest petitions, and an activist faction on the faculty, led by Monroe Freedman, came to Banzhaf's defense. The vote was reversed. The Banzhaf revolution continues.

Phil Moore wears paint-smeared denims and hiking boots to work. An evil-smelling cigar juts from under his sandy-brown mustache much of the day—the sort of environmental pollutant John Banzhaf sues about. The Sundance Kid in wire-rimmed glasses. You'll be fooled by Phil Moore just for a minute, for he's too calm to be dangerous. This . . . this *kid? This* is the guy who sends GM chairman James Roche racing for the Gelusil, and who forced America's largest industrial corporation to spend more than $400,000 in a proxy fight with its own shareholders—which is to say, its owners. Phil Moore, corporate guerrilla, patiently maneuvering General Motors toward a consumerist Dien Bien Phu. Calm, quiet—like Trotsky, or Unitas with the Colts third-and-seven inside the twenty; or Nader. We sat in a walkup sprawl of rooms on Connecticut Avenue below Dupont Circle and talked about the Project for Corporate Responsibility, which Phil Moore runs.

"When I was at Harvard, a group of us used to talk about entering the graduate business school, and then go into corporations and reform them from inside. But we decided that by the time we would be in a position to change things, our whole attitudes would have changed, too. I mean, how do you get to the top otherwise? The corporations drum uniformity into you from the first day; you couldn't stay there and keep your head, you'd flip. So we thrashed around for another idea. I really didn't know what to do.

"I went on out to the University of Chicago Law School and

got my degree in 1967. Then I joined a public-interest law firm, a very respectable place on LaSalle Street—Devoe, Shader, Mikva,* and Plotkin, it's called. But that wasn't the answer, either. Single legal actions don't really change things; you have to get to the heart of the corporation—the way things are run inside, the people who set policy."

Moore got his chance in early 1970. Ralph Nader was increasingly frustrated with the quasi-victories in his fights with GM over safety and pollution. (See chapter 9, "Mr. Cutler, Meet Mr. Nader: Making It Personal.") Did each of these issues have to be resolved on an ad hoc basis? Could not GM management decide, as a matter of corporate policy, to make the company a responsible member of industrial society? Were profits truly paramount to the public weal? Management shunned personal and individual responsibility for what GM did by hiding behind a carefully constructed corporate shield. Okay. The decisions are made at the top, so let's not only go to the top, but *seize* the top—or enough of it to change the way things are done. Shareholder Power. "Nearly a million and a half . . . citizens and institutions are shareholders in the company," Nader says. "In theory, they own the company; in fact, they have about the same rights as the owner of company debentures. The procedures, the information, the organization, the manpower, and the funds are management's to deploy. But the fiction of shareholder democracy continues to plague the reality. By highlighting the fiction a new reality can be born that will tame the corporate tiger."

Nader chose Moore as the man to tame the tiger. The Project for Corporate Responsibility was created as an umbrella group for public-interest lawyers and organizations eager to try their hand at giant-killing. In February 1970 the Project bought twelve shares of GM stock and proposed three shareholder reso-

* The Mikva was Representative Abner J. Mikva (D., Ill.), who resigned from the firm upon his election to Congress in 1968.

lutions to be voted upon at GM's annual meeting: to enlarge the board to include three "representatives of the public"; to establish a watchdog committee for corporate responsibility; and to require GM to improve auto safety, cut pollution, and take other actions "in the public interest." For the board the Project nominated Betty Furness, biologist René Dubos, and the Rev. Channing Phillips, a black who is Democratic national committeeman from the District of Columbia. (Nader withdrew from the Project to avoid any conflict of interest because his invasion-of-privacy suit against GM was still before the courts.) The vast majority of shareholders do not attend annual meetings, but vote via a proxy which GM mails in advance. The Project asked that its resolutions be included in the proxy material. GM refused, in a resounding cannonade of legal opinions (sixteen pages from Davis, Polk and Wardwell; twenty-nine more from general counsel Ross L. Malone) that made learned references to such things as SEC Proxy Rule 14a–8(c) (2) and Article IX, Section 1, of the Constitution of the State of Delaware, and concluded all the Project wanted was to publicize its "concepts with reference to . . . general economic, political, racial, social and similar causes." This is the way big-time law is practiced; it drives away cranks and people who think twelve shares entitles them to say something. But the Project fought on at the SEC and won the right to have GM circulate the proposals on enlarging the board and creating the watchdog committee.

Phil Moore, guerrilla warrior. The Project didn't do worth a damn, numerically, at the annual meeting, getting less than three percent of the shares voted. But Project people had sport with Roche, reading from a list of questions prepared by Moore:

> ▮▮ "What is the purpose of the bumper on GM cars if, as your vice president Mack Worden testified last year, they cannot withstand impacts of more than 2.8 mph without losing their shape and requiring repair?"

■■ "How much money did you spend—directly or through the Automobile Manufacturers Association—to prevent diversion of highway taxes to Bay Area Rapid Transit in San Francisco?"

■■ "According to your own figures, fewer than four percent of your salaried workers are nonwhite—and the salaried category includes many clerical and janitorial employees. How many employees of GM earn over $20,000 per year? How many of these are nonwhite? How many of them are women?"

Right after the meeting, Roche acknowledged, "I don't think we won a victory here. We won a vote of confidence. We could lose that vote of confidence very quickly unless we respond in the way our shareholders expect us to." Within the next few months GM (a) announced formation of a "public-policy committee" composed of five board members; and (b) elected as a director the Rev. Leon Sullivan, of Philadelphia, a black.

The 1970 campaign had fundamental flaws, which Moore is glad to enumerate. Too radical, for one thing, to appeal to conservative money managers—the men Moore must win if a GM campaign is ever to succeed. Don't meddle in specific corporate decisions, the money managers told the Project time and again; even "socially aware" men at the foundations and the big universities. The publicity, although good, came too late; hit shareholders earlier, before they returned the proxy stuff. So 1971 was different. Moore focused this time on shareholder rights: to have shareholder nominees on the proxy ballots along with men nominated by management; to allow each of three GM "constituencies"—workers, dealers, and vehicle owners—to nominate a candidate for director; and to require GM to disclose in its annual report what it is doing about minority-hiring, air pollution, and vehicle safety. The Project also singled out the twenty institutions—banks, insurance companies, foundations, and universities—which are the largest GM shareholders, and subjected them to moral and political pressure. Again, negligible support, but enough momentum to carry the Project into a third GM campaign, to be waged in 1972.

Despite two "failures," Phil Moore remains optimistic. The General Motors campaign has spin-offs all over the country. The Project's March 1971 newsletter lists a few: in Los Angeles, the Center for New Corporate Priorities is attacking the Bank of America on alleged "issues of war profiteering, racism, repression of farm laborers and . . . anti-union stands." In Detroit, the Domestic and Foreign Mission Society of the Episopal Church pressed GM to "get out of South Africa as soon as possible." The United Presbyterian Church harassed Gulf Oil for its involvement in Portuguese Africa. Dow Chemical, Honeywell, Niagara Mohawk Power Company in Buffalo, New York; Polaroid's South African operations. So the list grows. Phil Moore strokes his mustache and watches, and gives advice on legal stratagems and publicity when needed. He is broke. The Project received two $30,000 grants from Washington philanthropist Phil Stern in 1970 and 1971, plus a handful of small contributions. He is getting minimal support from Washington Lawyers. Arnold and Porter huffily withdrew altogether. Conversely, sev- from the Internal Revenue Service, but wouldn't touch the GM campaign for fear of conflict with other corporate clients. When the Project snapped at Arnold and Porter's client, Coca-Cola, for allegedly exploiting Florida workers at its citrus facilities, Arnold and Porter huffily withdrew altogether. Conversely, several Covington and Burling partners and associates helped the committee formed to fight Dow's manufacture of napalm.

"Lawyers are fundamentally changing. There will be more branch offices of law firms that are completely independent of the commercial practice. If public-interest lawyers are dependent upon grants, they won't be self-sustaining, and the movement will end.

"What we have are 'emerging consciousness' law firms. 'The Abe Fortases of the future,' someone has referred to us. But I don't believe that at all. We're not going to cop out, the way the Consciousness II people did."

Phil Moore puffed his evil cigar again. "We are opening up a new front with these public-interest proxy groups. I'm not a do-gooder, you know; from the standpoint of personal interest and satisfaction, this life is much better than my old LaSalle Street law firm." Puff puff. The floor isn't carpeted, as floors are farther down Connecticut Avenue, where the corporate lawyers work, and Phil Moore's boots clump. "But it's a war of attrition—think of it, $120,000 it would take us to put out one mailing to GM shareholders, and we have the rent due two days ago and I'll be damned if I know what we're going to do unless some foundation springs for bread."

On the way out I put a dollar in a cannister on the receptionist's desk.

There are some features of the old life that William Dobrivir misses. Before 1968, if someone he phoned in government wasn't in, the call-back number of 293-3300 that Dobrivir would leave meant he heard from the man before the end of the day, or surely first thing the next morning. And the logistical amenities: the photocopy machines, a bank of them, spitting out copies of documents at a hundred-page a minute clip; the messenger service, so you could whisk briefs across town in a few minutes, rather than risk the mails; the secretaries, always one available, even at 11:40 p.m. Dobrivir sighs, "That was Covington and Burling. When you're on your own, you do it with mirrors." If he wants a copy made of something, his secretary must go down to the Drug Fair store on the corner and drop a coin in the machine. If he wants to research a brief, Dobrivir uses the D.C. Bar Association library, or a Federal agency. Many evenings a lawyer friend from a large firm, or from government, will come around for nonpaid moonlighting to help Dobrivir with a suit; "they are delighted at the chance to get involved in an interesting case," he says.

Bill Dobrivir is engaged in a unique experiment: to determine whether public-interest law has expanded to the point where a man can make a living doing nothing else, on whatever fees and retainers come along. And one case alone proves a thesis shared by Dobrivir and other public-interest lawyers: *One* lawyer and *one* lawsuit can make a difference.

The membership of Congressmen in military reserve units has long been one of Washington's more publicized—and ignored—scandals. Seven of the sixteen Senators on the Armed Services Committee hold reserve commissions; so do seven of the forty-one Representatives. So do House Speaker Carl D. Albert (D., Okla.) and House Democratic leader Hale Boggs (D., La.). Senator Strom Thurmond (R., S.C.) is not only a retired reserve major general who receives a pension, but at one time served as president of the Reserve Officers Association, the reservists' chief lobbying group on Capitol Hill. In the 1971–72 Congress, no less than 117 Congressmen and Senators held commissions. The Pentagon catered to the "Congressional Commandoes" by assigning many of them annual "active duty" tours at such grim outposts as Paris, Rome, Hong Kong, Hawaii, and Lisbon.

The legislator-reservist is a cold-war phenomenon. Until veterans flocked to Congress at the end of the Second World War, both houses paid attention to Section 6, Article I, of the Constitution, which states, "no person holding any office under the

United States shall be a member of either house during his con-
tinuance in office." When a Kansas Senator named James Henry
Lane accepted a brigadier's commission in the Civil War, the
Senate promptly ejected him from Congress. Nor would the Justice Department permit Lyndon Johnson or Warren Magnuson
to serve simultaneously in Congress and the Navy during the
Second World War.

In early 1971 Dobrivir was approached by the Reservists
Committee to Stop the War, a group of some 2,000 present and
former reservists opposed to U.S. involvement in Indochina. The
chairman, Adam Hochschild, of Santa Cruz, California, felt
membership in the reserves deprived war opponents of "the un-
biased consideration by Congress of measures affecting the military establishment." Dobrivir agreed. He filed suit charging the
reserve memberships violated the constitution. And U.S. District
Court Judge Gerhard A. Gesell ruled on April 1, 1971, that
holding a reserve commission was tantamount to holding a separate office in the executive branch. "Given the enormous involvement of Congress in matters affecting the military, Gesell
wrote, "the potential conflict between an office in the military
and an office in Congress is not inconsequential." Gesell stopped
short of ordering present reservists to resign, for judges historically have not told Congress how to run its business—only advised it on the law. "There is no reason to believe that Congress
and the Executive will be unable to accommodate themselves
voluntarily to the decision," Gesell said.*

Dobrivir says, "This was an attempt, in a small way, to di-

---

* The Department of Defense is appealing the decision, but without
detectable enthusiasm. One person involved in the case opined: "The
Pentagon was glad to see this suit, for it has been itching for a chance to
get rid of the Congressmen reservists. There's too much trouble in hand-
feeding them, arranging for junkets, finding a jet plane for Barry Goldwater to fly. These people will vote for Pentagon appropriations regardless,
because they are pro-military anyway."

vorce Congress from the military. I think we accomplished a desirable end."

For his first thirty-five years Bill Dobrivir appeared to be on the track that leads to a comfortable living as a corporate Washington Lawyer. After graduation from Harvard Law School, he spent a year in Chile as a Fulbright Scholar, and then another year in Colombia as member of a Harvard advisory committee on tax reform. Covington and Burling hired Dobrivir on the basis both of his Harvard record and his fluency in Spanish, and assigned him to help represent the Venezuelan government in its successful effort to extradite former dictator Perez Jimenez for trial for corruption in office. (Dean Acheson was the lead-lawyer in the case.) General litigation, administrative law ("running things through Federal agencies for routine approval"), *pro bono* work for the ACLU—the well-established pattern.

Then the turmoil of 1968. Dobrivir walked out of C&B to work for Robert Kennedy, directed a commission that studied the administration of justice in the D.C. courts, and roamed Europe for five months. Back in Washington, he began looking for something to do. "As a radical Democrat, I didn't think a Republican Administration would be congenial to me as a Federal lawyer, and a policy-making job obviously was not available." Edgar Cahn, of the Citizen's Advocate Center, suggested that the burgeoning public-interest groups needed a lawyer to handle court litigation. "Everybody thought it was a great idea —but no one was ready to finance such a lawyer," Dobrivir says. Then Reuben Robinson, a onetime C&B colleague, took Dobrivir to Ralph Nader. "Ralph said, in effect, 'I'll take half of you.'" Dobrivir agreed to do Nader's litigation for a year, as an independent attorney free to take other work as he saw fit. "I talked around town to other public-interest lawyers, foundations, friends, and so forth, and cases began to come in. I didn't want to be a hired hand; I wanted to take on only what I wanted to do. My definition of a public-interest case is anything that turns me on, that serves a cause I believe in. I don't want to bother with anything else." Some examples:

■■ A suit under the Freedom of Information Act to force the Department of Labor to disclose records of the enforcement (or non-enforcement) of the Walsh-Healy Act, which requires government contractors to comply with Federal safety and health standards. Dobrivir won.

■■ A suit against the Department of the Interior to carry out mandatory inspection provisions of the Coal Mine Health and Safety Act. The court dismissed the suit when the Department changed procedures to comply with the law.

■■ A suit attacking advertising claims on the efficacy of aspirin. Friendly reception by the FTC, which at this writing was revising rules.

■■ A suit against the Department of Agriculture which forced suspension of the use of the herbicide 2,4,5-T on food crops as "an imminent hazard to the public" which caused birth defects in test animals.

■■ A petition to the FDA to ban open-flushing toilets on railroad passenger trains, locomotives, and cabooses, as a health hazard. The FDA in mid-1971 told the railroads to install chemical toilets on new trains after 1972.

Dobrivir feels fees will be the salvation of public-interest law, that foundation support is too transitory. But where will the fee money come from? Persons and organizations that seek out a public-interest lawyer are impecunious; otherwise they'd look elsewhere. An expanded class-action law—one providing for attorney fees in winning suits—would be one answer. (One lawyer compares class-action to the contingency-fee system which permitted the negligence lawyers to flourish.) Dobrivir also talks —with a hint of a dream in his eye—of major antitrust suits with treble-damage recoveries. "One good victory would finance the entire public-interest bar for years. But this kind of suit requires years to prosecute, and a phenomenal investment of money. You need an ongoing organization to conduct them." So Dobrivir and some lawyer-friends are putting together something called Advocates for Economic Justice, which intends to look for a suitable target and go after it, with the expectation of using any damages recovered as "seed money" for public-interest work.

Economically, Dobrivir is surviving, although his income is perhaps only a quarter of that earned by contemporaries at Covington and Burling who stayed on as partners. But he likes the camaraderie of public-interest work. "We are a small and beleaguered minority who keep together—but there seems to be more of us every month."

"Just what is 'public-interest' law, anyway?" Philip Elman asked. "It means all things to all men. Some lawyers resent the term—and rightfully so, I think—because it implies they are on the other side of the public interest, that representing a corporate client is not part of the public interest. When you start a case, you don't know *where* the public interest lies. An attorney representing a corporate client is not necessarily against the public interest. And it is possible to have a conflict between two public-interest groups.

"Suppose the Civil Aeronautics Board is considering a proposal for a new airport. The airport could provide transportation that is sorely needed, but it could add to the traffic congestion. Or the trans-Alaska pipeline. It could bring down the price of oil for the public. Or a new power plant for New York, which could relieve the electricity shortage there. Perhaps it would be wise for the oil industry and the power companies to call their attorneys 'public-interest lawyers,' because they can make a strong argument that they in fact *are* public-interest lawyers, the definition being as vague as it is.

"Soon after I went into practice for myself, I was approached by a steamship company that felt the Maritime Administration had treated it poorly in a complex rate case. I investigated the matter very thoroughly and concluded they had in fact been wronged, so I'm handling an appeal. This is a situation that would result in higher costs being passed to the consumer. Now this case won't fit many people's definition of 'public interest,' for the steamship company was certainly able to pay me, and well. But taking this kind of case enables me to engage in the kind of law I want to practice."

Phil Elman is unique for several reasons. He is a former member of the Federal Trade Commission who was not besieged with industry offers when he left office. He is a self-described "rascal fighter" who can look tolerantly at his adversaries, even when he disagrees with them. He is diffident to the point of grayness, conservative in dress and personality, yet he is idolized by the hustling fire-eaters who are the rank and file of the New Washington Lawyers. And he is a former insider whose "know-who" is being used for the benefit of consumers, not the corporations.

Elman understands the New Washington Lawyers because he sees in them a reincarnation of the New Deal spirit he found when he came to Washington in the 1930s as a clerk to his old friend and professor Felix Frankfurter. From 1946 to 1961 he was in the Solicitor General's Office, arguing more than fifty cases before the Supreme Court, and briefing hundreds of others —the initial school desegregation case, Little Rock, D.C. school integration, a host of antitrust, tax, and regulatory matters. President Kennedy put him on the FTC in 1961 as a watchdog over

Paul Rand Dixon, who was appointed chairman as a favor to Senator Estes Kefauver, his longtime mentor, but whose regulatory zeal was questioned by the White House. To everyone's surprise, Elman watched more than Dixon, and he soon developed a reputation as a maverick. It was Elman who first proposed that cigarette packages contain health warnings, who staggered the advertising industry by ruling illegal such Madison Avenue gimmicks as scraping sand off Plexiglas to back a claim that a lather would "shave sandpaper," who consistently opposed further monopolization of the American economy. "A perpetual one-man minority," he says of his FTC years.

By the time Elman had left the FTC in October 1970 he had reached two conclusions: (a) the regulatory agencies "have, in general, failed to develop and implement regulatory policies fully responsive to public needs and the public interest"; and (b) "a basic reason for such failure is the lack of adequate citizen involvement and participation in agency proceedings." Citizen involvement and participation means lawyers, and that is what Elman is trying to provide. He is teaching the New Washington Lawyers the mechanics of agency practice—how to prepare and present their cases, and how to find their way to the proper desk in the bureaucracy when they need information or action. As a part-time professor at the Georgetown University Law Center, he has organized "Operation Truth," under which students monitor TV advertising and watch for deceptive claims. Complaints go to the FTC. "Good practice for them, and the FTC is grateful because it doesn't have the staff for continuous surveillance."

Some younger lawyers don't understand what Elman is all about. "How could anybody work at the FTC as long as he did and come out with any soul whatsoever?" one youngster asked me. "So what if he did have a reputation as a dissenter? Anybody who cooperates with such a wretched system is fooling himself if he thinks he is improving things." And one of Elman's children quipped, "You're selling out, Daddy," when he went into quasi-private practice. Elman doesn't flinch; no one can truly know how wretched a regulatory agency is unless he has worked inside it, he says. Further, he feels he is setting an example for other lawyers who leave government—that is, work for the public interest, not just the business world. And Phil Elman likes to point to a quotation from Oliver Wendell Holmes that is framed on his wall:

> If a man has the soul of Sancho Panza, the world to him will be Sancho Panza's world. But if he has the soul of an idealist he will make—I do not say find—his world ideal.

A sub-theme of this book, as should be apparent by now, is that government regulation is not a panacea for what is wrong with our nation. Thus I shall not be hypocritical or inconsistent and recommend a set of rules that will make uniformly decent citizens of the Washington Lawyers and solve overnight the problems they help create and perpetuate in for our society. Each man is the keeper of his own conscience, and each Washington Lawyer ultimately must make his own choices about what he does in a government practice, and how. I agree with Charles Horsky that "we cannot legislate a moral attitude or a cure for influence-peddling." But some existing structures could certainly be put to better use.

The legal profession prides itself on being a self-governing society. The bar writes rules of conduct for attorneys, and the courts enforce them. But a vast number of Washington Lawyers fall outside the disciplinary jurisdiction of the bar in part because they are not members of any local bar association. A lawyer need not be a member of the D.C. Bar Association so long as he does not practice in the District Court or represent himself to be engaged in general practice. Neither does a lawyer who maintains offices in another city but comes to Washington frequently to practice before the Federal government. Bars elsewhere are unlikely even to hear of violations their members commit in Washington, much less take disciplinary action. Several Federal agencies make their own rules as to who may practice before them, and publish procedural guides. But disbarment procedures, even when they exist, are so seldom invoked as to be meaningless (with the notable exception of the Internal Revenue Service). But no general grievance committee exists with the power to deter or punish unethical conduct by lawyers who practice before the Federal government.

Lloyd N. Cutler has proposed one solution via the *Yale Law Journal*:

> Would it not be advisable for the Federal government to establish a single Federal bar, and to require that all lawyers representing clients before any government agency become members of that bar? Membership might be open to any member of a state bar, but applicants might be disbarred or suspended after hearing on a showing of professional misconduct. The power to disbar or suspend might be vested in a representative board of outstanding private and government lawyers practicing throughout the country; and in subordinate regional boards . . . jointly selected by the government and by the bar associations.

Cutler concluded this proposal by saying, "It may be time for all lawyers, and particularly Washington lawyers, to devote serious study to such a plan."

The article was published in 1953—almost two decades ago. "The bar paid absolutely no attention to it whatsoever," said Cutler. A D.C. Bar Association official told me in mid-1971 that the idea of a unified Federal bar "is alive, but I really couldn't say if and when it will come into existence." Cutler's idea has both merits and pitfalls. On the positive side, it would discourage the more blatent legal clip joints, if only by enforcing the canon that provides that a lawyer "shall not state or imply that he is able to influence improperly or upon irrelevant grounds any tribunal, legislative body, or public official." If some of the things that were told to me in recent months are true, I know of at least nine, and possibly seventeen, lawyers who would be out of business overnight were they to obey this rule.

The emergence of a strong, unified bar, however, could be the death knell for the public-interest law movement. When lawyers speak of a city with a "strong bar"—Philadelphia, Chicago, and St. Louis—they mean a "conservative bar," one dominated by the large, corporate-oriented firms. Because they have the time and the manpower, such firms as Covington and Burling; Hogan and Hartson; and Wald, Harkrader and Rockefeller in all probability would make short shrift of any bar election. And what established Washington bar presently exists is openly antagonistic toward the public-interest law centers. Indeed, Monroe Freedman, of the Stern Community Law Firm, spent almost a year fighting a disbarment attempt on grounds of soliciting business. Freedman's "sin," in the eyes of a vocal segment of the bar, was that the firm placed ads in neighborhood newspapers and other media announcing its existence and purpose, and inviting citizens to come in if they had problems. Freedman won only after a spirited contest. By normal bar standards, the public-interest lawyers are in technical violation of any number of canons almost daily, particularly those on out-of-court publicity. They respond that the public has a right to know about public-policy issues; further, many governmental decisions are political decisions, and hence should not be immune from spirited discussion. Nonetheless, a conservative local bar could destroy the public-interest lawyers through a war of attrition.

Any self-policing should start at the top, which is to say, within the American Bar Association itself. The ABA is a caricature of what is wrong with Washington Lawyers—domination by corporate interests, scant concern for the consumer, self-important pomposity. Whatever credibility the ABA has outside its own membership it doesn't deserve, and that is the most that can be said of Corporate America's private legal club.* "Of the 410 lawyers who were members of consumer-related ABA committees in 1970," says Representative Benjamin Rosenthal (D., N.Y.), "only five derived their principal income from the academic community and none, to the best of my knowledge, were members of public-interest law firms. Certainly, it would seem to be desirable to utilize the considerable talents of academicians and public-interest lawyers whose economic interests are unlikely to be in conflict with the public-interest responsibilities of the bar association." Rosenthal ticked off the 1970 affiliations of the members of the ABA's Division of Food, Drug and Cosmetic Law:

. . . The vice chairman of the division was general counsel and vice president of the manufacturer of Hellman's Mayonnaise, Mazola Corn Oil and other food products; the secretary was vice president and general counsel for a major drug manufacturer; the chairman of the standing committee on food additives was employed by a manufacturer of food additives and pharmaceuticals; the chairman of the drug law committee was employed by the Pharmaceutical Manufacturers Association; the chairman of the

* Several attorneys who read drafts of this section contended the ABA did not deserve such harsh language because of various "reforms" the past few years. Pending further evidence, I do not amend my original judgment.

committee on beverage law was in the legal department of Coca-Cola.

The list goes on indefinitely. The chairman of a subcommittee on advertising of the antitrust law section was in a law firm whose clients include the Association of National Advertisers, the Advertising Research Foundation, and the Direct Mail Advertising Association. The subcommittee on public utilities and holding companies was headed by an executive vice president of the American Electric Power Service Corporation. A lawyer for Trans World Airlines ran the aviation law committee; a lawyer for Continental Oil Company, the environmental quality committee; a vice president and general counsel of AT&T, the communications law committee. The *Washington Newsletter* of the Banking committee of the ABA's Section of Corporation, Banking and Business Law since its inception in 1959 "has been written and edited . . . by registered lobbyists of the banking industry," asserts Representative Wright Patman (D., Tex.). The editor's position has been held by such persons as Charles R. McNeill, head of the Washington office of the American Bankers Association, for which he has registered as a lobbyist; and by Donald L. Rogers, registered lobbyist for the Association of Registered Bank Holding Companies. "As a lawyer myself," comments Patman, "I think it is certainly unprofessional and unworthy of the calling that people in high places among a very powerful and influential association permit the circulation of biased and prejudiced reports of so vital an area as banking." He calls the banking committee "a front" for the banking industry. He says the *Washington Newletter* contains "very slanted views —those views being the special interests of the bankers' lobby."

That the ABA would so stack its committees, and then present their judgments as "objective and representative of the American bar," is damnable. But it happens, year after year.

Oh, but you must understand, the ABA responds, these committees are selected through democratic procedures within the association. If the committee composition is the end result of ABA-style democracy, the ABA sorely needs another system of government.

Perhaps because so many of its members are attorneys, Congress has little interest in the role of Washington Lawyers in government. The House Interstate and Foreign Commerce Committee, with broad jurisdiction over the regulatory agencies, occasionally chastises an attorney for whispering over a transom to an official or plying him with bourbon and handshakes. But it has never paused for a much-needed philosophical discussion about the Washington Lawyer's place in the scheme of things. Similarly, a House government operations subcommittee has compiled more volumes of testimony than I care to count on FDA regulation of the drug industry. The onus invariably has been placed upon the bureaucrats for permitting hokum drugs to go onto the market and to remain there even when exposed. The subcommittee would learn much more about shortcomings of drug regulation by putting Stanley Temko, of Covington and Burling, or Stuart Land, of Arnold and Porter, on the witness stand for an afternoon of brisk questioning. A breach of lawyer-client confidentiality? I think not, for much of the drug lawyers' work consists of face-to-face meetings with Federal officials, with clients present. What arguments did Temko use with Dr. Herbert L. Ley, Jr., the FDA Commissioner, on behalf of Panalba? And what did Temko say to HEW Under Secretary John Veneman, a layman, to persuade him to reverse the studied judgment of Ley, a scientist and physician?

Only once has a Congressional committee even suggested that Washington Lawyers talk about their work in philosophical terms. In 1969 Ralph Nader spent considerable time denouncing "the lobbying infrastructure" that retards effective consumer law. He told a Senate government operations subcommittee that lawyers in such firms as Covington and Burling, and Hogan and Hartson

> . . . are eminent specialists in cutting down consumer programs in their incipiency or undermining them if they mature. They are the masters of the ex parte contact, the private deals and tradeoffs, the greasing of the corporate wheels and the softening of the bureaucrats' wills. They could tell this committee a great deal about the obstacles and tasks which consumer protection administrators must deal with . . .
>
> I am sure that such citizens as Lloyd Cutler and Thomas Austern and Edwin Rockefeller—all of whom deal with the consumer in their distinctive ways as corporate attorneys— would be pleased to come before this subcommittee and provide its members with their views and expertise . . . They do not have to reveal any confidences . . . just let them talk on their strategies . . .

Senator Abraham Ribicoff (D., Conn.), the subcommittee chairman, asked five lawyers and three trade associations named by Nader if they would care to respond. None cared to come before the subcommittee, although Thurman Arnold of Arnold and Porter (now deceased) did offer one suggestion for improving the administrative process: "Perhaps a rule that counsel should not make any representation on behalf of his client without the prior approval of Mr. Nader would satisfy him."

Anyone who has watched the Federal government at close range, even as an outsider, recognizes the necessity of informal contacts. They will continue, even if outlawed, so why bother? The business of government is so vast, so amorphous, that conducting it in formal proceedings is a practical impossibility. But the public is justifiably suspicious of a "private" or "secret" or "off-the-record" meeting, even if it is nothing more furtive than a lawyer walking into an FCC bureau chief's office and asking about the progress of a case. Lawyers and bureaucrats alike insist there is nothing "secretive" in such meetings. So let us remove the public opprobrium. Any *ex parte* contact on a matter before a Federal agency or department should be made a matter of public record, even if only in cursory log form, and be preserved for two to five years and be open to inspection by any citizen who asks for it. The record would reveal who was interested in a case, and on behalf of what party, and what they said about it. In all probability the bulk of this record would go uninspected. But both government officials and Washington Lawyers would conduct their talks with the knowledge that they *could* become public knowledge. Disclosure—or even the possibility of it—is essential to good government. Any bureaucrat who acts in the public's name should be prepared to explain to the public what he has done, and why.

The above recommendations, however, are mere carpentry work on an existing structure. Some fundamental alterations are also necessary. What Washington Law needs, more than anything else, is competition. And a way must be found to provide it.

Within their very real limits, the Nader-oriented public-interest centers and individual lawyers have done much to balance the scales of justice in Washington. If nothing else, they have proved the Washington Lawyer is not omnipotent; and once an institution loses its mystique, almost anything can happen to it. When John Banzhaf went into court on the cigarette advertising case—a single man, mind you, two years out of law school—he faced a legal army drawn from the top firms of both Washington and New York: McKenna and Wilkinson, for ABC;

Wilmer, Cutler and Pickering, for CBS; Smith, Pepper, Shack and L'Heureux, for WLLE, Inc.; Arnold and Porter, for Philip Morris and the Tobacco Institute; Chadbourne, Parke, Whiteside and Wolff, for American Tobacco; Wald, Harkrader, and Rockefeller, for Lorillard, all of Washington; Cahill, Gordon, Sonnett, Reindel and Ohl, for NBC; Davis, Polk and Wardwell, for R. J. Reynolds Tobacco; Webster, Sheffield, Fleischmann, Hitchcock and Brookfield, for Liggett and Myers; and Forsyth, Decker and Murray, for United States Tobacco, all of New York. For those who are not familiar with the names of national law firms, suffice to say that Banzhaf had formidable and talented competition. And he won, on his own.

But how can the public ensure that there will always be a Banzhaf, or a Nader, or a Benny Kass, or a Bill Dobrivir? Public funding is one solution, provided a proper format can be found. Since 1969 Congress has studied various proposals for channeling Federal funds into "public representation" before regulatory agencies. Many of the present New Washington Lawyers are skeptical of Federal benevolence; they point to the continuous Congressional harassment of legal programs sponsored by the Office of Economic Opportunity and ask whether a "consumer counsel" or variation thereof would be given the necessary independence. But the tide of consumerism is flowing so strongly in the nation that such an agency ultimately will be established.

Finally, The Washington Lawyer is running scared. He is being discussed publicly; he is being held accountable for what he does on behalf of clients; he is feeling the same sting of "responsibility" as are corporate executives; he is learning to live with the awesome awareness that his self-proscribed privacy no longer insulates him from the rest of the world.

Capitalism survived the nonviolent revolution of the 1930s by reforming itself sufficiently to allay public anger. Are the Wash-

ington Lawyers equally intelligent? They should be, for their very profession is at stake. H. Thomas Austern has framed on his office wall a quotation from Dick the Butcher in Shakespeare's Henry VI: *"The first thing we do, let's kill all the lawyers." The public opinion of Washington Lawyers has not reached that point. Not yet, anyway.*

Acknowledgments and Sources

During one of the 90-odd interviews which form the core of *The Superlawyers*, I asked a Washington Lawyer what he charged per hour. He glanced at his watch and said, "You've already used about $240 of my time. Figure it out for yourself." Not every attorney bills his clients at $120 per hour; nonetheless I benefited from more thousands of dollars of free time than I care to compute. As is obvious from the text, many interviewees, both lawyers and government officials, preferred to speak on a not-for-attribution basis. Others would not be quoted in any fashion; still others are identified in the book. To those who talked, regardless of the ground rules, my thanks.

My appreciation also to Truman M. Talley, of Weybright and Talley, who had the idea; to Jack Limpert and Laughlin Phillips, of *Washingtonian*, for helping it take shape; to Carl D. Brandt and Charity Randall, for psychic and other boosts when needed; and to Jody, editor, typist, and wife.

Sources in addition to interviews follow.

Chapter One

The Acheson quotes on the early years of Covington and Burling are from *Morning and Noon*, by Dean Acheson, Houghton Mifflin Company, Boston, 1965. Burling's 90th birthday interview was published in *The Washington Post* February 1, 1960.

Background on the creation of the Civil Aeronautics Board is from hearings before Rep. Emanuel Celler's antitrust subcommittee of the House Judiciary Committee in February–June 1956, *Monopoly Hearings in Regulated Industries: Airlines, Parts 1 and 2.*

Briefs and transcripts of proceedings in the electrical equipment price-fixing case were supplied to me by two attorneys involved in the case. A good journalistic overview of the case is *The Great Price Conspiracy*, by John Herling, Robert B. Luce, Inc., Washington, 1962. The Kefauver hearings were before the antitrust and monopoly subcommittee of the Senate Judiciary Committee in May and June 1961, *Administered Prices: Price Fixing and Bid Rigging in the Electrical Manufacturing Industry, Parts 27 and 28.*

The Acheson commentary on the genesis of the Marshall Plan is from his *Present at the Creation*, W. W. Norton and Company, New York, 1969. The agreement between the Greek government and Covington and Burling is in the firm's foreign agent registration statements filed with the Internal Security Division of the Department of Justice. Fees paid Covington and Burling by various foreign clients, and descriptions of the work done for them, are from the registration statements.

Although not quoted directly in this chapter, *The Washington Lawyer*, by Charles Horsky, a Covington and Burling partner (Little, Brown and Company, Boston, 1952) was of value in tracing the development of the "national" Washington law firm. Many of Horsky's general statements in the book are directly applicable to Covington and Burling. The Horsky quotations are from a personal interview.

Chapter Two

The bulk of this chapter came from interviews with Clark Clifford on May 24 and June 30, 1971. Secondary sources on his work in the Truman Administration and the 1949 campaign were *The President's Men*, by Patrick Anderson, Doubleday and Company, New York, 1968; *The Truman Presidency*, by Cabell Phillips, Macmillan and Company, New York, 1967; and *Out of the Jaws of Victory*, by Jules Abels, Henry Holt and Company, New York, 1959.

The Lilienthal quotation is from *The Journals of David E. Lilienthal*, Harper & Row, New York, 1964.

Adverse Senate reaction to the duPont-Christiana legislation was expressed in hearings before the Senate Finance Committee on March 17 and 24, 1965; and in floor debate the next two months. A somewhat more conspiratorial account is given in *Clark Clifford: Attorney at War*, by David Welsh and David Horowitz, *Ramparts*, April 1968.

Clifford detailed his turnabout on Vietnam in "A Vietnam Reappraisal," *Foreign Affairs*, July 1969; the quotes are from this article and the interviews cited above.

Chapter Three

Background on the formation and early years of Arnold and Porter came from *Fair Fights and Foul*, by Thurman Arnold, Harcourt, Brace and World, New York, 1965. The Tugwell letter was quoted in the *Congressional Record*, September 27, 1968.

The Miami television dispute was aired before the House Interstate and Foreign Commerce Committee in its 1958–59 hearings, *Investigation of Regulatory Commissions and Agencies, Parts 4 and 5.*

The Fortas quotations on his relations with former President Johnson are from his confirmation hearing as a Supreme Court Justice before the Senate Judiciary Committee in 1965.

Arnold and Porter's longtime connections with Braniff International Airways are recorded in the line's annual filings with the Civil Aeronautics Board.

Information on the Serc case came from Unimed decertification hearings before a Food and Drug Administration examiner in October and November 1969; and hearings before Rep. L. H. Fountain's subcommittee of the House Interstate and Foreign Commerce Committee in

May 1969, *Drug Efficacy, Part 2*. The Measurin data are from hearings before the same subcommittee, *Drug Safety, Part 5*, March 1966.

The Lexington, Kentucky, bank merger case was discussed in hearings before the domestic finance subcommittee of the House Banking and Currency Committee, *To Amend the Bank Merger Act of 1960, Part 2*, 1965.

FTC commissioner MacIntyre's comments on the Federated Department Stores case came in his dissenting opinion in FTC docket C-1057, March 5, 1969. The case is also discussed in *The Closed Enterprise System*, by Mark Green, Beverly C. Moore, Jr., and Bruce Wasserstein, a preliminary draft of which was circulated by the Center for the Study of Responsive Law in June 1971.

Secondary sources include two *New York Times Magazine* articles on Fortas, "The Complexities of Mr. Justice Fortas," by Fred Rodell, July 28, 1968; and "The Many-Sided Mr. Fortas," by Fred P. Graham, June 4, 1967; and "Law and Power in Washington," by Andrew Kopkind and James Ridgeway, *Hard Times*, June 16–23, 1969.

Chapter Four

Corcoran's description of the informality of his practice was given in hearings of a subcommittee of the House Interstate and Foreign Commerce Committee, *Ex Parte Communications and Other Problems: Federal Power Commission*, May 1960. As noted in the text, Corcoran declined repeated requests for an interview. The criticisms by the subcommittee's Republican minority are in a report, *Independent Regulatory Commissions*, January 3, 1961. The Tennessee Gas Transmission case is detailed in these documents also.

Background on Corcoran's New Deal days and early law practice are from *The President's Men*, Anderson; "Young Man Who Practices Law Out of His Hat," by Andreas Spenser, *Washington Times-Herald*, August 10, 1941; and "Tom Corcoran's Success," *United States News*, April 12, 1940.

Corcoran's ties with the China Lobby are discussed in "The China Lobby," *The Reporter* Magazine, April 15 and 29, 1952.

The FPC's disallowance of Corcoran's fees from Tennessee Gas Transmission was in *18 FPC Reports 497*.

Chapter Five

Richard Olney's prophecy on the efficacy of regulatory commissions is quoted, among other places, in *The Politics of Oil*, by Robert Engler, Macmillan Company, New York, 1961.

The Friendly quotation is from *The Federal Administrative Agencies*, by Henry J. Friendly, Harvard University Press, Cambridge, 1962.

Austern's comments on mandatory food standards and economic versus political judgments are from "Food Standards: The Balance Between Certainty and Innovation," *Food Drug Cosmetic Law Journal*, September 1969. His statement to the National Canners Association is quoted in *American Chamber of Horrors*, by Ruth De Forest Lamb, Farrar and Rinehart, New York, 1936.

The peanut-butter case was summarized in *The Federal Register*, July 24, 1968; the final order is in the *Register* for March 3, 1971. Rankin's speech, entitled "Food Additives Today and Tomorrow," was to the Southern California Section of the Institute of Food Technologists, November 20, 1969. Austern's statements on procedural fairness are from "Expertise In Vivo," *Administrative Law Review*, winter-spring issue 1963.

The Motor Carrier Lawyers Association material and the Wilhite episode were explored by the House Interstate and Foreign Commerce Committee in hearings, *Inquiry Into Certain Procedures of the Interstate Commerce Commission, Parts 1 and 2*, January–August 1970. The Ottinger quotation is from hearings before the subcommittee on transportation and aeronautics of the House Interstate and Foreign Commerce Committee, *Passenger Train Service*, November 1969.

Austern's statements on staff-commissioner relations within the regulatory agencies are from "Some Aberrations in Administrative Law," a lecture he delivered at the New York University School of Law on October 27, 1970, as adjunct professor.

The Seven States case account was given by Louis J. Hector, former CAB member, in "Problems of the Civil Aeronautics Board and the Independent Regulatory Commissions," *69 Yale Law Journal 931*.

Austern's comments on the lack of judicial review are from a talk to the Food Law Institute on December 11, 1969, in Washington.

The Panalba material is from Food and Drug Administration files in a case styled, "In the matter of Novobiocin-tetracycline combination drugs; calcium Novobiocin-sulfamethizole tablets"; and hearings before the Fountain subcommittee, *Drug Efficacy, Part 2*, May 1969. Morton Mintz detailed the Mintener appointment in his *The Therapeutic Nightmare*, Houghton Mifflin Company, Boston, 1965. Kuykendall's lobbying against revision of the Federal Power Act is recounted in Engler, *The Politics of Oil*.

Austern's quotation on consumerism is from "The Formulation of Mandatory Food Standards," *Food Drug Cosmetic Law Quarterly*, December 1947; on Federal antitrust activities, from proceedings of the Antitrust Law Symposium of the Antitrust Law Section, New York State Bar Association, Commercial Clearing House, Chicago, 1954; on pharmaceuticals, from "Drug Regulation and the Public Health," *New York University Law Review*, November 1964.

Chapter Six

President Nixon's affiliation with the Mudge Rose firm is told in *Nixon: A Political Portrait*, by Earl Mazo and Stephen Hess, Harper and Row, New York, 1968. The Fisher-Treadwell study is quoted in this book.

The staffs of several Congressional committees—controlled by the Democratic majorities—have maintained a continuing watch on Mudge Rose for conflict-of-interest situations. Only one document has resulted: a staff report from the postal service subcommittee of the House Post Office and Civil Service Committee, *Report on the Circumstances Surrounding the Proposed Sale of United States Postal Service Bonds*, September 27, 1971. Rep. Morris K. Udall (D., Ariz.) commented on these bonds in press releases on July 29 and August 1, 1971.

Secondary sources on the Liquidonics merger were articles by Jim Hampton in the *National Observer*, January 19, 1970; and Donald Rothberg, of The Associated Press Washington bureau, February 9, 1970.

Chapter Seven

The Ablard quotation is from "The Washington Lawyer-Lobbyist," by Charles D. Ablard, *The George Washington Law Review*, May 1970. This issue (GWLR hereafter), a symposium on Washington Lawyers, is interesting self-examination.

The data on the Sugar Lawyers is from hearings before the House Agriculture Committee, *Extension of the Sugar Act*, February–May 1971; a staff report of the same committee, *The United States Sugar Program*, December 31, 1970; and foreign agent registration statements filed with the Internal Security Division of the Department of Justice. The Surrey-Karasik episode was developed in hearings before the Senate Foreign Relations Committee, *Activities of Nondiplomatic Representatives of Foreign Principals in the United States*, 1963.

Unruh's statement on former Senator Thomas Kuchel is from the *Sacramento Bee*, September 3, 1970. The Carey anecdote is from his *Politics and the Regulatory Agencies*, cited above. The Cohen quotations are from the GWLR issue cited above and an interview.

My discussion of Congressional ethics vis-à-vis law practices relies heavily upon *Congress and the Public Trust*, by James C. Kirby, Jr., Armin Rosencranz, and Ellen W. Ober, a report by the Special Committee on Congressional Ethics of the Association of the Bar of the City of New York (Atheneum, New York, 1970). Another secondary source on the general subject was *The Case Against Congress*, by Jack Anderson and Drew Pearson, Simon and Schuster, New York, 1968. Clients of Congressmen turned lawyer-lobbyists are listed in quarterly reports filed with the House of Representatives and published in the *Congressional Record*.

Smathers's Senate record, and his law practice, were exhaustively explored in a *Newsday* series in October 1971. The articles of October 11 and 12 were particularly helpful.

Chapter Eight

Judge Bromley's speech, entitled "Judicial Control of Antitrust Cases," was part of a Seminar on Protracted Cases at the Stanford Law School, August 25–30, 1958; printed in *23 Federal Rules Decisions 417* (1959).

Freedman's statements were in a memorandum entitled "Solicitation of Clients by Public Interest Lawyers," submitted to the legal ethics and grievance committee of the District of Columbia Bar Association on behalf of the Stern Community Law Firm, of which he was then the director. The Learned Hand statement is quoted in *57 Yale Law Journal 167*.

The Caplin quotations are from his "The Washington Tax Lawyer," in the GWLR symposium issue, and an interview.

Chapter Nine

Ralph Nader and Lloyd Cutler each gave me their versions of their ongoing public confrontation; I also benefited from interviews with numerous associates of both men.

The auto case was formally styled The United States versus The Automobile Manufacturers Association, Inc.; General Motors Corporation, Ford Motor Company, Chrysler Corporation, and American Motors Corporation, No. 69–75–JWC, in the United States District Court in the Central District of California.

The Kefauver drug hearings are recounted in *The Real Voice*, by Richard Harris, Macmillan, New York, 1964; and in *The Therapeutic Nightmare*, by Morton Mintz, *op. cit.*

Cutler's role in the Bay of Pigs prisoner swap is told in *The Bay of Pigs*, by Haynes Johnson, Norton, New York, 1964; and *Kennedy Justice*, by Victor Navasky, Atheneum, New York, 1971.

Some of the early background on the auto safety dispute within the industry is from *Ford: An Unconventional Biography of the Men and Their Times*, by Booton Herndon, Weybright & Talley, 1970. The Markley quotations are from the Herndon book.

Nader's side of the auto pollution case, and his correspondence with various Justice Department officials, is contained in *The Closed Enterprise System, op. cit.* Much of this material also was published in the *Congressional Record* on various dates in early September 1969, immediately prior to approval of the consent decree.

Chapter Ten

The Rosenthal speech was in *The Congressional Record* for September 19, 1970. The Nader quotation is from testimony before the subcommittee on executive reorganization of the Senate Government Operations Committee, "Hearings on S-860 and S-2045: To Establish a Department of Consumer Affairs," March–July 1969, page 386 *supra*. The Thurman Arnold response is in the same hearings.

The "public-interest" law centers, because they must raise money from foundations and other private sources, issue an unceasing flow of reports, proposals, and press releases; many of the quotations contained in this chapter on specific projects and litigation were gleaned from these documents. The core of the material on the four lawyers profiled —Banzhaf, Dobrivir, Moore, and Elman—came from personal interviews. Material on *pro bono* work of the conventional firms cited came from interviews and internal reports.

The Patman quotations on the bankers' newsletter are in hearings before the subcommittee on domestic finance of the House Banking and Currency Committee, *To Amend the Bank Merger Act of 1960*, September 1965.

Index

399